THE KING
AND HIS DOMINION GOVERNORS

THE KING
AND HIS
DOMINION GOVERNORS

A STUDY OF THE RESERVE POWERS
OF THE CROWN
IN GREAT BRITAIN AND THE DOMINIONS

HERBERT VERE EVATT

with a new introduction by
ZELMAN COWEN

SECOND EDITION

Routledge
Taylor & Francis Group
LONDON AND NEW YORK

First Published 1936 by
FRANK CASS AND COMPANY LIMITED

Published 2013 by Routledge
2 Park Square, Milton Park, Abingdon, Oxfordshire OX14 4RN
711 Third Avenue, New York, NY 10017

First issued in paperback 2014

Routledge is an imprint of the Taylor & Francis Group, an informa business

ISBN 13: 978-0-714-61471-7 (hbk)
ISBN 13: 978-0-415-76048-5 (pbk)

FOREWORD

By HAROLD J. LASKI

MY friend Mr. Justice Evatt has done me great honour in asking me to write a brief foreword to his book; but he has also laid upon me a heavy responsibility. For while he brings to the delicate and difficult subject he has here analysed with learning and pungency, not merely the insight of a disguished constitutional lawyer, but also the authority which belongs to his high judicial position, I can claim to discuss the problem only as an academic student of politics. My title to speak upon these matters is therefore indirect only, as far as they are matters of law.

But it seems to me that, in essence, they are less matters of law than of those unstated postulates of our Constitution upon which, in the last analysis, law itself always rests. From this angle Mr. Justice Evatt's plea that the reserve powers of the Crown should be reduced to known and positive principles seems to me of great importance. The strength of the Crown rests upon the conviction that its neutrality is, in all cases, beyond suspicion. It is difficult to maintain that conviction when not only is the extent of its powers unknown, but when, also, in the passion of party strife, demands for their use are made which go far beyond those limits which would enable the conviction of neutrality to be preserved. In the light of such knowledge of the Crown's activities as we have, it seems to me that any Ministry taking office should know beforehand what limitations upon its policy the habits of the Crown may impose. More, it seems to me that such knowledge should be public in order that electoral opinion may habituate itself to a body of defined and established expectation which would serve to prevent the perversion of the prerogative to party ends. Unless that is done, it will not, I think, be easy to prevent the Crown from becoming involved in controversies fatal to the respect in which it is held. Any one who remembers the manifold difficulties of the Home Rule crisis of 1911–14 will, I suggest, appreciate this view. I cannot myself explain the attitude which men so eminent as Sir William Anson and Professor Dicey took both over that conflict and the earlier struggle over the Budget of 1909 except upon the assumption that the present elasticity of the Crown's powers leaves dangerous room for the differences between men over ends to cloud their judgement about the legitimacy of the means the Crown might be persuaded to invoke upon a critical occasion. The issues at stake are now too momentous for doubts to be left unresolved.

This attitude seems to me, *a fortiori*, to apply to the position of governors and lieutenant-governors of the Dominions, and the mass of evidence collected by Mr. Justice Evatt upon their exercise of their functions seems to me decisive upon this point. To decide, however, that definition is desirable is not to decide what definition we should adopt. That seems to me a matter upon which no action can be taken which does not command the full and unfettered assent of political parties both here and in the Dominions. To secure that assent the careful exploration of the problem is essential. It is not the least of the services Mr. Justice Evatt has rendered by writing this book that he has at least made known the grounds upon which the statement of its principles must be built.

H. J. L. 1936

AUTHOR'S PREFACE

THE method or system of government in the United Kingdom and the self-governing Dominions may be described with sufficient accuracy as that of a political democracy under the Crown. This study is published because I am convinced that constant research into, and analysis of, all the present-day implications and tendencies of such method or system are essential; otherwise it may change, or be changed, without popular approval given with full knowledge, into something very different. I have attempted to describe, by reference to actual cases and precedents, certain vital aspects of our constitutional apparatus, also to suggest the provision of certain safeguards. It is obvious that such an analysis and criticism must be based upon postulates, expressed or implied. Here there are two such postulates and two only; first, the permanence of the Crown, second, the doctrine (never openly denied) that the clearly expressed will of a majority of the citizens is entitled to prevail throughout the particular constitutional unit to which they belong.

In this study I have taken important modern instances where the exercise of the reserve power of the Crown has given rise to dispute; in such a field it is essential that the material facts of the precedent should be appreciated before any generalization or criticism is attempted.

There has been included, by way of Appendix, a separate and independent discussion of the important constitutional changes recently effected in the Dominion of South Africa.

Upon the subject of constitutional history and practice several have made contributions, which were not only of great value in themselves, but affected the development of such practice. The modern student, though often compelled to disagree with them, is under a great debt to these historians of the Constitution, amongst whom Professor Keith holds a leading place.

I am also under obligation to Professor Laski of the London School of Economics, and to Professor K. H.

Bailey, Dean of the Faculty of Law in the University of Melbourne, for much encouragement and advice. The latter has been kind enough to contribute a special introduction.

For assistance in checking references, proof reading, and index preparation, I desire to thank Mr. J. J. O'Brien of the New South Wales Parliamentary Library, Mr. John Brennan, LL.B., and Mr. P. Burgess of the High Court staff, and, not least, my brother, Mr. Clive Evatt, K.C. For assistance in typing I thank Mr. K. O. Cooke and Miss H. Gover.

H. V. Evatt 1936

CONTENTS

INTRODUCTION TO THE KING AND HIS DOMINION GOVERNORS

by

ZELMAN COWEN

INTRODUCTION TO THE SECOND EDITION

Herbert Vere Evatt was appointed a Justice of the High Court of Australia in December 1930 at the age of 36, and he resigned his seat in September 1940 to contest election to the Federal House of Representatives. These ten years on the High Court Bench were very fruitful. Evatt's judgments established for him a permanent place in Australian jurisprudence; they reflect great industry, a wide learning and a range of inquiry which often extended into the fields of history, politics and sociology. Some of them, surely, are classics. His immense energy also found outlet in the writing of books, and four were published during these ten years. They were: *The King and His Dominion Governors* (1936); *Injustice Within the Law: A Study of the Case of the Dorsetshire Labourers* (1937;) *Rum Rebellion* (1938) and *Australian Labour Leader: The Story of W. A. Holman and the Labour Movement* (1940).

The King and His Dominion Governors has been out of print for some years. It has been decided to reprint it without textual amendment, and to take some note in this introduction of developments since it first appeared. Evatt's purpose was

> 'to reexamine some of the constitutional rules and practices whereby, both in Britain and in the self-governing Dominions, doctrines of overwhelming importance are treated as being too vague to be defined at all, or, if defined, defined in an unsatisfactory manner, and never regarded as enforceable by the Courts of the land. These rules and practices relate, in general, to what may be called . . . the "Reserve powers" of the Crown.'[1]

These reserve powers (exercisable by the Queen or by her representative in a Commonwealth country) include the powers to dismiss a ministry, to grant or refuse a dissolution of a legislative chamber, to designate a Prime Minister, and to appoint or to refuse to appoint Peers in the House of Lords or in a comparable Upper House.

Evatt's detailed examination of past practice and of the

[1] See p. 1 *post*.

writings of learned authorities disclosed 'the immense amount of sheer uncertainty and confusion in which the whole subject is involved'.[1] He argued that the appropriate course was to deal with the matter by restating practice in the form of rules of law.

> 'The best methods by which the constitutional practice, determining the relationship between the Crown, the first and other Ministers, the Parliament and each House thereof, and the electorate may be defined is by the passing of legislation by the Parliament possessing jurisdiction within the appropriate constitutional unit.'[2]

Both the late Professor Harold Laski and Sir Kenneth Bailey, who wrote separate introductions to the original edition, stressed the importance of more precise definition, and Bailey pointed to the heavy personal responsibilities which rested upon the Crown and its representatives in exercising these powers.

In the thirty years which have elapsed since *The King and His Dominion Governors* was published, there have been significant changes in the Commonwealth. In 1936 it comprised six member states, the United Kingdom, Australia, New Zealand, Canada, South Africa and the Irish Free State. At this writing it numbers twenty two, and Ireland and South Africa are not among that number, having left the association in 1949 and 1961 respectively. In 1936 it was unthinkable that the Commonwealth could include states which were not bound by a common allegiance to the Crown; since 1949 it is accepted that a member state may be a Republic or have its separate monarch, although the replacement of the Crown by another Head of State does not necessarily make a study of reserve powers irrelevant.

The climate of Commonwealth relations has changed in other respects. In 1936 Bailey wrote in his introduction that 'the formulation in the Dominions of constitutional conventions in harmony with the principles of responsible government has naturally been materially hampered and delayed by the persistence in our own times of something of the Crown Colony outlook, certainly not less among some sections of local opinion than in Great Britain'. In

[1] p. xxxvii *post.*
[2] p. 289 *post.*

1936 the redefinitions of the Commonwealth relationship which had been effected by the Imperial Conferences of 1926 and 1930 and by the Statute of Westminster, 1931, were still fresh, and some of their implications were uncertain and imperfectly accepted. In 1966 the very title of *The King and His Dominion Governors* is antique. The use of 'Dominion' flourished up to 1939, and it applied to the self-governing member states of the Commonwealth other than the United Kingdom. But, as Wheare points out in his *Constitutional Structure of the Commonwealth*, usage changed after the war. The Dominions Office became the Commonwealth Relations Office. The last notable usage of the word Dominion was in the Indian Independence Act 1947 which constituted two new Dominions of India and Pakistan. But that was the end of the road. There were, as Wheare notes, various objections to the use of 'Dominion'.[1] While at an earlier time it was used to distinguish the self-governing from the dependent colony or territory, it came to suggest subordination, because the United Kingdom was not a Dominion in this sense. What was called for was a terminology which comprehended all member states of the Commonwealth, including the United Kingdom, and acknowledged the equality of all. 'If', says Wheare, 'it was wise to replace "Colony" by "Dominion", why should it not be wise to replace "Dominion" by "Member of the Commonwealth?" '[2]

Of course it is not simply a matter of vocabulary. The modern Commonwealth insists on independence in substance as well as in form. Had Evatt rewritten his book in 1966 it would have had a rather different flavour, though the main argument would have stood. But the attitudes, as well as the constitutional dogmatics of a Berriedale Keith, to which Evatt made such copious reference, are quite out of fashion in the contemporary Commonwealth.

II.

Evatt's views have been considered by subsequent writers. In his able study of the *Statute of Westminster and*

[1] The Constitutional Structure of the Commonwealth (O.U.P. 1960) at pp. 13–17.
[2] *ibid* at p. 17.

Dominion Status, Wheare discussed the problems of the reserve powers of the Crown and said that it was obvious that the existence of a variety of usages without any single obligatory convention must lead to vagueness, confusion and misunderstanding in the exercise by the King of some of his most important powers. To this he appended a note that this 'is the paramount conclusion of Mr. Justice Evatt. His remedy would be not to commit agreed conventions to writing in a non-legal form (which, in the view of the present writer, has much to commend it), but to enact the appropriate rules, to translate them into strictly legal form'.[1] This reflects general agreement with Evatt's argument, if not with the precise form of the remedy.

A more detailed examination of many of Evatt's propositions and cases was made by Dr. Eugene Forsey in his *Royal Power of Dissolution of Parliament in the British Commonwealth*. This book, published in 1943, is the most elaborate study of this important reserve power so far written. While Forsey accepted many of Evatt's views and conclusions, he disagreed with some, and particularly with his analysis of the celebrated Canadian dissolution case of 1926, which was discussed by Evatt in Chapter VII of *The King and His Dominion Governors*. Forsey deals with this case in much greater detail and devotes almost half of his book to it. The Governor-General of Canada, Lord Byng, refused a dissolution to Mr. MacKenzie King who thereupon resigned. Mr. Meighen, the Conservative leader, was commissioned to form a government but found that he could not command a stable majority in the House, and within a very few days requested and was granted a dissolution. Evatt's view was that the Governor-General was wrong in granting a dissolution to Meighen, having refused it a few days earlier to King. In these circumstances, Evatt said that the Governor-General should have recommissioned King and granted him the dissolution. Forsey, on the basis of his more detailed examination, disagrees and argues that Lord Byng's action was in accordance with sound constitutional practice. Within the limits of a general introduction,

[1] *The Statute of Westminster and Dominion Status* (O.U.P. 5th ed. 1953) at p. 12.

it is not appropriate to pursue the arguments in detail, but readers of *The King and His Dominion Governors* should certainly take account of Forsey's fuller study. The disagreement between these two well-informed scholars underlines Evatt's argument that uncertainty surrounds the exercise of this very important reserve power. Forsey's general conclusions relating to the dissolution power, which are drawn from the study of many cases, show that the issues are complex and difficult. All this supports the case for settling and stating as clearly as possible the principles upon which this reserve power should be exercised.

The King and His Dominion Governors was cited and elaborately discussed in the judgment of the Chief Justice of Pakistan, Munir C.J., in the notable constitutional case of *Federation of Pakistan v. Moulvi Tamizuddin Khan* (1955).[1] The issues which were presented in this case and in the cases which followed it arose out of the dissolution of the Pakistani Constituent Assembly by the Governor of Pakistan, Mr. Ghulam Muhammad. The political background was complex. Earlier, in 1953, the Governor General had dismissed the Nazimuddin government and a new Cabinet with Mr. Mohammed Ali as Prime Minister was sworn in. Late in 1954, the Governor-General dissolved the Constituent Assembly and Mohammed Ali continued as Prime Minister with a reconstructed Cabinet. The events were summarized in the judgment of Munir C.J. in the later case of *Special Reference No. 1 of 1955*[2]

> 'The Proclamation of 24 October 1954, which is relied upon as the order dissolving the Assembly, stated that the constitutional machinery had broken down; that a state of emergency had been declared throughout Pakistan; that the Constituent Assembly, as then constituted, having lost the confidence of the people, could no longer function; and that the Prime Minister had accepted the invitation to reform the Cabinet with a view to giving the country a vigorous and stable administration. The question whether in acting in the manner that he did, the Governor-General acted in his discretion, does not arise because the acceptance of the invitation by the Prime Minister must, on the strength of several constitutional precedents in the Commonwealth, be taken as assumption by him of the responsibility for dissolution.'

[1] The judgments in this case and in the cases which followed are printed in full in Jennings: Constitutional Problems in Pakistan (Cambridge U.P. 1957) at pp. 79 et seq.

[2] Jennings op. cit, 259 at pp. 264–265.

In *Moulvi Tamizuddin's* case, the validity of the Governor-General's act did not come directly in question. It was challenged by Moulvi Tamizuddin Khan, the President of the dissolved Assembly, and the question before the Federal Supreme Court was the plaintiff's entitlement to the specific relief he sought. That in turn rested upon the validity of legislation authorizing the grant of such relief, which had been passed by the Constituent Assembly but had not been presented to the Governor-General for his assent. The Assembly had acted upon the assumption that in the exercise of its powers as a *Constituent* Assembly, its acts did not require the assent. The majority in the Federal Supreme Court held that all acts of the Assembly required the assent of the Governor-General, with the consequence that the plaintiff was not entitled to the relief sought.

The judgments ranged over wide fields of Commonwealth constitutional law and practice, and Munir C.J. dealt in considerable detail with the position of a Governor-General in a Commonwealth country. He reviewed the position of Governors as established by the conventional agreements of the Imperial Conferences of 1926 and 1930, and referred specifically to Chapter XIV of *The King and His Dominion Governors* in which Evatt dealt with the New South Wales constitutional crisis of 1926. At that time, Mr. Amery, as Secretary of State, had affirmed that it was not in accordance with constitutional principle for the Imperial government to intervene in an issue between the Governor and the New South Wales Government, involving the exercise of the Governor's constitutional duties. Munir C.J. also referred to Evatt's discussion of the reserve power in relation to the Imperial Conference Declarations of 1926 and 1930 (*The King and His Dominion Govenors*, Chapter XXI) to support the propositions that the appointment and dismissal of a Governor-General rest with the Dominion government, and that 'speaking generally, he (the Governor-general) has ceased to possess the right of exercising the reserve powers of the King against the wishes of the Dominion Government.'[1]

[1] ibid at p. 98.

Munir C.J. made various points relating to the status of a Governor-General. He observed that the Statute of Westminster itself said nothing about the Governor-General but 'took for granted the well recognized convention'[1] that the Governor-General was not in a position effectively to interfere with the administration of a Dominion contrary to the wishes of that Dominion. This did not mean that the Governor-General's position was 'either that of a nodding automaton or that of an autocrat'.[2]

> 'There may be occasions, however remote their conception may be, where the Governor-General would be entitled to withold his assent from a (sic) particular legislation. In the United Kingdom, if the House of Commons passes a law which strikes at the very foundations of the constitution, as for instance where Parliament indefinitely prolongs its life or trifles with the right of the electors to vote, the Sovereign may, and perhaps would, whether the Ministry advises it or not, exercise his reserve powers of withholding assent or dissolution. The same is the position of a Governor-General in the Dominions.'[3]

The Chief Justice did not cite authority for these propositions. They contemplate an extreme situation, though perhaps one which may possibly arise in some less politically stable areas of the far-flung Commonwealth. It would be an interesting exercise to write the law or the conventions to provide guide lines for the exercise of such powers.

The decision in *Moulvi Tamizuddin Khan* had far reaching implications in its holding that acts of the Constituent Assembly which had not received the Governor-General's assent were invalid. Many of these acts were very important and their invalidity exposed a chaotic prospect. In *Special Reference No. 1 of 1955*, the court considered what must follow in a situation in which 'we have come to the brink of a chasm'.[4] In that case, on a Reference by the Governor-General, the Court held, after elaborate discussion, that the dissolution of the Assembly by the Governor-General was, in the circumstances, a lawful exercise of power. It was further held that constitutional authority was vested in the Governor-General to deal with the emergency situation

[1] at p. 100
[2] at p. 146
[3] at p. 146
[4] Jennings op. cit. at p. 259.

resulting from the decision in *Moulvi Tamizuddin Khan*. The doctrine was stated in very broad terms by Munir C.J.

'. . . . the free exercise of a discretion or prerogative power at a critical juncture is essential to the executive government of every civilized country, the indispensable condition being that the exercise of that power is always subject to the legislative authority of Parliament, to be exercised *ex post facto*

. . . The disaster that stared the Governor-General in the face, consequent on the illegal manner in which the Constituent Assembly exercised its legislative authority, is apparent from the results described in the *Reference* as having followed from this Court's decision in Mr. *Tamizuddin Khan's* case and the subsequent case of *Usif Patel*. The Governor-General must, therefore, be *held* to have acted in order to avert an impending disaster and to prevent the State and society from dissolution. His proclamation of 16 April 1955, declaring that the laws mentioned in the Schedule to the Emergency Powers Ordinance 1955 shall be retrospectively enforceable is accordingly valid during the interim period, i.e. until the validity of these laws is decided upon by the new Constituent Assembly. Needless to say that since the validity of these laws during the interim period is founded on necessity, there should be no delay in calling the Constituent Assembly.'[1]

This is a very special reserve power, based squarely on necessity and emergency, and one which, if it commands general acceptance, raises formidable difficulties of precise formulation. These Pakistani cases raise a range of fascinating problems and Evatt would surely have relished the opportunity to analyse them.

III.

In Chapter V of *The King and His Dominion Governors* Evatt discussed the double dissolution of the Australian Commonwealth parliament in 1914. That dissolution was granted by the Governor-General, Sir Ronald Munro Ferguson, on the advice of the Prime Minister, Mr. Joseph Cook, under the terms of section 57 of the Commonwealth Constitution. Evatt wrote that that case must be regarded as establishing four propositions

(1) that so long as the conditions mentioned in section 57 are complied with, the Governor-General will grant a double dissolution to Ministers who possess the confidence of the House of Representatives

[1] at p. 307

(2) that it is not material to consider the importance or significance of the bill which, being the subject of dispute between the two Houses, becomes the occasion of the double dissolution

(3) that, in particular, it is not necessary that the Senate's rejection of the specified bill should have created a condition of financial deadlock between the Houses.

(4) that it is immaterial that the Ministers deliberately set out to create the occasion mentioned in section 57 which is exactly what the Cook government did.[1]

A double dissolution, under the authority of section 57, was granted by the Governor-General, Sir William McKell, in March 1951. Sir William had been appointed in 1947, and his appointment was sharply criticized at that time on the ground that he had come to the office directly from an active career in State politics. The Prime Minister, Mr. Chifley, stated that the appointment had been made in accordance with the terms and procedures laid down at the Imperial Conference of 1930.[2]

The papers relating to the double dissolution of 1951 were not tabled by the government in the House of Representatives until May 1956. In 1951, the Menzies (Liberal-Country Party) government commanded a majority in the House of Representatives, while Labour controlled the Senate. The Commonwealth Bank Bill 1950 which, inter alia, provided for the re-establishment of a Board of Directors for the Commonwealth Bank was introduced into the House of Representatives in March 1950, and was passed without amendment by that House in May 1950. The Senate passed the bill in June 1950 with amendments which included the deletion of the provisions for the re-establishment of the Bank Board. On June 22, when the bill was returned to the House of Representatives, the House carried a resolution 'that the amendments be disagreed to' and the reasons for disagreement were drawn up and approved. The bill was returned to the Senate which adopted a resolution insisting on its amendments and on June 23, the House resolved

[1] p. 45 *post*

[2] Parliamentary Debates (House of Representatives) Vol. 191 at p. 2051.

'that the House insists on disagreeing to the Amendments insisted on by the Senate' and the bill was then returned to the Senate.

In the same session, in October 1950, the Commonwealth Bank Bill was once again introduced in the House of Representatives in its original form, and it was passed and transmitted to the Senate. There followed a long delay in the Senate which discussed the bill from time to time. The second reading was finally carried in the Senate on March ·1951, and on that day the Senate passed a resolution that the bill be referred to a Select Committee which was to report to the Senate in four weeks. From the date of its second presentation to the Senate up to this point, rather more than five months had elapsed. In his memorandum of advice to the Governor-General, dated March 16, 1951, the Prime Minister, Mr. Menzies, said that the device of remitting the bill to a select committee was, in light of the history, 'clearly nothing more than a delaying procedure', which could be continued indefinitely. This was a 'failure to pass' within the meaning of section 57; the terms of the section both as to this requirement and as to time were satisfied and Mr. Menzies 'unhesitatingly' advised the Governor-General to exercise his powers to dissolve both Houses simultaneously.

In addition, Mr. Menzies observed that

> 'on the one former occasion upon which, in 1914, a Double Dissolution was sought and obtained, some importance appears to have been attached to the unworkable condition of the Parliament as a whole. Possibly such considerations were given a weight 37 years ago which they would not now be given having regard to modern constitutional developments. But if they are material then there can be no doubt that the present position in the Commonwealth Parliament is such that good government, secure administration and the reasonably speedy enactment of a legislative programme are being made extremely difficult, if not actually impossible.'

This was followed by a brief recital of the legislative history of the Social Services Consolidation Bill, the Communist Party Dissolution Bill and the National Service Bill. This, the Prime Minister said, disclosed a history of delay and frustration which stemmed from the opposed political configurations of the two Houses.

> 'Under these circumstances', said Mr. Menzies 'if the only conditior

upon which a Double Dissolution could be granted was, broadly expressed, that a serious conflict between the two Houses ought to be ended by the votes of the electors, then I would have no doubt whatever that as Prime Minister I should be more than justified in asking you to take the necessary steps to have determined by those electors a disagreement which tends so strongly against the giving of prompt expression to the public will.'

Opinions were also furnished to the Governor-General by the Attorney-General, Senator Spicer, and the Solicitor-General, Professor K. H. Bailey. The Attorney-General's opinion was brief and stated that the requirements of section 57 were satisfied since the Senate had 'failed to pass' the bill, and the required time had elapsed. In a more elaborate opinion, Professor Bailey reached the same conclusion. The opinion dealt principally with the requirement that the Senate should 'fail to pass' the bill. The Solicitor-General observed that while 'the preliminary question on which the Governor-General must be satisfied can properly be said to be a question of fact, its ascertainment is a matter rather of political interpretation or elucidation than the mere establishment of acts and events.'

On March 17 the Governor-General wrote to the Prime Minister acknowledging receipt of his advice and the opinions, and stated that he was prepared forthwith to grant a simultaneous dissolution of both Houses of Parliament under the provisions of section 57 of the Constitution.

While these events were unfolding, the question was actively discussed in the Press. It was said that Labour members believed that the Governor-General would not accept the Prime Minister's advice, and it was also suggested that the Governor-General might seek the independent legal advice of the Chief Justice of the High Court, Sir John Latham. There was much discussion of the 1914 case when Sir Ronald Munro Ferguson had consulted the Chief Justice, Sir Samuel Griffith, who had furnished him with a detailed memorandum.

In fact the Governor-General did not seek independent advice and accepted the advice of the Prime Minister, supported by the opinions of the Attorney-General and Solicitor-General. It is noteworthy that no reference was made in these documents to any obligation or supposed obligation of the Governor-General to accept ministerial advice. In

1914 Mr. Cook had urged this obligation on Sir Ronald Munro Ferguson as a ground for granting the requested dissolution.[1]

Dr. Evatt, as Deputy Leader of the Opposition, was reported[2] as saying that the government's use of the Banking Bills as a device for gaining a double dissolution was a 'hollow sham'. But he welcomed the opportunity to present the issues to the people, an anticipation which was not confirmed by the event, when Liberal-Country Party majorities were returned in both Houses.

On June 13, 1951, soon after the new parliament reassembled, Dr. Evatt asked on the floor of the House of Representatives whether the Prime Minister would table the documents and opinions relating to the double dissolution. He said that it had been the 'practice' in the past 'to make such documents public as guides to constitutional practice'.[3] There had been only one earlier double dissolution, though there were many cases of single dissolutions, and the disclosure of the 1914 documents was made late in 1914 by Mr. Fisher who came to office after the double dissolution election which Mr. Cook lost. Mr. Menzies gave a cautious answer to Dr. Evatt, and in September 1951, Dr. Evatt renewed his question. He pointed to the 'importance of the constitutional precedent that was involved'. It was important to know

> 'the assertions of fact or of constitutional law or practice that were made by responsible ministers . . . It is on that basis that the constitutional practice in this country is established and without the information that I seek nobody can say what the constitutional practice is.'[4]

The Prime Minister agreed that the documents were 'of first-class historic and constitutional importance'. He said, however, that while they would be tabled at a proper time, they would not be published at a time when discussion might embarrass Sir William McKell. In the event, they were tabled almost five years later.

The facts of the 1951 double dissolution satisfy the propositions formulated by Evatt as emerging from the

[1] p. 42 *post*
[2] Age Newspaper, Melbourne, March 19, 1951.
[3] Parliamentary Debates (House of Representatives) vol. 213 at p. 49.
[4] ibid. Vol. 214 at p. 37.

1914 case. The government in its advice to the Governor-General in 1951 argued that the precise terms of section 57 had been complied with. This satisfied the Governor-General who saw no need to call for independent advice which his predecessor had sought in 1914. There was nothing on the face of the documents which gave expression to a ministerial view that the Governor-General had no right to call for such independent advice, and there was no assertion in the government documents of any constitutional obligation to act on the advice of ministers. The Prime Minister added to his specific arguments based on section 57, more general propositions relating to 'the unworkable condition of the Parliament as a whole'. In 1914, the Governor-General placed what Evatt describes as 'complete reliance . . . upon the special parliamentary situation existing at the time of the request for a double dissolution'[1]. But while Mr. Menzies put forward this additional argument and documented it, he observed that it might now not carry the weight it had carried in 1914.

The 1951 double dissolution does not add significantly to the learning on the exercise of the reserve powers; it chiefly contributes to the definition of the words 'fails to pass' in section 57. Twice now a double dissolution has been requested and recommended and twice it has been granted. It would certainly be difficult to argue that Sir William McKell's action in granting a double dissolution was wanting in constitutional justification.

IV.

The reserve power to designate a Prime Minister was not given any detailed consideration by Evatt. In Australia and New Zealand it appears to be the practice that the Governor-General will commission the man elected by the majority party (or major element in a coalition) as its leader. So in Australia on the death of Mr. J. A. Lyons in 1939 Dr. Earle Page took over as caretaker Prime Minister, until Mr. Menzies was elected leader of the United Australia Party. When Mr. John Curtin died in office, Mr. Forde,

[1] p. 49 *post*

the Deputy leader, was commissioned until the new election of a Labour leader took place. That ballot, which was contested by Mr. Forde, resulted in the election of Mr. Chifley who was then commissioned. A like practice was followed in New Zealand when Mr. Holland announced his impending retirement and the National Party elected Mr. Holyoake who was then invited to form a government.

English practice has not been so clear. When Sir Anthony Eden retired in 1957, Mr. Macmillan was commissioned by the Queen. That was not as a result of an open election by the parliamentary party, and the Queen took the advice of a number of Conservative leaders. Lord Salisbury is said to have conveyed to the Queen the results of a rather formal Cabinet poll and there had been a less formal sounding out of Conservative backbenchers. After the choice of Mr. Macmillan was announced, the Opposition (Labour) shadow cabinet issued a statement in which it was said that

> 'The Parliamentary Committee . . . considers that, if at any time a Labour Prime Minister resigns or dies while in office and while the Government retains its majority in the House of Commons, the appropriate course to follow would be for the Parliamentary Labour party first to proceed to the election of a new leader who would then be ready to accept the invitation of the Crown to become Prime Minister.'

In 1963 on the retirement of Mr. Macmillan, Sir Alec Douglas Home was commissioned by the Queen. There was widespread criticism of the conservative party processes as a result of which the selection was made, and there was a call to bring the procedure into line with Labour practice.[1] On the retirement of Sir Alec Douglas Home this course was in fact followed, and it was by parliamentary election that Mr. Edward Heath was designated as leader of the Conservative party. It seems clear that this is a desirable procedure, for the commissioning of a Prime Minister is not a case in which the Crown or its representative should be required to make a real choice.

V.

Evatt's main argument in *The King and His Dominion Governors* was, as we have seen, that the reserve powers of

[1] See London *Economist* March 2, 1963, at p. 77; October 26, 1963, at p. 351.

the Crown should, in Sir Kenneth Bailey's apt words, be subjected to the normal and natural process of analysis and definition and reduction to rules of positive law. Whether it was the voice of Evatt which persuaded, or whether it was the intrinsic worth of the argument, some modern Commonwealth constitutions have essayed the task of writing conventions or usages into positive law. One example was the Western Nigerian constitution considered by the Privy Council in *Adegbenro v. Akintola*.[1] The provision considered in that case was section 33(10) of the constitution, which, as it then stood, provided that Ministers of the Government should hold office during the Governor's pleasure provided that

(a) the Governor shall not remove the Premier from office unless it appears to him that the Premier no longer commands the support of a majority of the members of the House of Assembly.

Other sections of the constitution related to the appointment of the Premier by the Governor, to the exercise of the functions of the Governor and particularly to the circumstances in which the Governor was required to act on ministerial advice and to those in which he might act in accordance 'with his own deliberate judgment'. Section 31(4) was a legislative formulation of the exercise of the reserve power to dissolve parliament. It provided

31(4) In the exercise of his powers to dissolve the Legislative Houses of the Region, the Governor shall act in accordance with the advice of the Premier

Provided that—

(a) if the Premier recommends a dissolution and the Governor considers that the government of the Region can be carried on without a dissolution and that a dissolution would not be in the interests of the Region he may refuse to dissolve the Legislative Houses;

(b) if the House of Assembly passes a resolution that it has no confidence in the Government of the Region and the Premier does not within three days either resign or advise a dissolution, the Governor may dissolve the Legislative Houses; and

(c) if the office of Premier is vacant and the Governor considers that there is no prospect of his being able to appoint a person who can command the support of a majority of the members of the House of Assembly to that office within a reasonable time, the Governor may dissolve the Legislative Houses.

[1] [1963] A.C. 614.

It was provided by sec. 38(1) (proviso (a)) that in the exercise of these powers, the Governor should act in accordance with his own deliberate judgment.

This is an interesting attempt to spell out in terms of positive law the rules governing the exercise of an important reserve power. Inevitably it is very widely drawn; wide discretions are still reposed in the Governor though general guide lines are furnished for him. But as *Adegbenro v. Akintola* shows, the interpretation of such a provision may give rise to acute differences of opinion. In that case, the power to dismiss was in issue, in the context of section 33(10)(a), which denied power to the Governor to dismiss unless it appeared to him that the Premier no longer commanded the support of a majority in the Assembly. There was sharp political dispute in the Western Region and the Governor dismissed the premier, Chief Akintola, having received a letter from 66 members of the Assembly (a majority) stating that they no longer had confidence in Akintola, and appointed Adegbenro in his place. The dismissal of Akintola was challenged and it was argued in the Federal Supreme Court, and on appeal in the Privy Council, that section 33(10)(a) required a prior decision or resolution on the floor of the House showing that the Premier no longer commanded the support of a majority of the House. On the other hand it was argued that there was no requirement on the face of the section of a determination of the issue in the House, and that the Governor could exercise the power of dismissal by reference to other information or intelligence. Speaking for the majority in the Federal Supreme Court, Ademola C.J., held that it was the clear intention of section 33(10)(a) to require reference to proceedings in the House.[1]

> To my mind the conclusion is inescapable that the framers of the constitution wanted the House to be responsible at every level for the ultimate fate of the Government and the Premier. The horizon must be higher than leaving it to one man. The Governor might eventually be the instrument used to effect this, but his position as final arbiter must be dictated by events in the House or events emanating from the House and not by a letter, however well meaning, signed by a body of members of the House. Law

[1] Federal Supreme Court 187/1962.

and convention cannot be replaced by party political moves outside the House.

I believe that the Constitution contemplated proceedings in the House as being the touchstone of whether the Premier (and his Government) commands the support of a majority of the members or no longer commands such support.

. . . It will be an unduly narrow and restrictive interpretation of the powers of the House, and a correspondingly unduly wide interpretation of the powers of the Governor, if, in the circumstances, section 33(10) is interpreted in any other way except in a way which makes it clear that the evidence emanates from proceedings in the House.

The majority said that section 33(10) was, together with other provisions of the constitution, an attempt to frame United Kingdom constitutional conventions in terms of positive law, and that the proper reading of the relevant United Kingdom convention was that there must be a reference to events occurring on the floor of the legislature.

The Privy Council, speaking through Lord Radcliffe, reversed this decision. The phrase 'the Premier no longer commands the support of a majority of the members' was derived from United Kingdom constitutional understandings. But, as Lord Radcliffe observed, 'the practical application of these principles to a given situation, if it arose in the United Kingdom, would depend less upon any simple statement of principle than upon the actual facts of that situation and the good sense and political sensitivity of the main actors called upon to take part.'[1] It was observed that there were very real dangers in removing a Premier on the basis of evidence and indications other than an adverse vote of the House, but this was a counsel of caution to the Governor, and not a consideration going to the proper interpretation of the clause.

Lord Radcliffe then considered the Federal Supreme Court's reliance on United Kingdom usage. The passage calls for extended quotation:[2]

'Another argument has been advanced to the effect that the Nigerian Constitutions are modelled on the current constitutional doctrines of the United Kingdom, and, since the British Sovereign would not be regarded as acting with constitutional propriety in dismissing a Prime Minister from office without the foundation of an adverse vote on a major issue in the

[1] [1963] A.C. 614 at p. 628.
[2] at pp. 631-2.

House of Commons, so the Governor in Western Nigeria must similarly be treated as precluded from exercising his power of removal in the absence of a vote of the same kind. This approach to the matter appears to their Lordships to have had some influence upon the view taken by the majority of the Federal Supreme Court in this case, and, since it seems capable of conveying an implication that could be misleading in other situations apart from the present one, their Lordships wish to make two observations upon it.

The first is that British constitutional history does not offer any but a general negative guide as to the circumstances in which a Sovereign can dismiss a Prime Minister. Since the principles which are accepted today began to take shape with the passing of the Reform Bill of 1832 no British Sovereign has in fact dismissed or removed a Prime Minister, even allowing for the ambiguous exchanges which took place between William IV and Lord Melbourne in 1834. Discussion of constitutional doctrine bearing upon a Prime Minister's loss of support in the House of Commons concentrates therefore upon a Prime Minister's duty to ask for liberty to resign or for a dissolution, rather than upon the Sovereign's right of removal, an exercise of which is not treated as being within the scope of practical politics. In this state of affairs it is vain to look to British Precedent for guidance upon the circumstances in which or the eventual material upon which a Prime Minister can be dismissed, where dismissal is an actual possibility: and the right of removal which is explicitly recognized in the Nigerian Constitutions must be interpreted according to the wording of its own limitations and not to limitations which that wording does not import.

The second observation is perhaps only another way of making the same point. It is true that the Western Nigerian Constitution, allowance made for the federal structure, does embody much of the constitutional practice and principle of the United Kingdom. That appears from a study of its terms. There are identifiable differences of scheme to be found in certain sections, but no one, it seems, questions the general similarity or the origin of many of its provisions. But, accepting that, it must be remembered that, as Lord Bryce once said, the British Constitution 'works by a body of understandings which no writer can formulate'; whereas the Constitution of Western Nigeria is now contained in a written instrument in which it has been sought to formulate with precision the powers and duties of the various agencies that it holds in balance. That instrument now stands in its own right; and, while it may well be useful on occasions to draw on British practice or doctrine in interpreting a doubtful phrase whose origin can be traced or to study decisions on the Constitutions of Australia or the United States where federal issues are involved, it is in the end the wording of the Constitution itself that is to be interpreted and applied, and this wording can never be overridden by the extraneous principles of other Constitutions which are not explicitly incorporated in the formulae that have been chosen as the frame of this Constitution.'

A reading of section 33(10) in the context of the constitution as a whole led to the conclusion that the Governor might exercise his power to remove a premier without the requirement of a vote on the floor of the House.

The judgment of the Privy Council makes two important points. First, United Kingdom usage and practice affords no certain guidance in the exercise of this reserve power. Indeed the Nigerian court and the Privy Council differed on the reading of that practice. Second, once a practice is written into positive law, it must stand as it is written. This is not the occasion to embark on a discussion of canons of constitutional interpretation, and the two courts which were called upon to interpret section 33(10) reached differing conclusions as to its meaning. The case aptly illustrates Evatt's argument. It also exposes the problems which confront the draftsman who takes heed of that argument and seeks to reduce convention, practice, or usage to positive law.

The issues on which the Federal Supreme Court and the Privy Council passed aroused great political feeling, and the decision of the Privy Council was followed by a constitutional amendment expressed to operate from a date prior to the dismissal of Akintola, which provided that the Governor might exercise his power of removal only in consequence of a vote of no confidence by the House of Assembly. In the subsequent republican Constitution of Nigeria the President and the Governors of the Region were deprived of this power of dismissal.[1]

VI.

In this introduction no attempt has been made to note every amendment which the text of *The King and His Dominion Governors* requires to be brought completely up to date. For example, each Australian State now elects ten senators, not six as stated in Chapter V, on the double dissolution of 1914.[2] But these are minor matters, and Evatt's general thesis remains persuasive. Uncertainty and vagueness in the definition of reserve powers may lead to inconsistent action and may embroil the Crown and its representatives in unhappy political controversy. But, as

[1] Nwabueze: Constitutional Law of the Nigerian Republic (Butterworths 1964) at p. 202.
[2] p. 37 *post*.

the Nigerian experience shows, there may be difficulty in reducing the reserve powers to certainty by legislative definition. In any event, that definition may be and in some cases will necessarily be complex and discretions will not wholly be eradicated. It remains only to say that it is a fitting memorial to a distinguished scholar and lawyer that this important book should once again be made available, and the present writer echoes the words of his own teacher, Sir Kenneth Bailey, in his introduction to the original edition, that 'as a teacher of constitutional law I welcome very much the (re) appearance of so valuable a piece of work as this book is.'

INTRODUCTION TO THE FIRST EDITION

By K. H. BAILEY

AN age of great controversies puts to the test all institutions, however soundly established. When vital questions come to issue, each side is fain to invoke the full exercise of constitutional powers, and seeks to resolve in its own favour all that is obscure or ambiguous in the existing situation. The fate of the constitution itself will depend on the adequacy of the provision it makes for what may be called emergency or crisis or reserve powers. One of the distinctive features of the British constitution, as has often been remarked, is the combination of the democratic principle that all political authority comes from the people, and hence that the will of the people must prevail, with the maintenance of a monarchy armed with legal powers to dismiss ministers drawn from among the people's elected representatives, and even to dissolve the elected legislature itself. In normal times the very existence of those powers can simply be ignored. In times of crisis, however, it immediately becomes of vital importance to know what they are and how they will be exercised. Readers of Mr. Mitchison's recent book, *The First Workers' Government 1936*, will recollect the central place of the Crown in the plan there unfolded, and the history of the adjustments made in Great Britain and the Dominions to meet the effects of economic depression shows the superficiality of the current view that convention has rendered negligible the Crown's personal place in politics. It is not too much to say that the whole future of the British constitutional system is likely to depend on the extent to which, in the next few years, it is demonstrated that the reserve powers of the Crown are not the antithesis but the corollary of the democratic principle that political authority is derived from the people.

In view of the fundamental issues of social reconstruction which are defining themselves in the politics alike of Great Britain and of the Dominions, Mr. Justice Evatt's book is a very timely one. In a detailed, independent, and comprehensive survey of recent constitutional history, the learned author seeks to elucidate the principles which have guided the King and his representatives overseas in exercising the reserve powers committed to the Crown by the constitution, with a view to clarifying and defining the conventions which in this most obscure field should regulate the exercise of the prerogative. The subject pertains strictly to the custom rather than to the law of the constitution. But no British constitutional lawyer can make any satisfactory separation between the two, and on any constitutional subject the position and standing of Mr. Justice Evatt alike command attention for his views. Both in his judgments in the High Court of Australia and in his general contributions to learning he has shown his deep concern in the development of the constitutional structure. The University of Sydney awarded him its Doctorate of Laws some years ago, in respect of a thesis—the only one ever awarded the University Medal—on the law of the prerogative in Britain and in the Dominions. A formidable critic of received opinions, with a vigorous and well-defined social philosophy, Mr. Justice Evatt presents conclusions, in this book as elsewhere, which challenge consideration even where they do not command agreement. It is almost superfluous, but may not be thought an impertinence, to remark on the thorough documentation of the whole, which enables the reader who finds some of the analysis disturbing to check for himself the objectivity of the survey.

The formulation in the Dominions of constitutional conventions in harmony with the principles of responsible government has naturally been materially hampered and delayed by the persistence into our own times of something of the Crown Colony outlook, certainly not less among some sections of local opinion than in Great Britain. Even quite recent precedents have to be scrutinized with especial care before any general principle for future guidance can be drawn from them. Indeed perhaps the most interesting and important sections of this book, both from the Dominion and from the British point of view, are those which analyse the action of the Crown in Great Britain during the critical years 1909–14. For one thing, it is now the recorded convention of Dominion constitutions (and in this regard, as the learned author contends, no distinction should be drawn between the constitution of a Dominion itself and that of one of the component States or Provinces in a Federal Dominion), that the King's representative holds 'in all essential respects the same position in relation to the administration of public affairs in the Dominion as is held by His Majesty the King in Great Britain'. Accordingly it is necessary in the Dominions now to discover the principles which have underlain the action of the King himself in recent constitutional crises. Further, the exigencies of three-party government no less than the emergencies of the depression period have brought into fresh prominence in Great Britain the unsolved questions that arise concerning the reserve powers of the Crown.

The most striking conclusion that emerges from a survey of past practice is the immense amount of sheer uncertainty and confusion in which the whole subject is involved. At the moment of writing a ministry has resigned in Victoria in the first week of a new Parliament, owing to the withdrawal of support (since the elections) by the party which had in the previous Parliament participated in a composite ministry. The Premier did not actually ask for a dissolution; but the state of public opinion, during the day or two during which it was widely supposed that he would, has amply confirmed Mr. Justice Evatt's remark that 'it is often impossible to tell whether the conventions are being obeyed, because no one can say with sufficient certainty what the conventions are'. It is small wonder that the continental publicists who, in the years of constitution-making at the end of the Great War, drew freely on the British system in their desire to establish Parliamentary government, found themselves hopelessly at odds in their interpretation of what was necessary to reproduce the British model.

The thesis maintained by Mr. Justice Evatt is that the reserve powers of the Crown should be subjected to the normal and natural process of analysis and definition and reduction to rules of positive law, just as the relations between the two Houses of the Imperial Parliament, or of the Commonwealth Parliament in Australia, have been defined and expressed in the form of law. The interpretation and maintenance of those rules would then normally become the function of some competent tribunal, judicial or arbitral. The idea that there is something radically un-British about this process, so happily disposed of in Mr. K. C. Wheare's book on the Statute of Westminster, is dealt with also in this book, from a different point of view. The risks of the process are of course great. A constitution in an emergency period has need of emergency powers, not over-rigidly defined. But the risks of undefined elasticity are also great. They are great even in the United Kingdom, but they are greater still in the Dominions. The importance in this regard of the new conventions regulating the appointment of the King's representative in a Dominion can scarcely be over-emphasized. Any exercise of reserve powers by the Crown must inevitably involve the King, or his Dominion representative, in the assumption of very heavy personal responsibility, to his advisers, to Parliament, and to the people. It will inevitably entail unpopularity in some quarters. That is a serious matter even in the case of the Sovereign. But it is an absolutely vital matter in the case of a Governor, who is a temporary officer, and who now, it appears, holds his office upon the advice of his own ministers. Under such circumstances the Governor can readily be stripped of all personal discretion, and left entirely without reserve powers. Such considerations as these—fully discussed in this book—lend additional weight and urgency to the contentions of Mr. Justice Evatt.

It remains that the writer of this brief Introduction should express his sense of the honour which the learned author has conferred upon him in inviting him to write it. As a teacher of constitutional law I welcome very much the appearance of so valuable a piece of work as this book is.

K. H. B. 1936

I

THE GENERAL PROBLEM OF THE RESERVE POWER OF THE CROWN

IT is desirable to re-examine some of the constitutional rules and practices whereby, both in Britain and in the self-governing Dominions, doctrines of overwhelming importance are treated as being too vague to be defined at all, or, if defined, defined in an unsatisfactory manner, and never regarded as enforceable by the Courts of the land. These rules and practices relate, in general, to what may be called, not for the first time, the 'Reserve Powers' of the Crown. Reference is made, not to the purely legal question whether or not any given power authorizes action on the part of the Monarch or his Dominion representative, for such a question is determined by the Courts by the standard of the common law or the relevant Statute. Nor is reference intended to the mere manner of carrying into effect any given legal power of the Executive. What concerns us is the real relationship between the King or his Dominion representative on the one hand, and, on the other, the four remaining elements which go to make up the polity in the typical British self-governing community. These four elements may include (1) the Cabinet or Ministry, (2) the House of Commons or representative Assembly, (3) the House of Lords or Upper House, and (4) the electorate or the people.

The mention of the main elements into which the apparatus of a typical British State or constitutional unit may be resolved, at once suggests the desirability of ascertaining and defining the relationship existing between such elements.

For instance there is the great question whether the King or his representative in a Dominion is possessed of a sufficient discretionary authority to ignore the advice of a Ministry which is no longer in possession of the confidence of the representative Assembly. Is the King or the Governor always bound to grant to a Ministry in office a dissolution of Parliament? May the King refuse to appoint Peers in the United Kingdom or may his representative refuse to appoint to the Upper House of a Dominion? Such a question may arise where the legal power to appoint is vested in the King or the Dominion Governor, and there is no statutory limitation upon the number of persons who may be appointed. May the King or the Governor constitutionally refuse assent to legislation which has passed both Houses?

And there is the even more important question whether, and under what conditions, the King or the Governor possesses sufficient constitutional authority to act *against* the advice of the Ministers fully possessing the confidence of the popular House, by (1) dismissing the Ministers, and (2) dissolving the Assembly.

That such questions are of the utmost significance is shown by the very recent case of the dismissal by a Governor of a Ministry in full possession of the confidence of the majority of the representative Assembly in a self-governing State. Such dismissal occurred in New South Wales in May 1932, and was followed by the even more important act of dissolving the representative Assembly, although almost one-half of its normal constitutional existence remained.[1]

In connexion with such grave constitutional problems, one observes a very curious growth of 'authority'. The helpful precedent is selected and the general statement advanced until, as time goes on, the loose generalization is itself treated as the true and only gospel. Further, what is really the appropriate subject for specially trained constitutional lawyers and historians tends to become the hunting-ground of mere political party polemics. I am convinced that this tends to prejudice, if not to endanger, the true constitutional position both of the Monarch and of his representatives, and that, in spite of the difficulties of the task, it is important that many of the supposed rules amd maxims affecting the reserve power of the Crown should be investigated anew.

The student engaged in such a research is almost overwhelmed by the assertions and deductions of those who are more inclined to make a general statement than to support it by careful reasoning or a close investigation of the facts.

[1] See *post*, Chap. XIX.

And even those who have devoted considerable time, labour, and skill to the effort of explaining the mysteries of these reserve prerogatives become dogmatic upon the questions, and either fail to take account of the special character of the individual precedent, or refuse to face modern developments because of some particular preconception.

In this field, Professor Keith occupies a very special position because of his many and multifarious books, articles, and letters. He has not only contributed greatly to the knowledge and information of those interested; he has also taken a prominent part in some of the recent constitutional struggles. None the less, there is a great danger involved in accepting his writings as necessarily authoritative.

Frequent reference will have to be made to Keith's works. Introducing himself to the topic of Colonial Government, with which Todd had dealt some twenty-five years before, Keith at first struck a note of inquiry and criticism. But since the publication of the first edition of his work *Responsible Government in the Dominions*[1] there has been a very noticeable change in tone. Indeed some of his later writings are freely interspersed with condemnatory references of an extreme, almost violent, character to those who entertained opposing views upon important constitutional problems.

In the scarcity of authoritative writings, it is inevitable that Keith's works should be quoted by participants in such controversies. This often leads to unfortunate results. It may happen that, even in the first stage of a dispute when one political party in a Dominion desires either to effect or to resist a political *coup*, the authority of Keith is invoked. Soon, the Professor's observations are cabled to the Dominion. It is almost unavoidable that a mixture of political facts and political comment will affect this process of constitutional 'spot diagnosis', the physician being ten thousand miles away from the spot.

Moreover, in these matters it is only the infallible who can safely dogmatize, and no one is infallible. Thus in the 1928 edition of his *Responsible Government in the Dominions* Keith sought to minimize the significance of the Report of the Imperial Conference of 1926, asserting that it was

[1] In the year 1909.

'sentimental rather than substantial',[1] and that General Hertzog had exaggerated its importance. For instance he asserted that:

> 'The suggestion that the King can act directly on the advice of Dominion Ministers is a constitutional monstrosity, which would be fatal to the security of the position of the Crown.'[2]

With these bold assertions may be contrasted the suggestion of Professor Jenks, published in 1927 in a discussion of the 1926 Conference. He then said:

> 'Who then is to advise the King upon the appointment of a Governor-General, say of Canada, Australia, or New Zealand. The answer (I may be wrong) seems as a matter of principle to me to be reasonably plain, namely, that, just as the King in matters affecting the United Kingdom takes the advice of his Prime Minister in London, so, in matters affecting Canada, he will take the advice of his Prime Minister in the Dominion, and in the case of Australia, that of his Prime Minister in the Commonwealth of Australia, and so forth. And I see no difficulty in applying the principle in that way.'[3]

Jenks's view was clear, logical, and at any rate reasonably practical. The alternative was, as Jenks himself pointed out, that Lord Stamfordham or his successor, as private secretary to the King, should 'run' the Empire. As will be seen later, the event has proved Jenks to be right. Is it still a 'constitutional monstrosity'?[4]

An illustration of the extreme heat which was engendered in some of these constitutional matters was Keith's reference to Mr. Asquith's expression of opinion that the King was not necessarily bound to accede to a request by an existing Cabinet for a dissolution. Keith said that this was a 'dictum . . . evidencing the spokesman's obvious and regrettable decline in mental power and sense of political realities'.[5]

Mr. Asquith's speech (reported in *The Times* of December 19th, 1923) will be discussed later, and it will be shown that

[1] A. B. Keith, *Responsible Government in the Dominions* (1928), (Preface), p. xviii.

[2] Ibid. (pp. xii–xiii).

[3] *Cambridge Law Journal*, vol. iii (1927), p. 21.

[4] See pp. 195–6 *post*.

[5] A. B. Keith, *Responsible Government in the Dominions*, vol. i (1928), p. 148.

there was no warrant for such a criticism.[1] All that is necessary to say here is that other authorities have approved the Asquith opinion, Sir John Marriott, for instance, stating that the existing constitutional position was expressed by Mr. Asquith in 'terms of unimpeachable accuracy'.[2]

Recent expressions of Keith's views seem to have been even more saturated with prejudicial matter. Whether this has its source in his own political opinions, or in that of his correspondents, is beside the point. For instance, his recent work, called *Constitutional Law of the British Dominions* (1933) contains an unjustified criticism of the appointment of Sir Isaac Isaacs as Governor-General of the Commonwealth. The objection is vaguely stated, but it seems to include 'great age', 'the objections of the Opposition', and the probability of 'accusations of partisanship'.[3] Keith also condemns the action of the Chief Justice of Tasmania, whilst Acting-Governor in 1924, as being 'in flat defiance of his duty to preserve the law'.[4] As will be seen, the Chief Justice acted not only after consultation with his advisers but also with the express approval of the then Secretary of State for the Colonies.[5] Keith says that in 1920 the Acting-Governor of Queensland, Mr. Lennon, 'a Labour nominee swamped unconstitutionally the Legislative Council of Queensland in order to secure the passage of legislation of a confiscatory character.'[6] He adds that Mr. Lennon having been 'formerly a Labour Minister', his appointment as Lieutenant-Governor 'was clearly improper since necessarily he was a partisan'.[7]

Keith does not propose that no person who has ever been actively engaged in politics should ever occupy the position of representative of the King, because that would disqualify so many of the most able and distinguished of such representatives. Is it that Keith's objection to Mr. Lennon was to the particular political party which had appointed him?[8]

[1] See *post*, Chaps. VII and VIII.

[2] Marriott, *The Mechanism of the Modern State*, vol. ii, p. 35.

[3] A. B. Keith, *The Constitutional Law of the British Dominions* (1933), p. 135.

[4] Ibid., pp. 136.

[5] See *post*, Chap. XX (*c*).

[6] A. B. Keith, *The Constitutional Law of the British Dominions* (1933), pp. 135, 136.

[7] Ibid., p. 155.

[8] See *post*, Chap. XVI.

With such instances may be contrasted Keith's almost lyrical praise of Sir P. Game, the Governor of New South Wales who in 1932 dismissed a Labour Ministry from office in New South Wales, although it then possessed the confidence of the popular Assembly.[1] It becomes very difficult to disentangle Keith's declarations and statements of constitutional practice when his comment is mingled with such irrelevant allegations of fact as 'the extremist views' and the 'wild promises of prosperity' of a Labour leader.[2]

Enough has already been said to show some of the difficulties with which students of the Crown's 'Reserve Powers' are confronted. The difficulties are closely related to what Keith calls the 'fundamental elasticity' of the British constitution[3] when he emphasizes that the temptation to define the powers of the King has been resisted to a sufficient extent to enable him to intervene at a time of crisis.

Questions of constitutional practice are not or should not be party questions. Sir Robert Borden, then Prime Minister of Canada, in his speech at the Imperial Conference of 1917 declared that the consideration of inter-Imperial relations 'ought not to be made . . . a question of party strife or party controversy if it can possibly be prevented'.[4] But it is unwise to rest content in the hope that there will never be a division of political opinion even as to the extent to which the status of the self-governing Dominions has developed unless the relevant constitutional rule can readily be referred to, and immediately applied, when any dispute arises. It is notorious that there was and is some division of opinion amongst the parties in some of the Dominions as to whether the full Dominion self-governing powers should be exercised. It is useless to expect unanimity upon such points. The best that can be hoped for is to know what the binding rule is.

The same observation applies much more strongly to matters of internal constitutional dispute, both in England

[1] See *post*, Chap. XIX.

[2] A. B. Keith, *The Constitutional Law of the British Dominions* (1933), pp. 155, 159.

[3] A. B. Keith, *The Sovereignty of the British Dominions*, p. 3.

[4] A. B. Keith, *Selected Speeches and Documents on British Colonial Policy*, vol. ii, p. 380.

and in the Dominions. Thus, both the Byng crisis in Canada in 1926, and the dismissal of the Lang Ministry in New South Wales in 1932, are cases where the constitutional discussions seemed to be coloured by the political views of the critics.[1] But it is difficult to avoid this unfortunate result when the disputed rule or practice is nowhere authoritatively enunciated so that reference has to be made to works containing bitter and prejudicial comment of a political character.

All this seems to suggest the desirability of some authoritative definition of the Crown's reserve powers, preferably in Statute form. The possibility of such action was envisaged in Canada, where conflicts as to the position of the Colonial Governor in the pre-Revolutionary American colonies had not been forgotten. Thus the Act of Union (3 & 4 Vic., c. 35) which in 1840 re-united the Provinces of Upper and Lower Canada, provided in section 40 how the authority of the Lieutenant-Governor should be preserved, and section 3 of the amending Act of 1854 (17 & 18 Vic., c. 118) by providing that any bill altering the power of the Governor to dissolve the Council or Assembly should be reserved by the Governor for the signification of Her Majesty's pleasure, recognized that the Legislature of Canada might deal with the great question of the power of the King's representative in relation to dissolution.[2]

On the other hand it seems to have been usually agreed that the practices and maxims of Parliamentary Government which in the colonies came to be called by the name of 'Responsible Government' could not be expressed in written form. Thus Lord John Russell in his dispatch of September 7th, 1839, to Poulett Thomson (afterwards Lord Sydenham) said:

> 'The intelligence which has reached me from Upper Canada makes it probable that you may be called on for some explanation of the views of the Ministers of the Crown on a question respecting which the Bill to which I have referred is necessarily silent. I allude to the nature and extent of the control which the popular branch of the United legislature will be admitted to exercise over the conduct of the executive government, and the continuance in the public

[1] See *post*, Chaps. VII, XIX. [2] See *post*, Chaps. XXXI, XXXII.

service of its principal officers. But it is evidently impossible to reduce into the form of a positive enactment a constitutional principle of this nature.'[1]

Until the reserve powers are adequately defined there is a special difficulty facing students in that much of the learning and many of the facts of leading precedents are contained in documents which do not at once become public and, in some instances, never do so. Lowell said that:

> 'The forces to be studied do not lie upon the surface, and some of them are not described in any document or found in any treatise. They can be learned only from men connected with the machinery of public life. A student must, therefore, rely largely upon conversations which he can use but cannot cite as authorities, and the soundness of his conclusions must be measured less by his references in footnotes than by the judgment of the small portion of the public that knows at first hand the things whereof he speaks. The precise effect of the various forces at work must be a matter of opinion on which well-informed people may differ, and the writer has drawn the picture as it appeared to him.'[2]

Lowell refers of course to his more general description of English Government, but he intends to include in his comment the rules governing the relationship between the Crown on the one hand, and the other elements of British polity on the other.

The main objection to definition is said to be that rules controlling the exercise of the reserve power are, to some extent at least, changing their content as new situations arise. Thus Low, after referring to such writers as Hearn, Todd, Bagehot, and Dicey, rejects the view that the last word on these important topics has been said. His words are:

> 'It may perhaps be said that since the subject has been handled by authorities so well-equipped, so learned, and so able, there can be no necessity to deal with any portion of it again. But it is of the essence of the English system of Government that it is in a state of constant development.'[3]

But there is no inconsistency between a demand for definition and suitable provision for adaptability and amendment

[1] W. P. M. Kennedy, *Documents of the Canadian Constitution (1759–1915)*, (1918 ed.), p. 517.

[2] A. Laurence Lowell, *Government of England* (1917 ed.), vol. i, p. vi.

[3] Sidney Low, *The Governance of England* (1914 ed.), p. 12.

to be contained in such definition. And a striking illustration of the necessity for the delimitation of the leading constitutional conventions is provided by the attitude of Dicey. In his famous work on the constitution Dicey disclaimed the role of Burke or Hallam, Bagehot or Hearn. He said:

> 'At the present day students of the constitution wish neither to criticise, nor to venerate, but to understand; and a professor whose duty it is to lecture on constitutional law, must feel that he is called upon to perform the part neither of a critic nor of an apologist, nor of an eulogist, but simply of an expounder; his duty is neither to attack nor to defend the constitution, but simply to explain its laws.'[1]

Dicey accordingly dismisses Hearn and Bagehot by asserting that such questions as whether the Ministry is entitled to dissolve Parliament belong to the realm of political understandings or conventions rather than to that of legal rules. The former rules raise great and weighty issues, but 'they are not inquiries which will ever be debated in the law courts', and they raise matters 'too high for me',[2] a 'mere legist'.[3] Dicey regards as the height of absurdity the possibility of the Chancery Division granting an injunction to restrain the creation of five hundred peers. But his opinion as to the sharp line of division between strict law and mere constitutional maxims or 'conventions' did not, as we shall see, prevent him from entering the latter as well as the former field and from laying down some very far-reaching and questionable propositions.[4] But the point to be made at present is the prima facie desirability of defining the matters which at one time he regarded as 'too high for me'.

The recent publication (in 1933) of the life of the Earl of Birkenhead, by his son, deals with the passing of the Parliament Act and with the Asquith Government's use of that Act in order to pass into law the Home Rule for Ireland Bill without a further appeal to the electorate. Lord Birkenhead (then Mr. F. E. Smith) had declared, in July 1912, that the fate of the Home Rule Bill would be determined, not in the House of Commons, but in the streets of Belfast. The recent work reveals that Dicey congratulated Smith upon

[1] A. V. Dicey, *Law of the Constitution* (8th ed.), pp. 3–4.
[2] Ibid., p. 20. [3] Ibid., p. 21.
[4] See *post*, Chaps. XI–XII.

this speech, expressed the opinion that the resistance of Ulster to an Act passed without a general election was morally justifiable, and added that 'it is all but impossible to do this [i.e. insist upon the moral justification of Ulster's resistance] without the use of language which may be technically treasonable'.[1]

This letter proves and illustrates the danger of allowing constitutional practice and convention to remain undefined in certain vital aspects. Whether an additional election was required in 1912, 1913, or 1914 should have been determinable at once by reference to some established rule or practice.[2] But the Liberals and the Conservatives were in dispute both as to what was the true rule, and as to the extent of the 'mandate' which had been conferred upon the Liberal Government by the two elections of January 1910 and December 1910. What the relevant 'convention' was, could have been discovered in a properly drawn constitutional enactment. If the terms of such an enactment involved a decision as to the precise authority committed to the Ministry by the electorate, that question was essentially one of fact, and was as capable of determination by the Chancery or any other Division of the High Court as was the true meaning of the relevant constitutional rule. In other words, a situation involving the dangers of revolution and treason, only averted by the outbreak of war in August 1914, would never have arisen if there had been in existence definite constitutional rules enforceable, if necessary, by the ordinary Courts of law. Dicey's example of the Chancery Division issuing an injunction to prevent the creation of peers is not very convincing when it is remembered that in recent years a Court of law has issued an injunction restraining the King's Ministers from presenting for the Royal Assent a Bill passed by both Houses of a Dominion Parliament.[3]

A further illustration may be given. In his recent study on the Constitutional Crisis in England in 1931 (*Crisis and the Constitution*), Professor Laski, after setting out the circumstances under which Mr. MacDonald retained the

[1] Birkenhead, *Frederick Edwin Earl of Birkenhead*, vol. i, p. 285.

[2] See *post*, Chap. X.

[3] Attorney General v. Trethowan, 1932, A.C. 526, *post*, pp. 289–90.

Premiership, although almost the whole of the members of the House of Commons who comprised his former party at once went into Opposition, said:

> 'For such a sequence of events there is no parallel in British history. . . . Mr. MacDonald formed a Coalition with four out of twenty-one colleagues, and the support, known only after the event, of one-nineteenth of his parliamentary party.'[1]

According to Laski, the action taken was made possible through the fact that the commission to form a Ministry proceeded from the King to his Prime Minister, and the result was to nullify the wishes of the great majority of the Cabinet, of the Parliamentary party behind the Cabinet, and of the party supporters in the electorate. The point which is noteworthy at present is not at all the particular action taken, but the fact that the undefined content of the conventions of the Constitution rendered it possible. Mr. MacDonald, according to Laski, became the King's personal nominee for the role of Prime Minister, and the precedent was regarded by Mr. Leonard Woolf as one which

> 'might be developed so that the Crown could be used to break down the democratic system of party government, and to introduce . . . a system not materially different from that of a dictatorship.'[2]

That observers so acute as Laski and Woolf, albeit opponents of Mr. MacDonald, consider it not impossible that 'theories of constitutional form will be adjusted overnight to suit the interests of Conservatism',[3] seems to show that, in the interest both of the Monarch and of his people, the correct relationship between the Crown and its Ministers should be determined by definite rules which will make it impossible to impute the slightest unfairness or favouritism to the exercise of any legal prerogative. It is true that in Shaw's *The Applecart* King Magnus is made to say 'Are you inexorably determined to force this issue to its logical end? You know how unEnglish it is to do that?' However 'un-English' precise definition may be, the writer hopes to illustrate how dangerous it may be to allow uncontrolled discretion, and the anarchy resulting from the absence of any binding rule, to prevail in the future.

[1] Laski, *Crisis and the Constitution*, pp. 13–14.

[2] Ibid, p. 35.

[3] Ibid., p. 56.

II

THE RESERVE POWER IN RELATION TO THE DOCTRINE OF 'RESPONSIBLE GOVERNMENT'

THE term 'Responsible Government' is frequently used to describe the method of government in which executive powers are required by custom to be exercised upon the advice of Ministers controlling a majority in the popularly elected House of Parliament. The term has been applied, in the main, to the British Dominions. But there are several aspects of the matter which should be distinguished. First of all, it may be that certain powers and prerogatives have not been committed to the Dominions at all, because reserved for Imperial control under certain conditions. Secondly, the problem may be that of determining in the Dominion how a power, admittedly within the competence of some local authority, ought to be exercised, e.g. whether the Governor-General or Governor retains a sufficient reserve of discretionary authority either to act against, or to refrain from acting upon, the advice of Ministers in office. It is with the second of these two aspects of Dominion Responsible Government that we are, in the main, concerned. Each element directly affects the well-being of the Dominion, but the distinction, which may be loosely described as that between Self-government and Responsible Government, has to be kept in mind.

In the self-governing Dominions, the doctrine of the reserve power of the Crown has been invoked far more frequently than in England. As a rule the controversy centres around the status and functions of the Dominion or Colonial Governor, who has been said to possess a 'dual capacity'. In one aspect, the Governor has occupied in relation to matters of Dominion government a position analogous to that of the Sovereign himself in relation to matters of British significance only. In another aspect, the Governor has been regarded as the agent or deputy of the British Government, and as being obliged to carry out its directions if the occasion required. In Britain there is nothing corresponding to the latter aspect of the Governor's function. In the former aspect the analogy between the position of Governor and Sovereign has frequently been drawn with a varying degree of accuracy. As Jenkyns has pointed out:

> 'the dependence of the Executive on Parliament is perfectly consistent with a restricted range of legislative power, and therefore is reproduced in a self-governing colony without difficulty. Such a colony has more than *representative* government; its characteristic feature is not merely a control of local taxation and an influence over local legislation exercised by a popularly elected Chamber. Such a Colony has also responsible government: i.e. the heads of administrative departments form a Ministry which continues in office so long as it commands the confidence of the legislature. It is this dependence of the colonial executive on the colonial Parliament which constitutes at once the essential resemblance between the constitutions of our self-governing colonies and that of the mother country, and the essential divergence between the constitutions of our self-governing colonies and all foreign systems.'[1]

Further, that aspect of responsible government, which concerns the exercise of the Crown's reserve power, assumes greater prominence in the Dominions than in Britain itself. In Britain official documents and dispatches seldom touch the question, because the intervention of the Sovereign is purely personal; or, if written memoranda come into existence, they are seldom made public until many years after the events to which they relate. In many of the Dominions, on the other hand, dispatches, rulings, directions, and correspondence dealing with such questions have frequently been published to the Parliament concerned, having, indeed, often been drafted in the expectation or knowledge of immediate disclosure to the public. In this way a good deal of material has become available to the student of Dominion constitutional affairs. At the same time, references to English practices and usage are so often to be found in the Dominion precedents that they occasionally throw light upon English constitutional rule and custom. Of course, English constitutional practice is often referred to in the Dominion documents in order to

[1] Jenkyns, *British Rule and Jurisdiction Beyond the Seas* (1902), p. 55.

differentiate it from the rule being asserted as applicable in the Dominion concerned, and great care has therefore to be observed in any attempt to derive general principles from such precedents.

III

THE RESERVE POWER IN RELATION TO THE ORIGIN OF COLONIAL RESPONSIBLE GOVERNMENT

IN his famous Report, Lord Durham denied that 'representative and irresponsible government could be successfully combined',[1] asserted that the policy of establishing representative government had been 'irrevocably' adopted, and recommended that, in the future, the colonial Governor should be instructed 'to secure the co-operation of the Assembly in his policy, by entrusting its administration to such men as could command a majority',[2] or, if the form of legal enactments were preferred, they should provide that the official acts of the Governor 'should be countersigned by some public functionary'[3] so as to 'induce responsibility for every act of the Government'.[4] These aspects of Durham's thesis are emphasized in the numerous works which deal with the significance of his report. Thus Jenkyns says:

> 'In the North American Colonies, therefore, representative institutions, dating back in the case of the old provinces of Canada to 1791, and in the case of Newfoundland to 1832, were silently transformed, without formal constitutional change, in the decade 1846 to 1855 into a system of responsible government.'[5]

And Duncan Hall says:

> 'The essential features of Responsible Government as stated by Durham, and afterwards elaborated by Buller, Wakefield, and Molesworth, were the division between imperial and local matters, and the giving over of the latter without reserve into the hands of the colonial legislature. Matters thus given over were to be administered by an Executive responsible to the Assembly. Imperial concerns on the other hand were to be retained absolutely in the control of the British Government; and in regard to these matters the colonies were to remain mere dependencies. In accordance with this twofold

[1] A. B. Keith, *Selected Speeches and Documents on British Colonial Policy*, vol. i, p. 130.
[2] Ibid., p. 137.
[3] Ibid.
[4] Ibid.
[5] Jenkyns, *British Rule and Jurisdiction Beyond the Seas* (1902), p. 58.

division of powers, the functions of the Governor were to be dual. As regards Imperial matters he was to remain an Imperial officer responsible to the British Government, but as regards domestic affairs he was to assume a role comparable to that of a constitutional monarch.'[1]

But insufficient attention has been paid to the nature of those limitations and qualifications upon the form of 'responsible government' proposed to be granted which were also contained in the Durham Report. For instance, Durham says:

> 'I would not impair a single prerogative of the Crown; on the contrary, I believe that the interests of the people of these colonies require the protection of prerogatives, which have not hitherto been exercised.'[2]

In another part of the Report, Durham states that he admits that his system 'would, in fact, place the internal government of the Colony in the hands of the Colonists themselves'.[3] But the matters which he regards as *not* being of internal concern include the constitution of the form of government, the regulation of foreign relations, the regulation of external trade, and the regulation of the disposal of public lands. Referring to the 'present unrestricted powers of voting public money'[4] possessed by the Assembly, Durham also suggested the introduction of the British practice 'that no money vote should be proposed without the previous consent of the Crown'.[5] Obviously Durham's proposal vested in the Executive a power both of initiative and veto which in times of emergency might become available to a Governor himself in a conflict with the Legislature.

Durham asserted that his proposals, including the union of the two Canadas, would provide for 'the full establishment of responsible government'[6] and should also allow political ambitions to be satisfied 'by creating high prizes in a general and responsible Government'.[7] But he by no means contemplated a complete assimilation between the powers of the English Ministry and the powers he proposed to commit to Canadian Ministers. This is conclusively evidenced by the

[1] H. Duncan Hall, *The British Commonwealth of Nations*, p. 25.

[2] A. B. Keith, *Selected Speeches and Documents on British Colonial Policy*, vol. i, p. 135.

[3] Ibid., pp. 138–9.

[4] Ibid., p. 144.

[5] Ibid.

[6] Ibid., p. 147.

[7] Ibid., p. 155.

attitude adopted towards the Report by Lord John Russell, who accepted Durham's 'practical views', but also made it perfectly clear that the Report implied, as well as expressed, important qualifications.

In March 1837 Lord John Russell had proposed his famous ten resolutions. The fifth resolution was

> 'that while it is expedient to improve the composition of the Executive Council in Lower Canada, it is inadvisable to subject it to the responsibility demanded by the House of Assembly of that Province.'[1]

Upon division, this resolution was carried by 269 votes to 46.[2] Notwithstanding this rejection by the House of Commons of the Canadian demand for 'responsibility', Durham used the word or its synonym several times in his Report. But, in June 1839, on the introduction of the Act of Union, Russell again deprecated the use of the word 'responsibility', and gave some illustrations of its danger and ambiguity.

> 'It does not appear to me that you can subject the Executive Council of Canada to the responsibility which is fairly demanded of the Ministers of the Executive power in this country. In the first place, there is an obvious difference in matter of form with regard to the instructions under which the Governor of a colony acts. The Sovereign in this country receives the advice of the Ministers and acts by the advice of those Ministers, and, indeed, there is no important act of the Crown for which there is not some individual Minister responsible. There responsibility begins, and there it ends. But the Governor of Canada is acting, not in that high and unassailable position in which the Sovereign of this country is placed. He is a Governor receiving instructions from the Crown on the responsibility of a Secretary of State. Here then at once is an obvious and complete difference between the executive of this country and the executive of a Colony. The Governor might ask the Executive Council to propose a certain measure. They might say that they could not propose it unless the members of the House of Assembly would adopt it, but the Governor might reply that he had received instructions from home, commanding him to propose that measure. How, in that case, is he to proceed? Either one power or the other must be set aside—either the Governor or the House of Assembly;

[1] W. P. M. Kennedy, *Documents of the Canadian Constitution* (*1759–1915*), (1918), p. 435; W. Ross Livingston, *Responsible Government in Nova Scotia* (1930), p. 60.

[2] Ibid.

or else the Governor must become a mere cipher in the hands of the Assembly and not attempt to carry into effect the measure which he is commanded by the Home Government to do.'[1]

A few months after this speech, Russell (in October, 1839) gave a fuller explanation of his opinions in a dispatch to Lord Sydenham. He referred to 'the excitement which prevails on the question of what is called "Responsible Government" '.[2] He said that the Constitution of England 'has settled into a form of government in which the prerogative of the Crown is undisputed but is never exercised without advice'.[3] He repeated the point made in his earlier speech, pointing out that if the Governor

> 'is to obey his instructions from England, the parallel of constitutional responsibility entirely fails; if, on the other hand, he is to follow the advice of his Council, he is no longer a subordinate officer, but an independent Sovereign.'[4]

He said that the force of these objections was so manifest in relation to such external affairs as trade and diplomacy that 'it is now said that internal government is alone intended'.[5] He then made this important observation:

> *'But there are some cases of internal government in which the honour of the Crown or the faith of Parliament or the safety of the State are so seriously involved that it would not be possible for Her Majesty to delegate her authority to a Ministry in a Colony.'*[6]

He illustrates this reservation by the possibility of legislation discriminating against British immigrants and merchants. Subject to this criticism, Russell added:

> 'While I thus see insuperable objections to the adoption of the principle as it has been stated, I see little or none to the practical views of colonial government recommended by Lord Durham, as I understand them',[7]

and he advised Sydenham to maintain the harmony of the Executive with the legislative authority. He said it was impossible to draw any specific line of demarcation between

[1] W. P. M. Kennedy, *Documents of the Canadian Constitution (1759–1915)*, (1918), pp. 478–9 (Russell, 'Speech on Act of Union', June 3rd, 1839).
[2] Ibid., p. 522.
[3] Ibid.
[4] Ibid.
[5] Ibid.
[6] Italics are mine. Ibid., pp. 522–3.
[7] Ibid., p. 523.

the powers of the Governor and those of the Assembly, but this was necessarily the case 'in any mixed government'.[1] And he concluded:

> 'Every political constitution, in which different bodies share the supreme power, is only enabled to exist by the forbearance of those among whom this power is distributed. In this respect the example of England may well be imitated.'[2]

This vital dispatch of October 1839 'so vigorously opposed to responsible government'[3] (according to Livingston) was 'tactfully held back'[4] by the Governor-General. He did publish a Colonial Office circular communication bearing date October 16th, 1839, which had been originally prepared to deal with a South Australian dispute, and which merely laid down that the tenure of office of Ministers should not be regarded as being equivalent to a tenure during good behaviour. Apparently this circular was published by Sydenham as though it were a formal declaration by the British Government of a new Colonial policy, with the object of inducing the Liberal parties to accept the Act of Union.[5]

One Canadian document throws considerable light upon the constitutional issues which were raised by the Durham Report. The Report being brought under the notice of the Legislature of Upper Canada, the Legislative Council appointed a Select Committee which issued its report in May 1839. It should be remembered that in September 1838 Durham had learned that his ordinance of June 28th, 1838, had been disallowed by the British Government. This ordinance had embodied Durham's decision to deport to Bermuda for imprisonment without trial the eight persons who alone were excepted from the proclamations of amnesty to those concerned in the Papineau rebellion. On October 9th he vigorously defended his actions in a proclamation

[1] W. P. M. Kennedy, *Documents of the Canadian Constitution (1759–1915)*, (1918), p. 523.

[2] Ibid. ('Russell to Poulett Thomson', Oct. 14th, 1839).

[3] W. Ross Livingston, *Responsible Government in Nova Scotia* (1930), p. 110.

[4] Ibid.

[5] W. P. M. Kennedy, *Documents of the Canadian Constitution (1759–1915)*, (1918), p. 187.

to the colonists. This resulted in the decision to recall him, the British Government being 'cowed by Brougham's malignant invective'.[1] But Durham had already forwarded his resignation.

In the circumstances, advantage was taken of Durham's apparent disgrace and ruin by 'the family compact' party, to which the Report had slightingly referred, and the nominees of which controlled the Select Committee. More significant, however, is the criticism of the doctrine of complete responsible government. The opinion advanced by the Select Committee is that a Governor must either be responsible to the Crown or to the prevailing party in a Colony. In the latter case 'he becomes the sovereign of an independent realm —having no discretion, and therefore no responsibility'.[2] The position next contended for by the Committee is that the Governor, as representing the Crown and England, possesses and should retain the 'umpirage' between contending factions. It is asserted that such function must be exercised by some external authority, and that the only alternative is the United States—'if England refuse the umpirage between contending parties, there is a power at hand ready and anxious to join with either, and watching for the favourable opportunity'.[3] The Committee, dealing with Durham's plan to confine the functions of the local legislatures 'to affairs strictly colonial',[4] replies that this limitation is not practical because 'the honour and interests of the Empire are intimately involved with local administration'.[5] It is urged that the legislation of the Colony should be planned with some regard to the interests of future citizens arriving from England. Further, even in relation to 'foreign trade, immigration, disposal of lands, or any of the excluded topics',[6] disagreement between Cabinet and Legislature 'will just as readily induce a stoppage of the supplies, with all the consequences, as any of the questions within the range of local legislature'.[7] In either event the result will be the exclusion from office of an unpopular administration.

[1] *Encyclopaedia Britannica*, vol. viii, 11th ed., pp. 705–6.

[2] W. P. M. Kennedy, *Documents of the Canadian Constitution (1759–1915)*, (1918), p. 473.

[3] Ibid., p. 476.

[4] Ibid., p. 473.

[5] Ibid.

[6] Ibid., p. 475.

[7] Ibid.

There is a considerable amount of special pleading in the Report of this Select Committee, but the views expressed in it are obviously of considerable importance. There is realism in the statement that the views of one party in a colonial legislature may be more favourable to English interests than those entertained by the opposing party. And it is openly suggested that under circumstances, which must occur not infrequently, the English Government, acting through the agency of the Governor, should endeavour to see that its views prevail.

Whilst these criticisms of the Durham Report never received any official approval from the British Government, it is quite misleading to assert, as so many do, with reference to Durham's Report, that 'the Home Government accepted, frankly and unreservedly, the principles it enunciated, and made it the basis of their policy'.[1] Durham died in 1840, but it was many years after his death, during the Governorship of his son-in-law Elgin, before there was any general acceptance in England even of Durham's main principles.

Sydenham, as Governor, would not tolerate the colonial demand of unqualified responsible government. In a letter of December 1839 he said

> 'I am not a bit afraid of the responsible government cry. I have already done much to put it down in its inadmissible sense; namely, the demand that the council shall be responsible to the assembly, and that the Governor shall take their advice, and be bound by it.'[2]

He regarded the Executive Council as 'a *Council* for the Governor to *consult*, but no more'.[3]

Sydenham's method of administering Canada broke down, and the reasons for this were discussed by Governor Metcalfe in 1843. Metcalfe pointed out in a dispatch with reference to the phrase 'responsible government' that 'Lord Sydenham scouts it'.[4] Metcalfe also said 'the term Responsible Government, now in general use in this colony, was derived, I am told, from the marginal notes of Lord Durham's Report'.[5] This statement is not accurate, the term having a much

[1] Marriott, *The Mechanism of the Modern State* (1927), vol. i, p. 203.

[2] W. P. M. Kennedy, *Documents of the Canadian Constitution (1759–1915)*, (1918), p. 532.

[3] Ibid. [4] Ibid., p. 565. [5] Ibid., p. 566.

earlier origin;[1] but Durham's references to 'responsibility' and 'irresponsibility' inevitably made the words 'Responsible Government' the battle-cry of the Colonial Radicals from thenceforward. According to Metcalfe, Sydenham's practice conformed more to the English system than Durham's plan or Sydenham's own view of what was desirable. Metcalfe's analysis of the Canadian practice under Sydenham and Bagot, his two predecessors, may be stated thus:

1. 'This kind of responsible government . . . tends to produce the government of a party.'[2]
2. If the Governor and Ministry perform a popular act of administration, the credit will be assumed by the party in power, and if the Governor opposes a party in power, he becomes an object of distrust to the party in power.
3. The interests of the party in power and those of the British Government are, or may be, opposed, for 'in a colony subordinate to an Imperial Government it may happen that the predominant party is hostile in its feelings to the mother country, or has ulterior views inconsistent with her interests'.[3]
4. The Governor may be, as Metcalfe himself was at the time of the 1843 dispatch, not perfectly satisfied with his Council. In such case 'the only effectual remedy would be to dismiss them, or such of them as are most in the extreme on this point, and form another Council'.[4] This, however, would lead to a conflict with the Lower House, leading either to continual warfare with the Assembly or the Governor's taking back those he had dismissed.

Towards the end of 1843 Metcalfe finally broke with his Council. It is likely that, but for Disraeli's overthrowing of Peel in 1846, and the consequent accession to power of Earl Grey and Lord John Russell, the Metcalfe crisis would have led to further rebellion in Canada. Queen Victoria was sympathetic with Metcalfe, and Lord Stanley and Gladstone

[1] W. P. M. Kennedy, *Documents of the Canadian Constitution (1759–1915)*, (1918), p. 566, n. 1.

[2] Ibid., p. 568. [3] Ibid., p. 569. [4] Ibid., p. 568.

supported him. Had Peel remained in office and full power, it is possible that he would have acted upon his opinion of 1838 that 'when once you went into a measure of a despotic character it was well to err, if at all, on the side of sufficiency'.[1] But, as events had shaped themselves, Lord John Russell was now sympathetic and tender towards the statesmanship and memory of Durham, and Grey's views had advanced nearer to those of the 'Colonial Reformers'.

It was not until Elgin had completed his term of office as Governor-General of Canada that the situation in Canada could be regarded as settled along the general lines of the Durham Report.

In 1847 Elgin wrote that

> 'I still adhere to my opinion that the real and effectual vindication of Lord Durham's memory and proceedings would be *the success of a Governor-General of Canada who worked out his views of government fairly.*'[2]

In 1852, towards the close of his term of office, Elgin summed up his precepts of administration in the following words to his Ministers: 'While you continue my advisers you shall enjoy my unreserved confidence; and *en revanche* you shall be responsible for all acts of government.'[3] This, however, was subject to one qualification and one reserve, which he stated as being this: 'that no inducement on earth would prevail with me to acquiesce in any measure which seemed to me repugnant to public morals or Imperial interests.'[4]

Elgin regarded himself as carrying out the scheme of his famous father-in-law. Accordingly the reserve powers Elgin was asserting were regarded by him as being perfectly consistent with the Durham method of government.

This aspect of Durham's report is also emphasized by the work of an early colonial advocate of the principle of 'responsible government'. Its main reasoning is very different from that of the Upper Canada 'family compact', but it also shows that even the colonial radicals admitted that

[1] John Morley, *Life of Gladstone* (1903), vol. i, p. 642.

[2] W. P. M. Kennedy, *Documents of the Canadian Constitution (1759–1915)*, (1918), p. 579 (Letter, Elgin to Lady Elgin).

[3] Ibid., p. 589 (Sept. 1852). [4] Ibid., p. 589.

responsible government, according to the Durham doctrine, possessed certain important reservations and exceptions. I refer to the famous letters which Joseph Howe, the radical leader of Nova Scotia, addressed to Lord John Russell, discussing at length

> 'the blessings and advantages of responsible government, based upon the principles of that constitution which your Lordship's forefathers laboured to establish and ours have taught us to revere.'[1]

For present purposes, the importance of Howe's letters lies in his acknowledgement of the reserve power of the Crown, acting through the Governor, even under the constitutional government for which he was struggling. For he conceded the existence of a limit 'over which no representative of Majesty will consent to be driven',[2] and he suggested that these grounds should be clearly defined, either in the Act of Parliament establishing the new system, or in the instructions to the Governor. Howe definitely stated that if the Executive Council sought to lead the Governor into unlawful measures or 'exhibited a degree of grasping selfishness which was offensive and injurious',[3] the Governor could, and should, at once dissolve the Assembly and take the verdict of the people. This was an advantage to be gained, because the Governors

> 'would in fact have the power of freeing themselves from thraldom to the family compacts which none of them can now escape by the exercise of any safe expedient known to our existing Constitutions.'[4]

In the same letter, Howe again refers to the possibility of the Governor's dismissing the Ministry.[5]

That the views of Elgin in 1852, so far as they emphasize the element of reserve power in the Governor, were in direct accordance with those of Durham and the 'Colonial Reformers' is also shown by Grey's reasoned arguments when he intervened in a constitutional crisis in Nova Scotia itself. The occasion for such intervention arose when the Lieutenant-Governor, Sir John Harvey, in a private and confidential dispatch to Grey in September 1846, adopted

[1] W. P. M. Kennedy, *Documents of the Canadian Constitution* (*1759–1915*), (1918), pp. 480–1 (Letter, Sept. 18th, 1839).

[2] Ibid., p. 488.

[3] Ibid., p. 504.

[4] Ibid.

[5] Ibid., p. 505.

an attitude closely akin to that of Metcalfe in Canada. Harvey stated that he was opposed to 'responsible or party government' as being

> 'peculiarly inapplicable to the conditions of a small colony, if not inconsistent with its proper relations with the parent State, by its direct tendency to array one class of Her Majesty's subjects against another.'[1]

On November 3rd, 1846, Earl Grey forwarded a dispatch to Harvey which Grey himself subsequently described as 'the best explanation I can give of these views and of the principles which have guided our whole policy towards the North American colonies'.[2] With the contents of this dispatch to Harvey, Elgin was made familiar, as were Colonial Governors throughout the Empire. Grey stated that he had the opportunity of communicating with Harvey very fully before his departure to Canada in January 1847, and added that it was Elgin's object to withdraw from the position of depending for support on one party as Lord Metcalfe had done.

> 'He was to act generally upon the advice of his Executive Council, and to receive as Members of that body those persons who might be pointed out to him as entitled to be so by their possessing the confidence of the Assembly.'[3]

The significance of Grey's dispatch has been recognized, but only as a stepping-stone in the triumph of Durham's principles, and not in connexion with the discretionary authority which, Grey insists, is retained by the Governor when sufficient occasion warrants. The dispatch clearly asserts the Governor's power 'of refusing to sanction measures which may be submitted to you by your Council'.[4] The main principle is that 'the opinion of the inhabitants' should be resorted to so as to determine disputes between the Governor and his Council. It is nowhere stated that the Governor is bound to act so that such disputes can never arise. Indeed, Harvey was expressly advised that, as public

[1] W. Ross Livingston, *Responsible Government in Nova Scotia* (1930), p. 203.

[2] Earl Grey, *Colonial Policy of Russell's Administration* (1853), vol. i, pp. 208–9.

[3] Ibid., pp. 213–14.

[4] Ibid., p. 211.

opinion (expressed in a general election) would determine a dispute between himself and Ministers,

> 'You will carefully avoid allowing any matter not of very grave concern, or upon which you cannot reasonably calculate upon being in the end supported by that opinion, to be made the subject of such a difference.'[1]

The second direction to Harvey was that if a difference upon so important a matter did arise between Governor and Council 'you will take equal care that its cause and the grounds of your own decision are made clearly to appear in written documents capable of being publicly quoted'.[2] The object of this second direction is made quite clear. It is for the purpose of carrying to the minds of the electorate the conviction that the Governor is right 'if they see clearly that your conduct is guided, not by personal favour to any particular men or party, but by a sincere desire to promote the public good'.[3] Grey anticipates that if the documents show that the Governor is taking his stand upon such grounds, his objection 'will have great weight with the Council, or, should they prove unreasonable, with the Assembly, or, in the last resort, with the public'.[4]

This general advice of Grey to Harvey, containing as it does evidence of considerable political acumen, not to say electoral cunning, often provides a clue to a Colonial Governor's method of conducting to a successful issue disputes between his Ministers or Legislature and himself. 'Written documents capable of being publicly quoted', and in due course publicly quoted, have often been used as valuable electoral weapons, and their subject matter may constitute its chief issue. It is unavoidable that such a method of dealing with a constitutional crisis may lead, as it has led, to considerable turmoil and confusion. In England, both the name and opinion of the Monarch have been insulated from all the shock of political defence and attack so far as it is reasonably possible to do so. In the Colonies and Dominions, on the other hand, Grey's advice has led to the name and opinion of the King's representative being introduced

[1] W. Ross Livingston, *Responsible Government in Nova Scotia* (1930), pp. 254–5.
[2] Ibid., p. 255. [3] Ibid. [4] Ibid.

into political contests which, often on that very account, develop special vehemence. For the dispatch of Grey contemplates an ultimate decision by the electorate upon the question whether the Governor or the Cabinet is right in the dispute which has led to the election. The question at issue is necessarily of a political character. From time to time, the weight of a Governor's carefully prepared opinion has been sufficient to turn the balance in a keenly fought electoral contest. The inevitable result is that, where the Governor's opinion proves more persuasive, a new administration antagonistic to the old is summoned to office. The result may be, and has been, not merely the triumph of the Governor on the one political issue which divided him and his dismissed Ministers, but the passing of other legislation with which the Governor has had nothing to do, and upon which he has expressed no opinion whatever. In the end, it might prove more logical, and also more just that, if the Governor decided to take such a course as Grey suggested, and force a dispute with the Ministers and the majority of the Assembly, the decision of the people should be confined in some way to the matter which has led to the dispute. But such a course will not be practicable in those Dominions or Colonies where the instrument of referendum upon a single issue has not been made available.

There was therefore a very slow and gradual, not to say grudging, acceptance of the principles and recommendations of the Durham Report. But for the defeat of Peel, and the ensuing period of Whig supremacy, and the long governorship of Elgin (1846–54), it is at least doubtful whether Durham's Report would have been regarded as belonging to the list of great State papers. As it was, by an indirect relation, the Corn Laws repeal led to the ultimate acceptance of Durham's views.

Further, it is reasonably clear that Durham was intent rather upon ending a system of irresponsible government than upon describing in precise detail the limitations of the new system when it came to be operated and applied. His recommendations were opposed by the Conservative section of Canadian politicians, because his desire was to terminate their continued possession of office without the support, and often against the wishes, of the popular Assembly. Those politicians, in turn, used arguments which were directed rather against their opinion of one or more particular applications of the new system, than in favour of the continuation of their previous monopoly of office. On the other hand, many used Durham's Report as a slogan, without perceiving the reservations, explicit or implicit, in it. There were explicit reservations in it. Apart from that, there were also special difficulties in applying Durham's ideas whenever a conflict of policy arose between the parties as to matters where British interests were vitally affected. This fact was fully recognized by Metcalfe, but Sydenham and Bagot, as well as Metcalfe himself, all failed to give a successful operation to Durham's main ideals.

Elgin always insisted that the Governor-General should not only possess, but exercise, if occasion arose, a reserve power, and dismiss his Ministers, or veto some proposed act of legislation or administration. It is true that this reserve authority was not explicitly mentioned in Durham's Report, and what was explicit—the distinction between internal and external affairs—was not the same matter as that insisted upon by Elgin. Yet the two restrictions upon the area of Canadian responsible self-government would overlap if the occasion for personal intervention by the Governor-General against his Ministers was in order to protect what he considered to be paramount Imperial or external interests. In the main, the broad division made by Durham—that between internal and external matters—was a limit upon the area of colonial jurisdiction (whether legislative or administrative in character), and therefore a limit upon self-government. But the same principle of division might also operate as a limit upon Ministerial action, though legally *within* jurisdiction, because the obvious instrument to hand for executing any Imperial policy was the Governor himself.

In later years the distinction between the permitted extent of colonial legal powers and the policy involved in their exercise became clearer. The area of legislative competence of the colony became greatly extended by legal decision and otherwise, and with legislative there was a corresponding extension of executive authority. As a consequence, differences between a Governor and his Ministers seldom turned upon the purely legal competence of the Parliament or Executive concerned, as involving the Durham distinction between matters internal and external. They turned mainly upon the precise constitutional and extra-legal relationship between Governor and Ministry, it being assumed throughout that the action in dispute could not be objected to upon merely legal grounds, or upon the ground that it related solely to matters external. Accordingly, as the general right of Dominion self-government became more fully recognized, the questions of dispute between Governor and Ministers came to relate to such questions as the true extent of the Governor's discretionary authority, and the nature of the reserve power of the Crown exercised by the Governor.

IV

AN IMPORTANT TASMANIAN PRECEDENT OF 1914

AN important constitutional controversy, involving the Governor of Tasmania, his Ministers, and the Colonial Office, was raised in the year 1914. In the end, the Secretary of State (Mr. L. Harcourt) ruled that the action of the Governor, Sir William Ellison Macartney, was 'not in accordance with constitutional practice'.[1] The official correspondence published showed that the Governor offered a commission to Mr. Earle, the leader of the Labour party, upon the condition, amongst others, that an immediate dissolution of Parliament should take place. Previously, the outgoing Liberal Ministry, against whom a motion of no confidence had been carried by the Legislative Assembly, advised the Governor to dissolve, but such advice was not accepted. It also appeared from the correspondence that Mr. Earle, after having been sworn in as Premier, refrained from advising a dissolution, although he had accepted office upon the condition that he should. He stated, on April 7th, 1914, that a dissolution was opposed to his advice. The Assembly also addressed a communication to the Colonial Office protesting against the Governor's intervention in favour of a dissolution. The lengthy dispatch of the Secretary of State can be analysed as laying down the following propositions:

1. That a Governor cannot dissolve the Legislature except on the advice of His Ministers.[2]
2. That a Governor cannot impose on an incoming Ministry, as a condition of admitting them to office, the condition that they should advise a dissolution, any more than that they should tender any other advice.
3. That in the particular circumstances Mr. Earle must be held to have accepted, for the time being, full

[1] A. B. Keith, *Selected Speeches and Documents on British Colonial Policy*, vol. ii, p. 137.

[2] Ibid., p. 137 et seq.

responsibility for the Governor's action in imposing the condition.

4. That Mr. Earle, having altered his opinion and being opposed to a dissolution, the Governor could not insist upon receiving his advice to dissolve nor could he himself dissolve the Legislature unless such action was clothed with ministerial responsibility.

These four propositions all seem to be justifiable. The first and fourth are identical with the broad principle that the act of dissolution, though the legal power to do it is vested in the Governor by a Constitution Statute, requires the assent of Ministers who will accept responsibility for the act.

The second proposition may also be justified. In 1807, after the Grenville Ministry went out of office, resolutions were proposed to the Lords and to the Commons to the effect that it was

> 'contrary to the first duties of the confidential servants of the Crown to restrain themselves by any pledge, express or implied, from offering to the King any advice that the course of circumstances might render necessary for the welfare and security of any part of the Empire.'[1]

Though these resolutions were not carried, their doctrine seems to have met with subsequent approval. They were directed of course to George III having forced the resignation of the Ministry because they refused to give the King a pledge or assurance that never under any circumstance would a measure for the relief of Roman Catholics be suggested by them to the King. The general condemnation of the King's action as 'unconstitutional' by such writers as May[2] is perhaps sufficiently authoritative to justify Mr. Harcourt's ruling on the second point.

The third proposition, that Mr. Earle, by taking office, should be regarded as having accepted, temporarily at least, responsibility for the Governor's imposition of the condition, applies a principle of supreme importance in the working of parliamentary government. Since the dismissal or com-

[1] A. Todd, *Parliamentary Government in England* (ed. Spencer Walpole), vol. i (1892), (cited note 1), p. 282.

[2] May, *Constitutional History of England*, vol. i, pp. 96–8.

pulsory resignation[1] of the Melbourne Ministry in 1834, and the subsequent acceptance by Peel of a commission from William IV, it has been stated that, as a general rule, new Ministers 'shall be held responsible to Parliament for the policy which occasioned the retirement of their predecessors in office'.[2] A similar 'responsibility' was assumed by Pitt in 1784 after the dismissal by George III of the Fox-North coalition. But the reality of the situation was asserted by Perceval in 1807 in the debate on the Grenville episode. He declared that 'in the interim between successive Ministries, the action of the Crown was necessarily independent'.[3] May, however, expresses the accepted and conventional opinion that Ministers 'who accepted office in consequence of the refusal of that pledge'[4] should be regarded as having accepted 'the same responsibility as if they had advised it'.[5]

The Harcourt dispatch proceeds, therefore, upon the principle that May laid down and Peel recognized. Yet the dispatch was criticized with some vehemence by Keith, to whom it was 'confused and sophistical'.[6] The passage to which he specially objected was the statement that

> 'the observance of the principles of responsible government requires that a Governor must be clothed with ministerial responsibility for all acts in relation to public affairs to which he is a party as head of the Executive.'[7]

Keith says that whilst this is true of the King, it is not true of the Governor. He also asserts that the statement is 'palpably inconsistent' with the statement in the same dispatch that the Governor 'has a discretion to refuse a dissolution'.[8]

But Keith's criticism is not substantiated. He mentioned

[1] On the whole, the better opinion is that Melbourne was dismissed. See Lord Melbourne's Papers (ed. Sanders), pp. 222–3, 225, 230. Both Grey and Melbourne describe what took place as a 'dismissal'. Ibid., pp. 255, 257.

[2] A. Todd, *Parliamentary Government in England* (ed. Spencer Walpole), vol. i (1892), p. 112.

[3] Ibid. (note 3).

[4] May, *Constitutional History of England*, vol. i (1912 ed.), p. 78.

[5] Ibid.

[6] A. B. Keith, *Responsible Government in the Dominions* (1928), pp. 120–1.

[7] A. B. Keith, *Selected Speeches and Documents on British Colonial Policy*, vol. ii, p. 137 et seq.

[8] A. B. Keith, *Responsible Government in the Dominions*, vol. i (1928), p. 157.

that perhaps the word 'acts' in the sentence quoted was not intended to apply 'to a negative matter like a refusal of a dissolution'. But Mr. Harcourt never suggested such a distinction, and certainly that was not the meaning of the dispatch. Nor is the principle of the Harcourt dispatch inapplicable to a refusal by the Governor of a dissolution. Keith adds that the rule in the Dominions, as distinct from England, is that

> 'the Governor must act on ministerial responsibility . . . but this responsibility may be either assumed in advance by a Ministry in office whose advice he accepts, or assumed *ex post facto* by a Ministry which has taken office after he has forced one to resign.'[1]

It will be observed that Keith omits the case of a Ministry in office which tenders to a Governor advice to dissolve Parliament, which advice is not accepted by the Governor. What is Keith's view as to this? He asserts that 'the rule is really quite different' from that laid down by Harcourt. Applied to such a situation as I have supposed, the Harcourt principle is perfectly clear. His dispatch says that, in cases where Governors have rejected advice to dissolve the Legislature,

> 'The Ministers either acquiesce in the Governor's action, in which event they accept responsibility for it, or leave the Governor to find new Ministers who will accept the responsibility.'[2]

The result, according to Harcourt, is that these instances do not stand on any special constitutional footing, but come within the general rule that ministerial responsibility should clothe all acts and decisions of the Governor. Mr. Earle accepted office after the Governor had refused the advice of his predecessor to dissolve the Legislature. Mr. Earle was thereupon placed in the position, according to the accepted theory, of accepting responsibility for the Governor's decision that the existing Legislature should not be dissolved. Yet the Governor immediately imposed a condition upon Mr. Earle's acceptance of office 'that an immediate dissolution of Parliament shall take place'. This at once created an impossible situation, because it resulted in Mr. Earle being

[1] Ibid.

[2] A. B. Keith, *Imperial Unity and the Dominions* (1916), p. 101.

made responsible both (1) for not dissolving and (2) for dissolving the Legislature without the lapse of any appreciable interval of time between the two decisions. It would seem quite clear, therefore, that in the circumstances the Governor was in error in imposing such a condition upon Mr. Earle.[1] Even for that error Mr. Earle was responsible because he accepted 'for the time being' (the guarded phrase used by Mr. Harcourt), and for the time being only, responsibility for the anomalous position created by the Governor. But, so soon as the incoming Ministry decided to advise against dissolution, no dissolution could take place whilst such Ministry remained in office. The desirability of dissolution then became merely a 'personal opinion' of the Governor and 'no constitutional means' existed for giving effect to it unless the Earle Ministry changed its views or another Ministry favouring the dissolution succeeded to office.

My analysis restates from a different aspect the attitude taken up by Mr. Harcourt in his dispatch.[1] It is of little avail for Professor Keith to denounce the reasoning as containing 'sophistical arguments' which arose from

> 'the false doctrine which permits a discretion to a Governor and allows him to choose between acting on advice from Ministers, or disregarding their advice and seeking *ex post facto* for ratification.'[2]

This criticism seems itself to show some slight confusion of thought. So far as it is based upon the opinion that the Governor should not possess any discretion either to act without, or to refuse to act upon, the advice of existing Ministers, something is to be said in favour of it, though, in his later writings, Keith has frequently departed from it. But in reference to the Tasmanian precedent the opinion is quite beside the point. It is nowhere directly dealt with in the Harcourt dispatch, for all that is said is that the doctrine of general ministerial responsibility applies even to cases where the Governor has refused to accept the advice of Ministers in favour of a dissolution. It is true that the

[1] This argument of inconsistency was not used by any of the protagonists, so far as I know. But it is of practical value as a test of action. See *post*, in relation to Lord Byng's action in Canada in 1926, Chap. VII, p. 62.

[2] A. B. Keith, *Imperial Unity and the Dominions* (1916), p. 104.

application of the general theory of ministerial responsibility for all the public decisions of a Governor involves the imputation of responsibility *ex post facto* either to the Ministers who remain in office after their advice has been rejected, or to the Ministers who succeed them. But this is not, as Keith would suggest, some new-fangled doctrine applicable only to the Dominions, but, as we have seen, the accepted English doctrine, at any rate since Peel's acceptance of responsibility in 1834–5 after William IV had exercised his discretionary authority in forcing Melbourne to resign.

One might more easily adopt the argument that the Governor of Tasmania was in error in not acting upon the advice of Mr. Earle's predecessor to dissolve. It seems that Keith was approaching this view when the existence of the reserve power of the Colonial Governor was criticized by him in his preface to *British Colonial Policy*. He then stated that the position of the Dominion Governor was 'closely analogous' to that of the King in relation to the Cabinet of the United Kingdom, but 'the parallelism'[1] was not complete. For, in the Dominions, he said,

> 'even in matters wholly of internal interest, the Governor may refuse ministerial advice if he thinks fit, provided that he can find other Ministers to accept office and to assume responsibility for his action *ex post facto*.'[2]

Keith then said the position was 'anomalous' and gave rise to a number of 'inconveniences', illustrated by the Tasmanian case.

As the resolution of the Tasmanian Assembly itself showed, the advice to dissolve was not in accordance with the views of the majority of the Assembly. Keith's insistence that the Harcourt dispatch doctrine was 'inconsistent with full responsibility' and evidenced 'lack of political strength'[3] lacked point, unless he considered that there should be no discretion in a Governor to refuse a dissolution to an existing Ministry, no matter what circumstances exist when the advice is tendered. That this, indeed, was his view in 1916,

[1] A. B. Keith, *Selected Speeches and Documents on British Colonial Policy*, vol. i (intro.), p. ix.

[2] Ibid., p. x.

[3] A. B. Keith, *Imperial Unity and the Dominions* (1916), p. 104.

seems to be shown by his contrasting the Tasmanian case with the

> 'striking action of the Governor General of the Commonwealth in 1914 in granting the request of His Ministers for a double dissolution of the two Houses of the Parliament of the Commonwealth.'[1]

In 1917 Keith's comment was that the Tasmanian precedent showed that 'the inevitable tendency of assigning a personal responsibility to a Governor'[2] was 'to induce him to overstep the bounds set to his responsibility by constitutional usage'.[3] It is somewhat difficult to see the relevance of this observation, unless Keith's view was that, notwithstanding the parliamentary situation, and the possibility of an alternative Ministry, the Governor should have granted a dissolution to Mr. Earle's predecessor. If Keith's view was only that the Governor was wrong in imposing upon Mr. Earle the conditions of advising dissolution, it added nothing to the Harcourt dispatch.

[1] A. B. Keith, *Imperial Unity and the Dominions* (1916), p. 104.

[2] *Journal of Comparative Legislation*, vol. xvii, Nov. 1917, p. 230.

[3] Ibid.

V

THE DOUBLE DISSOLUTION OF THE COMMONWEALTH PARLIAMENT IN 1914

THE circumstances in connexion with the 1914 dissolution of both the Houses of Parliament of the Commonwealth will now be referred to.

As a result of the general elections in 1913, the Liberal party led by Mr. Joseph Cook[1] comprised 38 Members of the House of Representatives whilst the Labour party under Mr. Fisher had 37 members. One of the 38 Ministerial supporters occupied the position of Speaker, and another that of Chairman of Committees. Mr. Cook's continuance in office depended upon the readiness and willingness of the Speaker and the Chairman to give the Ministers support, and so preserve their majority of one. But this was regularly done; and therefore it would not have been possible for the Labour party to carry on the Government.

But the Labour party had an overwhelming majority in the Senate. Under the Commonwealth of Australia Constitution Act, Senators are directly chosen by the people of each State voting as one electorate, each State electing six Senators. The latter are chosen for a term of six years, and half retire every three years. At the general election of 1910, the election of the eighteen Senators resulted:

Labour party . . .	18
Liberal party . . .	None

The eighteen Senators not seeking re-election in 1910 were:

Labour party . . .	5
Liberal party . . .	13

Consequently, during the Fisher Labour Ministry of 1910–13, the position of parties in the Senate was:

Labour party . . .	23
Liberal party . . .	13

When, in 1913, the Fisher Ministry was defeated by a majority of one in the House of Representatives, and resigned

[1] Later, Sir Joseph Cook.

office, the eighteen Senate vacancies filled at the same time resulted:

Labour party	11
Liberal party	7

and, as the eighteen Senators elected in 1910 were not due to retire until 1916, the position of parties in the Senate after 1913 was:

Labour party	29
Liberal party	7

It is clear that as a result of the election of 1913 the Cook Ministry can hardly be said to have obtained an unequivocal popular mandate.

Section 57 of the Commonwealth Constitution provides that the Governor-General 'may' dissolve both the Senate and the House of Representatives simultaneously if certain events have occurred. They are (1) the passing of a Bill by the House of Representatives and the Senate's not agreeing to it, (2) similar action by the House of Representatives and Senate in respect of the same Bill in the same or the next session, providing there has been an interval of three months before the House of Representatives proceeds to pass the Bill for the second time.

On June 4th, 1914, the Governor-General, Sir Ronald Munro Ferguson, who had been recently appointed to the post, addressed a memorandum to Mr. Cook. The latter had requested a double dissolution, the conditions of Section 57 having been complied with in regard to the Government Preference Prohibition Bill. The memorandum stated:

> 'The Governor-General desires to inform the Prime Minister that having considered the parliamentary situation, he has decided to accede to the Prime Minister's request and will grant an immediate simultaneous dissolution of the Senate and the House of Representatives.'[1]

The Prime Minister, Mr. Cook, announced the Governor-General's decision on June 5th, 1914. On June 12th the Senate passed a resolution requesting that it be supplied with the full terms of the request for, and reasons stated in

[1] *Commonwealth Parliamentary Papers* (1914), vol. v, p. 129.

support of, the simultaneous double dissolution. Nothing was done by Ministers to comply with the request. Thereupon the Senate addressed a petition to the Governor-General himself. It was stated by Senators that, although Ministers asserted that all communications between them and the representative of the Crown ought to be regarded as confidential, there were many Australian instances in which similar communications were disclosed to Parliament. It was also stated in the address of the Senate that a double dissolution should never be granted unless a situation of 'actual legislative deadlock' has arisen. The address also mentioned that, in the session of 1913, the Senate had passed twenty-three Government Bills, eighteen without amendment, and that, of the five Bills it had rejected, three were subsequently laid aside in the House of Representatives.

On June 20th the Governor-General replied to the Senate's address, stating:

> 'I have submitted to my Advisers the Address . . . I am advised by them that the request therein contained . . . is one the compliance with which would not only be contrary to the usual practice, but would involve a breach of the confidential relation which should always exist in this as in all other matters between the representative of the Crown and his Constitutional Ministers. I am advised further that to accede to the request contained in your Address would imply a recognition of a right in the Senate to make the Ministers of State for the Commonwealth directly responsible to that Chamber for advice tendered to the Governor-General in relation to the exercise of an Executive power vested in him by the terms of the Constitution, and that such a recognition would not be in accordance with the accepted principles of responsible Government.'[1]

The Governor-General's answer concluded by stating that, without conceding the existence of any obligation to disclose the ground of the Minister's request: 'The grounds . . . appear from the communication already made by the Prime Minister with my permission and by my authority to the House of Representatives.'[2]

It may be interpolated that this reference to the Prime Minister's announcement[3] gave no information whatever

[1] *Commonwealth Parliamentary Debates*, vol. lxxiv, pp. 2419–20.

[2] Ibid., p. 2420.

[3] Ibid., p. 1917.

as to the *grounds* of Mr. Cook's request to the Governor-General. And it was not until the success of the Labour party at the elections following the double dissolution that the relevant papers were disclosed to the House and the country.[1]

The reasons advanced in the Governor-General's answer to the Senate, no doubt drafted by his advisers, are not convincing. Australian constitutional practice teems with instances where similar communications were disclosed. It is true that the documents relating to the three prior refusals of a single dissolution by the Governors-General were not disclosed to Parliament. But no request to dissolve any of them was made until October 1914, when the 1909 documents were at once disclosed by Mr. Fisher.

Moreover, Senators were not, either expressly or impliedly, asserting that Ministers were responsible to them. They merely desired to be informed of the grounds upon which there had been an exercise of the power committed to the Governor-General by Section 57 of the Constitution, in order to resolve serious disagreement between the Houses. The Senate was vitally interested in its own dissolution. The Governor-General had acted upon the Ministers' advice, so that the decision to dissolve both Houses was really theirs. The Senate was asking for nothing more than does a litigant who, having lost his case, seeks to obtain the reasons for the Court's judgment.

The memorandum of Mr. Cook to the Governor-General should now be analysed:

1. It stated that, as a result of the 1913 General Election, the Labour party was placed 'in a position of overwhelming superiority'[2] in the Senate.

2. It continued: 'When it had become abundantly clear to the Government and the country that no useful business could be done, we decided that a further appeal to the people should be made by means of a double dissolution, and accordingly set about forcing through the two short measures for the purpose of fulfilling the terms of the Constitution. Since then our intention has been well known and understood by Parliament and the country, and it has been per-

[1] *Parliamentary Papers*, vol. v, pp. 127, &c. The Senate elections resulted: Labour party, 31; Liberal party, 5.

[2] *Commonwealth Parliamentary Papers* (1914), vol. v, p. 129.

severed in and carried out by the Government in the face of the most strenuous opposition by the Labour Party. There has been no secret or subterfuge in the procedure adopted. It has been clearly recognised, and openly proclaimed by myself and colleagues, that no Liberal Government could continue to carry on without an abandonment of its leading principles.'[1]

It is perfectly clear from this statement that the deliberate object of Ministers was to bring about the conditions mentioned in Section 57 of the Constitution, so as to obtain the grant of a double dissolution. In other words, section 57 was not to operate upon a situation resulting naturally from the Senate's treatment of Government measures. On the contrary, a disagreement was specially manufactured, so that the terms of the Constitution might be satisfied.

3. The memorandum proceeded: 'It is generally admitted that neither Party could carry on under existing conditions—certainly the Labour Party could not carry on for a single hour in the House of Representatives. But it is urged that the remedy is a dissolution of the House of Representatives, and not a dissolution of both Houses. It may be supposed, though it has not been expressly so contended, that this argument rests on some analogy of the position of the Lords and Commons before the Parliament Bill was passed. It is obvious that such an analogy has no force, unless it can be assumed that, if the Liberals obtained on such a dissolution a majority in the House of Representatives, the Senate would be prepared to pass the measures which are essential to the Liberal policy. If this be the ground of the argument, it may be dismissed at once. For the reasons set out already, the Senate possesses no authority to depart from the absolutely definite platform of the Labour Conference. Hence the suggested alternative of a single dissolution is equivalent to a trial of strength in which one party may win, but in which the other Party—which, in fact, is the Party entitled to claim that it represents the majority of the electors—if it succeeds, will be in no better position than it is now.'[2]

It will be observed that a real weakness in the Ministers' argument is concealed in this part of their submission. For the argument is, that, if there is a Labour majority in the Senate, Ministers should be entitled to dissolve both Houses provided only that they would be entitled to a dissolution of the popular House. This results, it is argued, from the fact that

[1] Ibid., pp. 129–30. [2] Ibid.

the Members of the Labour party (unlike its opponents) are held down by a binding pledge to a definite platform. Of course, no such argument may have prevailed with the Governor-General, though it is impossible to ascertain which of the reasons advanced by Ministers made any impression upon him. Many, perhaps most, representatives of the Monarch would have hesitated to accept or act upon such reasoning because each party adhered with sufficient rigidity to its platform and announced policy.

> 4. Mr. Cook's memorandum then referred to precedent. 'May I also remind your Excellency that Sir Thomas Carmichael, Bart., Governor of Victoria, in a memorandum communicated to the Victorian Parliament on the 18th February, 1909, said—"It was my duty to act in local matters on the advice of the Ministry as expressed by the Premier, unless I was prepared to find other advisers better able than they to conduct His Majesty's Government, or unless I felt that their advice was contrary to the feeling of the country."
>
> 'In the present circumstances, it is quite impossible for Your Excellency to find other advisers who could command a majority in the House of Representatives for a single hour.'[1]

Incidentally this part of the memorandum showed that the Governor of Victoria was prepared to announce the reason why he had decided to exercise a prerogative power upon the advice of Ministers, and the reference to it is somewhat difficult to reconcile with the persistent refusal of Ministers to disclose their memorandum at the Senate's request. The actual Victorian precedent of 1908–9 was hardly in point, because it related to a single dissolution—that of the Legislative Assembly of Victoria.[2]

5. Mr. Cook found some difficulty in meeting the argument of Mr. Hughes, then Deputy Leader of the Labour party, that the Government Preference Prohibition Bill (which had been selected as the occasion for the invocation of Section 57) merely proposed that, in relation to Commonwealth Government employees, there should be no preference given, or discrimination made because of membership of unions or associations, and the Government by Executive

[1] *Commonwealth Parliamentary Papers* (1914), vol. v, p. 130.

[2] See *post.*, chap. XXIV.

minute had already acted upon the policy embodied in the Bill. However, the memorandum said:

'The present Government, on assuming office, decided that its mandate from the country would not be fulfilled by simply ceasing to apply the obnoxious principle, and that it was necessary to make it impossible for any Government again to resort to it without the express authority of the Parliament.'[1]

This statement reveals great weakness in the merits of the case for a double dissolution. By the double dissolution, eighteen Senators were to be deprived of a five years' term of office, and the remaining eighteen of a two years' term because of the Senate's failure to accept a Bill which would make no difference whatever to the existing practice of granting employment in the Government.[2] Further, the policy of preference to Trade Unionists, the accepted Labour policy, could only be brought into operation in the event of Mr. Fisher's succeeding at the next election of the House of Representatives. And such success would, almost certainly, have carried with it a majority in the Senate as well, so that he would be fairly entitled to enforce his declared policy. On the other hand, if Mr. Fisher lost the next election his opponents could still refuse to accord preference to unionists.

6. The memorandum then turned the argument towards a broader issue. It stated:

'It is submitted that the power vested in the Governor-General by Clause 57 of the Constitution to dissolve the Senate and the House of Representatives simultaneously in the conditions therein set out is one in the exercise of which he should, according to constitutional principles, be guided by the advice of Ministers possessing the confidence of the House of Representatives.'[3]

'This conclusion is clearly supported:

(*a*) By established principles of constitutional government relating to the exercise of the Royal prerogative of dissolution, so far as they are relevant to the provisions for a dissolution of the two Houses under the Australian Constitution; and

(*b*) By an examination of the scheme of the Constitution itself

[1] *Commonwealth Parliamentary Papers* (1914), vol. v, p. 132.

[2] The Proclamation of Dissolution recited the fact that the Government Preference Prohibition Bill was the occasion of the dissolution.

[3] *Commonwealth Parliamentary Papers* (1914), vol. v, p. 132.

and of the historical steps by which that scheme was arrived at and ultimately put in its present form.'[1]

7. Dealing with (*a*) the memorandum argued that:

'So far as the Imperial Parliament is concerned, though theoretically the King possesses a discretion as to granting or refusing a dissolution of the House of Commons, that discretion is always exercised in accordance with the advice of his responsible Ministers.'[2]

Elsewhere I demonstrate the error, perhaps the danger, in the assumption that even in relation to the dissolution of the House of Commons the Monarch acts automatically upon the advice of Ministers.[3] The real position is more accurately stated in the recent work of Dr. Jennings, that:

'The position is, therefore, that the King has a right to refuse a dissolution, though no doubt he would exercise the right only in exceptional circumstances. The fact that the present King granted a dissolution to Mr. MacDonald in 1924, merely indicates that he did not think it convenient to refuse.'[4]

8. But Mr. Cook admitted that, in the Dominions, requests by a Ministry for a dissolution had frequently been refused by the Governor. He then proceeded:

'The claim for a dissolution in such cases is made by a Ministry which has lost the confidence of the House, and is confessedly unable to carry on the Government, but seeks to show that it still possesses the confidence of the electorate',[5]

whereas the present application was that of Ministers 'in full possession of the confidence of the popular Chamber'.[6] The situation therefore was very different. Mr. Cook said:

'It would appear, therefore, that unless there is something in the Constitution itself which leads to a contrary conclusion, the practice which has prevailed for so long in Great Britain applies, and that it would be contrary to established constitutional usage for the Governor-General to reject the advice of his Ministers in the circumstances mentioned.'[7]

9. Finally, Mr. Cook argued that Section 57 bore 'little analogy to the ordinary dissolution of the popular House

[1] *Commonwealth Parliamentary Papers* (1914), vol. v, p. 132.
[2] Ibid.
[3] See *post*, Chaps. VII and VIII.
[4] W. Ivor Jennings, *The Law and the Constitution* (1933), p. 108.
[5] *Commonwealth Parliamentary Papers* (1914), vol. v, p. 132.
[6] Ibid.
[7] Ibid.

provided for by Section 5'.[1] On the contrary, Section 57 indicated that 'in a specified event, a specified remedy is available',[2] and that, unless the double dissolution was granted, the popular House would be left without any constitutional remedy in the event of a direct cleavage between it and the House representing sectional interests. Reference was finally made to the standard work of Sir John Quick and Sir Robert Garran on the Constitution, in which the opinion was expressed by those learned authors that the power under Section 57 would be exercised 'according to the advice of Ministers who have the confidence of Parliament'.[3]

On the whole, the reasoning of Mr. Cook does not appear entirely satisfactory. But the decision of Sir Ronald Munro Ferguson was definitely in favour of the Ministers' request and it must be regarded as establishing the following propositions:

(i) That so long as the conditions mentioned in Section 57 are complied with, the Governor-General will grant a double dissolution to Ministers who possess the confidence of the House of Representatives.

(ii) That it is not material to consider the importance or significance of the Bill which, being the subject of dispute between the two Houses, becomes the occasion of the double dissolution.

(iii) That, in particular, it is not necessary that the Senate's rejection of the specified Bill should have created a condition of financial deadlock between the Houses.

(iv) That it is immaterial that the Ministers deliberately set out to create the occasion mentioned in Section 57, for that is exactly what the Cook Government did.

The chief value of the decision of the Governor-General is that it established a definite rule in relation to Section 57. It should be noted that the decision could hardly have been the same if, in the situation of the House of Representatives, Ministers could have been supplanted by an alternative Ministry. Nor does it show, in any way, that in such event, Ministers would have been entitled even to a

[1] Ibid. [2] Ibid. [3] Ibid, p. 133.

single dissolution. The essence of the 'parliamentary situation' upon which the Governor-General confessedly relied was that the Ministers were 'in full possession of the confidence of the popular Chamber'.

In 1917 Keith commented on this precedent as follows:

> 'Still more striking is the refusal of the Governor-General of the Commonwealth in 1914 to accept the appeals made to him by the Labour party to refuse the Liberal party a double dissolution of the Commonwealth Parliament; every precedent pointed to refusal, ordinary dissolutions having on three previous occasions been refused in the Commonwealth on far less substantial grounds, and Sir Ronald Munro Ferguson's action is explicable and justifiable only on the ground of the practice in the United Kingdom.'[1]

This comment of Keith should be carefully considered. He says that 'every precedent pointed to a refusal'. In fact, however, there was no precedent, no case of a request for a double dissolution having previously arisen. Keith gives too little attention to the particular facts of the case and the facts are of supreme significance. Although the Prime Minister's party had a majority of one only in the popular House, there was, by 1914, a well-defined two-party system in operation. Moreover, there was no reasonable possibility that Mr. Fisher, the Labour leader, could form an administration without being immediately defeated in the popular House.

Hence a refusal of a single dissolution (i.e. of the House of Representatives) would have been out of the question. But no request for such a dissolution was ever made by the Cook Ministry, so that no analogy can be drawn between the prior refusals of single dissolutions and the 1914 case.

It has to be remembered that Keith's view (in 1917) of the 'rule in the United Kingdom' was:

> 'It is now clearly the established rule in the United Kingdom that the responsibility for the political government of the country rests with the Ministry, and that any advice which after full consideration they decide to offer on political matters will be accepted by the Crown, a doctrine which may be deemed to have been definitely and finally affirmed by the action of the King in accepting ministerial advice on the question of the concurrence of the House of Lords in the passing of the Parliament Act.'[2]

[1] *Journal of Comparative Legislation*, vol. xvii, Nov. 1917, p. 231.

[2] Ibid., p. 227.

Keith's argument therefore was (1) that in the United Kingdom the Monarch must act in all matters upon the advice of his Ministers for the time being, (2) that the 1914 double dissolution was explicable solely upon the theory that such a practice was also applicable to the Dominions. But the first proposition will be shown to be unsound.[1] Is the second part of the argument any sounder?

Now the Governor-General's memorandum was expressly based upon his 'having considered the parliamentary situation'. Therefore his decision in favour of granting a double dissolution certainly does not establish Keith's 1917 theory that the Dominion Governor (or the Sovereign himself) should always follow an existing Ministry's advice *whatever the parliamentary situation may be*. It establishes that, where no alternative Ministry is possible, a Governor should dissolve upon the advice of a Ministry which retains the confidence of the popular Assembly, and it also establishes that, so long as the Senate twice rejects a Bill passed by the Lower House in accordance with the conditions of Section 57, a simultaneous dissolution of the Senate is also obtainable by the Ministry.

Keith's inference from this action of the Governor-General of Australia was that it

> 'is only susceptible of explanation on the ground that he felt that it was best to adhere to the principles of responsible government as they exist in their purest form in the United Kingdom.'[2]

Consequently, his action was no less than 'a landmark in the history of responsible government in the Commonwealth'.[3] These bold assertions are not justified by the facts of the case. Let us assume, as Keith points out, that three of Sir Ronald Munro Ferguson's predecessors 'had declined dissolutions in cases where a fair claim for a dissolution had undoubtedly been made'.[4] But these three instances had occurred when, because of the existence of three parties in the House of Representatives, there was at least a distinct probability that the House could be controlled by Ministers other than those who were advising dissolution.[5]

[1] See *post*, Chaps. VII and VIII and p. 61.

[2] A. B. Keith, *Imperial Unity and the Dominions* (1916), p. 109.

[3] Ibid., p. 110. [4] Ibid. [5] See *post*, Chap. VI.

In his 1928 edition of *Responsible Government in the Dominions*, Keith seems to have abandoned his earlier view of the extreme significance of the 1914 precedent. Moreover, he changes his ground on the Tasmanian case, asserting of the Harcourt dispatch that the principle of universal responsibility applies only to the King—'It is not and never has been true heretofore of a Governor.'[1] Later, in his 1933 work, there is still another departure from his original position. The Harcourt dispatch is not touched upon at all, and it is said:

> 'that a Governor should act on ministerial advice has been admitted in the Dominions, but with an important proviso; a Governor may reject advice if he can secure, in the event of the resignation of the Ministry in consequence of his action, a new Ministry which will accept responsibility *ex post facto* for his rejection of advice.'[2]

It may be observed that everything in this amended proposition is consistent with the terms of the Harcourt dispatch.

In 1916 Keith had condemned

> 'the false doctrine which permits a discretion to a Governor and allows him to choose between acting on advice from ministers, or disregarding their advice and seeking *ex post facto* for ratification.'[3]

This condemnation may be contrasted with his 1933 proposition that

> 'it is, of course, too much to say that the Governor must grant a dissolution inevitably on a request from his Government. It is obvious that only one dissolution can be asked for by the same Ministry within a limited period; if it fails to secure a majority at a dissolution, it cannot imitate continental practice and endeavour to secure a complacent Legislature by a series of dissolutions. The King in a like case would clearly be compelled to refuse dissolution and would then find a new Government to support his action.'[4]

This important exception from his earlier proposition Keith is compelled to make. He proceeds to make another when he says:

[1] A. B. Keith, *Responsible Government in the Dominions*, vol. i (1928), p. 156.

[2] A. B. Keith, *The Constitutional Law of the British Dominions* (1933), p. 147.

[3] A. B. Keith, *Imperial Unity and the Dominions* (1916), p. 104.

[4] A. B. Keith, *The Constitutional Law of the British Dominions* (1933), pp. 150–1.

'If a Ministry at an election secures only a slight majority, and, after a substantial period seeks again a dissolution, the issue would be different and must be decided according to circumstance. Absolute rigidity is impracticable, especially in the case of such a Dominion as Newfoundland, where constitutional usage is far from settled on normal lines.'[1]

This is so vague that it may be asked whether the degree of rigidity should have to depend upon the degree of latitude or longitude where the question has been raised.

Therefore the conclusions originally reached by Keith cannot be accepted. They find no real support, so far as the Dominions are concerned, in the Munro Ferguson ruling of 1914, where complete reliance was placed by the Governor-General upon the special parliamentary situation existing at the time of the request for a double dissolution. And the Harcourt dispatch of 1914, whilst asserting the general principle that no exception can be admitted to the doctrine of ministerial responsibility for every official act or decision of the Governor, did not concern itself with an investigation of the circumstances and conditions which could justify a Governor in venturing upon an original exercise of discretion and subsequently obtaining Ministers to assume 'responsibility' for his decision.

[1] Ibid., p. 151.

VI

REFUSALS OF DISSOLUTION IN THE COMMONWEALTH PRIOR TO 1914

PRIOR to the double dissolution of 1914, three requests for single dissolutions of the Commonwealth House of Representatives had been made to the Governor-General for the time being.

(i) In August, 1904, Lord Northcote refused a dissolution of the House of Representatives after a request for it had been made by Mr. Watson, Leader of the Labour Party. At the time the Parliament was less than eight months old, and the state of parties was:

Labour party	24
Mr. Deakin's party (Protectionists) .	27
Mr. Reid's party (Free Trade) . .	24

No documents in relation to the refusal were made public. The case is obviously very different from that of 1914, because it could not be shown, as it was in 1914, that an alternative Ministry was impossible. In fact Mr. Reid was commissioned by the Governor-General to form, and did form, a Ministry.

(ii) In June, 1905, Mr. Reid was also refused a dissolution. At the time, Parliament still had half of its normal life of three years outstanding. The same Governor-General acted on similar principles and, as a result, Mr. Deakin not only became Prime Minister, but was able to form a Government which carried on until the House of Representatives was dissolved, after a full three years of life. The circumstances of this case also were very different from that of 1914.

(iii) A more important case of refusal of a dissolution took place in June 1909. After the general elections of December, 1906, the Deakin Ministry continued in office until it was replaced in November, 1908, by the Labour Ministry under Mr. Fisher. The Ministry at once wound up the session in order to prepare its programme, the session closing on December 11th. At the time the state of parties was:

Labour party	27
Deakin party (Protection) . . .	15
Reid-Cook party (Free Trade) . .	32

Before the commencement of the new session—on May 26th, 1909—negotiations for a coalition or fusion of the two non-Labour parties were completed. Some of Mr. Deakin's supporters refused to coalesce on the ground that the last vote of the electorate in December, 1906, had been given upon the definite assumption that there was no possibility of compromise between what were now two branches of the coalition. For instance, Sir William Lyne, who represented these dissentient followers of Mr. Deakin, said:

'Knowing the arrangement under which support was given by the Labour Party to the late Administration, of which the Honourable member for Ballarat [Mr. Deakin] was Leader, I am astounded at what has taken place. My political life has been, probably, as long as that of any other Honourable member, and during the whole of it I have striven to be consistent. I have never sold a colleague, and I have never sold my principles.'[1]

Upon a meeting of the House, the Fisher Ministry was immediately defeated upon a test vote by the Coalition which was arranged to function under the leadership of Mr. Deakin and Mr. Cook. A great parliamentary struggle ensued. Mr. Hughes (then Deputy Leader of the Labour party) made indignant, not to say passionate, protests against the Coalition. For instance, he said:

'The Honourable member for Ballarat has thought fit to criticise the policy of this Government. He has done so in a way of which, since he was never at a loss for words, it can only be said that there are no words even at his command, to explain his position and attitude. It is a thing beyond words. It is very fitting that a party which met in Corners and hatched in darkness this monstrous combination, and which announced its existence to the world in a Town Hall, to which admission was by ticket, should treat with contemptuous silence the Government policy—a policy which they cannot criticise, and dare not denounce. This policy is substantially that of the Honourable member himself, save that behind it this time are men desperately in earnest.'[2]

[1] *Commonwealth Parliamentary Debates*, vol. xlix, p. 127.
[2] Ibid., p. 133.

And Mr. Hughes also said:

> 'God save us from such friends. Last night the Honourable member abandoned the finer resources of political assassination and resorted to the bludgeon of the cannibal. Having perhaps exhausted all the finer possibilities of the art, or desiring to exhibit his versatility in his execrable profession, he came out and bludgeoned us in the open light of day. It was then that I heard from this side of the House some mention of Judas. I do not agree with that; it is not fair—to Judas, for whom there is this to be said, that he did not gag the man whom he betrayed, nor did he fail to hang himself afterwards.'[1]

Meanwhile an important memorandum was being dispatched by Ministers to the Governor-General. In this it was pointed out:

> 'Your Advisers claim that many of the measures set forth in the Speech of your Excellency are of a most important and urgent nature; that a large number of Members of the Parliament were directly returned at the last election to support these measures; and that some of the members now supporting Mr. Deakin are amongst that number; that a considerable majority of members of the House of Representatives were returned to support many of the proposals mentioned in Your Excellency's speech; that, apart from the members who were returned at the last election to support these measures, there is no majority against the policy of the Government, and that unless there is evidence, obvious and conclusive, that public opinion in the constituencies has changed, or that your Advisers have been guilty of such acts of corruption, maladministration, or ineptitude as to make their occupancy of the Treasury benches a danger to the welfare of the nation, these measures ought to receive both the attention and the approval of Parliament.'[2]

It was then contended that the precedents established that

> 'A dissolution may probably be had recourse to under any of the following circumstances:
>
> '(1) When a vote of "no-confidence", or what amounts to such, is carried against a Government which has not already appealed to the country.
>
> '(2) Where there is reasonable ground to believe that an adverse vote against the Government does not represent the opinions and wishes of the country, and would be reversed by a new Parliament.

[1] *Commonwealth Parliamentary Debates*, vol. xlix, p. 175.

[2] *Commonwealth Parliamentary Papers*, No. 5 of vol. ii (1914–17), p. 1225.

'(3) When the existing Parliament was elected under the auspices of the opponents of the Government.

'(4) When the majority against a Government is so small as to make it improbable that a strong Government can be formed from the Opposition.

'(5) When the majority against the Government is composed of members elected to oppose each other on measures of first importance, and in particular upon those submitted by the Government.

'(6) When the elements composing the majority are so incongruous as to make it improbable that their fusion will be permanent.

'(7) When there is good reason to believe that the people earnestly desire that the policy of the Government shall be given effect to.

'All these conditions, any one of which is held to justify a dissolution, unite in the present instance.'[1]

Considerable argument was advanced to the effect that Parliament would expire after one additional session, so that a refusal of a dissolution would give Mr. Deakin, for the third occasion, the advantage of facing the general elections as Prime Minister. It was also urged:

'We have already mentioned that we are not supported by the public journals of the Commonwealth, and we now desire to submit to Your Excellency that an appeal to the people, which to a party having a powerful Press at its service may be without inconvenience postponed, is to your Advisers, who have not the direct support of any daily paper—and what is more, are subject to daily misrepresentation of their acts and motives, and to the suppression of those facts by which public opinion might be informed—a matter of most serious and urgent moment; and must enable the policy of your Advisers and the action of members violating their express pledges to the people, and of the Opposition in declining to deal with this upon its merits being placed before the people for their decision.'[2]

Lord Dudley refused the application for a dissolution, and Parliament was not dissolved until February 1910. At the general elections, the Deakin-Cook fusion was overwhelmingly defeated by the Labour party, and Mr. Fisher became Prime Minister.

[1] Ibid.

[2] Ibid., p. 1234.

This precedent is of special significance. The strength of Mr. Fisher's case was that Parliament's life had to run for a comparatively short period only, and that it was reasonable that a coalition or fusion of two parties which had been strongly opposed to each other should obtain the endorsement of the people as a condition of being allowed to assume the government. On the other hand, Mr. Fisher was not in the position of being able to control the popular House, so that the onus was on him to make out a special case, if previous precedents in Australia were to be recognized. Therefore, the case is not the antithesis of that of 1914, but it shows the extreme difficulty of determining such questions according to the exercise of a just discretion.

Keith comments upon the precedent that the electorate's decision was 'an indication that the Governor-General acted unwisely in refusing a dissolution'.[1] This, however, does not follow at all. Mr. Fisher, the Labour leader, succeeded at the general election in April 1910, but he may not have done so at an earlier date, and, in any event, the electors' opinion was then concentrated upon the merits of the Deakin-Cook Coalition, and not upon constitutional doctrines. Keith says that the Governor-General's decision 'prima facie was contrary to constitutional usage'.[2] It is not easy to understand what is meant by the use of 'prima facie'. Certainly the action of the Governor-General proceeded upon a principle which was not out of accord with what had until then been accepted as Australian practice, although the discretion may not have been wisely exercised.

[1] A. B. Keith, *Responsible Government in the Dominions* (1928), vol. i, p. 165.

[2] Ibid.

VII

LORD BYNG AND THE CANADIAN CRISIS OF 1926

THE constitutional controversy of 1926, when Lord Byng, the Governor-General of Canada, refused to grant a dissolution to the Liberal leader, Mr. Mackenzie King, is of great importance and requires careful consideration.

As a result of the refusal of the dissolution, Mr. King resigned office on June 28th, 1926. On June 29th the Conservative leader, Mr. Meighen, accepted office, but, on July 2nd, the House of Commons passed a vote of censure upon Mr. Meighen's method of assuming office. In order to avoid the vacation of seats on the part of new Ministers, Mr. Meighen had persuaded the Governor-General to appoint seven acting Ministers, one Minister only (Mr. Meighen himself) holding a permanent office and requiring re-election. The censure of the Canadian Commons was directed to this unusual device. It was immediately followed by Lord Byng's dissolving Parliament on Mr. Meighen's advice.

Now the correctness of Lord Byng's action in refusing Mr. King a dissolution in the first instance raised a question quite distinct from that of his subsequent action in allowing Mr. Meighen to form his Conservative Ministry in the manner described, and in granting Mr. Meighen a dissolution after the popular House censured the device which had been adopted by the latter.

On July 8th Professor Keith made a statement to the *Manchester Guardian* containing the rhetorical statement that Lord Byng 'by refusing the dissolution asked for by Mr. Mackenzie King . . . has relegated Canada decisively to the colonial status which we believed she had outgrown'. He also said: 'Lord Byng's action is, of course, absolutely constitutional . . . if Canada has the same status as the States of Australia or her own provinces.'

Here it may be observed that this supposed distinction between the status of the central government in the Federal

Dominions of Canada and Australia, and that of the Provinces and States united for certain purposes in those federations, had been completely overlooked by Keith in his earlier treatment of Dominion status in relation to the dissolution power.[1] In such treatment, Keith showed very clearly that he never entertained the opinion that any such distinction was admissible. For instance, in an article in the *Journal of Comparative Legislation* in November 1917, Keith discussed the general principle of Dominion status by reference to certain Australian precedents, and upon the footing that no differentiation was to be made between the constitutional position of the King's representative in the Commonwealth and in the several States. Under the Australian Constitution there is committed to the Commonwealth jurisdiction only certain specified powers of legislation and administration, and the States still retain the residue of their former powers. In his 1917 article Keith, having discussed the Tasmanian and Commonwealth cases of 1914, and the recall of Sir Gerald Strickland[2] from the position of Governor of New South Wales in the year 1917 because of his refusal to assent to a Bill for the extension of the life of the New South Wales Legislature, advocated the introduction to 'the Dominions' of the practice that

> 'in all matters of internal affairs the Governor should act on the advice tendered to him by the Ministry in office, being definitely relieved from all personal responsibility.'[3]

Keith's argument in favour of the proposed new practice applied to Commonwealth and States indifferently. It asserted the desirability of developing the feeling of political responsibility and of attaining the ideal of the Imperial War Conference of 1917 that the Dominions should acquire that equality 'in political status with the United Kingdom which their statesmen have declared that they desire, and which the United Kingdom is ready and willing to concede'.[4]

Moreover, in his 1916 work called *Imperial Unity and the Dominions*, Keith advocated that, in respect of all self-governing Dominions, including in that category the States

[1] See *post*, Chap. XXII. [2] Later, Lord Strickland.

[3] *Journal of Comparative Legislation*, vol. xvii, Nov. 1917, p. 231.

[4] Ibid., p. 232.

of the Commonwealth of Australia, 'the Governor . . . might also well be instructed to act always on ministerial advice'.[1] Whilst Keith admitted that the existence of a Governor's discretion to disregard ministerial advice could not be denied, 'it is much more doubtful if the continuation of the practice is desirable for an indefinite period'.[2] He added that the practice was

> 'characteristic of immaturity and of defective development. The proper penalty for disobedience of the laws of responsible government by a Ministry is punishment by the electorate; it should not be any part of the duty of a Governor to remedy the defects of political conscience on the part of Ministries, any more than that it should be part of the duties of the Crown to remedy the defects of ministries in the United Kingdom.'[3]

Later he referred to 'the undesirability and unsoundness of the existing doctrine of the discretion of the Governor in granting a dissolution'.[4] Keith finally suggested (i.e. in 1916) that the change he advocated, i.e. the adoption in its full sense of the British doctrine of Ministerial responsibility, could be adopted by a mere change in the instructions to the Governor.[5]

Why, then, did Keith, in discussing the Byng episode of July 1926, attempt to differentiate between the status of Canada as a central constitutional unit and the States of Australia as local constitutional units? The careful student will perhaps find the explanation in the fact that, at the time of the Canadian controversy, there was also pending a serious constitutional issue involving the status of New South Wales, in which Mr. Amery, then Secretary of State for the Dominions, the Governor of New South Wales (Sir Dudley de Chair), and the Labour Ministry then in office were all concerned. Reference is made elsewhere to the New South Wales precedent.[6] It is sufficient to bear in mind that by the year 1926 Professor Keith seemed to be committed to an opinion hostile to the views of the New South Wales Labour Ministers, who were emphasizing the

[1] A. B. Keith, *Imperial Unity and the Dominions* (1916), p. 85.

[2] Ibid., p. 97.

[3] Ibid.

[4] Ibid., p. 112.

[5] Ibid., pp. 118–19.

[6] See *post*, Chap. XIV.

enlarged constitutional status of that State, as well as the Commonwealth.

Keith's article of July 8th, 1926, also stated that

> 'Mr. King's whole contention . . . is that the colonial status is outworn and that the Governor-General's action ought to be based on the principles observed in the United Kingdom.'

After referring to King George's granting of a dissolution to Mr. Ramsay MacDonald in 1924, and to Mr. Asquith's views as to the King's discretion in granting dissolutions, Keith mentioned the Munro Ferguson precedent of 1914, stating that:

> 'the demand [i.e. of Mr. Cook for a double dissolution] on ordinary colonial principles would have been rejected without hesitation. But the Governor-General gave effect to the new status of the Commonwealth; he accepted the advice of the Prime Minister despite the objections of the Opposition.'

This is a treatment of the 1914 precedent which is absolutely unwarranted by the original documents. Neither Mr. Cook, the Prime Minister, nor the Governor-General himself said a word about the 'new status' of the Commonwealth.[1] Keith suggested that the status was acquired by virtue of the Imperial Conference of 1911. But there is nothing in the proceedings of that Conference which warrants any valid distinction between the quality and nature of the self-governing powers enjoyed by the Commonwealth on the one hand, and the States on the other, each acting within its defined constitutional jurisdiction. Such a distinction would have been rejected unhesitatingly as quite inconsistent with the principle of division of functions which is basic to a Federal Constitution. As we have seen, the action of Sir Ronald Munro Ferguson in 1914 proceeded upon his view of the special parliamentary situation existing at the time of the request for a double dissolution.[2] Keith's reference to Sir Ronald Munro Ferguson's 'long parliamentary experience', and his suggestion that Lord Byng had ignored 'the new status of the Dominions' merely introduced a little flourish to his main argument.

The reasoning of Keith's article cannot be accepted as a

[1] See *ante*, Chap. V.

[2] See *ante*, Chap. V.

satisfactory exposition of the existing constitutional practice. Regarded as an argument in favour of what the rule should be, it may assume a very different aspect. According to Keith his letter was

> 'accepted by Mackenzie King Ottawa 23 July 1926; *The Times* in its account of the struggle systematically and stupidly misrepresented the issues, treating Mr. King as anti-Imperial and ignoring Mr. Meighen's anti-British tariff and defence principles.'[1]

It was not surprising that Mr. King should accept support from Professor Keith, particularly as he was raising the issue whether Canada was 'still to be regarded as possessing the status of a Crown colony'. But subsequent history does not suggest that Mr. King ever agreed with Keith that in any relevant sense the Canadian Provinces were inferior in constitutional status to the Dominion itself.

The constitutional question in Canada in 1926 was greatly confused by the introduction of very general propositions as to 'status'. Moreover, it was also confused by the assumption that the question was necessarily determined by Mr. King's success at the general elections which followed.

Early in 1927 the correspondence which had passed between Lord Byng and Mr. King was tabled. This correspondence showed that in a letter dated June 28th, 1926, Mr. King suggested to the Governor-General that the latter should

> 'before definitely deciding upon this step, cable the Secretary of State for the Dominions asking the British Government, from whom you have come to Canada under instructions, what, in the opinion of the Secretary of State for the Dominions, your course should be in the event of the Prime Minister presenting you with an Order-in-Council having regard to dissolution.'[2]

Lord Byng rejected the suggestion, stating that he had himself dealt with the problem as fairly as possible. As the *Scotsman* points out, the letter of Mr. King seems to recognize that Lord Byng's position was that of a Governor 'under instructions' from the British Government.

In a comment upon the publication of these disclosures in

[1] A. B. Keith, *Responsible Government in the Dominions*, vol. i (1928), p. 146, n. 3.

[2] *Scotsman*, March 15th, 1927.

the *Scotsman*, Professor Keith adopted a much milder tone than that of July 1926, and said

> 'I confess that, while I have always held that Lord Byng erred in his decision, it appears to me that much of the responsibility really rests with a system under which a Governor-General is sent out without any clear instructions as to the place which he is to occupy in the structure of government. Happily, the resolution of the Imperial Conference of 1926 should effectively prevent any Governor-General in future being placed in so uncomfortable a position as was Lord Byng.'[1]

Now this comment recognizes, for the first time, that there was no clearly established constitutional error on Lord Byng's part in his original refusal of a dissolution to Mr. King. Let it be remembered that the parliamentary situation in the Dominion Parliament of 1926 appeared obscure. At the general election of 1925 many members of the King Ministry had been defeated. In the existing circumstances it seemed by no means impossible that Mr. Meighen, who had a larger direct following than Mr. King, would be able to obtain support from the third (Progressive) party to form a Ministry and carry on the Government. Even the vote of censure upon Mr. Meighen's method of forming the provisional Government was carried by a majority of only one vote.

Keith's second statement, that the Governor-General's constitutional position in reference to grants of dissolution was finally cleared up by the 1926 Imperial Conference, is not borne out by the Report of that year.[2] No doubt, it should be accepted that since 1926 the functions of the Governor-General are to be regarded as being assimilated to those of the King. Such a fact excludes the possibility of general or particular instructions to the Governor-General by the British Government, the Governor-General not being in any sense its 'representative or agent':[3] indeed, not being even one of 'the parties interested'.[4] But this generalization only shifts the difficulty farther back, making it necessary to determine whether the Sovereign should, in circumstances

[1] *Scotsman*, March 16th, 1927.

[2] See *post*, Chap. XXI.

[3] *Parliamentary Papers*, vol. xi (1926), Cmd. 2768, p. 560.

[4] Ibid., vol. xiv (1930–1), Cmd. 3717, p. 595.

analogous to those which faced Lord Byng in 1926, have granted an immediate dissolution to a Ministry which appeared to be tottering, and which might, it seemed reasonably possible, be replaced by a stable Ministry possessing the confidence of a Parliament which had been elected only twelve months before.

The facts of the Canadian crisis were carefully discussed during a debate in 1927. Mr. Cahan, K.C., then pointed out that, at the time when Mr. King was refused a dissolution, a censure motion was pending in Parliament upon an important branch of the administration. He argued that

> 'no Ministry has the right to attempt to dissolve the court before which it is being tried until a verdict has been rendered upon the issue in question. No cases can be found in which the Sovereign, or any viceroy representing the Sovereign, has attempted at the request of a Prime Minister to destroy the very Court before which he and his colleagues were compelled to appear.'[1]

Mr. Cahan strongly contended against 'the new rule that at all times and under all circumstances the Prime Minister of this country is to have a dissolution upon request'.[2]

In answer to this criticism, Professor Keith disclaimed his acceptance of such a rule. But I have already quoted passages from his earlier writings and from his first statement of his views on the Canadian crisis, which do not march comfortably with this disclaimer. Keith went on to say that the position of the Governor-General should be the same as that of the Sovereign himself in Great Britain, but that the Sovereign could properly refuse a second dissolution to a Prime Minister who had obtained a dissolution and been defeated at the Polls. He then, for the first time, suggested that his criticism of Lord Byng 'was based not merely on his refusal to grant a dissolution to Mr. King, but on that refusal coupled with the grant to Mr. Meighen'.[3] He admitted that 'colonial precedents would have justified the refusal to Mr. King had Mr. Meighen been able to form a Government and command a majority in the Commons'.[4]

Now this last pronouncement of Keith is important. Though the argument is not elaborated, it does indicate the

[1] *Scotsman*, May 10th, 1927.
[2] Ibid.
[3] Ibid., May 11th, 1927.
[4] Ibid.

point at which Lord Byng's action ceased to be justifiable on accepted constitutional practice. Mr. King had himself admitted in July 1926[1] that the refusal to dissolve might have been regarded as proper if Mr. Meighen had been successful in forming a stable government. The ground of attack upon Lord Byng was inevitably directed to the grant of a dissolution to Mr. Meighen, following so closely upon its refusal to Mr. King. An analysis of the situation created by Lord Byng, upon lines similar to that made in connexion with the Tasmanian precedent of 1914, discloses a real inconsistency between his two decisions.[2]

By accepting office after the refusal of a dissolution to Mr. King, Mr. Meighen had to be regarded as accepting full responsibility for the Governor-General's refusal. But responsibility was meaningless, unless it involved his definite acceptance of the opinion that, in the interests of Canada, it was not desirable that Parliament should be dissolved. And yet, before three sitting days elapsed, Mr. Meighen placed himself in the position of advising in favour of the very course which he had, by taking office, advised against, but which his predecessor had favoured. The change of front on the part of Mr. Meighen must have satisfied Lord Byng that a dissolution was inevitable, in other words, that Mr. King's original advice was sound and should be acted upon. The question which remained, whether Mr. King or Mr. Meighen should obtain the dissolution and face the country as Prime Minister, presented no difficulty. Not only did the balance of convenience and justice point strongly in favour of Mr. King, but Mr. Meighen's failure to form a stable government suggested that it was the advice and opinion of Mr. King which had to be adopted. Therefore, Lord Byng should have refused Mr. Meighen's request for a dissolution, and recommissioned Mr. King as Prime Minister, not, of course, imposing any condition of a dissolution, but being reasonably certain that Mr. King would repeat his former tender of advice, upon which a dissolution would ensue.

Such is the analysis which seems to me both inevitable and logical. Keith advanced no such reasoning, but in May 1927

[1] See *post*, p. 67. [2] See *ante*, Chap. IV, pp. 33–4.

he accepted its general implications. Unfortunately, in his subsequent discussion of the crisis, Keith departed from firm ground and reverted to the original tenor of his 1926 criticisms. He repeated his pleasing assertion[1] that

> 'in the opinion of Lord Byng as Governor-General, Canada was in constitutional usage as in law no more than a Colony, subject to the rules applicable to Newfoundland or an Australian State.'[2]

He also said that there was no answer to Mr. King's position, and recalled

> 'the precedent of the King's immediate grant to Mr. Ramsay MacDonald of a dissolution in 1924 *without even considering whether the Government could be carried on without a dissolution.*'[3]

Keith characterized the opinion of Lord Oxford and Asquith (viz. 'that the King still preserved an independent judgment in matters of dissolution'),[4] as showing 'the spokesman's obvious and regrettable decline in mental power and sense of political realities'.[5] This precedent is discussed elsewhere,[6] but the general conclusion which Keith drew was that, as a sequel to Mr. King's victory at the polls, the Imperial Conference decided in 1926

> 'that the true position of the Governor-General or Governor of a Dominion (not of the Governor of a State) was similar in all essentials to that of the King in the United Kingdom in respect of the administration of public affairs.'[7]

Keith further stated that the Imperial Conference accepted 'the view pressed for many years by the writer'. This last statement is quite inaccurate if it was intended to suggest that the Governor of a State should not be included in the rule of responsibility originally advocated by Keith.[8]

Moreover, the Imperial Conference of 1926 was not concerned with the status of State or Provincial Governors, and it would be a great mistake to infer that a special rule should

[1] Analysed and criticized elsewhere. See *ante*, p. 55, *post*, Chap. XXII.

[2] A. B. Keith, *Responsible Government in the Dominions*, vol. i (1928), p. 146.

[3] Ibid., pp. 147–8. Italics are mine (see *post*, Chap. VIII, and cf. p. 232).

[4] Ibid., p. 148. [5] Ibid. [6] See *post*, Chap. VIII.

[7] A. B. Keith, *Responsible Government in the Dominions*, vol. i (1928), p. 152. See Chaps. XXI, XXII.

[8] See *post*, Chap. XXII, *ante*, pp. 56–7.

be applied in the application of the doctrine of responsible government to their affairs. Indeed, as a general comment upon the Canadian case it may fairly be stated that neither in England nor in any of the self-governing Dominions, States, or Provinces, would constitutional practice warrant the Sovereign or his representative in granting a dissolution to one party, almost immediately after refusing it to another, in circumstances analogous to those of 1926.

VIII

THE RAMSAY MACDONALD DISSOLUTION OF 1924

IT is now convenient to deal with the question of the King's granting Mr. Ramsay MacDonald a dissolution in the year 1924. The first point to make is that there are no documents showing the grounds upon which His Majesty proceeded, or the representations which were made to him as to the existing parliamentary situation.

In an important speech delivered shortly after the general elections of 1923, Mr. Asquith had discussed the prerogative of dissolution. He said:

> 'It does not mean that the Crown should act arbitrarily and without the advice of responsible Ministers, but it does mean that the Crown is not bound to take the advice of a particular Minister to put its subjects to the tumult and turmoil of a series of General Elections so long as it can find other Ministers who are prepared to give it a trial. The notion that a Minister—a Minister who cannot command a majority in the House of Commons . . . in those circumstances is invested with the right to demand a dissolution is as subversive of constitutional usage as it would, in my opinion, be pernicious to the general and paramount interests of the nation at large.'[1]

Now it should be remembered that Mr. Asquith was addressing this observation to a parliamentary situation of a rather special kind. Sir John Marriott, who regarded the Asquith pronouncement as being couched in words 'as lucid as they are unequivocal',[2] was definitely of opinion that if Mr. Baldwin, before resigning office, as he did in January 1924 following upon his defeat in the House of Commons on a vote of no confidence, or Mr. MacDonald after accepting office, as he did in the same month, were 'so ill-advised as to ask for a dissolution of Parliament, the King might certainly have declined to assent to it'.[3]

What is Keith's justification for his violent attack upon

[1] *The Times*, Dec. 19th, 1923.

[2] Marriott, *The Mechanism of the Modern State* (1927), vol. ii, p. 35.

[3] Ibid., p. 34.

Asquith's statement.[1] The attack occurred in a discussion of the Canadian precedent of 1926, after Keith had said that Mr. King

> 'very properly advised Lord Byng to grant a dissolution of Parliament on the score that it was clear that the Government, to carry on effectively its duties, ought to be supported by a vote of the electorate. He very justly insisted that the status of Canada was co-equal in these matters with that of the United Kingdom; that the duty of the Governor-General was to act on the same principles as would have applied to the King.'[1]

And Keith added:

> 'There is no answer to Mr. King's arguments; the precedent of the King's immediate grant to Mr. Ramsay MacDonald of a dissolution in 1924 without even considering whether the Government could be carried on without a dissolution, ought to have been conclusive.'[2]

How is Keith in a position to deny that the King may have, not only considered, but also excluded, the possibility of an alternative Ministry?[3]

Keith's significant statement in 1929, in his work on *Dominion Autonomy in Practice*, not only omits the derogatory reference to Mr. Asquith, but goes some way towards admitting the general accuracy of the latter's opinion. Keith discusses the position of the Governor-General since the declaration of 1926:

> 'It does not mean that he is deprived of all authority to refuse to act on ministerial advice, for, if for instance after one unsuccessful dissolution Ministers asked him to grant another, he would clearly be bound to refuse thus to violate the Constitution. But it means that he should, save in extreme crises, accept the advice of Ministers, as readily as did the King in 1924, when he dissolved Parliament at the request of Mr. Ramsay MacDonald without trying to find an alternative government.'[4]

Not only was Mr. Asquith's opinion directed to the circumstances existing immediately after the dissolution of Parliament in November 1923, but its general validity was

[1] A. B. Keith, *Responsible Government in the Dominions*, vol. i (1928), p. 147. See *ante*, p. 4, *post*, p. 236. [2] Ibid., pp. 147–8.

[3] There is no warrant for Keith's asserting that the King did not 'even consider' the parliamentary situation. See *ante*, p. 63, *post*, p. 232.

[4] A. B. Keith, *Dominion Autonomy in Practice* (1929), p. 5.

not disputed by Mr. King in his policy speech of July 1926, after Lord Byng had granted the dissolution to Mr. Meighen. In that speech Mr. King said:

> 'I am prepared to say that there may be circumstances in which a Governor-General might find subsequent justification for a refusal to grant a dissolution of parliament. Such might be the case, where Parliament is in session and the leader of another party having accepted the responsibility of the refusal of dissolution, demonstrates after compliance with all constitutional obligations that he is able to carry on the business of Parliament by the majority he is in a position to command in the House of Commons. Clearly, any such possibility was not the case in the present instance.'[1]

This statement is quite irreconcilable with the very sweeping and very general assertions as to the Canadian crisis first made by Keith and elsewhere referred to. Mr. Asquith's considered statement was made when there were three parties strongly represented in the House of Commons, and no single party could hope to carry on the Government without reasonable support from one of the other two. The notion that the Prime Minister for the time being possessed an unqualified right to demand a dissolution had grown up during the long period when either two great parties only were represented in the Commons, or, at any rate, such third parties as existed bore allegiance to one of the two great parties. That situation was altered as soon as the Labour party became more powerful than the Liberals in the country and in the Commons. Previously, it was fairly certain that Labour would support the Liberals in preference to the Conservatives. But it was not equally certain that the Liberals would give the like support to Labour in preference to the Conservatives. The significance of this new development in British parties was appreciated by Mr. Asquith.

Mr. Asquith's main purpose was to negative the proposition that, in the existing state of constitutional practice, the King was irrevocably bound to grant a dissolution of Parliament to the Prime Minister for the time being. He pointed out that when, in 1910, he twice dissolved, his position in the Commons was 'absolutely impregnable', so

[1] A. B. Keith, *Speeches and Documents on the British Dominions (1918–31)*, p. 153–4.

that there was 'absolutely no analogy between that case and the circumstances of the present time'.[1]

What was the position when the King granted Mr. MacDonald's request for a dissolution? Obviously Mr. Baldwin, as Conservative leader, favoured a dissolution because, as the events showed, the electoral prospects of his party seemed to be very good. There was no reasonable probability that Labour would support a Liberal Ministry after the Liberals' criticism of the withdrawal of the Campbell prosecution. No doubt all the circumstances of the case were considered before the King reached the conclusion that it was a proper case for a dissolution to be granted.

Is it possible to induce a general principle from this single instance? The answer should be, No. Keith asserts that, if the King had refused a dissolution to Mr. Macdonald and sent for the Liberal leader, 'this course . . . would have been wholly unconstitutional, bringing the King into party politics and alienating as many of his subjects as it gratified'.[2] It is impossible to accept such a line of reasoning any more than the mere unsupported assertion of fact that the King acted 'without a moment's hesitation'[3] and that 'happily the matter was never in doubt'.[4] How can it be argued that the King's refusal of a request of a dissolution by the leader of one of the three parties who happens to be Prime Minister, must have the effect of bringing the King into party politics because it is bound to displease many party followers? Will not the granting of a dissolution in the like circumstances cause equal displeasure to followers of other parties? A refusal of a dissolution may be as popular as its grant. Everything depends upon the circumstances.

Recently, Mr. Emden has pointed out that if the factor of a third party proves to be permanent or important

> 'it seems that it will be necessary to have a revision of the rules governing the times when it is appropriate to make appeals to the people. Either the sovereign will have to exercise a real power of

[1] *The Times*, Dec. 19th, 1923.

[2] A. B. Keith, *Responsible Government in the Dominions*, vol. i (1928), p. 155.

[3] Ibid. [4] Ibid.

refusing a dissolution, or it will have to be laid down that a dissolution can only be claimed in certain recognised circumstances.'[1]

The same author states that, when the Labour Ministry obtained a dissolution in October 1924, the circumstances were 'allowed on every side to be sufficient, so that the question of a right to a dissolution was not put to a trial'.[2]

It is now plain that Keith was not justified in using the 1924 dissolution as disproving the general thesis asserted by Mr. Asquith in December 1923. On the contrary, the reasoning of Mr. King and his opponents in Canada in 1926–7, and Keith's significant admission that Lord Byng's error lay, not in the refusal of a dissolution to Mr. King, but in that refusal coupled with the grant of it to Mr. Meighen,[3] tend to support Asquith's opinion that the King was not bound always to accede to the request of his Prime Minister for a dissolution. By October 1924 the parliamentary position was very different from that to which Mr. Asquith addressed himself in December 1923.

It is desirable in the interests of the Crown and of its Dominion representatives that there should be more precise rules governing the circumstances and conditions under which a dissolution should be granted and should be refused. The absence of such rules does not necessarily bring the King or the Governor-General into the realm of political discussion and criticism, but its presence would be a complete safeguard against the possibility of misunderstanding and possible condemnation.

[1] C. S. Emden, *The People and the Constitution* (1933), p. 280.
[2] Ibid.
[3] *Scotsman*, May 11th, 1927.

IX

THE MONARCH'S RESERVE POWER: THE STRUGGLE OF 1909–11

THE constitutional controversies which commenced with the rejection by the House of Lords of the Liberal Government's Budget of 1909 assumed several distinct aspects. The most important questions which came to issue were (1) the claim of the Lords to force the House of Commons to a dissolution upon any important question, financial or otherwise, which did not have the definite endorsement of the electorate, and (2) the supposed right (or even duty) of the Sovereign to compel a dissolution in order to make sure that an important legislative and constitutional change should receive definite endorsement from the electorate. The first question was determined adversely to the House of Lords by the Parliament Act of 1911. The second question arose after that Act had disarmed the Lords. The two questions were closely related, each being concerned with the power of Dissolution, and each illustrating the great significance of the personal intervention of the Sovereign, and the delicacy and care involved in the exercise of his prerogatives.

It had long been accepted constitutional theory that it was not within the power of the Lords to reject the financial proposals of the Ministry as approved by the House of Commons, and to compel a dissolution of the Commons in order to obtain the verdict of the electors on such proposals. But a large and influential group of Conservative statesmen disagreed strongly with this theory of the Constitution. This group included Lord Cawdor, who took a very strong view on the subject and was in such a position that his views received anxious consideration from the then Sovereign, King Edward VII.[1] The Conservative leaders were vehemently opposed to the Budget of 1909, which provided for some taxation of the 'unearned' increment in land values.

[1] Newton, *Life of Lord Lansdowne*, p. 380; Lee, *King Edward VII*, pp. 666–7.

On October 6th, 1909, Mr. Asquith, the Liberal Prime Minister, saw King Edward VII, who asked him 'whether . . . he was well within constitutional lines in taking upon himself to give advice to, and if necessary put pressure upon, the Tory Leaders at this juncture'.[1] Mr. Asquith agreed that the King's proposed action was

> 'perfectly correct, from a constitutional point of view; that the nearest analogy was the situation and action of William IV, at the time of the Reform Bill; in both cases the country was threatened with a revolution at the hands of the House of Lords.'[2]

The King then said that the Conservative leaders (Mr. Balfour and Lord Lansdowne) might naturally ask whether, if they persuaded the Lords to pass the Budget, they could rely upon an appeal by the Government to the country. Now this was the very demand to which Mr. Asquith would not yield, being convinced that the Lords had no right whatever to force a dissolution, either by rejecting, or threatening to reject, the financial proposals of the Commons. All the surrounding circumstances indicate that the Conservative leaders were intent upon securing an early dissolution of Parliament. If the dissolution followed the passing by the Lords of the financial proposals, these could not be put into effective operation before the general elections, so that, in the event of a Conservative victory at the polls, they would never be put into operation at all. Further, the Conservative party would have been placed in a stronger electoral position if dissolution had followed the passing of the Budget, as it could not then be said that the electoral issue was the Commons' exclusive control of money questions. But the Conservative leaders were determined upon dissolution, even if they had to obtain it by accepting the responsibility of rejecting the Budget. This responsibility they decided to accept.

On October 12th the King granted an interview to Lord Lansdowne and Mr. Balfour. The King could hold out no hope of a dissolution if the Budget was accepted; and they, in turn, informed the King that no decision had yet been come to in relation to the Lords' proposed rejection of the Budget.

[1] J. A. Spender and Asquith, *Life of Lord Oxford and Asquith*, vol. i, p. 257.
[2] Ibid.

According to one commentator, the influence which carried the day in the decision of the Conservatives to force a dissolution was the 'pressure of rich men who feared for their property'.[1] Whatever motive predominated, the Lords rejected a second reading on November 30th by a majority of 350 to 75, there being no precedent for such action for over two hundred years.

Sir Frederick Pollock described the action of the House of Lords as 'the most audacious attempt to subvert the foundations of Parliamentary government since the revolution of 1688'.[2] But it should also be stated that other constitutional authorities, such as Dicey and Anson (who were Conservatives) took a different view of the situation.

On December 2nd the House of Commons resolved

> 'that the action of the House of Lords in refusing to pass into law the financial provision made by this House for the service of the year is a breach of the Constitution and a usurpation of the rights of the Commons.'[3]

On December 3rd Parliament was dissolved. On December 10th Mr. Asquith, in his electoral speech, said:

> 'We shall not assume office and we shall not hold office unless we can secure the safeguards which experience shows us to be necessary. . . . The absolute veto which it [i.e. the House of Lords] at present possesses must go. The power which it claims from time to time of, in effect, compelling us to choose between a dissolution and—so far as legislative projects are concerned—legislative sterility, must go also. . . . The will of the people, as deliberately expressed by their elected representatives, must, within the limits of the lifetime of a single parliament, be made effective.'[4]

On December 15th Mr. Asquith's secretary made a memorandum of a conversation with the Private Secretary of the King. It stated:

> 'Lord Knollys . . . began by saying that the King had come to the conclusion that he would not be justified in creating new peers (say 300) until after a second general election. . . . The King regards the policy of the Government as tantamount to the destruction of the

[1] J. A. Spender and Asquith, *Life of Lord Oxford and Asquith*, vol. i, p. 258.
[2] *Spectator*, quoted Lee, *King Edward VII*, vol. ii, p. 668.
[3] J. A. Spender and Asquith, *Life of Lord Oxford and Asquith*, vol. i, p. 261.
[4] Ibid., pp. 268–9.

House of Lords and he thinks that before a large creation of Peers is embarked upon or threatened the country should be acquainted with the particular project for accomplishing such destruction as well as with the general line of action as to which the country will be consulted at the forthcoming Elections.'[1]

Mr. Asquith did not, so far as appears, make any reply to this communication from the King, although his own secretary had suggested the advisability of an interview with the King *before* the elections. On the other hand, Mr. Asquith's biographers are quite right in emphasizing that he deliberately made the 'curtailment of the legislative powers of the House of Lords' one of the issues of the elections in January 1910.

The reality of the constitutional situation cannot be appreciated without rejecting the notion that King Edward himself did not hold very definite opinions upon the main questions which divided the Conservative party from the Liberal party with their Labour and Irish allies. This will not be surprising to any well-informed student of British constitutional history. For instance, William IV's opposition to the Trade Unions was very strong.[2] It is well known that Queen Victoria entertained strong opinions on great political questions. On one occasion she stated that she was 'very anxious that the elections should go right',[3] i.e. 'right' for the Conservative party. When Prince of Wales, King Edward was personally opposed to the Home Rule policy of Gladstone and he was in favour of the policy known as 'Coercion'.[4] And it is now a matter of history that Edward VII's personal view was one of hostility to the Budget, and of general approval of the attitude of the House of Lords in the crisis.[5] His biographer, Sir Sidney Lee, points out that 'a good deal of coolness'[6] arose between the King and Mr. Asquith before the new Parliament opened. The King had the greatest objection to such an exercise of the prerogative as was involved in the creation of a large number of Peers in order to swamp the Upper House. Lord Esher had advised the King that, if the great constitutional

[1] Ibid., p. 261.

[2] *Lord Melbourne's Papers* (Sanders), pp. 158–60.

[3] Buckle, *Disraeli*, vol. v, p. 86. (See also vol. v, pp. 29, 77, 100, 491; vol. vi, pp. 148, 152, 525, 528, 537.)

[4] Lee, *King Edward VII*, vol. i, p. 242.

[5] Ibid., vol. ii, pp. 664–5, 667.

[6] Ibid., p. 669.

crisis of 1832 had not been settled by the acquiescence of the Lords without the creation of new Peers, such a creation 'would have involved a decision by the King', and 'it was by no means certain that King William IV would, in the last resort, have made' a creation of Peers necessary to carry the Bill.[1]

Having taken considerable care to inform himself as to the constitutional precedents from Lord Esher, Lord Cawdor, and others, the King strove earnestly to attain an agreed settlement of the crisis, the Prime Minister being made fully aware of the King's personal views as to the merits of the competing views. The memorandum of December 15th was a definite caveat to Asquith that he should not, and could not, rely upon his success at the then pending election as necessarily giving him a sufficient mandate to warrant *any* kind of restriction of the Lords' powers which the Government might subsequently adopt. The position was accepted by Mr. Asquith after he succeeded at the election of January 1910, his minute of February 11th, 1910, to the King stating that Ministers

> 'do not propose to advise or request any exercise of the Royal prerogative in existing circumstances, or until they have submitted their plan to Parliament. If in their judgment, it should become their duty to tender any such advice, they would do so when—and not before—the actual necessity may arise.'[2]

Accordingly, on February 21st, Mr. Asquith informed the House of Commons, in answer to the suggestion that he had already been guaranteed a right to call upon the King for the exercise of his prerogative of creation of Peers, 'I have received no such guarantee and . . . I have asked for no such guarantee'.[3]

The King's view was that the election of January could not fairly be regarded as settling more than the main issue of the Budget of 1909, and perhaps as authorizing some reasonable proposal for restricting the powers of the Lords in relation to finance. He certainly regarded the Parliament Bill as quite unsupported by the electoral mandate of January 1910.

[1] Lee, *King Edward VII*, vol. ii, p. 671.

[2] J. A. Spender and Asquith, *Life of Lord Oxford and Asquith*, vol. i, p. 273.

[3] Ibid.

During the early part of 1910, the King was greatly concerned that his name and supposed opinion upon the matters of controversy between the parties should not be publicly discussed, his secretary informing the Ministers that speeches 'attributing various opinions to His Majesty' were 'most distasteful to the King'[1] and expressing the wish that Ministers 'will refrain from mentioning His Majesty's name in their speeches,[2] or referring to his opinions at all'. This was in April, during which month the constitutional theories of Lord Esher were being repeatedly brought before the King's notice. Lord Esher, strongly Conservative in his views, kept advising the King 'to assert his royal power—to refuse to create the peers—to decline to accept the formal advice of his Ministers'.[3] Above all, Lord Esher, quoting Grey's statement of May 9th, 1832, argued that the Sovereign was not bound to accept 'advice' if he could find another set of Ministers to carry on the Government.[4]

On April 14th Asquith introduced into the Commons the Parliament Bill resolutions. In the course of his speech he stated that if the Government was unable to give effect to the policy of the Bill in the existing Parliament

> 'we shall then either resign our offices or recommend a dissolution of Parliament. And let me add this: that in no case would we recommend Dissolution except under such conditions as will secure that in the new Parliament the judgment of the people as expressed in the election will be carried into law.'[5]

Mr. Spender has expressed the opinion that, in the end, King Edward would have acquiesced in a creation of Peers sufficient to carry the Parliament Bill, subject, of course, to the condition mentioned in the memorandum recording Lord Knollys's intimation of December 15th, 1919, i.e. a general election in which the particular proposal or Bill was known to the electorate. It is not possible to dogmatize on such a question.

Sir Sidney Lee also states that King George V was 'constitutionally correct in accepting such advice'.[6] But he

[1] Sir Sidney Lee, *King Edward VII* (1927), vol. ii, p. 705.
[2] Ibid. [3] Ibid., p. 713. [4] Ibid.
[5] J. A. Spender and Asquith, *Life of Lord Oxford and Asquith*, vol. i, p. 279.
[6] Sir Sidney Lee, *King Edward VII*, vol. ii, p. 714.

refrains from asserting that King Edward would necessarily have taken the same course, and there is much in his biography to suggest that the King might have carried his resistance to a point much farther than King George V went. It is important to note that the statement of Lord Knollys does not contain the slightest undertaking that, even if the Parliament Bill was approved by the electors at a second election, the King would assent to the creation of Peers in order to effect what he regarded as 'the destruction of the House of Lords'. When King Edward received from Mr. Asquith the first draft of the Parliament Bill, he acknowledged its receipt but added: 'The King notices that the date of this Bill is the first of this month.'[1] The month was April 1910! In all the circumstances, it is only possible to guess what King Edward would have done if he had encountered the final crisis over the Parliament Bill. As it was, the accession of King George V in May 1910 resulted in a conference of the Opposition leaders with the object of reaching a settlement of the dispute.

At the Conference difficulties quickly arose. Lord Lansdowne, in a memorandum to Mr. Balfour dated September 9th, 1910, said:

> 'The fact is that the difficulty of forming a complete catalogue of constitutional questions, in a country without a written Constitution, is enormous, and, for that reason, analogies taken from the Constitutions of other countries are not really helpful.'[2]

Mr. Asquith's view was that

> 'No differentiation was possible between that [i.e. constitutional legislation] and ordinary legislation. But the Government were willing that Bills affecting the Crown or the Protestant Succession or the Act which is to embody this agreement should be subject to special safeguards.'[3]

The safeguard suggested was a plebiscite in the event of the two Houses agreeing.

On October 16th, 1910, the Conference broke up, the real difficulty being the proposed application of the Parliament Bill to the question of Irish Home Rule.[4] The

[1] J. A. Spender and Asquith, *Life of Lord Oxford and Asquith*, vol. i, p. 278.

[2] Lord Newton, *Lord Lansdowne* (1929), p. 399.

[3] Ibid., p. 403.

[4] Ibid.

Parliament Bill was then introduced, and on November 15th a memorandum from the Cabinet to the King recommended a second dissolution within the year. It stated:

> 'His Majesty's Ministers cannot, however, take the responsibility of advising a dissolution unless they may understand that in the event of the policy of the Government being approved by an adequate majority in the new House of Commons, His Majesty will be ready to exercise his constitutional powers (which may involve the prerogative of creating Peers) if needed, to secure that effect shall be given to the decision of the country.'[1]

Previously, Mr. Asquith had seen the King, and pointed out that the proposed election would be the second time in the course of twelve months that the question of the relations between the two Houses was being submitted to the electorate, so that, if the Government policy was again endorsed, the matter should be put in train for final settlement. As the House of Lords could not be dissolved, the only constitutional and practical method of bringing it into harmony with the Commons was by adding to its members.[2] Mr. Asquith and Lord Crewe saw the King on November 16th, and he then expressed his assent to the memorandum of the 15th.

The Government was successful at the elections, but the constitutional struggle was by no means regarded as at an end. For instance, Lord Morley (a member of the Asquith Cabinet) is reported to have said that the King might refuse to create so large a number as five hundred Peers, in which event 'Arthur Balfour would take office . . . another dissolution would follow (and) . . . the country, in despair of any other expedient, would give the Unionists a majority.'[3]

In December, immediately after the elections, the Prime Minister prepared an elaborate memorandum as to the constitutional powers and functions of the Sovereign. This memorandum is seen to contain some important propositions as to constitutional practice,[4] and it demands analysis.

(i) The general duty of the King, Mr. Asquith said, was

[1] J. A. Spender and Asquith, *Life of Lord Oxford and Asquith*, vol. i, p. 297.

[2] Ibid., p. 296.

[3] Fitzroy, *Memoirs*, vol. ii, p. 427.

[4] J. A. Spender and Asquith, *Life of Lord Oxford and Asquith*, vol. i, pp. 305–6.

'to act upon the advice of the Ministers who for the time being possess the confidence of the House of Commons',[1] whatever the personal judgment or opinion of the Sovereign himself might be.

It will be observed that Mr. Asquith limits his proposition to the case of Ministers who possess the confidence of the popular House. His proposition, therefore, had no bearing on such a case as that of Lord Byng in Canada in 1926, when, at the moment when Mr. King was advising a dissolution, an amendment in the nature of a censure upon the Government was under the consideration of the Canadian Commons, and it was doubtful whether the Ministers who were tendering advice to the Governor-General still possessed the confidence of the House. The proposition of Mr. Asquith is also entirely consistent with his statement of December 1923, when, after Mr. Baldwin's defeat at the general elections, Mr. MacDonald, as Labour leader, was about to join with the Liberals under Mr. Asquith in defeating the Government. Mr. Asquith then argued that the King was not necessarily bound to accept the advice tendered by Ministers merely because they were holding office. For instance, such Ministers might have been defeated on a censure motion, and then asked the King to grant them a dissolution.

(ii) Mr. Asquith said that it followed from his first proposition

> 'that it is not the function of a Constitutional Sovereign to act as arbiter or mediator between rival parties and policies; still less to take advice from the leaders on both sides, with the view to forming a conclusion of his own.'[2]

It is no use burking the fact that Mr. Asquith was, by this time, greatly concerned with the repeated efforts which had been and were still being made by the Conservative leaders to influence the Sovereign's exercise of his prerogative so that the terms of the Parliament Bill would be qualified. As already noted, Mr. Asquith assented to King Edward's first attempt at intervention when the Lords threatened to reject the Budget of 1909. However, the intervention of the King had not been fruitful, and to Mr. Asquith it seemed

[1] J. A. Spender and Asquith, *Life of Lord Oxford and Asquith*, vol. i, pp. 305–6.

[2] Ibid., p. 306.

likely that, as a result of the incident, the Conservative leaders became aware of the King's personal distaste for the Government's proposals, and so received encouragement to which they were not entitled, and which was embarrassing to the Ministers.

Mr. Asquith's fear as to the Conservative strategy is now seen to have had a substantial basis. On January 27th, 1911, Lord Lansdowne had a conversation with the King of which he reports:

> 'His Majesty told me that he had had some controversy with the Prime Minister as to the propriety of interviews between himself and the Leaders of the Opposition. . . . His Majesty dwelt on the improbability of Mr. Balfour's being able to form a Ministry and to go to the country, supposing the King were to send for him.'[1]

At this interview Lord Lansdowne expressed his agreement with the King that if the elections were held immediately, 'I did not see that Mr. Balfour would stand any chance',[2] but 'it might, however, happen that, as the situation developed, the issue might undergo a change'.[3] This interview explains Balfour's letter to Lord Lansdowne of December 27th, 1910, in which he stated:

> 'I do not believe, however, as at present advised, that it would be fair to the King to suggest that he will better his position by attempting, under present circumstances, to change his government.'[4]

The correspondence between Balfour and Lord Lansdowne, and the interview of the latter with the King, suggest two points. The Conservative leaders were looking forward to the possibility of some such amendment to the Parliament Bill as would secure the Constitution against a drastic alteration during the period which must necessarily elapse between the passing of the Bill into law, and the coming into existence in accordance with its preamble of a reformed House of Lords. For instance, it was now obvious that the Home Rule legislation might be passed without the assent of the House of Lords, and—unless the Parliament Bill was amended or a third dissolution forced—without any other appeal to the electorate.

[1] Lord Newton, *Lord Lansdowne* (1929), pp. 409–10.

[2] Ibid., p. 410.

[3] Ibid.

[4] Ibid., p. 408.

A further point is that the conversation recorded by Lord Lansdowne suggests that the King had not committed himself, at any rate irrevocably, to an appointment of Peers which would make impossible the incorporation of a safeguarding amendment in the Bill itself. Newton does not overlook this point,[1] and although Mr. Asquith's biographers state that the King assented to the Cabinet memorandum of November 15th, 1910, they also state that, at the interview with Mr. Asquith and Lord Crewe on November 16th, the King deprecated the use of the word 'guarantee' in relation to his future action.[2] Further, they also emphasize the importance of the interview of January 27th, 1911, between the King and Lord Lansdowne, and infer from the latter's warning the King of the danger of committing himself that the Conservatives were endeavouring to create 'a new issue which might plausibly be said to require yet another election'.[3] Naturally, Mr. Asquith strongly resisted the suggestion of a third election on the relation between the two Houses. On July 14th, in a Cabinet minute, he stated that such question had been 'a dominant issue' at both the elections of 1910, and that 'a third dissolution is wholly out of the question'.

The second proposition of Mr. Asquith accurately describes the Whig view of the Constitution, which in many quarters had become accepted; but such a theory is and will be regarded by many as an attempt to reduce the power of the Monarch to a nullity in those very times of great crisis when his intervention alone might save the country from disaster.

(iii) Mr. Asquith next stated that 'it is technically possible for the Sovereign to dismiss Ministers who tender to him unpalatable advice'.[4]

Stated as a bald legal doctrine, for that clearly is what Mr. Asquith intends by the word 'technically', the proposition is merely that the common law prerogative of appointing and dismissing Ministers is vested in His Majesty. After dealing with the case when William IV dismissed or com-

[1] Lord Newton, *Lord Lansdowne* (1929), p. 411.

[2] J. A. Spender and Asquith, *Life of Lord Oxford and Asquith*, vol. i, pp. 297–8. [3] Ibid., p. 307. [4] Ibid., p. 306.

pelled the resignation of Lord Melbourne, but was himself compelled to recall that Minister to office when Peel was defeated after the dissolution of 1834, Mr. Asquith pointed out that the result in such a case was 'from the King's point of view, singularly unsatisfactory'[1] and Queen Victoria had never attempted to follow so dangerous a precedent.

(iv) Mr. Asquith went on to describe the basis of the constitutional doctrine which he was promulgating. He found it in the power of the House of Commons over supply, which places 'every Ministry at its mercy'.

Elsewhere an analysis of this theory is attempted.[2] The power of 'stopping the supplies' is emphasized by many constitutional writers, including Dicey, but, as Dicey himself concedes, no stoppage of supplies has occurred for over two hundred years. In the case of a Ministry which is supported by the House of Commons, and which is advising the exercise by the King of some prerogative, the power of the Commons over supply is of no importance. In the case of the King's dismissing or compelling the resignation of a Ministry which enjoys the confidence of the Commons, the power of stopping supplies technically exists, and the Commons may conceivably be tempted to exercise it in order to injure or remove a Ministry supported only by the Crown and by a minority of the House. Again, however, the exercise of the power would probably cause indescribable confusion throughout the country, and, if the Ministry sought dissolution at an appropriate moment, as Pitt did in 1784, it is quite possible that very many members of the Commons would be defeated at the election on the very ground of their stoppage of supply. Further, the King's Civil List is not dependent upon annual parliamentary appropriation, and it would probably be suicidal for the Commons to hold back the pay of the ordinary servants of the Crown, or to withhold grants for social purposes, merely in the hope of compelling the Sovereign to act in a certain way.

Therefore, the ground upon which constitutional practice rests does not lie only, if it lies mainly or at all, in the legal power of the Commons to withhold grants of public money.

[1] Ibid.

[2] See *post*, Chaps. XII and XIII.

By way of caution, it should be remembered that the general validity of Mr. Asquith's statement of principles is not dependent upon his having adopted the ordinary conventional view as to their supposed sanction.[1]

Mr. Asquith's minute to the King of July 14th, 1911, forecasted that the House of Commons would reject *en bloc* all the Lords' amendments to the Parliament Bill, and said that then

> 'it will be the duty of Ministers to advise the Crown to exercise its Prerogative so as to get rid of the deadlock and secure the passing of the Bill. In such circumstances Ministers cannot entertain any doubt that the Sovereign would feel it to be his Constitutional duty to accept their advice.'[2]

Three days later the King informed Ministers that their advice would be accepted by him.

In the speech intended for delivery by Mr. Asquith in the House of Commons on July 24th, 1911, but not delivered owing to continued interruptions, he dealt at length with the constitutional struggle, and pointed out that although, in their amendments, the Lords were seeking to put in a special category and outside the main operation of the Bill the question of creating a national Parliament in any part of the United Kingdom, they were not seeking to protect in a similar way the laws relating to the electoral franchise or laws changing the constitution of the Upper House itself; and the result of the amendment would be that in the event of a Unionist majority in the Commons there would be 'unchecked and undiluted Single-Chamber Government'.[3] He also dealt with the proposed exercise of the prerogative, pointing out that it was the one constitutional escape from absolute deadlock when, as was the case here, 'the House of Commons must be presumed to represent on the matter in dispute the deliberate action of the nation'.[4] He quoted Lord Grey's statement that

> 'the Commons have a control over the power of the Crown by the privilege, in extreme cases, of refusing the Supplies, and the Crown has, by means of its power to dissolve the House of Commons, a

[1] See *post*, Chaps. XII and XIII analysing the conventional view.

[2] J. A. Spender and Asquith, *Life of Lord Oxford and Asquith*, vol. i, p. 310.

[3] Ibid., p. 318.

[4] Ibid.

control upon any violent and rash proceedings on the part of the Commons; but if a majority of this House [i.e. the House of Lords] is to have the power whenever they please of opposing the declared and decided wishes both of the Crown and the people, without any means of modifying that power, then this country is placed entirely under the influence of an uncontrollable oligarchy.'[1]

Shortly afterwards, a sufficient number of the Lords yielded in order to avoid a swamping, and so the Parliament Bill became law.

It is now convenient to discuss certain aspects of the long dispute.

In the first place, it cannot be taken for granted, as is so usually done, that the King's personal view of what is a just and proper exercise of the royal prerogative does not count. What may fairly be called the extreme Whig view of the Monarchy, whatever validity it is thought to have in point of theory, is not true in point of fact. It is absolutely clear, for instance, that King Edward would have insisted upon the second dissolution of 1910 before assenting to the proposed swamping of the Lords. It is by no means certain that, even then, he could have been induced to allow Lord Morley to declare, as he did during the final debate in the Lords when the Bill was accepted, that their persistence in rejecting it would lead to an immediate creation of sufficient Peers to secure its passage. Mr. Balfour complained, though the justice of the complaint is hard to see, that the Government had taken advantage of 'a sovereign who had only just come to the throne'.[2] The truth is that Mr. Balfour was reasonably confident that nothing would have induced King Edward to act as King George did.

In the second place the question arises, did constitutional practice require the second election of 1910? Here nothing is certain except the uncertainty of the application of constitutional practice to the particular circumstances. Before the election of January 1910, Mr. Asquith publicly declared that the claim of the Lords to enforce a dissolution by rejecting vital legislation should be finally dismissed, and that the will of the people should be made effective 'within the limits of the lifetime of a single Parliament'. But these statements

[1] Ibid., p. 320.

[2] Ibid., p. 321.

were general in character, and did not condescend to particulars as to the details or main heads of the legal changes proposed. Moreover, the first election of 1910 was also concerned (1) with the merits of the Budget proposals themselves, and (2) with the special claim of the Lords to amend or reject financial proposals, even assuming that they possessed greater rights in reference to other legislative proposals. Under the circumstances it was hardly possible to conclude from the electoral verdict that a clear mandate was obtained to carry into law such a Bill as the Parliament Bill. And the action of the Sovereign, in insisting that a second dissolution should take place when the precise terms of the Parliament Bill had been formulated, was designed to secure a definite decision upon that single issue.

It may here be noted that a general election is by no means a perfect instrument for obtaining a popular decision upon a single issue, since other factors are bound to obtrude themselves. In applying constitutional maxims, practices, and conventions, one is continually faced with the difficulties involved in applying the doctrine of the electoral 'mandate'. Although the main issue at the elections of December 1910 was the question of the relationship between the two Houses of Parliament, and although that question and that of the Budget were the two prominent issues at the elections of January 1910, success by the Conservative party at either election would have given it office for a period possibly extending into seven years. Yet the electors might not have favoured a single piece of Conservative legislation, but merely hesitated to alter the existing constitutional relationship between the two Houses. And this is only one aspect of the matter. Even if the elections had resulted in a Conservative majority in the House of Commons, the majority of electors might have favoured the Liberal policy as to the House of Lords. This was because, under the existing distribution of electorates, there was no necessary correspondence between the number of successful candidates of a particular party and the total vote of that party.[1]

What was involved in the success of the Liberal party at the election of December 1910? Logically no inference

[1] These matters are referred to in Chaps. XXXI and XXXII.

could be drawn from the votes of electors favouring House of Lords reform as to their views upon such other Legislative schemes as Home Rule for Ireland. Only the adoption of the referendum in relation to a specified question enables a severance of issues and decisions to be made.

It has already been pointed out that the underlying claim in 1909 by the House of Lords was its right to insist upon a dissolution of the Commons whenever it considered that far-reaching legislative proposals, passed by the Commons, had not obtained the approval of the electorate. Although the special position occupied by the Commons in relation to finance had a considerable historical backing, a good deal was to be said for the argument of the Lords that it is often impossible to sever financial policy from general social policy, and that such a Budget as that of 1909 presented both aspects of policy, some Liberal leaders being very insistent that the taxation of increments in land values was motived by general considerations of land policy as well as by actual financial needs. In other words, 'the power to tax is the power to destroy', and the power to rebuild, as well as the power to raise a revenue. Whatever the merits or demerits of the Budget policy of 1909, it is difficult to assert that, if the House of Lords was right in its general claim to reject legislative proposals, such claim could never extend to financial measures, whatever their character or social tendency might be. Perhaps the greatest merit of Mr. Asquith's contributions to the discussions lay in his logical and unequivocal denial of the claim of the Lords to enforce a dissolution by rejecting *any* policy measure of the Commons, whether financial or otherwise.

All the aspects of the crisis which already have been discussed illustrate the position that each constitutional controversy as to the actual or threatened exercise of the royal prerogative should be regarded in the light of the particular circumstances existing at the time. For instance, however broadly Mr. Asquith stated the issue to the electors in January 1910, the action of the Lords could not be dissociated from the outstanding fact that they were challenging a proposal in relation to finance, over which subject the Commons were generally understood to have exclusive rights and privileges. Therefore, whilst the individual electors were being given an opportunity of voting against the Government for any reason which might suggest itself as suitable, the special circumstances presented the Liberals with a fighting issue upon which they could take high constitutional ground. And all the existing circumstances played some part in the Liberal victories.

This shows the difficulty and danger of deducing from the ultimate result of the controversy between the Houses conclusions as to the pre-existing constitutional practice governing the relations between the Houses. It is often stated, for instance, that the controversy in England must be regarded as having negatived the claim of every Upper House either to deal with questions affecting finance, or to do more than delay other legislation passed by a popular Assembly. Of course, it is impossible to prevent persons interested from drawing analogies, and, provided due regard is had to all the circumstances of the supposed analogy, such a method of using precedent is proper and permissible and such precedents form the main source of the supposed constitutional rules or maxims.

One aspect of this great precedent is that it shows the necessity of defining constitutional maxims and the danger of relying upon any general agreement even as to their terms, let alone their application to particular controversies. It is clear that, had it not been for the passing into law of the Parliament Bill itself, constitutional 'authorities' would have adopted conflicting views as to the effect, if any, of the two 1910 elections upon the constitutional relationship between the two Houses. The supreme value of the Parliament Act lay in its making such a conflict impossible. We often hear objections raised to any embodiment in clear language of constitutional maxims or conventions. Such, indeed, were the main objections raised to the Imperial Conference declaration of 1926 as to the relationship between Great Britain and the Dominions. When, in 1931, some portion of the constitutional conventions was embodied in the Statute of Westminster, repeated objection was taken to writing down such 'intimate relationships' in 'the unyielding form of an Act of Parliament'.[1] Fortunately, objections of this character did not

[1] See *post*, p. 270.

commend themselves to those who were responsible for the Parliament Act of 1911.

The passing of the Parliament Bill into law in 1911 thus represented an instalment in the gradual conversion of unwritten constitutional understandings into statutory law, enforceable, if necessary, by the Courts. The fact that by the Parliament Act, 1911, the Speaker of the House of Commons was made the authority to determine what should be regarded as a money Bill, and whether the statutory requirement for the passing into law of other public Bills had been followed, and that his certificate was made 'conclusive for all purposes' and not to be questioned in any Court of law,[1] does not detract from its significance: the decision might equally have been committed to the ordinary Courts of law.

I am not aware that any difficulty has been met with in interpreting the clear provisions of the Parliament Act, though, of course, many may object to the policy of the provisions themselves. That is beside the present point, which is that the Parliament Act settled the question of 'conventional' relationship between the two Houses of Parliament by depriving the Lords of all authority in connexion with money Bills, and by limiting its jurisdiction over all other public Bills to the right of a suspensive veto. It is not suggested that the Parliament Act, 1911, represents the last word on the question, even if the House of Lords continues to exist in its present form. Some, no doubt, consider that the Act gives the Lords excessive powers. The two years which must elapse under section 2 (1) of the Act, if the Lords continue to reject a Bill passed by the Commons, may, under circumstances easily imagined, be too long and too dangerous. On the other hand, there are many who would give to the Lords greater authority, and, at any rate, give it some authority to delay certain forms of money Bills. All these points go to the political merits of the Act. The great achievement involved in its passage into law was the formation into definite written rules, easily understood and possessing binding force, of some of the unwritten 'conventions' which are still so prominent and important a feature of the constitution of Great Britain and most of the Dominions.

[1] 1 & 2 George V, c. 15, s. 3.

Again, a point has to be stressed. It is not impossible that the right of personal intervention by the Monarch should be preserved but its proper scope and ambit carefully defined and restricted so that all concerned may attend and govern themselves accordingly. This course has not yet been attempted, and the failure to take it may yet create situations of embarrassment or even danger both to the Crown and to the people.

In the meantime, the exercise of prerogatives remains embarrassed by the generalizations of constitutional writers. One of the features of the common law of England has been the close consideration by the judges rather of the precise *ratio decidendi* of cases previously decided than of the general deductions of text-writers. A similar method of approach is demanded of all those to whom the exercise of royal prerogatives and privileges is committed. Until the time comes when constitutional practice assumes the form of written declarations or enacted law, and is made enforceable by proper tribunals, it would appear safer for prerogative powers to be exercised by reference, so far as it is possible, to analogous precedents, and not to mere assertions by constitutional commentators. The validity of this comment will be proved by an analysis of the important constitutional controversy which took place in 1913 in relation to the Home Rule Bill.

Meanwhile it is quite impossible to accept such generalization as that of Professor Keith. He says that 'it is now clearly the established rule'[1] in the United Kingdom that 'any advice which after full consideration'[2] Ministers offer to the King 'will be accepted';[3] and further that this is a

> 'doctrine . . . definitely and finally affirmed by the action of the King in accepting ministerial advice on the question of the concurrence of the House of Lords in the passing of the Parliament Act.'[4]

On the contrary, as has been shown, the final action of the Monarch was the culminating point of a very complicated series of events; and it is perfectly clear from the precedent that not always is the exercise of the prerogative either automatically nor even easily controlled by Ministers.

[1] *Journal of Comparative Legislation*, vol. xvii, Nov. 1917, p. 227.
[2] Ibid. [3] Ibid. [4] Ibid.

X

THE MONARCH'S PREROGATIVE OF DISMISSAL IN RELATION TO THE HOME RULE BILL

NO sooner was the Parliament Act passed, than the question was raised whether it would be fair or proper to apply it to a Bill providing for the granting of Home Rule to Ireland. As to the strictly legal applicability of the Parliament Act to such a Bill, no possible question could arise. The Act operated as and from August 18th, 1911, the day upon which the King's assent was given, and thenceforward the extent of the effective veto of the House of Lords was limited by its terms. Further, as we have seen, the special motive underlying the policy of the Conservatives after the second general election of 1910 was to secure such an amendment of the Parliament Bill as would prevent a Home Rule Bill from becoming law over the opposition of the Lords before the next ensuing general election, which would take place not later than December 1915, the maximum duration of Parliament having been reduced from seven years to five years by the Parliament Act itself. But it gradually became clear that the conditions presented by the Parliament Act, namely, passing by the House of Commons in three successive sessions, and the lapse of two years between the first and third passing of the Bill by the House of Commons, could easily be fulfilled in relation to any Government Bill during the lifetime of the existing House of Commons. Hence it became understood, not only at the Conference proceedings of 1911, but at the time when Lord Morley announced to the Lords the proposed exercise of the prerogative of creating Peers, that the passing of the Parliament Bill in the form desired by the Government might be followed by the passing into law in the year 1914 of a Home Rule Bill for Ireland.

A very important, but now almost forgotten, public discussion of certain grave constitutional issues connected with the Home Rule Bill was entered upon as the time approached when the Government of Ireland Bill might lawfully be presented to the King for assent, notwithstanding its rejection by the Lords. The discussion took the form of letters to *The Times* in the autumn of 1913. The Conservative demand for the submission of the Home Rule Bill to the test of a general election was then becoming insistent. A dispute as to the existence of a Home Rule 'mandate' at once arose. Mr. Birrell, the Secretary for Ireland in the Asquith Ministry, had said in reference to the second election of 1910 that

> 'there was not an elector in Bristol [his constituency] or anywhere else who was not aware that the approval at the polls of the Parliament Bill meant the immediate introduction and the probable passage into law of a Bill setting up an Irish Parliament and Executive.'[1]

In a reply to this statement, Mr. Birrell's opponent at the elections of December 1910 quoted him as having then said:

> 'Home Rule was one of the questions which ought to be left, and should be left, to the judgment of the whole people. . . . If they thought they could smuggle a Home Rule Bill through the House of Commons in the three years following, all he could say was that their ignorance was beyond all conception.'[2]

The Conservative leaders at once interpreted Mr. Birrell's statement as indicating that the Government had determined against a general election, notwithstanding what Mr. Cave called 'the probability' of civil war in Ireland as a result of its passage into law in its then form.[3]

Mr. Cave went on to say that, if Ministers proved obdurate, the prospect was not a pleasant one, but he suggested that, if a final decision against a general election was made, 'the Sovereign will exercise his undoubted right and dissolve Parliament before the commencement of the next session'.[4] He added,

> 'a refusal of the Royal Assent to the Home Rule Bill after its third passing might no doubt be represented as a challenge to the democracy; but no such reproach could be levelled against a decision of the Sovereign to satisfy himself, before the House of Commons is finally committed to a decision which must change the history of his Kingdom, that that House does indeed represent the democracy of to-day.'[5]

Mr. Balfour then contributed an important statement

[1] *The Times*, Sept. 4th, 1913. [2] Ibid.
[3] Ibid., Sept. 6th, 1913. [4] Ibid. [5] Ibid.

which was published in *The Times* of September 8th. He pointed out that the country was being governed under an 'interim constitution', the Parliament Act having recited the intention to substitute a second Chamber 'constituted on a popular instead of a hereditary basis', and nothing having yet been done to carry out such an intention. He argued strongly against the Government's deferring the dissolution until *after* the Home Rule Bill had been placed upon the Statute Book, and declared that if dissolution took place *before* any attempt to advise the Sovereign to pass the Bill it would be impossible to say 'that Ulster is the victim of a revolution on which the people of this country were never consulted'.[1]

On September 10th Anson stated his view of the constitutional position of the King. He asserted as a fact that certain measures of high importance 'have never been fairly submitted to the consideration of the electorate',[2] and he added that, against the danger of civil war, 'our only safeguard . . . is to be found in the exercise of the prerogatives of the Crown'.[3]

Anson made the following three points:

(i) He would not admit that any prerogative of the King had become atrophied by disuse, but said that the prerogative could only be exercised under certain conditions.

(ii) 'For every public act of the King his Ministers must accept responsibility.' If the King desired to dissolve *before* the Irish and Welsh Bills should be submitted to the Commons in the third successive session, and the present Ministers did not accept the King's views, there must be 'an alternative Ministry . . . prepared to accept the responsibility for a dissolution'.

(iii) Anson agreed with Mr. Cave 'that a dissolution would be a milder exercise of the prerogative than a refusal of the Royal Assent to a Bill'; but he added that in each case new Ministers must be obtained to accept the responsibility for the King's determination.[4]

Dicey now expressed his 'complete agreement with Sir William Anson's masterly exposition of the principles regu-

[1] *The Times*, Sept. 8th, 1913.
[2] Ibid., Sept. 10th, 1913.
[3] Ibid.
[4] Ibid.

lating the exercise of the prerogative of dissolution'.[1] He referred to his own work on the Constitution, stating that his opinion as to the occasion on which a dissolution 'may rightly take place' had 'never been assailed'.[2] His contribution may be expressed in four propositions:

(i) By the whole current of modern constitutional custom, the final decision of 'every grave political question now belongs, not to the House of Commons, but to the electors'.[3]

(ii) A dissolution by the King *before* the commencement of the 1914 session in conformity with the advice of Ministers ready to assume the responsibility for such a decision would be amply justified, following the precedents set up by Pitt in 1784 and Peel in 1834.

(iii) A dissolution *after* the commencement of the 1914 session, before the King assented to the Home Rule Bill, would prevent the Bill becoming law, even if Mr. Asquith succeeded at the elections, because of the requirements of the Parliament Act itself as to 'successive' sessions. This was in the nature of an appeal to Mr. Asquith himself to advise dissolution *before* the commencement of the 1914 session. The curious argument assumed, of course, that even although Mr. Asquith had obtained a definite majority at the elections in favour of the Bill, the House of Lords would still persist in rejecting it, and, presumably, the prerogative of appointment of Peers could not be successfully invoked, so that the machinery of the Parliament Act would have to be invoked *de novo*.

(iv) Dicey greatly preferred the exercise of the prerogative of dissolution to that of the King's refusing his assent to the Bill after its third passing by the Commons, and third rejection by the Lords. Whether the King could 'rightly or wisely' refuse his assent was at present 'a purely academic inquiry'.[4] None the less, Dicey adopted the *obiter dicta* of Burke that 'the King's negative to Bills is one of the most undisputed of the Royal Prerogatives, and it extends to all cases whatsoever',[5] and that 'its existence may be the means of saving the

[1] Ibid., Sept. 15th, 1913.
[2] Ibid. Dicey's theory is analysed *post*, Chap. XI.
[3] *The Times*, Sept. 15th, 1913.
[4] Ibid. [5] Ibid.

Constitution itself on an occasion worthy of bringing it forth'.[1]

Before discussing the final outcome of the controversy, it is desirable to refer to the other opinions which were expressed.

(i) Mr. Balfour distinguished between two cases—first, where the King was opposed to his Ministers, second, where 'though impartial or even agreeing with his Ministers' he still thought that an election should be held.[2] In the second case, not in the first, the King could properly insist upon a dissolution. The Home Rule Bill could, he thought, be brought under the second case. If the King addressed his subjects, explaining why he acted and his readiness to accept the result, his position would be unaffected. Mr. Asquith's biographers regarded Mr. Balfour's distinction between two types of case as 'characteristic', but do not comment further.

Now, whether the King agreed or disagreed with the policy of Home Rule could not be ascertained, except by some authoritative expression of his views. If Mr. Balfour's suggestion as to the King being in agreement or disagreement with his Ministers referred merely to the question of dissolving, the existence of disagreement would be clearly evidenced by the dismissal or resignation of Ministers, and their replacement by Conservative Ministers, followed by the dissolution of Parliament on the advice of the latter. On the other hand, if there was agreement on the question of dissolving at once, there was no room or occasion for the King addressing his subjects. But if Mr. Balfour's comments were directed to the Sovereign's opinion as to the merits of the Home Rule Bill itself, he was advancing an almost impossible thesis. How could the King, for instance, address his subjects and say that he agreed with the Home Rule Bill, but thought the country should first be 'consulted' on the question? The very act of dissolution required some Ministers to 'accept responsibility' for the decision, such Ministers would have to be found from the Conservative party, which could never accept responsibility for any state-

[1] *The Times*, Sept. 15th, 1913.

[2] J. A. Spender and Asquith, *Life of Lord Oxford and Asquith*, vol. ii, p. 26.

ment of Royal *approval* of the Home Rule Bill. The event of Royal *disapproval* of the Bill was, according to Mr. Balfour, to be followed by no action whatsoever on the part of the Sovereign.

Really, it seems an extraordinary suggestion that, if the King was convinced that his Ministers were in the wrong, he could not properly exercise his tremendous reserve power, but that he might properly do so if he was 'impartial' or thought that his Ministers were in the right.

(ii) Mr. Bonar Law

> 'had no doubt that the King had the right to dismiss his present Ministers and appoint others, who would accept the responsibility of advising him differently, and that acting on the advice of these new Ministers he could dissolve Parliament, so that the wishes of his people could be clearly ascertained.'[1]

This opinion was in agreement with that of Anson and Dicey.

A realist might be pardoned for asking what real responsibility would be borne by Ministers in such a case. *Ex hypothesi* they would represent only a minority of the Commons. By taking office under such circumstances as to enable the Sovereign to act in constitutional form, what real risk would they run? If the electorate expressed itself in their favour they would hold office for five years. If, on the other hand, the electorate proved hostile, as it did to Peel in 1834, their position would be little worse. They would quietly resume their places in the Commons as Opposition leaders, and patiently wait for something to turn up.

Mr. Bonar Law seems to have appreciated that real 'responsibility' for this action of dismissal and dissolution would not be borne by the Conservative leaders. 'He said frankly that whatever course he took, the King could not avoid personal responsibility and the risks attaching to it.'[2]

(iii) Lord Rosebery was of opinion that the King could not decline the Royal Assent to the Home Rule Bill, if duly passed under the terms of the Parliament Act. In his opinion, such a step 'would be unconstitutional and a *coup d'état*'.[3] No doubt, as Mr. Cave had observed, Royal intervention, if delayed until the stage had been reached for assent, would

[1] Ibid. [2] Ibid. [3] Ibid.

One other feature of the 1909–11 crisis which calls for attention is the serious discussion, after the second election of 1910, of the possibility of a third general election which would have followed upon the resignation of Mr. Asquith if the Sovereign had declined to exercise the prerogative for the purpose of carrying the Parliament Bill in the Lords. It has been noted that important discussions as to Mr. Balfour's readiness to assume office took place shortly after the second election of 1910. Mr. Asquith was always aware of the possibility of such a move, and he subsequently discussed the situation which might have been created had the King accepted his (Mr. Asquith's) resignation and immediately granted a further dissolution to Mr. Balfour. We have noted the comment of Lord Morley to the effect that the third election might have resulted in a Conservative victory, especially in the event, certain in the circumstances supposed, of the King's name and opinions being introduced by both sides into the contest. Mr. Asquith's comment was that, even if the King's action had been upheld by a majority, the

> 'politics of a great mass of people would have been embittered by the belief that in a great popular crisis the power of the Crown had been exercised against the people and the Constitution.'[1]

He added that 'one does not see how the extirpation of this conviction could have been accomplished'.[2]

This comment is important and significant. It states in somewhat guarded terms that the action supposed on the part of the Monarch would have definitely involved his entry into the political controversy, and his being regarded as upholding the side of the Conservative party. Would it have been constitutional for King George to have taken the action supposed and gone over the heads of a newly elected Commons as well as the Asquith Ministry to ask the people to ratify his action in declining to swamp the Lords and in entrusting the conduct of his case to Mr. Balfour? Old precedents could have been quoted in favour of, as well as against, such action. Yet it is not possible to calculate the adverse effect of such an intervention by the Sovereign in electoral contests conducted upon a full democratic franchise.

[1] J. A. Spender and Asquith, *Life of Lord Oxford and Asquith*, vol. i, p. 340

[2] Ibid.

appear to be less justified than if occurring at the earlier stage suggested by the Conservative leaders. It would also have involved the resignation or dismissal of existing Ministers, new Ministers accepting office (and 'responsibility' for the refusal of the Royal assent) and an immediate dissolution.

(iv) Mr. Asquith's opinion was as follows:

> (*a*) 'However it might be wrapped up, either the refusal of the Royal Assent to the Home Rule Bill or the dismissal of Ministers, would be as dangerous to the Crown as the rejection of the Budget had been to the House of Lords.'[1]

(*b*) If the King, acting on the prompting of a Conservative Opposition in a Liberal-controlled Commons, dissolved the latter body, he would be expected to take similar action in a Conservative-controlled Commons in the case of every important legislative proposal.[2] Intervention by the King would be expected in all important legislative acts which would have to be regarded as necessarily 'bearing the personal *imprimatur* of the Sovereign'.[3]

(*c*) Since early in Anne's reign there had been no withholding of the Royal Assent to a Bill.

(*d*) 'The Sovereign undoubtedly has the power of changing its advisers', but only once during the last hundred and thirty years had the King dismissed a Ministry possessing the confidence of the Commons.

(*e*) The Parliament Act did not affect the constitutional position of the King. The Act was a dead letter when the two Houses were in agreement, and this was always the case when there was a Conservative majority in the Commons.[4]

As Mr. Spender says:

> 'most of the elder statesmen were now contributing their opinions about the possible action of the Crown within the limits of the Constitution . . . but, as the records show, their views of what the Crown might do were generally in accord with what they wished it to do.'[5]

Two such theories or opinions may be noted, one of Lord Lansdowne, the other of Dicey.

[1] J. A. Spender and Asquith, *Life of Lord Oxford and Asquith*, vol. ii, p. 27.
[2] Ibid. [3] Ibid., p. 31. [4] Ibid., p. 30. [5] Ibid., p. 25.

Lord Lansdowne was

> 'strong on the theory that since the Parliament Act had destroyed the power hitherto inherent in the House of Lords to kill a Bill and compel an election, that power now belonged to the Crown alone.'[1]

I discuss this below.

In his 1914 edition of *The Law of the Constitution*, Dicey argued that the Parliament Act

> 'greatly restrains, if it does not absolutely abolish, the use of the Royal prerogative to create Peers . . . in order to force through the House a Bill rejected by the majority of the Peers.'[2]

It is, of course, an accepted commonplace of constitutional law that a prerogative, using the term in the sense of the King's common law powers, ceases to exist when a Statute assented to by the King deals with the subject-matter of the particular prerogative in such a way as to show Parliament's intent that henceforth it should be exercised either not at all, or only in the way permitted by the Statute. Looking at the Parliament Act from this point of view, it does deal with the question or subject-matter of the reciprocal powers and duties of the two Houses in connexion with the passage of public Bills. But it does not purport to deal with any prerogative of the Crown at all. It expressly disclaims (in section 6) any intention to 'diminish or qualify the existing rights and privileges of the House of Commons'. It is also an accepted commonplace of constitutional law that no prerogative of the Crown is deemed to be adversely affected by a Statute unless clear words or necessary intendment require such a conclusion. As a matter of strict law, of course, Dicey's suggestion has no foundation. But what he really meant was this, that, after the passing of the Parliament Act, the King, if asked to 'swamp' the House of Lords by an exercise of the prerogative of creating Peers, was enabled to refuse because, in Dicey's words, the Ministers 'can certainly in about two years turn it [that is, the proposed Bill] into an Act of Parliament without the consent of the Lords'.[3]

[1] Ibid., pp. 25–6.

[2] A. V. Dicey, *The Law of the Constitution*, 8th ed., Intro., p. lii.

[3] Ibid.

The weakness of this argument is the implication of the phrase 'certainly in about two years'. For it may well happen that, in the opinion of the electorate, and of the Ministers, and of the Commons, time is of the essence of the particular legislative proposal. That proposal may be of such a character that the Lords will not accept it, but the people will insist upon it, and will be ready to give conclusive evidence of their insistence. One purpose of the Parliament Act was to set up a legal obstacle in the way of the Lords holding up non-financial legislation for more than approximately two years. But the Act did not confer upon the Lords a 'constitutional' right to delay all such non-financial legislation until so long a period had elapsed.

The Parliament Act said nothing about the composition of the House of Lords except that it was intended to reform it. It would be a curious perversion of the constitutional struggle which preceded the passing of the Act if it were regarded as giving the House of Lords a new 'constitutional' immunity against drastic additions to its numbers, and a 'constitutional' right to delay the operation of all Liberal or Radical legislation until the procedure of the Act had been followed and the necessary time had expired.

Dicey's point, however, is valid to this extent, that, upon a request for swamping, where there is no mandate for the immediate passing of legislation, the King is, by the terms of the Parliament Act, afforded a plausible argument in favour of refusing.

There remains for consideration the question whether the Parliament Act can be regarded as affecting the question of the King's constitutional right or duty to exercise the prerogative of dissolution and dismissal, providing he is able to find Ministers ready and willing to vouch for the formal acts.

Lord Lansdowne's suggestion that the Act merely transferred from the House of Lords to the Sovereign the 'constitutional' right to compel an election in reference to any Bill of importance, is clearly untenable. The Liberal view was that the election of December 1910, and the passing of the Parliament Act, had *destroyed* the claim of the Lords to exercise the right of dissolving Parliament by the method of rejecting vital legislative proposals. Moreover, it was not unreasonable to contend that the period of two years fixed by the Parliament Act as having to elapse before a Bill could become law against the opposition of the Lords, and the relation of such period to the new period of Parliament's life—five years—both indicated something more than a mere negation of the Peers' claim to force a dissolution by their opposition to important legislation. Indeed, the Parliament Act proceeded upon the assumption, positive in character, that, subject perhaps to very exceptional cases, all the legislative proposals of a newly elected Ministry 'which can survive the ordeal of three sessions, prolonged over two years, in the House of Commons, ought, without the need of another election, to pass into law'.[1] If such an inference could fairly be drawn from the history and result of the constitutional struggle, it annihilated the Lansdowne theory that the passage into law of a Government's proposals might still be prevented, the method of prevention being the exercise of the prerogative by the Monarch instead of rejection by the Lords.

The utmost that could have been urged by those who asserted the right or duty of the Sovereign to force a dissolution before the session of 1914 was that the Parliament Act should not be regarded as concluding the question of constitutional right *against* the Sovereign, and should be regarded as being irrelevant in the circumstances existing. The real strength of the Conservative position lay, certainly not in the terms of the Parliament Act according to the Lansdowne theory, but in the contention that both the elections of 1910, outside Ireland itself, were not sufficiently related to the issue of Home Rule for Ireland. This view was strongly expressed both by Dicey, in a letter to Mr. F. E. Smith, referred to elsewhere,[2] and also by Anson.[3] It was for this reason that Dicey said that 'the Parliament Act enables a majority of the House of Commons to resist or over-rule the will of the electors or, in other words, of the nation',[4] and, in particular reference to the Home Rule Bill, he added that 'no impartial observer

[1] J. A. Spender and Asquith, *Life of Lord Oxford and Asquith*, vol. ii, p. 33.
[2] *Ante*, p. 10; Birkenhead, *Frederick Edwin Earl of Birkenhead*, vol. i, p. 285.
[3] *The Times*, Sept. 10th, 1913.
[4] A. V. Dicey, *The Law of the Constitution*, 8th ed., Intro., p. liii.

can therefore deny the possibility that a fundamental change in our Constitution may be carried out against the will of the nation'.[1] These statements proceed upon the assumption that no electoral mandate was obtained for the Home Rule Bill by the Liberal party.

The question thus raised is essentially one of fact. Dicey's contention finds some support in the evidence furnished by Mr. Birrell's pre-election assurance of December 1910. On the other hand, evidence in the contrary direction is not wanting.

Dicey's criticism also suggests the desirability under certain circumstances of restricting legislative capacity to those proposals which are supported by electoral mandate, and the necessity of determining in some satisfactory way whether or not the authority committed by the electorate to a Legislature is about to be exceeded. The fallacy lurking in the condemnation by Dicey of the Parliament Act is that the House of Lords should be the proper authority to restrain such excess, and that, prior to the Parliament Act, that House interposed its veto only in cases of such excess.

The attempt of the Conservative leaders and constitutional authorities to induce intervention by the King in order to secure a dissolution before the session of 1914 failed. Nor was the possibility of the King's further intervention by refusing assent to the Bill ever seriously entertained, so far as is known. But the normal conclusion of the constitutional controversy in relation to the Government of Ireland Bill was prevented by the outbreak of war in August 1914. The Bill had been originally introduced in the Commons on April 11th, 1912, and, the conditions of the Parliament Bill being satisfied, June 9th, 1914, became the earliest day on which the Bill could legally be presented to the King for his assent. Assent took place on September 18th, 1914, after the outbreak of war, but the operation of the Act was immediately suspended by another Act of Parliament.

What, then, is the proper conclusion to draw from the constitutional controversy which commenced in the discussions of the autumn of 1913? The precedent is negative in character. As no action was taken by the King, it is not

[1] A. V. Dicey, *The Law of the Constitution*, 8th ed., Intro., p. liii.

easy to deduce any general principle from such a case. Where action takes place, and the prerogative is exercised, it is more easy to infer that some general principle has been applied. On the other hand, logically speaking, a similar inference should not be impossible in the case of inaction where action has been openly urged and invited. In 1913–14 the King refrained from exercising his legal prerogatives of dismissal and dissolution notwithstanding the direct and undisguised promptings of the Conservative leaders and constitutional experts. It can fairly be taken that he was not prepared to dissolve the Commons by compelling the resignation or securing the dismissal of the Asquith Ministry, and by committing the formal responsibility for such exercise of the prerogative to the Conservative leaders whose readiness and willingness were quite obvious. While the importance of the precedent is considerable, it is difficult to conclude whether the King proceeded upon his own view of the facts or upon a general principle which he regarded as controlling the exercise of his reserve legal powers. It is conceivable that he was satisfied that the Home Rule Bill was sufficiently embodied in the Liberal programme to warrant the conclusion that, in the second election of 1910, the electors had committed to the Government the carrying out of such part of their programme. It is quite possible that, in spite of the bold prophecies that the country would have ejected the Government from office if a general election was held either in 1913 or 1914, the King was not satisfied that such would be the case if a dissolution was insisted upon by him. Mr. Asquith's argument that the Sovereign himself would have been embroiled in a bitter political fight, and that the Crown would be thereby weakened, may well have carried conviction. The King must have been affected to some extent by Mr. Bonar Law's frank admission that, if the King took action against Ministers, personal responsibility could not be avoided, despite the choice of new Ministers to vouch for the act. Dicey's argument in favour of action was based upon the discussion in his *Law of the Constitution* of the precedents of 1784 and 1834, but the latter precedent was a very unsatisfactory one from the point of view of the Monarch. Anson, on the other hand, merely laid down the necessity for the Conservative leaders' assuming 'responsibility' for the exercise of the prerogative. What real responsibility was involved was left in doubt, for, as has already been indicated, seizing a chance of electoral success and subsequent power with nothing to lose in the event of failure is not 'responsibility' of a very onerous character. In truth, Anson was only emphasizing well-accepted constitutional practice, better remembered because oftener applied in the Dominions than in Britain itself. But that very emphasis perhaps served to call the King's attention to the fact that the burden of the exercise of the King's legal power would probably be regarded by the people as resting upon his own shoulders; for the student of the Constitution does a disservice to the Monarchy if he fails to perceive and stress the tremendous responsibility necessarily involved in the exercise of reserve legal powers by the Monarch against a Ministry which clearly retains the confidence of the popular House.

Finally, it may well be that the King would have acted otherwise than he did had the precise conditions and limits of royal action been an accepted constitutional thesis, and if he could have had the assistance of the judicial power in the ascertainment of the principles and facts upon which either action or inaction might properly proceed. This being out of the question, his inaction in the circumstances, whilst important and significant, cannot be relied upon as itself establishing any general rule.

Whilst the precedent of 1913 does not necessarily negative Dicey's opinion as to the true limits of the exercise of his reserve power by the King, yet it does cast considerable doubt upon the general validity of Dicey's doctrines, especially as Dicey in his letter to the King chose to introduce his own statement of principle. A re-examination of Dicey's position should therefore be made.

XI

DICEY'S TREATMENT OF THE CROWN'S RESERVE POWER OF DISMISSAL

DICEY treats the action of King George III in the dismissing of Fox and North as an appeal 'from the sovereignty of Parliament . . . to [the] sovereignty of the people.'[1] He adds:

> 'Whether this appeal be termed constitutional or revolutionary is now of little moment; it affirmed decisively the fundamental principle of our existing Constitution that not Parliament but the nation is, politically speaking, the supreme power in the State.'[2]

He deduces from it, and the precedent of William IV's dismissing Melbourne or compelling him to resign in 1834,[3] the principle that the King may dismiss a Ministry commanding a parliamentary majority, and may subsequently dissolve the Parliament where there is 'fair reason to suppose that the opinion of the House is not the opinion of the electors'.[4] He restates the condition as follows: 'a dissolution is allowable or necessary, whenever the wishes of the legislature are, or may *fairly be presumed to be*, different from the wishes of the nation'.[5] Dicey considers that the constitutionality of the dismissal and dissolution of 1834

> 'turns at bottom upon the still disputable question of fact, whether the King and his advisers had *reasonable ground for supposing* that the reformed House of Commons had lost the confidence of the nation.'[6]

He regards the two precedents as 'decisive', i.e. as showing that the rules as to the dissolution of Parliament 'are, like other conventions of the constitution, intended to secure the ultimate supremacy of the electorate as the true political sovereign of the State'.[7]

Dicey's discussion of William IV's action in 1834 is revealing. From the constitutional point of view he admits that

[1] A. V. Dicey, *The Law of the Constitution*, 8th ed., p. 431. [2] Ibid.
[3] See *ante*, p. 32, note 1. [4] A. V. Dicey, *The Law of the Constitution*, 8th ed., p. 428. [5] Ibid., p. 429. Italics are mine. [6] Ibid., p. 432. Italics are mine. [7] Ibid., p. 432.

it was 'a mistake'.[1] He adds 'it was justified (if at all) by the King's belief that the House of Commons did not represent the will of the nation'.[2] He argues that if it is right for the King to dismiss Ministers and dissolve Parliament when it is shown to be out of harmony with its constituents, 'there is great difficulty in maintaining that a dissolution is unconstitutional simply because the electors do, when appealed to, support the opinions of their representatives'.[3] He concludes, therefore, that a compulsory dissolution against the will of Ministry and Commons is constitutional 'whenever there is valid and reasonable ground for supposing that their parliamentary representatives have ceased to represent their wishes'.[4]

It is obvious that Dicey, endeavouring to unify and rationalize the two precedents of 1784 and 1834 under one governing principle, was faced with the great difficulty of reconciling the failure of William IV and Peel to gauge popular opinion with the success of George III and Pitt in 1784. Accordingly he is forced to conclude that ultimate electoral success is not required to justify the exercise by the King of the prerogative of dismissal and dissolution.[5] So long as there is a 'fair presumption', 'valid and reasonable ground for supposing' that the Commons is out of step with its constituents, the King is justified in his action.

The first difficulty which arises from this view of constitutional practice is, who is to decide whether there is fair, valid, and reasonable ground for the supposition or presumption? At p. 432 Dicey mentions 'the King *and his advisers*' as the authority to decide this difficult question of fact. Such reference to 'advisers' is necessarily to those Opposition leaders who have, *ex hypothesi*, to be summoned to office for the purpose of 'accepting the responsibility' for the King's action in dismissing those who previously held the confidence of the King. What sources of information are to be tapped for the purpose of making a sound electoral forecast? The

[1] A. V. Dicey, *The Law of the Constitution*, 8th ed., p. 431.

[2] Ibid. [3] Ibid., p. 432. [4] Ibid.

[5] It may well be asked why, if the mere absence of electoral success does not prove that the exercise of the prerogative was erroneous, the mere presence of such success should ever be regarded as proving that the exercise of the prerogative was proper.

great resources of a political machine may be available, in which event the reports of Opposition canvassers may find a place in the material upon which a judgment is to be delivered. It is obvious that Dicey's doctrine, if carried out logically, must tend to place the Sovereign in the invidious position of consulting the Opposition leaders upon the question whether the proposed coup and rush election will be successful. It is quite clear that George III, and, to a lesser extent William IV, placed themselves in such a position.

Further, according to Dicey, even if the coup is not successful, and Ministers who have been dismissed from office by the King are returned triumphantly to their former office by the people, the latter have no reasonable cause of complaint so long as the King and the Opposition leaders had 'reason to believe' that a moment had arrived when the Government party was sufficiently unpopular to be rejected by the people.

In his letter to *The Times* in September 1913, Dicey ventured to assert that this exposition of this reserve power of the Monarch has 'assuredly never been controverted by any writer of authority'.[1] But in this connexion it has to be remembered that very special circumstances existed in 1784, and that no occasion even arose for a close examination of this aspect of the prerogative between 1834 and 1913—a period of nearly eighty years.

Is the doctrine of Dicey justified when fairly analysed? It certainly assimilates the functions of the Monarch to that of a political prophet, although his serene and remote position necessarily prevents him from being armed with the soundest materials for such a forecast. Failure of the new Ministry at the elections would place the Monarch, to put it at the lowest, in 'a position of some embarrassment'.[2] Under similar circumstances a Colonial Governor is 'reasonably supposed' to be liable to recall from office.

If Dicey's test as to the existence of 'reasonable ground for supposing' is taken, it leads to some absurdity. Picture the reassembling of the Commons under the leadership of a

[1] *The Times*, Sept. 15, 1913.

[2] J. A. R. Marriott, *The Mechanism of the Modern State* (1927), vol. ii, p. 34.

dismissed Ministry which is recalled to office after the elections. The Opposition leader will have to justify his action and that of the King by saying: 'We made a mistake—but I put it that William IV also made a mistake. I furnished to His Majesty a summary of reports from expert officials in my party organization. In their opinion we should have won. Moreover, as the people knew perfectly well that the King had intervened upon our side, we expected to rally all doubtful voters to our support.[1] I ask for a finding that I did not act unreasonably in measuring the probability of electoral success.'

Such a defence would seem to contain its own refutation. It reduces to a question of mere negligence the correct standard of ministerial 'responsibility'. And what if the Commons considered that Opposition leaders had been negligent, and that there was not *reasonable ground for thinking* that the Government formerly holding office would be turned out by the electors? It is difficult to escape the conclusion that a victorious Commons, the members of which had been put to very considerable trouble and expense for no purpose, might be inclined to say: 'These Opposition leaders voluntarily chose to accept "responsibility" for the exercise of these prerogatives. Let them assume some real responsibility, and let us proceed to discuss sanctions.' It is not difficult to imagine how, under the modern conditions of political warfare, the device of impeachment or some analogous proceeding might again be brought into play.

The overwhelming success of Pitt and George III in 1784 has been allowed to convey a false impression as to the situation of the Monarch in relation to the modern democracy. The coalition of North and Fox was regarded by the people as being little short of infamous. In 1782 Fox had suggested that North should be brought to the scaffold. In the circumstances the fusion of the pair shocked the conscience of the country and gave the King a unique opportunity of revenging himself. Moreover, Fox's India Bill, which was one of the

[1] This was exactly the point of view of the supporters of Peel during the elections of 1834. Melbourne regarded Peel's good showing as 'principally owing to the natural influence of the Government and of the King's name'. (*Melbourne's Papers*, ed. Sanders, p. 238.)

immediate issues of the election of 1784, involved a delegation of governing powers over India and an enormous patronage to a commission which might be out of the reach both of the King and a future Cabinet. Further, the Bill was regarded as a general attack upon property rights, the East India Company broadcasting the slogan, 'Our property and charter are invaded, look to your own'.[1] Pitt's superb parliamentary tactics, in refusing to dissolve immediately upon the dismissal of his predecessors in December 1783, played an important part in the election results. Threatening to stop the supplies, the Commons gradually weakened and failed to adopt Fox's suggestion. Having displayed its fear of avoiding an ultimate issue with the Monarch, its prestige gradually vanished. In the circumstances success for North and Fox at the elections would have been miraculous.

If it is dangerous to draw any sweeping general principle from such a modern precedent as that of 1913, or from the precedent of 1834, it is quite impossible to do so from the coup of George III one hundred and fifty years ago, in which, according to one distinguished authority, Pitt became Prime Minister by 'a violent exercise of the prerogative'.[2]

[1] Rosebery, *Pitt*, p. 59.

[2] Ibid., p. 67.

XII

DICEY'S THEORY OF THE CONVENTIONS OF THE CONSTITUTION AS APPLIED TO THE POWER OF DISSOLUTION

AN unsatisfactory feature of Dicey's work on the Constitution is his treatment of the 'conventions' of the Constitution. In the earlier part of his work he distinguished between the enforceable rules of the Constitution and 'the conventions of the Constitution' or constitutional morality. The latter set of rules consists of

> 'conventions, understandings, habits or practices, which, though they may regulate the conduct of the several members of the sovereign power, of the Ministry, or of other officials, are not in reality laws at all, since they are not enforced by the Courts.'[1]

As he points out, 'some are as important as any laws, though some may be trivial, as may also be the case with a genuine law.'[2]

When, however, in Chapter XIV, Dicey comes to discuss the nature of these conventions, and in Chapter XV, the sanctions by which they are enforced, his account is inadequate, and, in some respects, distinctly misleading. First of all he asserts, correctly, that most of the rules determine 'the mode in which the discretionary powers of the Crown (or of the Ministers as servants of the Crown) ought to be exercised'.[3] The powers in question cover 'every kind of action which can legally be taken by the Crown, or by its servants, without the necessity for applying to Parliament for new statutory authority'.[4] Dicey expressly includes, *inter alia*, the power of the Crown to dissolve or convoke Parliament, to create new Peers, to dismiss a Minister from office, or to appoint his successor.[5]

Dicey's general thesis is that all the 'conventions' of the Constitution have 'one ultimate object',[6] namely, 'to secure

[1] A. V. Dicey, *The Law of the Constitution*, 8th ed., p. 23.
[2] Ibid., p. 27. [3] Ibid., p. 418. [4] Ibid., p. 419.
[5] Rosebery, *Pitt*, p. 419.
[6] Dicey, *The Law of the Constitution*, 8th ed., p. 424.

that Parliament or the Cabinet . . . shall in the long run give effect to the will of . . . the nation'.[1] He attempts to bring within this rule the 'convention' that 'a Ministry placed in a minority by a vote of the Commons have, in accordance with received doctrines, a right to demand a dissolution of Parliament'.[2] With this he brackets the convention that 'there are certainly combinations of circumstances under which the Crown has a right to dismiss a Ministry who command a Parliamentary majority, and to dissolve the Parliament by which the Ministry are supported'.[3] The principle uniting the two cases is, he suggests, the principle that 'a dissolution is allowable, or necessary, whenever the wishes of the legislature are, or may fairly be presumed to be, different from the wishes of the nation'.[4]

The question immediately arises whether the last suggested principle qualifies Dicey's prior statement that a Ministry, losing the confidence of the Commons, has 'a right to demand' a dissolution. If only one principle operates, and the test is, or should be, the same when a dissolution is asked for by a defeated Ministry, or required by the Crown when the Ministry still retains the confidence of the Commons, in each case the Sovereign, with or without the assistance of Ministers, has to determine the question whether the Legislature may fairly be presumed to be no longer representative of the electorate. The difficulties involved in such a doctrine have already been discussed.

Of course, in one sense, every appeal to the people, whatever circumstances exist when it takes place, represents an attempt to get a decision from the political sovereign. In this sense a series of repeated dissolutions of the Parliament may be said to represent the 'triumph' of the people as political sovereign. In actual fact, however, by means of defamation and intimidation and the deliberate inculcation of disillusion and disgust, a series of repeated dissolutions would probably be the very means of first delaying and ultimately defeating the true popular will, and so represent a triumph over, and not a triumph of, the electorate.

If Dicey's reference to the general principle of appeal to the political sovereign applies to such cases, it is a mere

[1] Ibid. [2] Ibid., p. 428. [3] Ibid. [4] Ibid., p. 429.

truism, a restatement in impressive words of the fact that, as the prerogative being exercised is that of dissolution, whenever and however a dissolution takes place, the principle must apply. But what is to be said when dissolution, according to Dicey's rule, should not take place at all? In such an event the existing Parliament should continue its life. If Dicey is understood to mean that *every* defeated Ministry has an absolute 'constitutional' right to a dissolution, irrespective of its chances of success at the polls, it is not an application of, but an exception to, the general principle that 'a dissolution is allowable, or necessary, whenever the wishes of the Legislature are, or may fairly be presumed to be, different from the wishes of the nation'.[1] If, however, Dicey merely asserts that such a dissolution should only be granted to a defeated Ministry where the Legislature is, or 'may fairly be presumed to be', at odds with the people, again the principle of recognition of 'the ultimate supremacy of the true political sovereign, or, in other words, of the electoral body'[2] involves the difficulties we have analysed in the last chapter.

[1] A. V. Dicey, *The Law of the Constitution*, 8th ed., p. 429.
[2] Ibid., p. 428.

XIII

THE RESERVE POWER IN RELATION TO THE QUESTION OF SANCTIONS

WHAT are the sanctions for the observance of that constitutional 'practice' which is said to govern the exercise of the reserve powers of the Crown? In the Grand Remonstrance, presented to the King in 1641,[1] it was recognized by Pym that the sanction which Parliament possessed of impeaching Ministers was not in itself sufficient to secure Parliament's control of administration. For even though the King's Ministers had to assume responsibility in a very real sense for the acts of the King, the position of Parliament would be improved if the King should 'employ such counsellors . . . as the Parliament may have cause to confide in'.

Yet the practice of impeachment for acts advised by the person impeached could not fail to assist in the development of the practice of ministerial responsibility to Parliament. The impeachment of Danby in 1679 first established the rule that neither the express written order of the King, nor the King's pardon in relation to the punishment in which the impeachment proceedings might terminate, was a valid plea in bar to such proceedings. This doctrine, and the violence of the two parties during Anne's reign leading to important impeachments, helped to induce a recognition of what was, quite literally, a *modus vivendi*.

The significance of impeachment as a possible weapon in the hands of Parliament has been under-estimated, because it has fallen into disuse for so long a period of British history. Some such practice as responsible or parliamentary government had to be evolved unless the leaders of the great factions were, in turn, to suffer death, exile, or other drastic punishment. It was quite inevitable that gradually they should understand, in the first place, that they must pay heed to the will of Parliament which could exercise the terrible power of impeachment if Ministers acted solely from loyalty to the Monarch; and, in the second place, that if they yielded too

[1] Gardiner, *Documents of the Puritan Revolution*, p. 231.

readily to an existing Parliament's desire to punish defeated opponents, their own turn would come. As Mr. Churchill has said:

> 'No such anxieties beset the Victorians or trouble us to-day. . . . The 'Ins' and 'Outs' take their turn in His Majesty's Government and in His Majesty's Opposition usually without a thought of personal vengeance, and often without a ruffle of private friendship.'[1]

Mr. Churchill's further comment that it is 'astonishing' that such a system of ministerial responsibility should have proved so serviceable for more than two hundred years, thwarting the natural desire of the Sovereign to govern without parties, is significant of an important modern tendency to overhaul and readjust the technique of government.

In Lord Durham's Report it is said that

> 'the ancient constitutional remedies, by impeachment and stoppage of the supplies, have never, since the reign of William III, been brought into operation for the purpose of removing a Ministry. . . . If Colonial Legislatures have frequently stopped the supplies, if they have harassed public servants by unjust or harsh impeachment, it was because the removal of an unpopular administration could not be effected in the Colonies by those milder indications of a want of confidence, which have always sufficed to attain the end in the mother country.'[2]

Durham then argued that the introduction of the English practice would prevent both the stoppage of supplies and the possibility of Parliament's impeachment of the Governor's advisers.[3]

Further reference is made below to the question of the efficacy of the weapon of stoppage of supplies by the Lower House in order to secure its desires. No doubt such a weapon could sometimes be employed in a Colony to compel the action or inaction of the Governor when payment of the latter's salary was dependent upon the annual grant of Parliament. In the pre-Revolutionary American Colonies pressure by the Assembly upon the Governor was frequently exerted by a refusal to vote his salary. As Greene says, the Governor's

[1] Winston Churchill, *Marlborough—His Life and Times*, vol. i, pp. 339–40.

[2] A. B. Keith, *Selected Speeches and Documents on British Colonial Policy*, vol. i, pp. 136–7.

[3] Ibid., p. 138.

position was 'trying in the extreme', it being at times almost impossible 'without a violation of instructions . . . to get his salary or the necessary grants for the conduct of Government or even the military supplies demanded by the Crown'.[1] Occasionally the Assembly became further entrenched in relation to finance by insisting upon the appointment by itself of the Treasurer of the Province. By the year 1715 the Governor of New York, although violently opposed to such system, was satisfied that it could not be departed from. The same situation existed in Virginia after 1704, in the proprietary Governments of Pennsylvania and South Carolina, and, for a time at least, in Maryland.[2] In Massachusetts the Governor's salary was voted from year to year, and permanent grants were refused in nearly all of the other colonies.[3]

It may be noted that Durham made it an essential part of his recommendations that all the revenues of the Crown except those derived from public lands and immigration should be surrendered to the united Legislature 'on the concession of an adequate civil list'.[4] He was greatly impressed by the fact that in 1836, under the Governorship of Sir Francis Head, the Assembly of Upper Canada refused the grant of the annual supply for the first time in the history of that colony. Head was very indignant that the device so often used in Lower Canada should be resorted to in the Upper province.

It is very difficult to reconcile Dicey's treatment of the reserve 'conventions' relating to dissolution and dismissal with his theory of the sanction 'by which obedience to the conventions of the Constitution is at bottom enforced'.[5] This 'most perplexing' question[6] of sanctions is answered by Dicey's proposition that the sanction consists in the fact that breach of the conventions 'will almost immediately bring the offender into conflict with the Courts and the law of the land'.[7] He illustrates this by reference to the maxim or con-

[1] E. B. Greene, *The Provincial Governor*, p. 51.

[2] E. B. Greene, *Provincial America*, pp. 76–7.

[3] Ibid., pp. 74–5.

[4] A. B. Keith, *Selected Speeches and Documents on British Colonial Policy*, vol. i, p. 169.

[5] A. V. Dicey, *The Law of the Constitution*, 8th ed., p. 435.

[6] Ibid.

[7] Ibid., p. 442.

vention that Parliament should assemble at least once a year. In such a case, breach of the rule will almost necessarily involve illegality, but it is, as Dicey concedes, 'a particularly plain case'.[1] This is so because of the practice of appropriating supplies annually, and of limiting the duration of the Army and Air Force (Annual) Act to twelve months.

Dicey then takes a second maxim as a test, namely, the maxim that a Ministry should retire when defeated upon a vote of no confidence by the Commons. He says that, in the absence of a dissolution, and in the event of the refusal of supplies by the Commons, and the failure to pass the annual Mutiny Act, conflicts of Ministers with the law of the land are bound to occur.

These are the two maxims which Dicey chooses to take as illustrations. The latter maxim should be analysed. The rule is that a defeated Ministry should retire from office when defeated by the vote of the Commons. It may well happen that supplies have been granted for months ahead, and also that the Army and Air Force (Annual) Act will continue to operate during that period of time. If we suppose that a defeated Ministry is able to prorogue Parliament and thus, as it is called, 'get into' recess, it may carry on the government of the country, and enjoy the full conduct of Foreign as well as of Home affairs without the slightest illegality occurring during the time I have mentioned.

I have recently read the valuable discussion of the 'conventions' by Dr. Jennings, particularly noting his statement that ordinarily the House of Commons does not meet between July and April.[2] His conclusion of the matter is that 'Dicey's argument applies only to those comparatively few, though important, conventions which determine the relations between the Cabinet and the House of Commons'.[3] The present discussion should show that the application is still more limited than even Dr. Jennings concedes.

Dicey's explanation of the case supposed leaves out entirely the element of time, which is so vital in affairs of government. Further, if the constitutional rule means any-

[1] A. V. Dicey, *The Law of the Constitution*, 8th ed., p. 445.

[2] W. Ivor Jennings, *The Law and the Constitution*, p. 100.

[3] Ibid., p. 101.

thing, it must mean that a defeated Ministry should *immediately* resign office. Under certain conditions, however, it may break this rule, and, without any breach of law, may retain office for a considerable period of time during which it may, in the name of the Crown, incur binding obligations in relation to external affairs, and may even make war or peace. Therefore, it is not correct to say that the sanctions of positive law necessarily support the constitutional rule under discussion.

And what shall be said of the two maxims or conventions already discussed relating to the prerogative of dissolution? How is their binding force related to the law of the land? One concerns the proper action of the Sovereign when a defeated Ministry asks for a dissolution, the other the limits of the Sovereign's right to insist upon a dissolution against the will of both Ministers and Commons. There is a rule of some kind governing each situation, or rather there should be a rule. If Dicey's statement of the rule is accepted, dissolution may or may not proceed quite regardless of any actual or threatened breach of positive law. Indeed, it is possible to imagine a case where a defeated Ministry prorogues Parliament, does not resign forthwith, holds office up to the very moment when supplies run out, and then dissolves Parliament because it knows that Parliament will refuse to grant supply. Such a state of facts assumes that two rules have been broken, the one, by the failure to resign forthwith, the other, by the grant of a dissolution without reference to the probable verdict of the electorate. How can it be said in such a case that the law of the land has operated in some mysterious way so as to prevent breaches of the maxims of the Constitution?

The truth is that the most important 'conventions' or rules of all, those relating to dissolution of Parliament and dismissal of Ministers, are concerned with the personal discretion of the Sovereign, and whatever the 'convention' or rule on the point may be, mere legal requirements have nothing to do with the matter. The reason is plain. The common law, in the case of Britain, and the Statute law, in the case of most of the Dominions, vests the relevant legal power in the King or the Governor. If the conventional rule is broken by the decision to dissolve, the legal power is merely applied. No question of *its* breach can arise.

One possible exception to this statement occurs when no supplies have been granted by Parliament to cover the cost of the elections. In such a case unauthorized expenditure of public money may take place, and has, on occasion, taken place. Even so, no relation exists between the application of Dicey's general rule and the law of the land. If the rule were that there should be no dissolution granted to Ministers not possessing the confidence of the Commons unless it was *certain* that they would be returned by the electorate, a relation would exist, because the unlawful expenditure of public moneys (in the case of refusal of supply for the elections) would *certainly* be validated after the elections. But the suggested rule is otherwise. Further, even where the popular House is of the same political complexion after a dismissal of Ministers and a dissolution, supply to cover election expenses is never refused.

Dicey touches upon the question why, if his view as to the true sanction of constitutional rules is right, Parliament has never refused to pass the annual Mutiny Act, or refused supplies. He denies the theory that Pitt's victory over the Fox-North coalition shows that Parliament cannot refuse either to grant supplies or to pass the annual Army Act. He explains that case by asserting that Parliament at last 'perceived that the majority of the House did not represent the will of the country',[1] and that it does not show that the Commons, when supported by the country, would not compel a Minister who defied the maxims of the Constitution to choose between 'resignation or revolution'.[2] This is somewhat unconvincing both from the point of view of origins as well as validity.[3]

The danger of impeachment is also mentioned by Dicey as a possible reason why conventions of the Constitution are obeyed. He concedes that 'the habit of obedience to the constitution was originally generated and confirmed by impeach-

[1] A. V. Dicey, *The Law of the Constitution*, 8th ed., p. 449.

[2] Ibid., p. 450.

[3] See *New South Wales* v. *Bardolph* (1933) 52 C.L.R. 455, at pp. 478–9, for a discussion of the action taken in 1784 in relation to supplies.

ments',[1] but points out that no impeachment for violations of mere constitutional conventions has occurred for more than a century and a half. He concludes that the weapon has 'grown rusty by disuse',[2] and that a Minister who dreaded it would advise the King not to convene Parliament at all. He draws the further inference that impeachment, the formal refusal of supplies, and the like 'have fallen into disuse' because the principle of 'obedience to the will of the nation, as expressed through Parliament, is so closely bound up with the law of the land that it can hardly be violated without a breach of the ordinary law'.[3]

One special weakness of Dicey's general theory as to sanctions is that it assumes too readily that the conventions of the Constitution are definitely known, so that all concerned are in a position either to make use of them, or to obey them. Unfortunately this is not so. A close study of the precedents relating to dissolution and dismissal, and to the Crown's exercise or refusal to exercise other powers, shows that it is often impossible to tell whether the conventions are being obeyed, because no one can say with sufficient certainty what the conventions are. In the Dominions, many rules, such as the annual convocation of Parliament, which in England rest upon convention, have become embodied in Statutes. Even that need not always result in their ready obedience, because of the difficulty of finding appropriate legal remedies suitable to the case. None the less, in some respects at least, the Statutes provide conclusive evidence as to what the binding rule is.

Dicey's discussion of impeachment is not quite satisfactory. The reason why, for a period of about two hundred years of British history, impeachment has not been used, is that the two main governing groups have possessed sufficient social and economic interests in common to warrant a tacit understanding that certain 'rules of the game' will be fairly obeyed, so that each in turn should be regarded as entitled to hold office and exercise power. A very potent factor in the early growth of such an understanding was the punishment

[1] Ibid., p. 439.

[2] Ibid. This phrase seems to derive from May, *post*, p. 258.

[3] Ibid., p. 450.

inflicted on certain Ministers who deliberately chose to defy the will of Parliament. As time went on, however, responsibility became more nominal, and the rules and understandings became more concerned with rights than with punishments and sanctions. It came to be understood that the political apparatus of the State should be operated by one or other of the parties, each knowing perfectly well that its adversary would sooner or later succeed it, and then itself be replaced. The laws of treason and sedition, which were formerly imputed to 'factious' opposition, were pushed into the background. The shield of the Crown gradually covered the Opposition as well as the Ministries in power. 'His Majesty's Opposition' became just as essential to the working of the State as 'His Majesty's Government'. Good form required that the understandings should be obeyed. It was inevitable that something like a code of political morality should be recognized, not merely because it was a code, but because there was danger to both parties involved in its breach. Herein lies the true explanation of many of the conventional understandings which have characterized the British and Dominion Constitutions. If, occasionally, they are, or appear to have been, broken, that is an incident of many games, but is never treated as detracting from the binding force of the rules. Hence impeachment was conveniently forgotten, and, for the very same reason, Parliament would never behave so unmannerly as to refuse supplies even when there had been a breach of the rules. Accordingly the grant of supply itself becomes less and less an annual affair. As time goes on permanent appropriations of money are made. There is included the remuneration of many who wield important power in the State. In many of the Dominions the salaries of Ministers are covered by permanent appropriations. Many persons and services become emancipated from review by means of the annual parliamentary vote. Taxation also becomes more and more permanent in character. Under such circumstances, even if Parliament is not called together at all, huge sums of money may lawfully be collected by the Executive Government, and much of it may lawfully be disbursed.

In such a development certain conventions of the Constitution became recognized, but only in a general and somewhat haphazard way. For instance, the great precedent of 1784 came to lose any absolute significance, if it was ever regarded as possessing it. That of 1834 was explained away in the light of William IV's hostility towards one or two of those who had taken the popular side in the great crisis of 1832. All this vagueness and uncertainty did very little harm, and it was 'good form' never to intrude too closely upon the lack of definition of the constitutional maxims. But the extended franchise of to-day has completely altered the position. The controversies as to prerogative between 1909 and 1914 evidence a process which is quite inevitable. It is the process of analysing, defining, and restating unwritten conventions, until they finally assume the form of positive law. The rise of parties and groups which question many of the foundations, which both the older parties took for granted, leads to a demand for the understanding of these vague doctrines of prerogative. The bitterness which infused itself into the political controversies of the twentieth century, and the gradual separation of parties and groups upon opinions previously accepted as indisputable, have rendered it almost dangerous to allow this anarchic part of the constitution to remain in its present state.

The rise of the Labour movement was itself a criticism of what has been called the 'delicate equipoise' of parliamentary government in England.[1] Its devotees were no longer satisfied with a mere reference to rules and understandings which were nowhere defined except so far as definition might be found in the essays of Bagehot or the daring but inaccurate generalizations of Dicey. The former had deprecated the growing solidarity of the working classes and prophesied the break-down of the English system of Government if the Liberal and Conservative parties raised 'questions which will excite the lower orders of mankind'. In 1914 Dicey formally took his stand with Bagehot, whose views on this topic he quoted with approval.[2] In the Dominions, moreover, as is elsewhere shown, the new parties would not, and do not, content themselves with an explanation which con-

[1] The phrase is that of Bryce, *post*, p. 267.

[2] A. V. Dicey, *The Law of the Constitution*, 8th ed., Intro., p. ciii.

sists of no more than a vague gesture towards some hinterland of constitutional and political morality. They cannot see the 'rules' written down in any authoritative way, and they come to suspect the rules the more if they are brought into operation against their desires.

If Parliamentary government is to endure, it is essential that the terrain of this constitutional no-man's-land should be finally explored. In defining the conventions and maxims great difficulty will, no doubt, be involved.[1] There will be greater dangers involved if the questions continue to be neglected. Although the declarations of the Imperial Conferences of 1926 and 1930, and the passing of the Statute of Westminster in 1931, have gone some little way towards carrying out the task in relation to certain aspects of Dominion self-government,[2] very much remains to be done both in Great Britain and most of the Dominions.

[1] See *post*, Chaps. XXX, XXXI, and XXXII.
[2] See *post*, Chap. XXI.

XIV

THE NEW SOUTH WALES CONSTITUTIONAL CRISIS OF 1926

IN June 1925 a Labour Ministry came into office following upon the general elections. At the time the Legislative Council or Upper House was a body the power to make appointments to which was vested in the Governor by the Constitution Act. Each appointment had to be made for the life of the member and there was no legal restriction upon the number of members who could be appointed. The Labour Ministry (under Mr. Lang) had a small but compact majority in the popular Assembly, but was in a minority in the Council. The Council rejected a number of the proposals of the Government, though the latter argued that it had obtained a 'mandate' for them from the electors at the elections of May 1925.

Requests for further appointments having been made, the Governor (Admiral Sir Dudley de Chair) intimated to the Premier on December 21st, 1925, that 'acting on the advice of his Ministers and on the advice given him by the Attorney-General with respect to the constitutional position'[1] he was prepared to make twenty-five appointments to the Council. The advice of the Attorney-General, Mr. McTiernan,[2] was

> 'that the observance of the principles of responsible self-government, which were in full force and effect in this State, required that the Governor should act as advised in this matter by His Ministers, who were supported by a majority of the members of the Legislative Assembly.'[3]

The twenty-five appointments were duly made. One of the Bills then passed by the Assembly provided for the abolition of the Council, but the Bill was rejected by the Council owing, in part at least, to the defection of several Labour supporters. The Government then desired to obtain further appointments which would secure for it a definite majority in the Council. On March 4th, 1926, the Premier and the Attorney-

[1] *N.S.W. Parliamentary Papers* (1926), vol. i, p. 313.

[2] Now Mr. Justice McTiernan of the High Court of Australia.

[3] *N.S.W. Parliamentary Papers* (1926), vol. i, p. 313.

General interviewed the Governor, who declined to act upon the advice to make the further appointments desired.

Here it should be mentioned that on December 3rd, 1925, prior to the making of the twenty-five appointments, Mr. Amery, the then Secretary of State for the Dominions, telegraphed to the Governor, Sir Dudley de Chair, in the following terms:

> 'I have carefully studied your telegram as to the recent discussion with your Premier regarding the proposed increase in the numbers of the Legislative Council. While I realise that a difficult situation has arisen, it seems to me that established constitutional principles require that the question should be settled between the Governor and the Ministry. Consequently, I do not feel able to give you any instruction. I have considered the terms of paragraph 6 of the Royal Instructions, but I do not find that they affect in any way the conclusion indicated above.'[1]

Previously, on November 26th, 1925, the Premier, Mr. Lang, stated to the Governor that he objected to any reference of the dispute to the Dominions Office, fearing that any such reference

> 'might be construed as an admission by me that further action was necessary on the part of the Home Government to give to the people of this State those rights of self-government which we believe we now enjoy. The view of Ministers is that the appointment of persons to the Legislative Council is a matter of ministerial responsibility.'[2]

Clause VI of the Royal Instructions to the Governor of New South Wales provided that the Governor should, in the exercise of his powers, 'be guided by the advice of the Executive Council', but it also provides that

> 'if in any case he [the Governor] shall see sufficient cause to dissent from the opinion of the said Council, he may act in the exercise of his said powers and authorities in opposition to the opinion of the Council, reporting the matter to Us without delay, with the reasons for his so acting.'[3]

The meaning of Mr. Amery's telegram was far from clear. It certainly stated that 'the question should be settled be-

[1] *N.S.W. Parliamentary Papers* (1926), vol. i, p. 315.

[2] Ibid., p. 320.

[3] *N.S.W. Parliamentary Handbook*, 13th ed. (1931), p. 183.

tween the Governor and the Ministry'. It seemed to follow that the British Government should not interfere in the dispute, particularly in view of the further statement that the Secretary of State did not feel able to give the Governor any instructions. So far the position taken up was reasonably plain, whatever constitutional doctrine was inherent in the ruling. But the further reference to paragraph VI of the Royal Instructions create great difficulty.

The telegram was quite capable of meaning that established constitutional practices no longer justify the retention of instructions from the British Government to the King's representative in a self-governing Dominion, and for that reason existing instructions may be ignored; but Sir Dudley de Chair treated the telegram as asserting a discretion in the Governor, stating to his Ministers that 'this places the powers of the Governor beyond question'.[1] From such view Ministers strongly dissented. In 1926, during his mission to England, Mr. McTiernan, the Labour Attorney-General, discussed Clause VI of the Instructions with Mr. Amery, being of opinion that the Clause was 'an accidental survival from the early times'.[2] As Mr. McTiernan said, the Clause was not contained in the Instructions issued to the Governor-General either of the Commonwealth of Australia or of the Dominion of Canada. Mr. McTiernan said that 'the manner in which the Governor is viewing Clause VI is the root-cause of the constitutional differences existing between him and his Ministers'.[3] He contended that the Clause should be recast to make it accord with correct constitutional practice, because, literally, it inferred that 'Downing-Street may govern the State whenever the Governor decides, in the exercise of his own discretion, to dissent from the opinion of his Ministers'.[4] Mr. Amery, however, in pronouncing his ruling from London was content to point out that, as Clause VI also appeared in the Instructions to the Governors of all the Australian States, as well as of certain other self-governing portions of the Empire, the proposal for its alteration 'is one which could hardly be considered with exclusive reference to the State of New South Wales'.[5]

[1] *N.S.W. Parliamentary Papers* (1926), vol. i, p. 315.
[2] Ibid., p. 318. [3] Ibid. [4] Ibid. [5] Ibid.

Forty years before, Chief Justice Higinbotham of Victoria had taken the strongest objection to Clauses VI and VII of the then Instructions to the Governor of Victoria. In a striking letter of 1887 to Lord Knutsford, Secretary of State for the Colonies, he said that the Instructions purporting to authorize the Governor to act in the exercise of his powers in opposition to the advice of Ministers was 'a distinct denial of the fundamental principle of the existing public law of Victoria'.[1] Higinbotham C.J. argued that the Instruction was a direct instigation to the Governor of Victoria to violate the law. He swept aside the suggestion that the Instructions were intended to be regarded as obsolete, and asserted that the contrary was the case. They were definitely in accord with

> 'the wish and intention of the Colonial Office that the Governor shall always and in everything fulfil the oath which he has taken to obey his instructions, whether they be legal or illegal, up to the point, but no further, at which compliance with his instructions and disobedience to the law of the land consequent thereon might involve the risk of comment, followed by exposure and rejection of the illegal claim of the Colonial Office'.[2]

In various forms the Chief Justice expressed his strong opinion that the Instructions to the Governor were unlawful, because inconsistent with the Constitution Statute of Victoria.[3] His argument was that the creation by Statute of the system of responsible government in Victoria operated to vest in the representative of the Crown

> 'such powers and prerogatives of the Crown, and only such, as are necessary in the conduct of the ordinary duties and functions of Government and the administration of existing laws within the colony.'[4]

He concluded that

> 'the radical vice of the Governor's letters patent, commission, and instructions, both public and private, appears to me to be this—that they studiously and persistently refuse to take note of the fundamental change made in the public laws of the Australian Colonies by the Constitution Acts of 1854–5.'[5]

[1] E. E. Morris, *Memoir of George Higinbotham* (1895), p. 215.
[2] Ibid., p. 217.
[3] Ibid., pp. 202, 214, 215, 220.
[4] Ibid., pp. 213–14.
[5] Ibid., p. 214.

It is impossible to accept this contention if considered as a strictly legal argument. There is a good deal to be said for the argument that certain portions of the then Instructions, being surplusage, were void, having regard to the terms of the Imperial Constitution Statute 18 & 19 Victoria, c. 55, and the Constitution Act of the Victorian Parliament itself, because, so far as the powers and functions of the Governor were dealt with by valid Statutes, no room was left for their being governed by Instructions.

But neither the Imperial nor the Victorian Statutes attempted to define and describe the general discretionary authority of the Governor in relation to his Ministers. The true position appears from the terms of the dispatch of Lord John Russell forwarded to Australia after the British Parliament had passed the Constitution Statute authorizing the Crown to assent to the locally passed Constitution Act. This dispatch recognized that it was intended to confer upon the leading Australian Colonies that which Russell was at last willing to describe as 'responsible government'. But the dispatch also showed that the provisions of the new legislation did not, of themselves, direct or require the Governor for the time being to act only upon the advice, and always upon the advice, of Ministers possessing the confidence of the popular Assembly, but that 'responsible government' was to rest, in part at least, upon the terms of the Royal Instructions. Russell's dispatch to the Governor of New South Wales stated, *inter alia*,

> 'You will shortly receive a fresh Commission and Instructions, amended in those particulars which the introduction of that system [i.e. responsible government] renders it necessary to change.'[1]

Therefore Higinbotham was as wrong in asserting the illegality of the Instructions to the Governor as he was obviously right in calling attention to their extraordinarily autocratic character and to the 'culpable inattention of all Australian Governments'[2] to the question of their continuance in full.

From 1850 to the year 1886, when Higinbotham's com-

[1] *N.S.W. Parliamentary Handbook* (1931 ed.), p. 233.

[2] E. E. Morris, *Memoir of George Higinbotham* (1895), p. 217.

munication was invited by Lord Knutsford, there had been no change in the Instructions. It was not until 1892 that new Instructions were issued, but Clause VI of these Instructions, which have since remained in force, repeated the substance of the old form of Instructions and, as we have seen in the case of New South Wales, authorized the Governor to act independently of Ministers if he thought the occasion warranted it.[1]

The real objection to Clause VI was that stated by Mr. McTiernan in 1926, when he pointed out that the then Governor placed a literal reliance upon the Clause, and that this was quite inconsistent with existing constitutional practice in the State and throughout the Dominions. By this it is not intended to suggest that, in the existing condition of constitutional practice in 1926, the Governor of the State was stripped of every element of personal discretion. But it is clear that Clause VI could not be seriously regarded as correctly stating the constitutional position of the Governor, for its terms are in direct conflict with New South Wales constitutional practice over a very long period of years. To take one instance only, in the year 1916 the Governor, Sir Gerald Strickland, was actually recalled by the Colonial Office because, purporting to exercise a personal discretion, or a reserve power, he was on the point of dismissing Ministers who were proposing to pass a Bill in the local Legislature for the purpose of prolonging its life. This case will be referred to in detail,[2] but it should be noted here that, if Clause VI was anything like a true description of his constitutional position, Sir Gerald Strickland merely proposed to act according to its terms.

In the circumstances Mr. Amery's refusal of the request of the New South Wales Government for some more satisfactory recasting of the Instructions to the Governor was not well founded. It should also be noted that the condition he implied—that the Instructions should not be amended with reference to New South Wales alone—merely avoided the existing constitutional issue. It is quite improbable that in Australia, where there are six State Governments, there will

[1] E. E. Morris, *Memoir of George Higinbotham* (1895), pp. 215, 234, 237.

[2] See *post*, Chap. XVII.

ever come a time when some State Government will not, because of its political policy or otherwise, be ready to baulk any attempt of the other five States to obtain united action upon such a question. It is idle, therefore, to deny that insistence upon unanimity was tantamount to the refusal of the request. Exactly the same condition—of unanimity—was made by Mr. Amery when in 1925 five of the Australian Governments suggested that, for the future, appointments to the position of State Governor should be made from Australian citizens. The five Governments concerned were Labour, the one opposing Government was anti-Labour. The condition was locally regarded as a refusal of the request.

Almost at any moment there may arise a constitutional crisis affecting one State only of the Commonwealth. Interest in great constitutional questions is then and there aroused. But other States will seldom be sufficiently interested to make common cause with the State affected and, even if some of them desire to take action, some dissentient can always be discovered. Moreover, it is a feature of recent Australian constitutional history that the States, although jealous of their powers when considered from the point of view of strict law and often prepared to test such powers in the Courts, have, to some extent, allowed their position and status in relation to questions of 'constitutional', in the sense of non-legal, significance to be prejudiced by their failure to insist upon their constitutional position as co-partners with the Commonwealth itself in all that concerns Australian self-government.[1]

Mr. Amery's main ruling of December 3rd, 1925, was that

> 'established constitutional principles require that the question should be settled between the Governor and the Ministry. Consequently, I do not feel able to give you [i.e. the Governor] any instruction.'[2]

Later,[3] he made the following statement in the House of Commons, and repeated it in a letter dealing with the pro-

[1] The matter is fully discussed in Chap. XXII.

[2] *N.S.W. Parliamentary Papers* (1926), vol. i, p. 315.

[3] On March 15th, 1926.

posed appointments to the Legislative Council which the Governor of New South Wales had declined to make.

'Since there seems to be some misconception as to the position of the Secretary of State in relation to matters of this kind, I should like to take this opportunity of making it clear that, in my view, it would not be proper for the Secretary of State to issue instructions to the Governor with regard to the exercise of his constitutional duties.'[1]

On July 14th, 1926, in a letter sent to the Attorney-General (Mr. McTiernan), Mr. Amery announced his final conclusions. They may be thus stated:

1. That he 'firmly adhered' to the position that he could not give the Governor any instructions. This referred to his telegram of December 3rd, 1925, and to his statement to the same effect in the House of Commons on March 15th, 1926.

2. 'If Ministers at home should purport to intervene' in the 'internal affairs' of New South Wales, that would be 'wholly incompatible with the status of New South Wales within the Empire'.

3. The matter in dispute as to the Legislative Council appointments was 'essentially one to be settled in New South Wales, and not in London'.

4. With reference to the argument that 'under the constitutional usage of New South Wales, the Governor has no option but to make appointments to the Legislative Council as and when advised by Ministers', Mr. Amery was 'not qualified to speak' even if he were so disposed; but, he added, 'it is at least clear that I could not accept your view without, in effect, instructing the Governor that he must make the appointment which he has declined to make'.[2]

What is the precise meaning of this last statement of Mr. Amery? Having disclaimed any intention of considering the constitutional duty of the Governor in relation to the advice of his Ministers, he went on to add, quite unnecessarily, that acceptance by him of Mr. McTiernan's view would amount to his instructing the Governor to make the desired appointments. But this line of reasoning assumed that there had been a request by the Ministers for such an instruction to the

[1] *N.S.W. Parliamentary Papers* (1926), vol. i, p. 318.
[2] Ibid.

Governor. Apparently Mr. Amery must have treated the visit to England of the Attorney-General in connexion with the dispute, in order that the case should be fully discussed with Mr. Amery, as a request for a specific instruction to the Governor upon the matter in dispute. The Attorney-General's report, and the correspondence tabled, merely suggest that some ruling as to the relationship between Governor and Ministers should be obtained, and that the Governor's claim 'that he represented the people of New South Wales and that the Premier only represented Parliament'[1] should not be allowed to pass unchallenged and uncondemned.

The more important portion of Mr. Amery's decision, which was made, there can be no doubt, with the full imprimatur of the Baldwin Ministry, was that, in view of the constitutional status of New South Wales:

1. The British Government did not regard a Governor, although appointed by the King on its recommendation, as being properly subject to any instructions from it as to the exercise of any power vested in him by law;
2. The British Government should not intervene in the internal affairs of New South Wales; and
3. The British Government considered that the particular dispute had to be settled in New South Wales, and not in London.

The first two propositions anticipated the principle of IV(*b*) of the Balfour Report as adopted by the Imperial Conference of 1926, that the position occupied by a Governor-General was not that of representative or agent of His Majesty's Government in Great Britain or of any department of that Government.[2] The second proposition adds nothing to the first, except to show that the question of Upper House appointments related to the internal affairs of the State. The third proposition merely repeated the earlier two, because the *place where* the dispute had to be settled was only selected in order to emphasize the persons who had to settle it, namely the Governor in New South Wales and the Ministers in New South Wales.

[1] *N.S.W. Parliamentary Papers* (1926), vol. i, p. 313.

[2] See *post*, Chap. XXI.

Nowhere in this letter is there any ruling as to whether and to what extent the Governor possesses a discretion to refuse to act upon the advice of his Ministers. It is consistent with the latter that Ministers in command of the Assembly may have their advice upon a purely local and internal matter rejected, assuming, of course, that, if Ministers resign, the Opposition leaders will be prepared to assume office, and 'accept responsibility'. The situation envisaged is an extraordinary one. What is the position if the Governor refuses to act upon the advice of Ministers who are elected in order to carry out the very policy to which the Governor objects? Previously, when the Governor was admittedly responsible to British Ministers, a Dominion Minister could complain to the principal that its agent had acted improperly, and could seek, either the Governor's recall, or, at least, a direction that he should act in another way. This is no longer possible if the Amery principle is accepted. A Governor is placed in a position, relatively at least, of complete irresponsibility. The King himself does not occupy such a position. During the crisis of 1913, in reference to the Home Rule Bill, King George 'sometimes reminded his Ministers that whereas the Government would in due course disappear, he would remain and his action be remembered'.[1] A Governor, on the other hand, departs from a Dominion, and is soon forgotten. He does not even remain to see the consequences of some act upon which he may have given a personal decision of vital importance to the people concerned. The possibility of such an impasse as has been suggested is greater in the Dominions than it is in Great Britain, where all parties know the King's deep and abiding concern for constitutional propriety.

The question whether a Dominion Governor is bound to act upon the advice of Ministers in relation to local matters is related to the question whether he may not call in aid opinions from quarters outside his Ministry. This is illustrated by Sir Dudley de Chair's statement in answer to the question put to him by the two legal members of the N.S.W. Labour Ministry (Messrs. McTiernan and McKell) in 1926, 'Since the Secretary of State declares that he is neither able nor willing to give you advice, whom do you accept as your con-

[1] J. A. Spender and Asquith, *Life of Lord Oxford and Asquith*, vol. ii, p. 28.

stitutional adviser on constitutional matters?'[1] The answer was '*Principally* you'.[2] This answer suggested that the Governor reserved a right to look for advice upon such questions to persons outside the Ministry. And there is some evidence that, from time to time, Governors have adopted such a course of procedure. In theory, there is nothing objectionable in examining conflicting views, provided the question at issue is openly and fully debated and the opposing interests present their respective sides of the controversy before a tribunal vested with authority to decide or advise. It is not impossible that, in the future development of constitutional practice, there will be an attempt to secure rulings upon moot points from a competent tribunal. But, in the meantime, the practice suggested by the Governor's answer tends to lead to recrimination and imputation of motives, especially where the British Government has opposing political opinions to those of the Ministers for the time being in office in the Dominion.

For Mr. McTiernan's view was that:

> 'From my conversation in political circles I feel that the attitude of a Liberal Minister may have been different from that of Mr. Amery. I believe that the attitude of a Labour Secretary of State for the Dominions would have been markedly different—that he would have strongly disapproved of the action of the Governor in ignoring the advice of his responsible Ministers, who are supported by the elected representatives of the people.'[3]

Mr. McTiernan stated that he was impressed by the great importance to the Dominions of the fact that the Secretary of State 'is a member of a political party'. He added that Mr. Amery's attitude was perhaps affected by the constitutional crisis in Canada after Lord Byng had declined to accept Mr. King's advice, and that 'Naturally the sympathy of the British Conservative Party was for the Canadian Conservatives'.[4]

Perhaps it was unfortunate from his point of view that, in connexion with the crisis, Mr. McTiernan chose to call in aid some of the opinions of Professor Keith. But the Attorney-General seemed to be well warranted in doing so,

[1] *N.S.W. Parliamentary Papers* (1926), vol. i, p. 321.

[2] Italics are mine.

[3] *N.S.W. Parliamentary Papers* (1926), vol. i, p. 313.

[4] Ibid.

having regard to Professor Keith's strong comments upon the earlier precedents in the Dominions, especially (1) the action of Sir Ronald Munro Ferguson in granting a double dissolution of the Federal Parliament in 1914, and (2) the recall of Sir Gerald Strickland in 1916–17. Mr. McTiernan quoted, amongst other documents, Keith's letter to *The Times* of September 18th, 1917. In this, Keith said, in reference to the Dominions, including therein the States of the Commonwealth, that 'the true solution of the difficulty is the establishment of the rule of action on Ministerial advice in every case', because any other practice threw upon the Governor 'a personal responsibility which is more and more out of harmony with modern conditions of political thought in Australia'.

But in 1926 Professor Keith intervened in the New South Wales dispute not in support of, but against, the Ministers who had made the mistake of accepting at full face value his 1917 opinion. And he now stated that 'the Governor took a somewhat extreme step when he granted an addition of twenty-five members to the Council'. He also urged 'that Mr. Amery ought not to consent to remove the Governor'.[1] And he distinguished his condemnation of Lord Byng's action in relation to Mr. King by saying that the former's error lay

> 'in seeking to effect an innovation in Canadian public life, the refusal of a dissolution to a Prime Minister who assured him—correctly as it proved—that the step was essential in the interests of the country.'[2]

Even here it should be observed that at first Keith made no attempt to suggest that the status of New South Wales, as a State of the Commonwealth, was in any essential respect different from that of Canada, but only sought to distinguish the two cases by reason of the differing circumstances. Keith's later attempt to reduce and belittle the status of the Australian States was quite inconsistent with all his prior writings and comments. Further, the above comment as to Lord Byng's 'error' leaves one in bewilderment. If the Prime Minister of Canada assured Lord Byng that the acceptance of his (the Prime Minister's) advice was essential to the

[1] There appears to be no official document suggesting any such request for recall or removal.

[2] *Scotsman*, Nov. 17th, 1926.

interests of the country, the New South Wales Ministers gave much the same assurance. Indeed, such an assurance is expressed or assumed whenever advice is deliberately given by Ministers. That Mr. King's assurance turned out to be correct does not necessarily prove that Lord Byng was in error in declining to act upon it.

Later, on March 4th, 1927, Keith again intervened in the dispute on the ground that 'the Governor of New South Wales is precluded from defending his action'. In Parliament both Mr. McTiernan and Mr. McKell had referred to and relied upon the declaration as to the status of the Governor-General in the Balfour Report adopted by the Imperial Conference of 1926, this report becoming available in Australia early in 1927. Keith's comment was that the Imperial Conference

> 'never attempted to deal with the position of the Governors of the States, a matter which, owing to its composition, lay entirely outside its province, and the mention [i.e. by Mr. McTiernan] of this resolution is wholly unfair to the Governor.'[1]

Again it will be observed that this statement of Keith, though true enough to be a truism, was beside the point. Mr. McTiernan's argument was that no distinction as to general constitutional status could or should be made between the Governor of a State and the Governor-General of the Commonwealth. Each was the representative of the Crown, though exercising different functions, determined by reference to the legislative topics committed by the Commonwealth Constitution to the States and Federal authorities respectively. This argument Keith made no attempt to deal with. But in his later works he took pains to suggest, not merely that the States were not affected directly by the 1926 Conference declarations, but that, on that account, their status became definitely subordinate to that of the Commonwealth. This does not follow in the least, for the 1926 Conference merely declared what the existing status was. The matter is fully considered elsewhere,[2] but it would seem that this New South Wales dispute is the *fons et origo* of Keith's unconvincing attempt to subordinate the status of the States because

[1] *Scotsman*, March 4th, 1927.

[2] See *post*, Chap. XXII.

such subordination seemed necessary in the exigency of the particular New South Wales dispute.

The other part of Keith's criticism is sounder. He pointed out that the Government's object in asking for additional members of the Council was, not to secure a working majority or a fair representation in that Chamber, but to abolish it. Under similar circumstances, the Government's majority being very small, the King could hardly be expected to swamp the House of Lords without a vote of the electorate. Keith said with great force that it was a

> 'fundamental principle of democracy that changes of substance in the Constitution should only be carried out after they have been definitely and distinctly made the subject of a general election.'[1]

Subsequently Keith discussed the New South Wales dispute further, stating:

> 'I consider that in similar circumstances it would have been unconstitutional for the King to swamp the House of Lords, and that Admiral Sir Dudley de Chair's attitude was in perfect harmony with his constitutional duty. . . . It is obvious that the temptation to dismiss Ministers must have been strong, but the Governor wisely held that so drastic a step was unnecessary and would merely prejudice the position as giving colour to accusations of partisan conduct.'[2]

His most recent comment on the matter is that

> 'An effort to secure the dismissal of the Governor on the score of his refusal to act to the full extent was made in Admiral de Chair's case, but the Colonial Secretary negatived the suggestion on the ground that the Royal Instructions expressly contemplated the possibility of the Governor acting against the advice of his Ministers. The formal reason is of negligible importance; it is the mere expression of a principle inherent in the position of the Governor or Governor-General, but clearly the refusal was sound.'[3]

In view of the uncertainty as to the constitutional practice existing in 1926 before the discussions entered upon at the Imperial Conference, it is not possible to say that Governor

[1] *Scotsman*, March 4th, 1927.

[2] A. B. Keith, *Responsible Government in the Dominions* (1928), vol. i, Intro., p. xviii.

[3] A. B. Keith, *The Constitutional Law of the British Dominions* (1933), p. 155.

de Chair's action was constitutionally 'wrong', just as it is not possible to assert that his action was 'right'. The situation as to the constitutional position was extremely obscure. Very few precedents of an authoritative character were available. The Government relied upon the action of Sir Ronald Munro Ferguson in 1914, not merely in granting a double dissolution to the Cook Ministry, but in refusing to direct the submission of proposed constitutional alterations of the Commonwealth Constitution to a referendum of the people under Section 128 of the Constitution. The Senate had proposed these Bills, and the formal requirement of a double passing and a double rejection had been satisfied. In 1926 it was argued that the Governor-General's action was explicable solely upon the ground that he was bound to act *in all matters* upon the advice of Ministers possessing the confidence of the popular House. It was also argued that this precedent of 1914 had a double significance. Action was taken and a double dissolution ordered when Section 57 of the Constitution was complied with.[1] But no action was taken, although Section 128 was complied with. The Constitution stated that the Governor-General 'may' dissolve both Houses and 'may' submit the Bills to a referendum. The Governor-General distinguished between his action and inaction because of the presence in one case and the absence in the other of advice from Ministers holding the confidence of the House of Representatives.

Yet there was no real parallel between the situation of 1914 and that existing in the years 1925–7 in New South Wales. In the latter case the Government would have abolished the Council if the additional appointments had been consented to by the Governor. That involved an important change in the Constitution of the State which, in the Governor's opinion, was not brought sufficiently, if at all, to the attention of the electors at the General Election of May 1925. There were elaborate arguments in the Houses of Parliament as to the extent of the reference to Legislative Council abolition by the Labour party at the election. That party urged that the proposal was a well-known part of their 'platform', and that they were always pledged to carry it out. On the other hand

[1] See *ante*, Chap. V.

it was urged that, in his policy speech, the Leader did not evidence any intention of abolishing the Council during the life of the next Parliament. The dispute was essentially upon a matter of fact. No constitutional means existed for obtaining a decision upon the question of fact. Consequently, the Governor determined it for himself, and decided against the contention of the Ministry.

It should be noted that the Labour Government never asserted that circumstances could never arise when the Governor might 'constitutionally' exercise a discretionary or reserve power. In his comment upon Mr. Amery's statement of constitutional usage, Mr. McTiernan expressly disclaimed the suggestion that he would necessarily hold that the Governor had no option

> 'where the circumstances differed from those which have existed in the State since the present Ministers took office. Whenever I gave an opinion on the matter, I have spoken with reference to circumstances which were known to me.'[1]

The matter may also be put in another form. Reference has already been made to the question of the Instructions to the Governor, and to the fact that they are quite out of harmony with the general constitutional position of the States of the Commonwealth. Yet it does not follow that, if the Instructions are assimilated to those of the Governor-General, so that no reference to the Governor's acting *against* the will of the Ministers will appear in the Instructions, every vestige of discretionary power will disappear. The extent of such discretionary or reserve power is a question of doubt and difficulty not only in relation to the Governor-General of Canada and Australia, but also in relation to the position of the Sovereign himself.

[1] *N.S.W. Parliamentary Papers* (1926), vol. i, p. 319.

XV

LORD CHELMSFORD'S EXERCISE OF RESERVE POWERS—THE QUEENSLAND CRISIS OF 1907–8

TOWARDS the end of 1907 Lord Chelmsford, when Governor of Queensland, became involved in a serious dispute with the Liberal Ministry under Mr. Kidston, which had the general support of the Labour party, and was opposed by the Conservative party under Mr. Philp. The Assembly was elected in May 1907, and met in July 1907. At this time the Legislative Council was a body whose members were nominated by the Governor, and there was no statutory restriction upon the number of members. Mr. Kidston requested the Governor that sufficient appointments should be made to ensure the carrying out of his policy. The Governor refused the request and sent for Mr. Philp, who agreed to form a Ministry. He met the Assembly on November 12th, 1907, but it refused to adjourn at his request, and passed a resolution expressing its disapproval at the contemplated change of Government. The Governor then sent for Mr. Kidston, and requested him to ask the Assembly to adjourn for several days in order to enable Mr. Philp to form a Ministry. Mr. Kidston duly made the request to the Assembly, and the House agreed to the adjournment. On November 19th the Philp Ministry met the Assembly and asked for supply, but although it was refused Mr. Philp continued to administer the Government. On November 20th he again moved the adjournment, but was again defeated. On November 22nd he endeavoured to pass a Supply Bill, but the Assembly refused to assent and addressed the Governor, stating that:

> 'While entertaining a most sincere respect for Your Excellency [it was] constrained by a sense of the duty it owes to the people of Queensland to again refuse Supply to a Ministry who have not the confidence of this House.'[1]

In the address it was also stated:

> 'We further submit to your Excellency that the Kidston Ministry has never been defeated, and still commands the support of a

[1] *Parliamentary Journals, Queensland* (1907), No. 55, p. 264.

majority of the whole of the members of this House. We therefore submit to Your Excellency that Your Excellency has been misinformed as to the possibilities of this House having been exhausted, or that it is impossible to carry on Your Excellency's Administration with the present Legislative Assembly.'[1]

And further:

'We respectfully submit to Your Excellency that it is probably unprecedented in any self-governing State of the British Empire that a House fresh from the people should be dissolved.'[2]

The address concluded:

'Being assured that Your Excellency has been misinformed as to the state of feeling in the House, and that you have been advised to take a course of action based on such misinformation, we pray that Your Excellency will take into consideration the facts herein set forth, and will be pleased to refrain from any exercise of your High Prerogative which would conflict with the expressed wishes of this House, and could only at the present time result in serious injury to the interests of this State.'[3]

On November 22 Lord Chelmsford made a reply to the Assembly. He stated that 'the constitutional position of the Upper House' was

'the great constitutional issue with which my late Premier invited me to deal. I declined because I considered the matter too grave for a Governor to touch without a mandate from the people.

'By the exercise of the Prerogative of Dissolution the people are asked to say what they wish done.

'I fully recognize the inadvisableness of frequent general elections. I appreciate the peculiar inconveniences of an election at this time, but I regard it as of paramount importance that the country should speak its mind on this question, and therefore I have to decline the prayer of your Address.

'I recognize to the full the responsibility I have taken on my shoulders throughout this disturbed political period.

'From time to time under the Constitution a Governor has to take responsibility, and I cannot shirk it when laid upon me.'[4]

Mr. Philp's party was defeated at the election, Mr. Kidston becoming Premier again. For a time it seemed probable that Supply would not be passed to cover the period between the

[1] *Parliamentary Journals, Queensland* (1907), No. 55, p. 264.
[2] Ibid. [3] Ibid. [4] Ibid., p. 265.

date of the accession of Mr. Philp to the Premiership and February 18th, 1908, when Mr. Kidston became Premier again. However, this course was not pursued, and Parliament agreed to the Kidston Constitutional Bill which provided for a reference direct to the people of Bills as to which there was persistent disagreement between the two Houses.

Lord Chelmsford's action has frequently been criticized, but his decision rested upon the application of the doctrine of popular mandate to the disputes which were frequently occurring in Queensland between the two Houses. He considered that the Kidston Ministry did not, until the elections following the dissolution granted to Mr. Philp, possess a sufficient mandate to warrant the appointment of such a number of members to the Council as would, *without any further reference to the electors*, carry out the Government's policy, not only in respect of any special constitutional legislation to use the referendum in order to settle disputes, *but also in respect of all other items of domestic policy*. In this sense the action taken by the Governor was designed to secure further consideration by the people of important legislation which was not clearly covered by an electoral 'mandate'.

The precedent also illustrates that, however excellent the object and motive of a Governor, actual intervention by the grant of a dissolution early in the life of a Parliament is almost bound to cause a grave constitutional crisis. In the circumstances Mr. Philp cannot be considered to have possessed any justification for requesting, or the Governor for granting, a dissolution, after the Assembly's expression of opinion was made known. At the very least Lord Chelmsford should have recalled Mr. Kidston to office without thereby necessarily committing himself to the acceptance of his future advice as to further Council appointments for the purpose of passing either constitutional or ordinary legislation. The error of Lord Chelmsford lay, not in his original refusal to make appointments, nor in his sending for Mr. Philp after such refusal, but in his determination to aid Mr. Philp in securing a dissolution of an Assembly, newly elected by the people, willing to continue support to Mr. Kidston, and so unwilling to support or condone the acts of the Philp Ministry that it refused him supply.

XVI

UPPER HOUSE APPOINTMENTS—THE QUEENSLAND PRECEDENT OF 1920

THE action of the Lieutenant-Governor of Queensland, Mr. Lennon, in the year 1920 may be considered as providing a contrast with the action of Sir Dudley de Chair in the New South Wales dispute of 1926–7. The Legislative Council occupied precisely the same position in the constitutional polity of Queensland as did the Council in New South Wales, each being a nominee body without any statutory restriction upon the extent of nominations. In May 1917 the number of Councillors in Queensland was thirty-seven. In October 1917 thirteen appointments were made by the Governor. This increased the number of members beyond all precedent. In August 1919 three additional appointments were made, bringing the total up to fifty. Subsequently, in February 1920, fourteen further appointments were made by the Lieutenant-Governor.

The object of the Government in securing the appointments was, undoubtedly, to obtain a sufficient majority in the Council to secure its abolition. Further, several years previously (in May 1917), a referendum of the electors had been held, and the result showed a substantial majority against the proposal to abolish the Council.

That referendum was the method specially devised in 1908, after the Chelmsford-Kidston crisis, for the purpose of settling disputes between the two Houses. The method of settling these disputes was embodied in the Parliamentary Bills Referendum Act of 1908. It provided that, if the Legislative Assembly in two successive sessions passed a Bill to which the Council failed to agree upon each occasion, the Executive Government could direct that the Bill should be remitted to a referendum of the electors, and that if the approval of the electors was given, the Bill could be assented to and could come into force, notwithstanding the Council's failure to agree. In *Taylor* v. *Attorney-General of Queensland*[1]

[1] (1917), 23 C.L.R. 457.

the High Court held that a Bill to abolish the Legislative Council might validly be passed under the terms of the Parliamentary Bills Referendum Act 1908.

A reference to Keith's comments upon the Lieutenant-Governor's action has already been made. He said that 'much indignation was created by this action of Mr. Lennon [in February, 1920] and there can be no doubt that it was unconstitutional'.[1] He adds that his (Keith's) view to this effect was adopted by those who petitioned the Imperial authorities to advise the King not to assent to the Bill for the abolition of the Council, which was passed subsequently.[2] Keith also contrasted the action of Mr. Lennon with that of Governor de Chair in New South Wales, saying that

> 'the upper chamber was deliberately swamped by the acting-governor under circumstances which made his action definitely unconstitutional. He was a nominee of the Labour Government and formerly a Labour Minister, and his appointment as Lieutenant-Governor was clearly improper, since necessarily he was a partisan.'[3]

He considered that such action was 'indefensible' because of the referendum vote of 1917, the result of the swamping being to make it possible 'to carry legislation so confiscatory in character that the London market was closed to Queensland borrowing until later concessions were made and part of the wrong undone'.[4] Keith summed up the position by asserting that 'the whole of the advantage of an upper house was thus lost through the unconstitutional neglect of duty by a political partisan'.[5]

The question remains whether Keith's condemnation of Mr. Lennon's action is justified. Assuming, as one perhaps should, that there was a constitutional discretion vested in the Lieutenant-Governor to refuse to make the appointments, how is it possible to say that his discretion was wrongly exercised, still less that his conduct was actuated by improper and disgraceful motives? The subsequent petition

1 Keith, *Responsible Government in the Dominions*, vol. i (1928), p. 143.
2 Ibid. (Note 1).
3 A. B. Keith, *The Constitutional Law of the British Dominions* (1933), p. 155.
4 Ibid., pp. 155–6.
5 Ibid., p. 156.

to the Imperial authorities, upon the formal reservation of the Abolition Bill for the Royal assent, brought the question of constitutional propriety prominently before the consideration of the Imperial Ministers responsible for advising His Majesty. Keith's criticism was invoked by the petitioners, equal stress being laid by them upon the defeat of the referendum. Its significance was overstated. The rejection had taken place three years before Mr. Lennon's action. The Labour Government under Mr. Ryan and Mr. Theodore had enjoyed a long tenure of office, and, after the referendum of 1917 and before the Abolition Bill was carried, the Government was twice elected to office, first in 1918, and second in 1920.

In the memorandum of the Labour Government's views prepared for the Colonial Secretary in 1921, it was stated that, at the General Election in 1918, both the Labour party and the Opposition made the question of Council abolition a direct issue, and the return of the former was 'a complete reversal of the vote of 1917', which vote, it was asserted, was taken under very exceptional conditions, preventing an accurate gauging of public opinion. It was also asserted in the memorandum that, at the General Election of 1920, 'the question was again made a prominent issue'.[1] Moreover, after the appointments had been made and the Council abolished, the Labour party was again returned to office, which it has retained in Queensland ever since the year 1915, with one break between 1929 and 1932.

The subsequent elections cannot be regarded as decisive, but it should be noted that, when dealing with the Byng precedent of 1926, Keith regarded a subsequent electoral verdict as settling doubts upon an issue of constitutional practice in favour of the party which gained success at the polls. Notwithstanding Keith's views upon the subject, the Imperial authorities, through Mr. Churchill, decided on March 11, 1922, against those who petitioned in favour of Imperial veto. Mr. Churchill said:

> 'After careful examination of all the circumstances, I cannot but regard the matter with which the Bill deals as essentially one for

[1] *Parliamentary Papers* (1922), vol. xvi, p. 326, Cmd. 1629.

determination locally. The policy of the Bill being on this view one of purely local concern, it would not be in accordance with established constitutional principles that His Majesty's Advisers should intervene to prevent the Bill from becoming operative. I have had accordingly no alternative but to advise His Majesty to assent to the Bill.'[1]

It should not, of course, be assumed that because Royal assent to the Abolition Bill was not withheld by the Imperial Government, the latter should necessarily be regarded as having approved of Mr. Lennon's action in agreeing to the additional appointments. On the other hand, it is reasonably clear that, had Keith's theory of an improper political conspiracy been adopted by the Imperial authorities, Mr. Churchill, as Secretary of State, would either have advised dissent or else taken some very strong action in another direction. Further, the ruling shows clearly that the question of the constitutional framework of the Queensland Legislature was regarded as being a matter of local and internal concern, a decision which is obviously right. Sir Matthew Nathan, who was Governor in 1921, reported that he could not say there was 'evidence of any very strong or widespread feeling in the country against this assent being given'.[2]

On the whole, Keith's attack upon the Lieutenant-Governor is unjustified. The precedent, when considered in conjunction with the de Chair precedent, is a striking illustration of the failure of Keith to differentiate between constitutional rule and political opinion. The very most that could fairly have been urged against Mr. Lennon was that he acted erroneously, because there was no sufficient evidence of prior approval by the electorate of the specific proposal to abolish the Council, which proposal the new Councillors were expected to carry out. Assuming the existence of a discretion in a Governor to refuse to make Council appointments, a fair ground for the exercise of such discretion *against* Ministers was presented by the possibility of submitting the Abolition Bill to the electors for their approval in accordance with the procedure laid down by the Parliamentary Bills Referendum Act 1908. That Act was passed in order to prevent the

[1] *Parliamentary Papers* (1922), vol. xvi, p. 344, Cmd. 1629.
[2] Ibid., p. 293.

recurrence of constitutional disputes between Council and Assembly by making the electors the authority to decide such disputes. *A fortiori* it provided an appropriate method for determining a dispute as to the desirability of terminating the existence of the Upper House.

On the other hand, Mr. Lennon was not disentitled to accept the advice that the electorate approved of such abolition, and it may be said that the electorate by twice returning the Labour Government to office after the referendum could be regarded as having approved.

The importance of the de Chair and Lennon precedents is that they so clearly illustrate the absence of any general rule either in New South Wales or Queensland as to the extent of the Governor's discretion to refuse to act on the advice of Ministers. Each of the two persons representing the King had to determine for himself what was just and expedient in the circumstances. When on December 17th, 1925, Governor de Chair informed his Ministers of his agreement to appoint twenty-five additional Legislative Councillors, he stated,

> 'but at the same time the Governor feels it his duty to inform the Premier that he only agrees to the appointment of twenty-five members under protest, as he is still of opinion that the number is more than is needed.'[1]

The Governor then proceeded to discuss how such protest might be recorded, and it was agreed that the correspondence should be tabled.

One possible view is that, in assenting to the appointments which he thought unnecessary, the Governor was not performing what he believed to be his constitutional duty. That was indeed suggested—by some of the political opponents of the Labour Government then in office. And it can be said that, if a discretion existed, the Governor should never have surrendered his right to exercise it, and been content with a mere formal protest. A consequence of such a view would be that Mr. Lennon's action was more in accord with constitutional practice than was that of Sir Dudley de Chair. The former merely accepted the position which Keith had ad-

[1] *N.S.W. Parliamentary Papers* (1925–6), vol. i, p. 349.

vocated in 1917, and took high ground in acting upon the advice of Ministers who had to assume full responsibility. Sir Dudley de Chair, on the other hand, asserted that he possessed a personal discretion, but, in spite of his considered view of the public interest, he contented himself with a futile gesture of protest, well calculated to embarrass both himself and his Ministers.

This is merely one conceivable view of the activities of the two persons concerned. It is, however, just as reasonable to put it forward as it is for Keith to indulge in his violent aspersion of the action and character of Mr. Lennon. What is required by the Crown and its representatives is a position where their exercise of great prerogative powers is controlled and regulated by general principles openly stated and applied with complete indifference to the welfare or detriment of particular parties or interests. Until then, unfortunately, it will be impossible to prevent the recurrence of attacks similar to those made by Keith on Mr. Lennon.

XVII

THE STRICKLAND-HOLMAN CRISIS OF 1916—RECALL OF THE GOVERNOR

IN the year 1916 Mr. Holman was Leader of the Labour party and Premier of New South Wales, Sir Gerald Strickland, afterwards Lord Strickland, being Governor of the State. The popular Assembly was approaching the end of its three years' life, having been elected at the end of 1913. Late in the year 1916 there was a serious split in the Labour party, following upon the introduction by Mr. Hughes, the Labour Prime Minister of the Commonwealth, of a proposal of conscription for war service overseas, which was submitted for the approval of the electors of Australia at a referendum. Mr. Holman and a minority of the New South Wales Labour party advocated an affirmative vote, but the majority of the party advocated the rejection of the proposal. At this time Mr. Wade was the Leader of the Liberal (Conservative) Opposition.

The crisis in the Labour party, both Federal and State, was accentuated when, on the taking of the referendum on October 28th, 1916, the Conscription proposal was defeated. The majority in favour of the 'No' vote in New South Wales was very substantial.[1] On November 10th the majority of the Labour party, which had the backing of its official organization and all the Trade Unions, submitted a resolution of no confidence in the Holman Ministry. Mr. Wade, as Opposition Leader, proposed an amendment to the effect that it was not then desirable to determine whether or not the Government possessed the confidence of the House because, 'in order to ensure the successful prosecution of the war, the best efforts of this State should be devoted to assisting the Commonwealth', and for that purpose there should be formed 'a National Party with a programme based on broad democratic lines'.

What was left of Mr. Holman's Labour following joined forces with the Opposition. The no-confidence motion was

[1] The N.S.W. figures were: Yes, 356,805; No, 474,544.

defeated and the amendment was carried, in each case by a large majority.

On or about November 10th Mr. Holman agreed with Mr. Wade that a National party should be formed, and that the life of the Parliament should be extended. It was desired to avoid an early election.

At this stage the Governor intervened. He stated to Mr. Holman that, as the Assembly as a whole had deliberately refrained from declaring its confidence in Ministers, he (the Governor) would cease transacting business with them, particularly as Mr. Holman

> 'had received the Governor's commission on the strength of his being the Leader of a Party (i.e. the Labour Party) whereof the majority had now expressed its want of confidence'[1]

in him, as Leader.

This was regarded by Mr. Holman as a demand for the return of his commission. He

> 'refused to comply and immediately appealed to the Colonial Office, with the result that the Governor was considered to have fallen into error, and was recalled'.[2]

According to Mr. Holman, Sir Gerald Strickland's action was taken because he (the Governor)

> 'was looking at something which took place in the House, and of which he had no right to take notice, and even if the facts had come before him officially he was not entitled to make the demand that he did'.[3]

Mr. Holman at once proceeded to form a 'National' Ministry, completed it on November 16th, and the first measure of Ministers was the Legislative Assembly Continuance Bill, which prolonged the life of the Assembly for an additional period of one year. The Official Labour Organization at once addressed a petition to the Governor, protesting against the measure. The petition declared that the Assembly no longer represented the views of the citizens of the State and that the Bill was 'a violation of the will of the majority . . . of the people of this State—the refusal to meet the electors being a tacit acknowledgment of the fact'.[4] It

[1] *Sydney Morning Herald*, Nov. 11th, 1916. [2] Ibid., May 16th, 1932.
[3] Ibid. [4] Ibid., Nov. 21st, 1916.

also alleged that 'the proposal to form a National Government is prompted by a desire merely to prolong the life of the Parliament'.[1]

By this time, however, the British Government's intervention had become decisive, and the Bill was assented to by the Governor, presumably by the British Government's direction, on November 23rd. Accordingly, in reply to the deputation which submitted the petition, the Governor stated:

> 'I will transmit the petition to my Ministers, and whatever advice they give me will be forwarded, together with the petition, to His Majesty the King, through the proper channels'.[2]

The appointment of a successor to Sir Gerald Strickland was not announced until September 1917, the Lieutenant-Governor acting as Governor from the time of the former's departure early in 1917. Although the life of Parliament had been prolonged from three years to four, the Holman Government decided to hold the General Election on March 24th, 1917, and it was successful.

In September 1917 an important discussion of the Holman-Strickland affair was published in *The Times*. Professor Keith took up the cudgels on behalf of Sir Gerald Strickland, pointing out that:

> 'It is . . . still the theory of Dominion Constitutions that a Governor may, and indeed perhaps should, decline to accept the advice of Ministers whom he considers not to represent the popular will, relying on his ability to replace them with other advisers should they resign as the result of his refusal.'[3]

The true solution of the difficulty was, according to Keith, 'the establishment of the rule of action on Ministerial advice in every case'.[4]

Sir Charles Wade (as he now was), who had been appointed Agent-General by the National Ministry, then wrote supporting in the main the new proposal of Keith, but not defending the Governor in any way. His views may be summarized thus:

1. In England 'the King acts in all matters according to the advice of the Government of the day', so that the Sovereign's action was 'automatic'.[5]

[1] *Sydney Morning Herald*, Nov. 21st, 1916. [2] Ibid.
[3] *The Times*, Sept. 18th, 1917. [4] Ibid. [5] Ibid., Sept. 20th, 1917.

This view, then entertained by Keith also, rests entirely upon assertion.

2. A Dominion Governor is empowered in theory to exercise a wide prerogative. He may, in his discretion, (1) dismiss Ministers; (2) veto legislation by refusing the Royal assent; (3) exercise the prerogative of mercy; (4) dissolve Parliament against the wishes of the Ministry; (5) refuse to dissolve Parliament on the recommendation of the Ministry. Sir Charles Wade said:

> 'In the course of the last fifty years, however, the exercise of a personal discretion in nearly all these matters has been replaced by the practice of acting on the advice of the Government of the day. In respect of the dissolution of Parliament, the exercise of a personal discretion by the Governor is still maintained. This custom, however, produces undesirable results.'[1]

3. If the Governor turns out to have 'backed the wrong horse' he is practically compelled to resign.

4. The reason for the acceptance of the position that a Governor could, in his discretion, refuse to dissolve upon advice, was to be found in the unpopularity amongst paid members of shortening the life of Parliament—'Frequent refusals to dissolve Parliament are not criticized by the Opposition'.[2]

5. On the other hand, 'If the Governor in his discretion decided to dissolve Parliament against the wish of the Ministry, the whole Legislature would rise in condemnation of the infringement of the rights of the people'.[3]

6. With triennial Parliaments in the Dominions the British practice could safely be adopted.[4]

Sir Charles Wade's views are revealing. He says: 'With triennial Parliaments the day of reckoning cannot for long be postponed.'[5] But one of Sir Gerald Strickland's reasons for intervention was obviously his desire to prevent the attempt of the Holman Ministry to 'postpone the day of reckoning' beyond the triennial period. Wade's view, like that of Keith, recognizes (*a*) that, up to the year 1917 at least, the existence of a discretion in the Governor was admitted, subject to the Governor's accepting the risk of recall following

[1] *The Times*, Sept. 20th, 1917. [2] Ibid. [3] Ibid.
[4] Ibid. [5] Ibid.

upon an adverse electoral verdict, and (*b*) that the Governor of a Dominion occupied a position in the State Governments of Australia not different from that of the Governor-General.

Professor Swift MacNeill suggested,[1] that one important qualification had to be made upon the assertion of Keith that the Sovereign in the United Kingdom always accepts the advice of the Ministry in office. This qualification, which was applicable both to the Monarch and to the Dominion Governor, was the power of dismissing an existing Ministry and appointing a new one. He quoted Anson's view to the effect that such a prerogative 'might conceivably be a resource when a Ministry and House of Commons were alike out of harmony with the country and were unwilling to admit the fact'.[2]

Professor Keith at once joined issue with Professor MacNeill's suggestion. He said: 'It is impossible now to maintain that it is an effective part of the constitutional law.'[3] Indeed, the attribution of such a power to the Monarch would throw on him a 'wholly impossible burden'.[4]

Then Keith added:

> 'I earnestly trust that no Dominion Governor will be seduced into an experiment of dismissal of a Ministry; though precedents of such action could be adduced from periods much more recent than 1783, the time has certainly gone when the attempt can be made without disaster to the Governor himself.'[5]

Commenting later upon the Strickland case, Keith said that there were two grounds of disagreement between the Governor and members, one relating to the question whether they still 'commanded the support of the legislature and the Constituencies',[6] the second relating to the proposed extension of the life of Parliament, the Labour party arguing '*probably correctly*, that a dissolution of Parliament at that moment would return it to power, while delay would tell in favour of its opponents'.[7] Keith's conclusion was that 'On the constitutional rules hitherto observed in Australia, the Governor was fully entitled to act as he did',[8] but the true

[1] *The Times*, Sept. 24th, 1917.
[2] Ibid.
[3] Ibid., Sept. 28th, 1917.
[4] Ibid.
[5] Ibid.
[6] *Journal of Comparative Legislation*, vol. xvii, Nov. 1917, p. 230.
[7] Ibid. The italics are mine.
[8] Ibid.

solution of such difficulties was to secure that the action of the Governor in the Dominions should be as automatic as that of the King in relation to the United Kingdom.

The two cases of Sir Philip Game's action in 1932,[1] and Sir Gerald Strickland's action in 1916 provide a somewhat extraordinary contrast. In the former case Ministers possessing the confidence of the Assembly were dismissed, and the Assembly itself dissolved, because of a supposedly illegal act on the part of Ministers, although redress in respect of such illegality was obtainable in the Courts of law. In the latter case the Imperial authorities intervened on the side of Ministers, although everything indicated that, at the time, they would have been decisively defeated upon an immediate appeal to the people. The object of Sir Gerald Strickland was to safeguard the electors against a Coalition Government which had never received any popular endorsement, and the first act of which was to suspend for a period of one year the electors' right to elect their representatives. Yet he was recalled from office in something like disgrace although, at the time, Dominion Self-Government had not developed to anything approaching the point reached in 1932. Even in 1917 Keith expressed the hope that 'No Dominion Governor' (including and meaning the Governor of an Australian State) would ever be 'seduced into an experiment' of dismissing a Ministry because 'the time has certainly gone' for such an experiment.[2] Yet, in 1932, Keith was able to justify the experiment after it was made, though certainly he took no part in any such 'seduction'.

The two precedents, difficult as they are to reconcile with any governing principle, show that, to use the phrase of Kohn, an 'element of legalized anarchy' characterizes certain features of the Dominion (and British) Constitutions.[3] In the one case (Strickland's) there was intervention from overseas at the instigation of Ministers who feared the exercise of the prerogative against themselves. The possibility of such an exercise was itself forestalled by an intervention equally uncontrolled by governing rule or practice. In the other case (Game's) intervention from overseas had become out of order,

[1] See *post*, Chap. XIX.
[2] *The Times*, Sept. 28th, 1917.
[3] Leo Kohn, *Constitution of the Irish Free State* (1932), p. 292.

nominally at least, by such rulings as the Amery decision of 1926,[1] and the subsequent Imperial Conference declarations.[2] The action of Governor Game did not cease to be anarchic because it purported to be based upon a breach of the ordinary law of the land.

The moral of the precedents is the need for definition, regulation, and enforcement of the Crown's reserve powers; for very damaging inferences are apt to be drawn from the fact that, in each of the two cases, which are so difficult to reconcile with each other, it was the Official Labour party and its supporters which was seriously disadvantaged both by the exercise of, and by the prevention of the exercise of, a reserve power.[3]

[1] See *ante*, Chap. XIV. [2] See *post*, Chap. XXI.

[3] See, for instance, the observations of the Labour party's press organ: *Labor Daily*, Feb. 23rd, 1935. Sir P. Game's successor (Sir Alexander Hore-Ruthven) had announced on his arrival that 'The Governor can advise his advisers. He can suggest. He can warn. But as long as his Ministers are the chosen representatives of the people, he must defer to their advice and assist them to the best of his ability in their deliberations, no matter what may be his private view or personal conviction.'

The paper commented: 'Apparently Downing Street now realizes the gravity of the error committed two and a half years ago, when a people's Government was assassinated in this State. All canons of constitutional conventions were then inconsistently smashed and the Dominions Office, by its silence, acquiesced in this repudiation of the State's charter of responsible government, if, in fact, it did not inspire it. If, in its anxiety to make amends, it has chosen a representative fully seized with the necessity of maintaining inviolate the pillars of responsible government, then it will have removed very effectively the principal *casus belli* between the Governor and the people. That, at least, will be something.'

XVIII

THE RESERVE POWER AND THE DOCTRINE OF THE PARLIAMENTARY SITUATION—A COMMONWEALTH PRECEDENT OF 1918

A CASE which occurred in the Commonwealth of Australia in the year 1918 and affected the Hughes Ministry, illustrates the tendency of some Governors to confine their attention to the parliamentary situation whenever questions arise as to the exercise of any reserve or discretionary power.

On February 17th, 1917, Mr. Hughes, the Prime Minister, who had been Leader of the Labour party, coalesced with Mr. Cook in a National party or Government. Previously, on October 28th, 1916, the Conscription referendum sponsored by Mr. Hughes had been defeated. On May 5th, 1917, the Federal General Elections were held, Mr. Hughes giving a pledge that compulsory military service overseas would not be legislated for without the approval of the electors at a second referendum. Later in the year it was decided to submit the question to a referendum of the electors. During the electoral campaign important statements were made by Mr. Hughes and Ministers as to what would be the result if the proposal of conscription was again defeated. Speaking at Bendigo, his then electorate, the Prime Minister said: 'I tell you plainly that the Government must have this power; it cannot govern the country without it, and will not attempt to do so.'[1]

At Sydney, on November 14th, Mr. Hughes said: 'The Win-the-War Government will not, and cannot, attempt to govern this country unless the people give us that power.'[2]

On November 26th, in a manifesto, he said:

> 'the safety of Australia imperatively demands that Australia should do its duty, that the proposals of the Government should be accepted. Unless it has the power to secure the reinforcements as set out in its proposal, the Government cannot carry on, and will not attempt to do so.'[3]

[1] *Commonwealth Parliamentary Debates*, vol. lxxxiii, p. 2923.
[2] Ibid.
[3] Ibid.

Speaking at Brisbane, Mr. Hughes added:

> 'He asked them to give him the power which the Government sought. If they did not he for one would not attempt to govern the country. Without that power it was impossible to govern the country.'[1]

At Sydney, on December 4th, he said:

> 'I also declare that unless the Government has this power, it will not attempt to—it cannot—govern this country. If it has not this power, you will choose the manner of men you wish should govern. Your duty has to be done. You have to do it.'[2]

On December 5th, at Hurstville, he said: 'If you reject these proposals, I wash my hands of all responsibility. I shall not attempt to carry on'.[3]

Announcements of a similar character were made by Mr. Cook and other Ministers. On December 20th the vote took place, and the majority against the Government's proposals was greater than upon the occasion of their previous defeat.[4] On January 9th Parliament reassembled, and Mr. Hughes at once announced that the Government had resigned and the House of Representatives adjourned. On the following day Mr. Hughes stated that, consequent upon the referendum result, 'the Government considered it its duty to resign unconditionally and to offer no advice to his Excellency.' He then presented to the House a memorandum of the Governor-General[5] stating that Mr. Hughes had offered no advice as to who should be asked to form an Administration. The memorandum proceeded as follows:

> 'The Governor-General considered that it was his paramount duty (*a*) to make provision for carrying on the business of the country in accordance with the principles of parliamentary government, (*b*) to avoid a situation arising which must lead to a further appeal to the country within twelve months of an election resulting in the return of two Houses of similar political complexion, which are still working in unison. The Governor-General was also of the opinion that in granting a commission for the formation of a new Administration his choice must be determined solely by the Parliamentary situation. Any other course would be a departure from constitutional practice, and an infringement of the rights of Parlia-

[1] *Commonwealth Parliamentary Debates*, vol. lxxxiii, p. 2923.

[2] Ibid., pp. 2923–4.

[3] Ibid., p. 2924.

[4] The majority for No, after the inclusion of soldiers' votes overseas, increased from 73,000 to 166,000.

[5] Sir Ronald Munro Ferguson.

ment. In the absence of such parliamentary indications as are given by a defeat of the Government in Parliament, the Governor-General endeavoured to ascertain what the situation was by seeking information from representatives of all sections of the House with a view to determining where the majority lay, and what prospects there were of forming an alternative Government.

'As a result of these interviews, in which the knowledge and views of all those he consulted were most freely and generously placed at his service, the Governor-General was of opinion that the majority of the National Party was likely to retain its cohesion, and that therefore a Government having the promise of stability could only be formed from that section of the House. Investigations failed to elicit proof of sufficient strength in any other quarter. It also became clear to him that the Leader in the National Party, who had the best prospect of securing unity among his followers and of therefore being able to form a Government having those elements of permanence so essential to the conduct of affairs during war, was the Right Honourable W. M. Hughes, whom the Governor-General therefore commissioned to form an administration.'[1]

This memorandum calls for the following comments:

1. The Government's pledge as to its course of conduct in the event of a referendum defeat might reasonably have been regarded as extending to an undertaking either to advise the dissolution of the House of Representatives or to make way for an administration that would so advise. Further, the pledge might even have been regarded as warranting the Governor-General's dismissal of the then Ministers unless such dissolution was advised and the consequential grant of a commission and immediate dissolution to Mr. Tudor, the Leader of the Labour party. But the Governor-General must have decided to ignore the pledge, and to set on one side all questions as to the promise or moral duty of the Government to the electors because such considerations bore no relation to 'the parliamentary situation'. The Governor-General regarded himself as bound by what he called 'the principles of *parliamentary* government', in order that 'the rights of Parliament' should not be infringed. It followed that he would not concern himself at all with any question as to what intention the constituencies must have entertained when the referendum was defeated.

[1] Ibid., pp. 2895–6.

2. Accordingly the Governor-General mentioned a possible dissolution only to reject the idea of 'a further appeal to the country within twelve months of an election'.

3. The Governor-General, having decided to explore the 'parliamentary situation' in order to measure the prospects of forming 'an alternative Government', inevitably concluded that the party which already possessed a majority in each House, and no other party, could carry on the Government of the country.

The case is very interesting. It shows that the action of one representative of the Crown may proceed upon principles entirely different from those upon which another founds himself. For the facts set out above might possibly have justified another Governor in boldly declaring that the referendum vote made it perfectly clear that the Government no longer possessed the confidence of the electors, especially as, by the political strategy of the Government, the issue had been deliberately broadened into one of confidence or no confidence. Of course, there was much to be said in favour of the Governor-General's decision not to attach general significance to the verdict upon the single matter referred to the electorate. But other Governors might have taken a very different attitude.

In some respects the case provides a contrast to the action proposed to be taken by Sir Gerald Strickland in 1916,[1] and to that actually taken by Sir Philip Game in 1932.[2] In the last-mentioned case the Governor did not confine his attention to the 'parliamentary situation' because the dismissed ministry had a majority in the popular Assembly comparable with that enjoyed by Mr. Hughes in the House of Representatives in 1918. And Sir Gerald Strickland also considered the question before him from the point of view of the duties and pledges of members of Parliament to the Electorate.

[1] See *ante*, Chap. XVII. [2] See *post*, Chap. XIX.

XIX

SIR PHILIP GAME'S EXERCISE OF THE POWER OF DISMISSAL IN 1932

IN order to appreciate the significance of the action taken by the Governor of New South Wales, Sir Philip Game, on May 13th, 1932, in dismissing from office the Lang administration, certain preliminary facts should be stated:

1. In October 1930, the Labour party, under Mr. Lang, was returned to power with a very large majority.

2. At that time the State of New South Wales, in common with the rest of Australia, was passing through a period of great depression, wool and wheat prices having collapsed.

3. In February 1931, at a Conference of State Premiers with the Federal Government, in which Mr. Scullin, the Labour Leader, was Prime Minister, Mr. Lang suggested that interest rates were too high, and proposed that the Australian Governments should refrain from paying interest to British bondholders 'until Britain has dealt with the Australian overseas debt in the same manner as she settled her own foreign debt with America'.[1]

4. At this time there was pending an appeal by the Lang Government to the Courts on the question whether the Legislative Council of New South Wales could lawfully be abolished without the approval of the electors at a referendum, the preceding Government[2] having amended the Constitution Act for the purpose of requiring such a referendum and of preventing the requirement itself from being amended without a like referendum.

5. On March 16th, 1931, the High Court of Australia decided by a majority of three Judges to two that a referendum was necessary.[3]

6. Mr. Lang was, at this time, in a minority in the Legislative Council. The latter body had passed the Bill for its

[1] This was the leading proposal in what came to be called the 'Lang plan'.

[2] That of Sir Thomas Bavin, leader of the Nationalist party.

[3] The majority comprised Rich, Starke, and Dixon, J.J. The minority Gavan Duffy, C.J. and McTiernan, J.

own abolition upon the assumption that approval by the electors at a special referendum was required by law and might not be given.

7. The Council rejected certain Government proposals, including a Bill for the purpose of reducing the rate of private interest to pre-war levels, the method of rejection adopted being to postpone consideration of the Bill for six months.

8. On March 23rd, 1931, after the Council had referred to a Select Committee of Inquiry the Government's Bill amending the Industrial Arbitration Act, Ministers advised the Governor to appoint additional members to the Council. This advice was rejected[1] and the Governor then suggested to the Premier that perhaps he should dismiss the Ministry. However, on March 26th, he wrote to the Premier stating that 'almost as soon as I was alone in a position to think quietly, it was borne in upon me that I should be entirely wrong if I were to ask you to surrender your Commission'.[2] The Governor added

> 'You have tendered me advice which I cannot see my way to accept, but there is no reason why I should demand your resignation, or indeed, take any action. Were I to do so it would inevitably give rise, as you yourself agree, to a popular outcry that I was taking sides, and I cannot put the King's representative in that position.'[3]

9. Mr. Lang resolved to appeal to the Privy Council against the High Court's decision, but in the meantime was still desirous of further appointments for the purpose of carrying his various legislative proposals into effect.

10. On June 29th, 1931, the Governor wrote to Mr. Lang suggesting that the King's example in convening a Conference over the Home Rule Bill should be followed in relation to the political struggle in New South Wales. He stated that the Premier's proposal to obtain funds by drastic taxation would not be accepted by the Legislative Council. The letter anticipated further requests by Mr. Lang for additional appointments to the Council, and stated:

> 'I am, as you are aware, very loath to take what I consider, rightly or wrongly, the extreme step of overriding the Legislative Council by the appointment of a large number of additional members.'[4]

[1] *N.S.W. Parliamentary Papers* (1930–2), vol. i, p. 501.
[2] Ibid. [3] Ibid. [4] Ibid., p. 505.

11. On June 30th the Premier replied, stating that:

> 'Exercising my constitutional right, I requested you at our meeting this afternoon to place me in the position referred to in the aforesaid paragraph of your letter . . . but Your Excellency refused my request.'[1]

The Premier rejected the Governor's suggestion of a Conference.

12. Further conflict between the Government and the Council followed, and, finally, on November 20th, 1931, the Governor appointed to the Council twenty-five Labour nominees upon the Premier's recommendation. This number was not sufficient to secure the passage of Government Legislation.

13. At the General Elections for the Commonwealth in December 1931, Mr. Scullin, the Labour Prime Minister, met defeat, and Mr. Lyons's Government[2] succeeded to office.

14. Early in 1932 the Federal Parliament passed legislation with a view to seizing the revenues of New South Wales for the purpose of meeting the interest liability of that State, which Mr. Lang was unable to pay but which, under the Financial Agreement, given constitutional sanction in 1929, was payable by the States to the Commonwealth for the purpose of transmission to bondholders overseas.

15. The validity of this special Federal legislation was unsuccessfully challenged by Mr. Lang in the High Court, the decision being announced on April 6th, 1932. The scheme of the legislation was to compel persons who owed taxes and other money to the State of New South Wales to pay their debts to certain Commonwealth agencies, such payment being made the only valid method of discharging liability.

16. Mr. Lang still resisted or evaded the Commonwealth scheme. For instance, he sought to prevent moneys being collected by the Commonwealth by adopting the expedient of delaying taxation assessments, and so preventing the creation of further debts upon which the Commonwealth Act might

[1] Ibid., p. 506. This was a reference by the Premier to his desire for further appointments to the Legislative Council.

[2] Mr. Lyons had been a member of the Scullin Ministry and was now leader of the United Australia party.

operate. This device produced no revenue for the State, but made it impossible for the Commonwealth to obtain the money expected from current taxation assessments.[1]

17. The Commonwealth next acted upon a provision in the Financial Agreements Enforcement Act, 1932, by requiring the various trading Banks to pay over to the Commonwealth the amounts of balances standing to the credit of the State of New South Wales in order to apply these sums towards the discharge of State interest liabilities. Mr. Lang challenged this action, but the High Court decided against him on April 22nd, 1932. It also decided that the Commonwealth could seize, in addition to the ordinary revenues of the State deposited with its bankers, moneys received by the State under certain statutes and orders of Court for specific purposes, and to meet particular claims, e.g. estates administered by the Master in Lunacy and the Public Trustee.

18. Mr. Lang sought to counter these decisions by directing State officers to refrain from paying moneys into the trading Banks where the accounts of the State had been kept.[2]

19. By this time it was plain that, unless drastic taxation expedients were immediately adopted, the State would be unable to pay its public servants, or meet the heavy expenses on account of social services, such as unemployment relief, child endowment, and widow's pensions.

On May 12th, 1932, Mr. Lang introduced into the Assembly a Bill which recited the Federal Financial Agreements Enforcement Act, and the necessity of imposing special taxation with a view to safeguarding New South Wales. The Bill imposed a tax on all mortgages at the rate of ten per centum of the total amount secured thereby, the tax being payable within fourteen days from the commencement of the Act. It was aimed mainly at the Banking and Insurance Companies, which, according to Mr. Lang, were endeavouring to prevent his obtaining a substantial reduction of interest on overseas loans, and to force him out of office by promoting the Commonwealth Enforcement Acts legislation.

21. The Mortgage Taxation Bill passed the Assembly by

[1] The assessments are directed to each taxpayer personally.

[2] This action involved non-compliance with a section of the New South Wales Audit Act.

a large majority, and, as a result of the rallying of a number of former Labour supporters, was also carried in the Council in the early hours of Friday, May 13th, 1932.

22. On May 13th the Governor of New South Wales, Sir Philip Game, received a deputation from representatives of British companies holding New South Wales mortgages. The object of the deputation was to request that the Governor should refuse assent to the Mortgage Taxation Bill or reserve the Bill for the signification of the Royal Assent.[1]

23. The Federal Government's advisers, anticipating the passing of the Bill by the State Parliament, had drafted a Bill designed for the purpose of nullifying the State Bill, and, also on May 13th, forced it through all stages in both Federal Houses. This was the Financial Emergency (State Legislation) Act, No. 11 of 1932, calling itself an Act

> 'for the peace, order, and good government of the Commonwealth with respect to Taxation, Insurance, Banking, Foreign Corporations, and Trading or Financial Corporations formed within the Limits of the Commonwealth'.

The validity of this last Federal measure was never tested in the Courts, because Mr. Lang was also dismissed from office on Friday, May 13th, and the Governor's assent was not given to the Mortgage Taxation Bill. It may be pointed out that, in relation to the Parliaments of the States, the Federal Parliament has not exclusive, but only concurrent jurisdiction over the subject of taxation.[2] There is no express power given to the Commonwealth to nullify any State enactment but, by section 109 of the Commonwealth Constitution, any law of a State is invalid so far as it is inconsistent with any law validly passed by the Commonwealth Parliament in relation to a specific subject committed by the Constitution to Federal jurisdiction.

As appears from its title, the Federal Act purported to deal with certain subjects expressly committed to Federal jurisdiction such as Banking, Corporations and Insurance, as well as with the subject of Taxation itself. Had the validity of

[1] *Sydney Morning Herald*, May 14th, 1932.

[2] See *post*, Chap. XXII, as to the relative constitutional position of the State and Federal Parliaments.

the Act been tested, the case would have raised the interesting question whether a law purporting to exempt Banks, Insurance Companies, Trading Corporations, and private individuals from State laws imposing taxation is, in truth and in fact, a law with respect to Banking, Insurance, or Taxation. Only if the answer was in the affirmative would the New South Wales Mortgage Taxation Bill have been rendered invalid as inconsistent with a valid Federal law.

It is very interesting, and not without an effect of irony, to note that the passing of this Act by the Commonwealth Parliament, for the purpose of nullifying Mr. Lang's Mortgage Taxation Bill was mentioned in the Western Australian Case for Secession.[1] The case in reply for the Commonwealth, prepared by a Committee of four, including Sir Robert Garran,[2] stated:

> 'The particular danger that the Act was designed to meet passed away within 24 hours, so that the Act never took effect, and the High Court was never called upon to pronounce upon its validity. There is no reason to believe that it could have been supported by the taxation power. It is true that, after the fashion of legal pleading, the title of the Act calls in aid everything that could be thought of, on the spur of the moment, as a possible support—Taxation, Insurance, Banking, Corporations, &c. The draughtsman was evidently scratching round for a peg on which to hang the Bill; but Taxation was certainly a forlorn hope. The power of the Commonwealth Parliament as to Taxation is a power to make laws "for the peace, order and good government of the Commonwealth", with respect to "Taxation, but so as not to discriminate between States or parts of States". It can hardly be questioned that these words refer only to Commonwealth Taxation, uniform throughout the Commonwealth, for Commonwealth purposes, and do not cover control of State taxation. Nothing in any decision of the High Court suggests a doubt of this; and indeed the principles of interpretation laid down by the Court make doubt impossible.'[3]

The documents passing between Mr. Lang and the Governor should now be considered. On May 12th (a Thursday) the Governor called the attention of the Premier to a Cabinet

[1] Para. 136.

[2] One of the leading authorities on the Australian Constitution, and law officer of the Commonwealth during a lengthy period.

[3] *The Case for Union*, pp. 25–6.

Circular (of April 12th, 1932) which the Ministers had issued to all Departments directing Officers (1) to refrain from meeting governmental expenditure by the drawing of cheques, (2) to hold all moneys collected, forwarding them to the Treasury, and (3) to insist upon payment to the Government in cash or by bearer cheques. The object of this direction was to avoid, so far as possible, the operation of the Federal law requiring Banks to pay moneys of the State to Federal Officers. But a Federal Regulation (Proclamation No. 42 of 1932) had also been issued by the Governor-General, which purported to direct officers of the State receiving revenue of a certain character to deal with the moneys in the manner directed by the Federal Treasurer.

There was a direct collision between this proclamation and the instruction issued by Mr. Lang requiring State officers receiving such revenue to deal with it as directed by the Circular. The contrary view has been suggested.[1] It was argued by Mr. Piddington that the Commonwealth Proclamation directing 'Officers or employees of the State' receiving moneys to deal with them as directed by the Federal Treasurer, referred, or could be construed as referring, only to such employees of the State as the Commonwealth chose to employ or pay. Mr. Piddington said: 'My own opinion is clear that, in the meaning of gratuitous service for the Commonwealth, Proclamation 42 was never law.'[2]

It is difficult to accept this view as a matter of construction.

But three points are outstanding. In the first place neither the validity of the Commonwealth proclamation nor its application was ever determined by a competent legal tribunal; secondly, there were competent Courts with jurisdiction to determine such questions; thirdly, if the question had been determined adversely to Mr. Lang, injunctions could have been issued, preventing both him and all others concerned from acting upon the circular objected to.

The correspondence between the Governor and the Premier soon developed towards an ultimate issue. On May 12th (still the Thursday) the Governor said, in reference to the

[1] A. B. Piddington, K.C., *The King and the People*, pp. 11–12.

[2] Ibid., p. 12.

circular of April 12th, 1932 (nearly a month old at the time), that

> 'it appears to me that the terms of this circular direct Public servants to commit a direct breach of the law as set out in Proclamation No. 42. . . . I feel it my bounden duty to remind you at once that you derive your authority from His Majesty through me, and that I cannot possibly allow the Crown to be placed in the position of breaking the law of the land.'[1]

The letter concluded with a request to the Premier 'either to furnish me with proof that the instructions in the circular are within the law, or, alternatively, to withdraw the circular at once'.[2] A definite reply was asked for by 11 a.m. on the following day, Friday, May 13th.

The reply of the Premier was dated May 13th. It complained of the Governor's ultimatum, and stated that 'the circular cannot possibly be withdrawn'. A reply came from the Governor stating 'I have just received your letter. . . . I gather from it that you do not dispute my view that the circular in question is a breach of the Federal law'.[3] It then went on to suggest an interview with the Premier 'to discuss the whole position'. This interview was held at 3 p.m. on the same day, when the Premier asked the Governor to communicate his views by letter. The letter was immediately sent, and stated:

> 'The position as I see it is that Ministers are committing a breach of the law. While you did not admit this, you did not deny it. . . . My position is that if my Ministers are unable to carry on essential services without breaking the law, my plain duty is to endeavour to obtain Ministers who feel able to do so. . . . If Ministers are not prepared to abide by the law, then I must state without any hesitation that it is their bounden duty under the law and practice of the Constitution to tender their resignations.'[4]

An early reply was requested. The Premier's answer, of the same day also, was 'If your letter of to-day's date means that you are requesting the resignation of Ministers, you are hereby informed that your request is refused'.[5] The final

[1] *Sydney Morning Herald*, May 14th, 1932.
[2] Ibid.
[3] Ibid.
[4] Ibid.
[5] Ibid.

letter from the Governor then came. It stated that, in view of the refusal of Ministers to resign or to withdraw the Circular,

> 'I feel it my bounden duty to inform you that I cannot retain my present Ministers in office, and that I am seeking other advisers. I must ask you to regard this as final.'[1]

Immediately after this letter was sent the Governor directed his Secretary to communicate with the Leader of the Opposition—Mr. Stevens. The latter arrived at Government House, and stated to the press, after interviewing the Governor, 'His Excellency has sworn me in as Premier, and had commissioned me to form a Government. I have asked for time, and will see His Excellency later.'[2] At the time of his dismissal Mr. Lang had 55 supporters in a House of 90, Mr. Stevens had about 20, and the Country party the balance of the House. Parliament had been in existence for only half of its normal period of three years. Mr. Stevens formed an administration, obtained a prorogation of Parliament which, as we have seen, was still in session.[3] During the period of prorogation the Governor dissolved Parliament, and his new advisers were successful at the Elections held shortly afterwards.

This very recent precedent is of great constitutional importance, but needs a careful and detached analysis.

At the outset it should be emphasized that the success of the Stevens Government at the elections should not of itself be regarded as concluding the matter. It can hardly be accepted as correct that the Sovereign or his representative may at any time dismiss a Ministry possessing the confidence of Parliament and force a dissolution and, so long as the popular verdict goes against the dismissed Ministers, the action of the King or Governor must necessarily be treated as right.

In point of fact, during the history of many, perhaps all Assemblies, there are occasions when, if an immediate election is held, the Ministers are very likely to be defeated. This is so well recognized that it is often noticed that 'un-

[1] Ibid. [2] Ibid.

[3] The Assembly had adjourned until Tuesday, May 17th.

popular' measures are passed into law at a comparatively early stage in the life of a Parliament, but, as the elections approach, 'window-dressing' proposals become the order of the day. If the time and occasion of a general election are to be selected by the adversaries of an administration, the chances of the Opposition are enormously increased. At the time of the General Election in New South Wales in 1932 the situation of the country was such that it would have been difficult for any existing Government to retain office. It should also be remembered that, as a dismissal from office is a very rare event, even in the Dominions, the very fact of dismissal is calculated to affect that substantial section of voters who argue, either that the lead given by the King's representative should be followed,[1] or that it will be futile to return to office a Premier who may possibly be dismissed from office upon a second occasion.

Regarding the matter logically, the success of an administration bearing the Governor's personal if indirect imprimatur should not be regarded as conclusive of the validity of the Governor's action in dismissing its predecessors. The case is otherwise if we accept the constitutional theory of Dicey—that the right of dismissal enures to the Crown through its representative whenever it is supposed upon reasonable grounds that, at the time of their dismissal, the Ministers will not be supported by the electors. But the fact of dissolution may frequently result in the Ministers being so seriously prejudiced in the minds of loyal voters, that their success at the polls will be rendered impossible, or highly improbable. The true test of the constitutional exercise of such a reserve power should direct itself to the circumstances existing when the power is exercised, disregarding the mere calculation as to the outcome of the subsequent electoral verdict.

But in any case it would seem clear that if the reserve power of the Crown is exercised upon a specifically stated ground, the propriety of the exercise should be discussed solely in reference to such ground. This last point is of great

[1] Lord Melbourne described this as 'the natural influence of . . . the King's name', in reference to the 'increase of Tories' at the dissolution following upon the dismissal of Melbourne by William IV in 1834. (*Melbourne's Papers*, ed. Sanders, p. 238.)

importance in connexion with this New South Wales precedent.

Long before May 13th, 1932, many and varied opinions as to the Governor's exercise of the power of dismissal had been published. Most of them were political addresses upon their face, and it will suffice to refer to the opinions advanced on grounds of constitutional principle. Sir W. Harrison Moore, for instance, made the point that the voting in New South Wales at the Federal election of December 1931 indicated a decisive rejection by the people of Mr. Lang's proposal not to meet overseas indebtedness until the rate of interest was reduced. Harrison Moore said:

> 'The ordinary presumption that a Ministry represents the people of the country becomes, since the verdict of the people of New South Wales in the Commonwealth election, a pure fiction.'[1]

He contended that the Lang Ministry, having defaulted to the Commonwealth in interest payments, was injuring the economic security of every State, and that its continuance in office represented a danger to the political unity of the Commonwealth. He distinguished unitary communities, such as the Irish Free State and the Union of South Africa, from the Federal Commonwealth, and concluded that

> 'the functions of the King's representative in Australia, whether Governor-General or Governor must, it is suggested, be exercised not as if the Federal system did not exist, but in the light of the responsibilities of the Crown in the maintenance of the Federal Union itself'.[2]

The argument thus presented would have curious results. Quite frequently during the history of the Commonwealth, a general election, either Federal or State, will appear to show that the electors have completely lost confidence in the party to which their State or Federal Ministers respectively belong. For many years the same parties have organized in respect of Federal politics just as in respect of State politics. Therefore an electoral verdict often provides very strong ground for supposing that a similar verdict will be returned in the elections which follow hard upon the first. For instance, late in

[1] Melbourne *Argus*, Feb. 4th, 1932. [2] Ibid.

1929 the Labour party swept the polls at the Federal election, the verdict being particularly pronounced in New South Wales. At this time the Government which held office in that State was opposed to Labour and Sir Philip Game occupied the position of Governor. At the General Election in 1930, as was expected, the Labour party under Mr. Lang repeated the Federal Labour victory. Could it be said that the Governor, attending to the 1929 result, was entitled to reduce the life of the existing State Parliament from three years to two on account of the strong evidence of popular feeling, and to dismiss the State Premier in order to secure the dissolution? In this respect the circumstances were analogous to Mr. Lang's position at the time of his dismissal when the State Parliament had nearly eighteen months of its normal life still remaining.

Other instances of a similar character could be cited to test the argument of Sir W. Harrison Moore. The argument is greatly weakened by the unbroken rule in Australia that Federal and State electoral verdicts are never used to warrant the shortening of the life of a Parliament not concerned in the elections. The same rule seems to be well recognized in Canada. The position created at the Federal election of December 1931 was not sufficiently special to remove it from the general rule.

Further, under the Constitution of the Commonwealth, powers of government and administration are divided between the Federal and State authorities. If there is a contest or collision as to legislation or administration, the Constitution itself provides a means for the settlement of the contest by reference to the organs of the judicial power which have been brought into existence, either by the Constitution itself, or by legislation passed thereunder. Indeed, it may be said, quite dogmatically, that any controversy of a legal character between the Commonwealth and any State is, by the Constitution, intended to be settled by recourse, not to the action of the Executive power as represented by the Governor-General or the Governor, but by reference to the judicial power which alone is entitled to say whether the Commonwealth or the State has trespassed beyond the limits of its lawful authority.

Professor Keith joined issue with Sir W. Harrison Moore. He said:

> 'I regret that Sir Harrison Moore should have lent his authority to a suggestion that it would be constitutional, and indeed proper, for the Governor of New South Wales [Sir Philip Game] to exercise the Royal prerogative and dismiss the Lang Ministry. . . . The Constitution . . . supplies adequate authority to meet the situation under judicial authority.'[1]

Professor Keith added that dismissal of a Premier by a Governor

> 'would be justifiable only if the Governor had a full assurance that the Premier had ceased to represent the people's wishes, and that the Governor's action would be endorsed by the election which would follow. If this was not the case the Governor's position would be impossible.'[2]

Sir Harrison Moore in reply elaborated his views. With reference to judicial remedies he regarded them as 'full of uncertainty and delay', and added,

> 'the difference between Professor Keith and myself appears to be less on any constitutional question than on the political expediency of the Governor forcing an election'.[3]

Professor Keith's rejoinder was that:

> 'The matter must be regarded from the Governor's point of view, and the whole recent tendency to assimilate increasingly and more closely the Governor's position with that of the Crown. His Majesty is notable for his absolute insistence personally on deferring in the last resort to his Ministers' advice.'[4]

He added that

> 'If the Governor's action did not receive a popular verdict his career would be ended, as in the case of Lord Strickland, then Sir Gerald Strickland, whose recall from the office of Governor of New South Wales should be a warning of the danger of departing from a course of action advised by Ministers. . . . If he [the Governor] refrains from acting it is not because he doubts his right to act, but because on deliberate consideration he holds that the moment is unpropitious.'[5]

At the time of this interesting controversy the High Court had not yet pronounced upon the validity of the Finan-

[1] *Scotsman*, quoted Melbourne *Argus*, Feb. 9th, 1932. [2] Ibid.

[3] Melbourne *Argus*, Feb. 10th, 1932.

[4] Melbourne *Argus*, March 17th, 1932. [5] Ibid.

cial Agreements Enforcement Act, judgment in favour of its validity not being given until April 6th, 1932. The illegality to which both publicists then referred was the non-payment by the Lang Government of the interest obligations of the State to the Commonwealth under the terms of the Financial Agreement itself. The object of the Financial Agreements Enforcement Act was to provide summary sanctions in case of default.

Keith's position was particularly interesting. On the one hand he considered that resort to judicial remedies which were available against the State was the constitutional way of dealing with default. Yet at the same time he implied that dismissal might take place if only the Governor could be sure of the consequences. Keith remembered Mr. King's skilful introduction of Lord Byng's action into the Canadian electoral issue of 1926, and he feared that the Governor might be taking a grave risk. It is not possible to reconcile these two views; for if the non-payment of external interest could be remedied by recourse to the judicial power, the justification for the exercise of the reserve prerogative at once disappeared.

After the actual dismissal Keith at once made further comments. He said:

> 'Mr. Lang's proposed tax on mortgages was so wholly unjust that it is impossible to regard it as being intended for any other purpose than to compel action by the Governor in order to give the people an opportunity of showing their attitude towards the Government and the Empire. . . . It is necessary before the Ottawa Conference to know whether New South Wales is prepared to honour its obligations and so enable a trade agreement to be made with the Commonwealth.'[1]

This kind of reasoning is a good example of the intrusion of mere political arguments into what are, or should be, questions of a legal or quasi-legal character. If the Governor's action was inspired by the Mortgage Taxation Bill he never said so; nor did the slightest hint of any relation between the two matters appear from the official correspondence. The reference to the Ottawa Conference, at which the Commonwealth alone was to be represented, is quite irrelevant. It had

[1] Melbourne *Argus*, May 14th, 1932.

nothing to do with the matter, except from the point of view of mere party politics.

However, Keith went on to say that Sir Philip Game's action was 'fairly justified'. He added that the proposed taxation of mortgages 'was clearly motived by his (Mr. Lang's) desire to inflict the maximum loss on his political opponents in the State'. In these circumstances,

> 'the Governor was under a clear obligation to ensure observance of the law of the Commonwealth, and if his Premier refused to obey that law the Governor would have incurred personal responsibility had he failed to take action'.[1]

Again there is the irrelevant reference to the Mortgage Taxation Bill, but that may be passed over. But how can the argument as to the observance of the law of the Commonwealth be reconciled with Keith's previous insistence upon the fact that the proper remedy for breach of law was recourse to the judicial power, and to the prescribed legal remedies? The Governor could hardly incur any responsibility for illegal instructions, except that he might reasonably have insisted upon Mr. Lang's calling the judicial power into action for the purpose of determining the validity of the Commonwealth Proclamation No. 42. But if the State Premier's circular was illegal (because the Commonwealth proclamation was valid) an injunction could have been obtained from the Courts.

Sir Edward Mitchell, K.C., and Mr. Justice Piddington, President of the Industrial Commission, who resigned as a protest against the Governor's action, also engaged in a public discussion as to the constitutional issue. The latter took the point that the sole reason for the Governor's action was the issue of a circular—illegal because it was directly opposed to the Federal Proclamation. He said, 'This is purely a question of law,' and added that, although the Financial Agreements Enforcement Act had been held valid, 'neither the High Court nor any other Federal Court has ever decided on the validity or interpretation of Regulation 42.'[2] He asserted that the Governor had purported to convert himself into a Court for the purpose of enforcing Commonwealth law

[1] Ibid., May 16th, 1932.

[2] A. B. Piddington, K.C., *The King and the People*, p. 14.

contrary to section 71 of the Commonwealth Constitution, which vests judicial power exclusively in the High Court, and the other Courts there specified. And Sir Edward Mitchell said,

> 'I would agree with Mr. Justice Piddington that, *if the circular stood alone and were not the culmination of a series of attempts to obstruct and disobey the laws so declared valid*, it would not be proper for His Excellency, on his own responsibility, to determine whether the Federal Regulations were valid or not.'[1]

This very important constitutional precedent illustrates the confusion and anarchy resulting from the absence of binding and settled rules for the exercise of the reserve power of the Crown in the British Dominions. I have not referred in any way to merely political attacks upon, and defences of, Sir Philip Game's action. Their number is legion. With extravagant praise from the one side was mingled violent blame from the other. For months prior to the dismissal of his Ministers the Governor was attacked by newspapers which were politically opposed to the Premier, because the latter was not dismissed. For months after his action the Governor was attacked by the Labour party for what he did. By the first group he was called a political poltroon because he allowed the Lang Ministry to retain office; by the latter he was called a political assassin because he decided to act. Such a controversy was calculated to injure the dignity and reputation of the office of King's representative. It is certain that the feared or actual exercise of exceptional prerogatives and reserve powers will often be followed by such consequences, unless the conditions and occasions of their exercise are perfectly well known to all concerned.

A noteworthy feature of the comments made is that no one who justified the Governor's action seems to have paid any attention to the official correspondence which alone discloses the precise ground upon which the action was taken. The Governor himself did not, so far as such correspondence shows, concern himself with anything but the illegality which, he considered, attached to the departmental circular issued by the Cabinet on April 12th, 1932. The Governor did not refer to, still less apply, the doctrine of Dicey, that if popular confidence in an administration has gone, the prerogatives of

[1] *Sydney Morning Herald*, May 26th, 1932. Italics are mine.

dissolution or dismissal may properly be exercised. Nor did the Governor accept for a moment the argument of Sir Edward Mitchell that the circular was merely a culminating point in a series of attempts to avoid the consequences of legally binding agreements and overriding Statute law. Nor did he, at any moment, glance at the argument by which Keith thought his action might be 'fairly justified'. And the Governor left out of account, so far as appears, any reliance upon the Federal election results to which Sir W. Harrison Moore attached so much significance.

Was the Governor constitutionally correct in his action? No judgment can be pronounced until what is constitutionally 'correct' is defined by competent authority. The subsequent electoral verdict, which may be regarded as giving political support to his action, can hardly be regarded as a conclusive answer to the problem which arose before the elections, despite the temptation to look at such constitutional disputes entirely *ex post facto*.

But the fair solution of such disputes should be discoverable before irrevocable action is taken. When the Sovereign or his representative desires to exercise the reserve powers on the ground that Ministers are breaking the law, it is difficult to justify the action because, very often, an untrained lawyer will be claiming the right to determine whether or not the law has been broken. In a unitary State or Dominion where such issues arise (e.g. during the crisis as to the deportation of Labour leaders which occurred in South Africa in 1913–14)[1] the duty of the Governor is, perhaps, to assume that Parliament which is legally supreme and which continues to entrust its confidence to Ministers will, by Act of Indemnity or otherwise, support the supposedly illegal action of Ministers. Cases may also arise where, the illegality of ministerial action being either admitted or beyond dispute, no remedy whatever is available, except the exercise of a prerogative by a Governor.[2] In New South Wales, however, legal proceedings could have been instituted before the ordinary Courts of law, and, upon the assumption that the questioned

[1] See *post*, Chap. XX (A).

[2] See *post*, Chap. XX (C) dealing with the Tasmanian case of 1924, and Chap. XX (E) which contains a ruling of Sir Isaac Isaacs as Governor-General.

circular was illegal, appropriate declarations obtained and injunctions issued to prevent action under the circular.[1]

Although no person can confidently assert that Sir P. Game was guilty of a breach of constitutional duty, that is mainly because the reserve powers have not yet been defined so as to exclude prerogative action when those interested in asserting illegality on the part of Ministers have it in their power to obtain redress from the ordinary Courts of law. The continual use by the Governor in his letters of the phrase *bounden duty* rather suggests that he was relying upon a constitutional doctrine asserted some fifty years earlier by Todd, who was fond of the phrase in the same connexion.[2] But, even assuming that Todd's opinion has any application to the modern self-governing Dominion, it must be remembered that Todd wrote at a time when, and was addressing himself to cases where, there was no available sanction for disobedience of law by Ministers. When the time comes for reserve prerogatives to be controlled by appropriate Statute law, close consideration of the propriety of action such as Sir Philip Game took, will have to be given. That the question is still a live one among constitutional students is shown by a discussion at a Special Meeting of the New South Wales Branch of the Empire Parliamentary Association held in November 1934. The subject was introduced by Mr. McKell, an able and experienced member of various Labour Cabinets.[3] If the matter is carefully and dispassionately considered, it will become reasonably plain that the power of dismissal can hardly be regarded as properly exercised if a Governor justifies it merely by reliance upon the Ministers having broken the law, and it appears that there is available a competent legal tribunal which can determine the question of legality, and which has jurisdiction to issue appropriate orders and injunctions, and see that they are enforced.

[1] The Supreme Court of New South Wales is not debarred from exercising its jurisdiction merely because questions of federal law are involved. If a question is raised as to the limits *inter se* of the constitutional powers of Commonwealth and State Parliament, it has to be referred to the High Court of Australia.

[2] See *post*, Chap. XXVII.

[3] He was closely associated with Mr. McTiernan in the Constitutional crisis in New South Wales in 1926 and was Minister of Justice in the Lang Ministry of 1932.

XX

EXERCISE OF THE RESERVE POWER ON THE GROUND OF ILLEGALITY

A. SOUTH AFRICAN CASE OF 1914

LONG prior to the New South Wales crisis of 1932 Keith had discussed the problem of the attitude to be adopted by the head of the Executive in reference to illegal action by Ministers. The action of General Smuts, in January 1914, in deporting ten Labour leaders from Natal, was condemned.[1] Keith said:

> 'To intimidate the strikers he decided to deport without legal authority ten leaders. . . . The step taken was wholly illegal. . . . It was found that General Smuts had admitted that he had had recourse to the illegal deportation because he knew that Parliament would never give him authority in cold blood to expel the men in question.'[2]

Mr. Harcourt, the then Colonial Secretary, deprecated any interference with South African policy by the Parliament at Westminster because of 'the existence of responsible self-government in South Africa'.[3] Referring to the acquiescence of the Governor-General, Lord Gladstone, Mr. Harcourt said that the Governor-General's position was 'in the main largely analogous to that of the constitutional sovereign of this country',[4] and that he

> 'properly assented to the only method which his responsible advisers recommended . . . on the assurance that his Ministers would immediately endeavour to obtain from their Parliament the ratification of, and an indemnity for, the action they proposed to take'.[5]

It appeared that, when the South African Ministry expelled the Labour leaders, the consent and concurrence of the Governor-General 'was neither sought for nor obtained', although the latter was informed of the action at the time when it was taking place. Lord Gladstone, according to Mr. Harcourt, did 'all he was entitled to do in his position

[1] A. B. Keith, *Responsible Government in the Dominions* (1927), vol. i, pp. 199–202.
[2] Ibid., pp. 200–1.
[3] A. B. Keith, *Selected Speeches and Documents on British Colonial Policy*, vol. ii, p. 109.
[4] Ibid., p. 119.
[5] Ibid., pp. 116–17.

as constitutional Governor with responsible representative Ministers'.[1] There was no other Government which could have succeeded to the Government, and, in the circumstances, the action of the Governor-General was 'entirely correct'.[2] Mr. Harcourt brushed aside the suggestion that Lord Gladstone should be instructed to reserve for Imperial consideration the Indemnity Bill so that the British Government could either veto or disallow it, describing such intervention as 'unprecedented and wholly unjustifiable', because 'such legislation is essentially one of the attributes and prerogatives of the responsible and popularly elected Parliament of South Africa'.[3] The Indemnity Bill was duly assented to by the Governor-General.[4]

B. EXPENDITURE OF PUBLIC FUNDS WITHOUT PARLIAMENTARY SANCTION

Keith's most recent pronouncement on the duties of the Governor when he suspects illegality is that

> 'if there is a doubt . . . regarding the legality of action, he [the Governor] is entitled to demand a legal opinion, but he may rely on it when given, unless it is so obviously wrong as to render it farcical, and few issues are so clear as to make such an event probable'.[5]

Keith's comment upon the Lang dismissal of 1932 is difficult to reconcile with his earlier emphasis upon the desirability of invoking the judicial power to enforce legal claims.[6] Keith subsequently said that

> 'marked skill was displayed in the handling of the situation by the Governor, who had refused to be induced to act until the issue of illegality became quite clear. Obviously so long as he was not asked to acquiesce in illegal action it would have been unconstitutional to dismiss his Ministry'.[7]

[1] A. B. Keith, *Selected Speeches and Documents on British Colonial Policy*, vol. ii, p. 118. [2] Ibid., p. 120. [3] Ibid., p. 121.

[4] This precedent warrants the inference that in any British or Dominion constitutional unit where the Legislature may validate illegal action on the part of Ministers, the Crown should not, as a rule, interfere while Ministers retain the confidence of the popular Assembly.

[5] A. B. Keith, *The Constitutional Law of the British Dominions* (1933), p. 156. [6] *Ante*, p. 169.

[7] A. B. Keith, *The Constitutional Law of the British Dominions* (1933), p. 159.

A very curious feature of the dismissal of the Lang administration was that, probably seeking to prevent the exercise of the power of dismissal, Mr. Lang adopted the practice of passing temporary Supply Acts, so that, at the time of his dismissal, the authority for paying moneys requiring parliamentary vote was due to terminate on May 31st, 1932. The dismissal took place on May 13th, and Mr. Lang's successor, Mr. Stevens, actually governed the country during most of the month of June without having any legal authority for most of the very considerable payments of moneys necessarily made by him out of the Consolidated Revenue Fund.

Keith confesses but seeks to avoid the implications of such action on a Governor's part by asserting that 'it is seldom easy for the Governor to refuse assent to irregular expenditure, for he is normally assured of later legislation'.[1]

In Queensland, in 1907, Lord Chelmsford, the Governor, who granted a dissolution to Mr. Philp in the extraordinary circumstances elsewhere mentioned,[2] authorized expenditure without sanction of Parliament. The Ministry was defeated, and there was certainly, as Keith says, 'great reluctance to secure supply and threats to move the Crown for the removal of the Governor'.[3] Similarly, in 1926, says Keith, Lord Byng's action in authorizing expenditure without parliamentary grant, 'was resented strongly in Liberal circles, and Parliamentary sanction was accorded with great reluctance'.[4]

Of course, it is very difficult for Ministers to refuse to propose grants of money to cover periods which have elapsed between the time of their dismissal or forced resignation at the hands of a Governor, and that of their restoration to office following upon a general election. Refusal to grant supply will only cause confusion and dismay to the public service without necessarily affecting the personal position of the Governor. And the Governor's own salary is covered by permanent appropriation.

The future sanction against 'unconstitutional' action on the part of the Governor is likely to be either his recall from office or even the devising of some appropriate sanction against the Ministers who have accepted 'responsibility' for

[1] Ibid., pp. 156–7. [2] *Ante*, Chap. XV. [3] A. B. Keith, *The Constitutional Law of the British Dominions* (1933), p. 157. [4] Ibid.

the Governor's action and held office pending the election. The possibility of the application of such sanctions shows the dangerous crisis to which 'constitutional' conflicts may approach. The great paradox is that a Governor may act 'unconstitutionally' and still escape all adverse consequences through the chances of an election going in a particular direction; but may act perfectly 'constitutionally', and yet be recalled.

C. THE TASMANIAN CASE OF 1924

Another precedent involving the question of the reserve power, and of a Governor's dealing with questions of law, was created by the action of the Acting Governor of Tasmania, Sir Herbert Nicholls, who, in 1924, assented to an Appropriation Bill, treating certain amendments made thereto by the Legislative Council as void, and then ignoring their existence. The Legislative Council of Tasmania is an elective body, and the Constitution Act[1] contains only one restriction upon its power in relation to Money Bills. That is section 33, which provides that all Bills for appropriating any part of the revenue or for the imposition of any taxation 'shall originate' in the House of Assembly. The Victorian Constitution provides, by way of contrast, that Money Bills 'shall originate in the Assembly and may be rejected but not altered by the Council'.[2]

The attitude taken up by the Tasmanian Labour administration (Mr. Lyons being Premier and Mr. Ogilvie Attorney-General) was based upon a ruling of the Privy Council given in April 1886. At that time the section of the Queensland Constitution Act dealing with Money Bills was in terms similar to those of the Constitution of Tasmania. Mr. Griffith (later Sir Samuel Griffith)[3] contended that the Queensland Constitution Act did not confer on the Council 'powers coordinate with those of the Legislative Assembly in the amendment of all Bills, including Money Bills'. Upon a reference of a case to the Privy Council, such contention was affirmed.[4] Naturally enough, much reliance was placed upon the ruling

[1] 18 Vic., No. 17.

[2] Constitution Act, 1855, sec. 56.

[3] First Chief Justice of the High Court of Australia.

[4] Unfortunately no reasons were given.

by Mr. Ogilvie in his opinion[1] which concluded by advising the Lieutenant-Governor to assent to the Appropriation Bill, and to treat the amendment of the Council as an 'unconstitutional nullity'.

Sir Herbert Nicholls cabled to the Secretary of State (Mr. Amery) on November 25th, 1924, pointing out that the Council had reduced 'practically every item in the Schedule to the Appropriation Bill', and that the State would probably be without supply at the end of the month. He added,

> 'The Premier has secretly intimated to me that if matters become desperate, he will present the Appropriation Bill for the Royal Assent after it has passed the Council, and demand that Council's amendments be ignored upon the ground that the Council has no right to amend Money Bills'.[2]

The Lieutenant-Governor added that the decision might affect other States and so 'ought to be given by the British Government'. He referred to Keith's views as follows: 'Keith misses the whole point and does not even mention in his book that the Council in Tasmania cannot be dissolved.'[3]

The Lieutenant-Governor's forecast of events proved to be correct. On November 26th and November 28th further cables were sent to England, stating that the Council had read the Bill for a third time, but had amended it very extensively. Sir Herbert stated: 'I shall be glad to hear whether you leave the matter to me or will issue instructions. If left to me I shall decide that Council's amendments are nullities.'[4] The Assembly, on November 27th, resolved that the Speaker should present the Bill to the Lieutenant-Governor for the Royal Assent in the form in which it passed the Assembly. The Lieutenant-Governor clearly indicated to the Colonial Secretary his intention of assenting to the Bill as passed by both Houses, ignoring the amendments of the Council. He cabled to the Secretary of State:

> 'You will see how undesirable it is that I should do this without your previous approval as if I assent and you disapprove it would mean your advising His Majesty later to disallow a Bill which would produce financial chaos.'[5]

[1] *Tasmanian Parliamentary Papers*, No. 41 of 1924, p. 1.
[2] Ibid., p. 2. [3] Ibid. [4] Ibid. [5] Ibid., p. 3.

The reply of the Secretary of State was given on November 29th, 1924. It was that the question as to the Council's legal powers was one on which he could not undertake to express any opinion. The cable then went on:

> 'Action to be taken on resolution which has been passed by the Assembly is in the first instance matter for consideration of your Ministers. If after such consideration and after their Law Officers have given their formal opinion in writing that assent can be properly given, they then advise you to assent and if you assent accordingly responsibility will rest exclusively with your Ministers and no question can arise as to the constitutionality of your action.'[1]

Thereupon the Lieutenant-Governor, having received the formal advice of Ministers and the unanimous opinion of the Attorney-General and all the Law Officers of the Crown 'and seeing no other way of securing that the Government of the State did not come to an end for want of supplies'[2] assented to the Appropriation Bill, ignoring the Council's amendments.

Keith's comment on the precedent was that the episode is 'amazing'. He said that 'the only way of obtaining a decision would be "by decisions of the Courts"'.[3] He added: 'Ministers naturally procured a written opinion from their Attorney-General—a political officer—that assent could be given',[4] a comment which ignores the fact that the Attorney-General's view was supported by all the permanent legal advisers.

A short time after a similar course of action was adopted by the newly arrived Governor of Tasmania, Sir James O'Grady, in reference to the Council's amendments to a Land and Income Taxation Bill.

Keith roundly condemned the action of the Secretary of State (Mr. Amery) as being 'regrettable and unconstitutional and certainly unprecedented',[5] and asserted that since Mr. Chamberlain's retirement such office 'has unhappily been regarded as of only second- or third-rate importance, and no Secretary of State has had adequate knowledge of constitu-

[1] *Tasmanian Parliamentary Papers*, No. 41 of 1924, p. 3.

[2] Ibid.

[3] A. B. Keith, *Responsible Government in the Dominions* (1927), vol. i, pp. 188–9. [4] Ibid., p. 189. [5] Ibid.

tional law'.[1] Keith's comments seem to rise in a crescendo of indignation:

> 'Granted that he [the Governor] can constitutionally shelter himself behind the legal advice of his Ministers when there is doubt, it does not seem that even a Governor should become so much of a cipher that he can be expected to believe that black is white on the bidding of a political partisan.'[2]

He said, also, 'it is significant that no legal adviser of the Governor except the Attorney-General could be induced to certify that assent could properly be given'.[3] But the fact was that the Attorney-General's opinion, on the face of it, showed that it had been 'perused and approved by all the Law Officers of the Crown in this State'.[4]

It is somewhat extraordinary to find that Keith is able to regard the action of the Chief Justice of Tasmania as being 'much more serious as a violation of law' than the action of Lord Chelmsford in 1907, Lord Byng in 1926, and Sir Philip Game in 1932, in allowing funds to be withdrawn from the Treasury without any parliamentary approval whatsoever.[5] So, too, Keith's attempt to belittle the precedent because of what he calls 'the widespread disapproval of it'[6] in Australia is unconvincing. Keith's statement that the Colonial Secretary 'cannot well be excused for his action'[7] is in the same strain. A fair comment seems to be that Keith was smarting under the references made by the Chief Justice to himself, and his language reflected his feelings.

Let us refer to the real point of the case. It may be conceded that, notwithstanding the breach of the Tasmanian Council of the general constitutional practice, which was regarded as assimilated to that of Britain, a passing of the Bill with amendments could not be treated as a passing of the Bill without amendments, so that, had the matter been

[1] Ibid. (note 1). The list of the condemned is a very distinguished one but need not be given here. [2] Ibid., p. 190. [3] Ibid.

[4] *Tasmanian Parliamentary Papers*, No. 41 of 1924, p. 5.

[5] A. B. Keith, *The Constitutional Law of the British Dominions* (1933), p. 157.

[6] As usual, the newspapers and publicists took their stand upon political rather than upon legal or constitutional grounds.

[7] A. B. Keith, *The Constitutional Law of the British Dominions* (1933), p. 158.

capable of immediate legal determination by some appropriate procedure, the validity of the Bill could have been successfully assailed. But that is not conclusive of the constitutional propriety of the action, either of Sir Herbert Nicholls or of Sir James O'Grady. The real issue was whether the Crown, through its representative, should act upon the advice of Ministers, leaving all strictly legal considerations for subsequent determination before the judicial organs. If the action of the Crown also involved a sharp rebuke to the Council, that was not sufficient, of itself, to make it constitutionally incorrect. Keith's condemnation of the long succession of Colonial Secretaries may be ignored; no doubt the Secretary at the time (Mr. Amery) acted on the advice of his departmental experts. The importance of his ruling is obvious —it was undoubtedly a precedent which carried to an extreme the doctrine of ministerial responsibility where Ministers possessed the confidence of the popular Assembly. The alternative presented to Sir Herbert Nicholls was the reduction to a chaotic condition of all public affairs in Tasmania. The latter's conduct throughout seems to have been absolutely open and just. At every stage the Colonial Office was kept informed, and the explanation of the action taken locally is to be found in the British ruling of November 29th, 1924.

The precedent again illustrates the necessity of relieving the Governor of personal responsibility in such cases by remitting the relevant issues in dispute to a competent tribunal. In Tasmania a tribunal might have enforced the constitutional practice previously recognized as controlling the Legislative Council's exercise of its strictly legal power over Money Bills. Just as, in 1886, the Privy Council had found itself able to determine the somewhat vaguely drafted reference from Queensland, so in 1924 a proper tribunal might have determined the real matter in controversy between the two Houses in Tasmania. In each case the question was one of constitutional practice, not of strict law.

As Sir Samuel Griffith declared, when the Queensland controversy was being submitted for determination:

> 'The literal interpretation of the words of the Constitution Act is regarded as a matter of small importance as compared with the larger question whether, on a true construction of the written and

unwritten Constitution of the Colony, the two Houses of the Legislature should be regarded as holding and exercising relatively to one another, position and functions analogous to those of the House of Lords and the House of Commons.'[1]

Governor Musgrave (of Queensland) entirely agreed with this opinion, stating that it would be

'difficult to overestimate the value which would attach to a declaration of the opinion of the Lords of the Judicial Committee of the Privy Council upon the questions involved'.[2]

In the absence of constitutional enactments, as distinct from mere conventions of the Constitution, and in the absence of a tribunal vested with jurisdiction to rule upon such conventions, the situation in Tasmania had to be met in the light of constitutional usage and principle. The decision of the Colonial Office went some considerable distance towards establishing a rule that the Governor is never to concern or busy himself with the final determination of any question of law so long as, if thought necessary, he arms himself with the opinion of his constitutional legal advisers. The decision certainly cannot be squared with the attitude taken up by Sir Dudley de Chair in 1926, that the proper persons to advise him upon legal and constitutional matters were not his constitutional legal advisers exclusively.[3]

The Tasmanian decision is also in line with the attitude of Sir Philip Game when he was asked by the Premier, in December 1930, to recommend the Imperial authorities to assent to a Bill abolishing the Legislative Council, notwithstanding the absence of any approval of the Bill by the electors. The latter said,[4] in his cable to the Secretary of State, with reference to the question of assent, that 'If you desire my views, I see no reason why advice of Ministers should not be accepted'.[5] As events turned out, no assent was given, because an injunction was issued against the Ministers by the Supreme Court of New South Wales. The decision of the Supreme Court was affirmed by the High Court and the Privy Council. This intervention by the ordinary Courts of law rather illustrates the governing principle laid

[1] Quoted. *Tasmanian Parliamentary Papers*, No. 41 of 1924, p. 5.
[2] Ibid. [3] See *ante*, p. 131.
[4] *N.S.W. Parliamentary Papers* (1930–2), vol. i, p. 514. [5] Ibid.

down in 1924—that questions of pure law should be left to be determined, not by the Governor, but by the Courts of law. On this occasion Sir Philip Game left the question of bare legality to be dealt with by the organs of the judicial power. The Royal Assent to the Bill for the abolition of the Legislative Council of New South Wales would not have converted the Bill into a valid law, as, indeed the decisions of the Courts subsequently showed. Similarly, the Royal Assent in Tasmania in 1924–5 to an Appropriation Bill and a Land and Income Tax Bill could not give them legal efficacy. But if, in either event, Royal Assent had been refused by the head of the Executive Government on the ground that such Assent would be a legal nullity, the jurisdiction of the Courts would have been ousted by the ruling of an Administrator on a point of law despite the advice and opinion of his constitutional and legal advisers.

D. IRISH FREE STATE LEGISLATION

In 1932 Keith ventured far in his statement of the duties of the King's representative, in relation to any proposed legislation or administration which is deemed by a Governor to be void or illegal. He suggested that the Governor-General of the Irish Free State 'might properly withhold assent' to the Bill to eliminate the Oath described in Article 17 of the Irish Free State Constitution, requiring members of the Legislature to take such oath, and to amend Article 50 thereof, precluding constitutional amendments from being made by the Legislature unless 'within the terms of the Scheduled Treaty'. Keith asserted that assent might be withheld on

> 'the obvious ground . . . that the bill purports to violate the power entrusted by the constitution to the legislature and therefore is null and void, and that its nullity is so clear that assent would be improper'.[1]

Keith added that 'in such a case the King could doubtless advise his representative through his Private Secretary'.[2] Doubtless, arguments and suggestions of this character were partly responsible for Mr. De Valera's securing the removal

[1] A. B. Keith, *The Constitutional Law of the British Dominions* (1933), p. 160.
[2] Ibid. (note 1).

of Mr. McNeill, the Governor-General, from his position, in October 1932.

The argument of Keith is untenable.[1] If the legislation was invalid, the matter fell to be dealt with in the exercise of the jurisdiction of the Courts, not by the intervention of the head of the Executive. Such intervention may amount to an attempt to deprive the ordinary Courts of law of their exclusive responsibility for exercising the judicial power. Kohn's argument on the point is quite convincing. He says:

> 'It would clearly not fall within the competence of a constitutional officer of the status of the Governor-General to adjudicate on his own authority upon the complex legal question of repugnancy. His position in relation to the administration of public affairs in the Dominion having been assimilated to that held by the King in Great Britain, he clearly has no other official adviser than the head of the Ministry. It is only the Courts which under Article 65 of the Constitution are competent to pronounce on the validity of the impugned legislation.'[2]

E. SIR ISAAC ISAACS' RULING IN 1931

In relation to executive or administrative action which is or may be impugned on the ground of illegality or invalidity, an interesting case occurred in Australia in 1931. Under the Commonwealth Transport Workers' Act, power was given to the Executive Government (in form the Governor-General) to make regulations prescribing the method of employment to be adopted in connexion with waterside labour engaged in inter-State trade. The validity of the Act and of the Regulations was affirmed by the High Court.[3] Subsequently the Senate (the Upper House) acting under the Acts Interpretation Act duly disallowed regulations which had been lawfully made by the Governor-General. The Labour (Scullin) Government had a majority in the House of Representatives, but was in a minority in the Senate. The opposition between the two Houses on the question created an almost absurd situation. The Senate would meet (say) on Wednesday. It would immediately proceed to disallow a regulation, where-

[1] See note on p. 191.

[2] Leo Kohn, *Constitution of the Irish Free State*, pp. 209–10.

[3] *Huddart Parker* v. *The Commonwealth* (44 Commonwealth Law Reports (1930–1), 492).

upon the regulation would be deprived of all force and effect under Section 10 of the Acts Interpretation Act.[1] The Government, fearing another disallowance, could do nothing until the Senate adjourned. So soon as the Senate adjourned (say) on the following Friday, the Cabinet would advise the Governor-General to issue a fresh regulation under the Transport Workers' Act. The latter would do so, and the regulation would have the force of law for three or four days, until the Senate next assembled. Then it would be promptly disallowed and the same process would be continued weekly during the parliamentary session.

Upon the conflicts recurring, the Senate forwarded an address to the Governor-General, praying the latter to refuse to approve during the existing session of Parliament of any regulations presented to the Executive Council

> 'being the same in substance as regulations which the Senate, in the lawful exercise of its powers as defined by Parliament in the Acts Interpretation Act, 1904–30, has, in this session, already disallowed'.[2]

It was submitted further that it was a rule of each House that no question should be presented which was substantially the same as one upon which an opinion had already been expressed during the current session, and that this principle should apply to delegated legislation by the Executive as much as to direct legislation passing through each House of the Parliament. The action of the Executive was said to be 'inconsistent with the spirit and intention of the Constitution'.[3]

The Governor-General's reply, dated June 6th, 1931, stated that he found it 'impossible conformably with my duty as I understand it, to comply with the request'.[4] The Governor-General said that he did not understand that the legality of the regulation was being questioned, but he added:

> 'I have, to the best of my ability, carefully re-examined the matter from this standpoint also, in order that no plain illegality should arise. My consideration of the relevant legislation and

[1] *Dignan* v. *Australian Steamships Pty. Ltd.* (45 Commonwealth Law Reports (1930–1) 188).

[2] *Commonwealth Parliamentary Debates*, vol. 129 (May 28th, 1931), p. 2343.

[3] Ibid.

[4] Ibid. (June 13th, 1931), p. 2595.

judicial decisions has led me to the belief that the advice of my legal adviser, the Honourable the Attorney-General, is correct—that unless and until disallowed by either House of Parliament such a regulation would be valid and have the force of law.'[1]

It will be noticed that the Governor-General did address himself to the question whether an obvious breach of law of 'plain illegality' characterized the action of the Executive. Although he excluded such a possibility, it should not be assumed that every representative of the King, whether proficient or not in legal learning, is entitled to determine for himself any legal issue which may be raised. Sir Isaac Isaacs was, of course, a Judge and a lawyer of great experience, and was therefore in a position very different from that occupied by the usual Governor or Governor-General. His conclusion upon this point was that

'with respect to legality, therefore, it is obviously my duty to take the only course which would enable the proper tribunal for that purpose, the judiciary, to determine the question should it arise'.[2]

This seems to indicate sound constitutional practice. Unless a Governor is himself sufficiently qualified to dismiss entirely the contentions of the Attorney-General for the time being as unarguable—a situation which can seldom arise—he should assent to the action proposed by his Ministers, so that all questions of legality may be determined by the Judiciary, which is, as Sir Isaac Isaacs pointed out, 'the proper tribunal for that purpose'.

Whilst the prayer of the Senate was refused, Sir Isaac Isaacs also made the following important pronouncements:

'As to the constitutional propriety of my approval to such a regulation as is postulated by the address, it cannot be doubted that normally by constitutional practice, confirmed, and perhaps strengthened, by the pronouncement of the Imperial Conference of 1926, I am bound to act upon the advice of my Ministers.'[3]

2. 'My plain duty in such circumstances, as it appears to me, acting, not as the representative of His Majesty the King as a constituent part of the Commonwealth Parliament, but as the designated executant of a statutory power created and conferred by the whole Parliament, is simply to adhere to the normal principle of respon-

[1] *Commonwealth Parliamentary Debates*, June 13th, 1931, p. 2596.
[2] Ibid.
[3] Ibid., June 10th, 1931, p. 2596.

sible government by following the advice of the Ministers who are constitutionally assigned to me for the time being as my advisers, and who must take the responsibility of that advice. If, as you request me to do, I should reject their advice, supported as it is by the considered opinion of the House of Representatives, and should act upon the equally considered contrary opinion of the Senate, my conduct would, I fear, even on ordinary constitutional grounds, amount to an open personal preference of one House against the other—in other words, an act of partisanship.'[1]

3. 'It is beyond my power, either legally to amend the legislation, directly or indirectly; or constitutionally, in existing circumstances, to do anything except to follow faithfully the path marked out in the statute itself, and according to the normal course of responsible government.'[2]

Subsequently the High Court had to consider whether it was lawful for the Governor-General to promulgate the regulations in substantially the same form as those disallowed. It was held that such regulations were valid and possessed the force of law during the period between their promulgation by the Governor-General and their subsequent disallowance by the Senate.[3] It followed also that during that portion of the year when Parliament was not in session the regulations retained the force of law.

Whilst Sir Isaac Isaacs applied to executive action under statutory power the same general principle of exclusive ministerial responsibility as was, in November 1924, applied to the Crown's participation in legislative action in Tasmania, it cannot be overlooked that he satisfied himself that the case was not one of 'plain illegality'.

These two precedents tend to create the principle that constitutional practice excludes from the consideration of the Governor in any Dominion the determination of all legal questions because direct responsibility for the action of the Governor in assenting to Bills or any proposed administrative act rests upon the Ministers holding office. The adoption of any other principle creates enormous practical difficulties. Unless the Governor is a specially trained lawyer (Sir Isaac

[1] *Commonwealth Parliamentary Debates*, June 10th, 1931, p. 2596.

[2] Ibid., p. 2597.

[3] *The Victorian Stevedoring and General Contracting Coy. Pty. Ltd.* v. *Dignan* (46 Commonwealth Law Reports (1931–2), 73).

Isaacs, of course, had a long judicial career), he will be unable to determine the disputed legal issue without seeking advice from outside the circle of his responsible Ministers. How can he be sure that the official advisers are wrong, and that the outside advisers are right? He is on perfectly safe ground if he allows all legal questions which are at all susceptible of argument to await determination at the hands of the judicial power. If he intervenes in the matter *against* Ministerial advice the result will usually be to prevent the Courts from exercising their jurisdiction by deciding the legal questions in dispute.

F. TODD'S DOCTRINE AS TO ILLEGALITY

Todd's work on *Parliamentary Government in the British Colonies* is responsible, to a large extent, for the theory of an independent discretion in the Governor on legal questions. According to Todd, if a Governor has

> 'reason to believe that their [that is the Cabinet Law Officers] legal judgment has been unconsciously biassed by political considerations, so that he cannot accept their interpretation of the law'[1]

he is not bound by such opinions, and 'is free to ask further assistance from elsewhere to aid him in his judgment'.[2] Todd said that the responsibility for action in such circumstances lies upon the Governor alone, for he 'must finally decide upon his personal responsibility'.[3]

This view of Todd finds some support in a dispatch of July 5th, 1878, from Sir M. Hicks-Beach, the Colonial Secretary. There it was stated that if a Governor is called upon to justify the legality of any questionable proceeding, he cannot shelter himself under the responsibility of his Ministers. However, the dispatch also stated that in all doubtful cases a Governor should require from the Colonial Law Officers a written memorandum certifying, as lawyers not as political advisers, that no infraction of the law is involved. If no such certificate can be given, the personal responsibility of the Governor 'may' require that he should delay acting upon the advice given until he can decide whether the emergency is sufficiently grave and urgent to justify his consenting to

[1] Todd, *Parliamentary Government in the British Colonies* (2nd ed.), pp. 58–9. [2] Ibid., p. 59. [3] Ibid., p. 59.

perform the act advised 'or whether he should inform his Ministers that he must decline to do so, even at the cost of having to accept their resignation of office'.[1]

The difficulty of the Governor's position under such circumstances was, however, extremely great. In a debate in the House of Lords on May 8th, 1868, upon the question of the grant to Sir Charles Darling,[2] Lord Carnarvon said that he must bear witness to the extremely difficult position in which the Governors found themselves, owing to questions arising 'which required not merely general knowledge of constitutional law, but of technical and professional details which few could command'.[3] He pointed out that the Governor's advisers were pledged to one political party or other, and suggested that, had he remained in office as Secretary of State for the Colonies, he would have striven earnestly for the appointment of some 'one permanent and impartial legal adviser, who might be in a position to advise a colonial Governor as emergencies arose'.[4]

The doctrine was vehemently condemned by Higinbotham, who pointed out that the legal advisers in England of the Sovereign were in precisely the same position, and added that it would be just as reasonable for the Victorian Ministry to seek to provide an additional legal adviser to the Queen in all urgent matters relating to the Colony of Victoria! The suggestion, he said, was 'illegal' and 'absurd'.[5]

Todd's views can no longer be regarded as satisfactory. The moment when it is supposed that a Governor, who is usually a lay person or a lawyer who has never practised or taken any special interest in legal matters, may be tempted to act against Ministers on the ground of actual or threatened illegality, there will be tendered to him, directly or indirectly, unofficial legal advice from many persons whose motives will be none the less political because not openly taking part in political conflicts. It is quite certain that, from time to time,

[1] Todd, *Parliamentary Government in the British Colonies* (2nd ed.), p. 727.

[2] Darling had been recalled from the position of Governor of Victoria, after supporting the popular Assembly against the Legislative Council. Subsequently the Assembly passed a special grant to Darling by way of compensation for his having been dismissed by the English authorities.

[3] E. E. Morris, *Memoir of George Higinbotham* (1895 ed.), p. 175.

[4] Ibid.

[5] Ibid., p. 176.

Dominion Governors have had to endure, and have sometimes embraced, advice from such quarters. Thus the warning of Merivale, who was permanent Under-Secretary for the Colonies during the early period of responsible government, was forgotten. He said of the Governor:

> 'His responsible Ministers may (and probably will) entertain views quite different from his own. And the temptation to surround himself with a *camarilla* of special advisers, distinct from these Ministers, is one which a Governor must carefully resist.'[1]

No doubt, difficult cases will occasionally arise where a Governor is convinced that the action taken or proposed to be taken is legally erroneous. But his position, and that of the Sovereign he represents, is enormously strengthened if, even in such cases, he limits his intervention to persuading or even compelling Ministers to have the legality of the challenged action tested before the Courts of the land.

[1] Todd, *Parliamentary Government in the British Colonies* (2nd ed.), p. 807.

Additional note to p. 185.

Subsequently, it was held by the Privy Council that, as a result of the passing of the Statute of Westminster 1931, the Irish Act No. 6 of 1933 (the Bill referred to by Keith) was valid. *Moore* v. *the Attorney General for the Irish Free State* 1935 A.C. 484.

XXI

THE RESERVE POWER IN RELATION TO THE IMPERIAL CONFERENCE DECLARATIONS OF 1926 AND 1930

AT the Imperial Conference of 1926, the Report[1] of the Inter-Imperial Relations Committee, which was adopted, stated in IV (*b*) in reference to the position of the Governors-General that it was an essential consequence of the equality of status existing among the members of the British Commonwealth of Nations

> 'that the Governor-General of a Dominion is the representative of the Crown, holding in all essential respects the same position in relation to the administration of public affairs in the Dominion as is held by His Majesty the King in Great Britain'.[2]

In particular it was declared that the Governor-General 'is not the representative or agent of His Majesty's Government in Great Britain or of any Department of that Government'.[3]

Next, at the Imperial Conference of 1930, the further declaration as to Inter-Imperial relations included the statement that 'the new position' of the Governor-General 'as representative of His Majesty only' involved certain consequences in relation to the appointment of Governors-General. These included the consequence that 'the constitutional practice that His Majesty acts on the advice of responsible Ministers applies also in this instance'.[4]

Other aspects of these decisive declarations are of supreme importance, but, for present purposes, it has to be noted that the decisions of the two Conferences assert the general principle that the King proceeds upon the advice of responsible Ministers. Moreover the general doctrine of Ministerial responsibility in its application to the affairs of a Dominion does not except from its operation, but definitely includes, the appointment of the King's representative therein.

[1] Cmd. 2768, vol. xi (1926), p. 545. (*Parliamentary Papers.*)
[2] Cmd. 2768, para. iv (*b*), p. 560.
[3] Ibid.
[4] *Parliamentary Papers*, vol. xiv, 1930–1, Cmd. 3717, p. 595.

Such matter thus becomes a Dominion affair, and a very important and vital one.

It is also declared that the relationship existing between the King and his Ministers in Great Britain is essentially the same relationship as that between the Governor-General and the King's Ministers in the Dominion. But what that relationship is, or may be, under particular circumstances, in Great Britain is only stated by a very general reference to the principle of ministerial responsibility, viz. *His Majesty acts on the advice of responsible Ministers.*[1]

Difficult situations may easily be imagined, even in reference to the appointment of a Dominion Governor-General. Suppose that, on the eve of a general election, a Dominion Ministry sees fit to submit advice to the King suggesting the appointment of a new Governor-General. Is the King, under such circumstances, bound to act upon such advice immediately, or may he await the result of the electoral contest in order to determine whether his advisers are endeavouring to secure an appointment to a vital office, although their own term of office is about to expire? The answer to such questions is not discoverable in the Reports of 1926 and 1930.

Therefore the declarations of 1926 and 1930, despite their great significance in other respects,[2] do not contain any final solution of the various problems of the reserve power, although it is recognized that the general principle of ministerial responsibility (illustrated by the Harcourt decision in the Tasmanian case of 1914)[3] governs the actions of the King and Governors-General alike; and also that in the appointment of the latter the relevant Ministers are those of the Dominion concerned.

Yet these declarations as to the Governor-General's position are of significance, because they followed upon the Canadian constitutional crisis of 1926. It will be recalled that the Amery decision, also of 1926 (already referred to),[4] as to the action of Governor de Chair foreshadowed one aspect of the Conference declaration by negativing the relation of

[1] The italics are mine. See *post*, p. 197.

[2] Especially in the supreme declaration as to Dominion status; *post*, p. 208, n (1).

[3] See *ante*, Chap. IV.

[4] See *ante*, Chap. XIV.

agency between the Governor of New South Wales and the British Government.

But the formal repudiation of the agency relationship, though in many respects valuable, tends to conceal some real contradictions and difficulties, which were not overlooked even in the days when Joseph Howe was struggling to enlarge the scope of local self-government in Nova Scotia. In one of his open letters of 1839 to Lord John Russell, Howe discussed the opinion as to the position of the Colonial Governor asserted by Sir Francis Head, who was Lieutenant-Governor of Upper Canada from January 1836 to 1838. Head had declared that responsibility for acts of Government in Upper Canada 'rests on me'.[1] Howe went on to suppose that the Queen had made him (Howe) Mayor of Liverpool, and then proceeded to analyse the situation which would arise, including the inevitable local discontent. But, he said, a Governor holding such views as those of Head remains 'perfectly safe so long as he commits no act so flagrant as to outrage the feelings of the nation'. Even if he has to retire, the position is only that 'His Excellency is removed to another Province, with a larger salary, to act the same farce over there'.[2] Howe's point was that, if a Governor is to be regarded as immune from responsibility to, and control by, the Colonial Office, the Colonists are deprived of a supervising authority which may, on occasion, curb a Governor's action.

Similarly the 1926 decisions as to the status of Dominion Governor and Governor-General seem to imply that, generally speaking, the Ministers holding the confidence of a Dominion Assembly have no easy means of redress against unconstitutional action by a Governor. Formerly the Ministers could appeal to the Colonial Office; the Assembly might also pass a motion for the Governor's recall, and have it transmitted through the proper authorities to the King, who would in such case act upon the advice of British Ministers. Upon certain occasions, notably in 1916–17, when the British Government recalled Sir Gerald Strickland from New South Wales, a drastic sanction was available, at any rate in cases

[1] W. P. M. Kennedy, *Documents of the Canadian Constitution (1759–1915)*, (1918), p. 489.

[2] Ibid., p. 490.

where the Dominion Ministers and British Ministers agreed that the Governor had acted unconstitutionally.[1] But in the case of a Governor-General or a Governor who is neither a representative nor agent of the British Government, the latter, if appealed to, is, or may be, enabled to say that it disclaims all responsibility, having no constitutional concern in the local dispute, which is essentially one for settlement in the Dominion itself. This is more than a possibility, as is shown by the disputes in Canada and New South Wales in the year 1926.[2] It must again be emphasized that the Imperial Conference's adoption of the Balfour Report did not make any provision for solving bona-fide disputes between Governor and Ministers, where the former insisted upon his possession of some real discretionary authority.

At the Conference of 1930 a nearer approach to the root of such problems was made in dealing with the question of the *appointment* of Governors-General. Previously, the real appointing authority in such cases was the British Government, although the practice had grown up of consulting the Dominion Government concerned in order to make a selection acceptable to them.[3] The extent of prior consultation depended upon the vigour and resolution of the Dominion Government, but it was recognized that, in the last resort, the views of the British Government would prevail.

The important connexion between the question of appointment and that of the relation after appointment had been foreseen by Jenks, who said in reference to the declaration of 1926 that the exclusion of the agency relation 'has caused some searchings of heart'.[4] He added:

> 'Does it really mean that in future the government of the Empire is to fall into the hands of the King's private secretary? Put picturesquely—are Lord Stamfordham and his successors to "run" the British Empire? I cannot conceive any rational foundation for such a suggestion. Who then is to advise the King upon the appointment of a Governor-General, say of Canada, Australia, or New Zealand? The answer (I may be wrong) seems as a matter of principle to me

[1] See *ante*, Chap. XVII. [2] See *ante*, Chaps. VII, XIV.

[3] A. B. Keith, *Speeches and Documents on the British Dominions (1918–31)* (Letter of Lloyd George to Mr. A. Griffith, Dec. 13th, 1921), pp. 101–2.

[4] *Cambridge Law Journal*, vol. iii (1927), p. 21.

to be reasonably plain, namely, that, just as the King in matters affecting the United Kingdom takes the advice of his Prime Minister in London, so in matters affecting Canada he will take the advice of his Prime Minister in the Dominion, and in the case of Australia that of his Prime Minister in the Commonwealth of Australia, and so forth. And I see no difficulty in applying the principle in that way.'[1]

This opinion was in direct opposition to that of Keith, although, as a matter of logical inference from general principle, Jenks was plainly in the right. Thus Keith wrote, on July 1st, 1927:

'The suggestion that the King can act directly on the advice of Dominion Ministers is a constitutional monstrosity, which would be fatal to the security of the position of the Crown. That His Majesty should on his personal discretion and responsibility accept or reject Dominion advice is absurd; but not less so the idea that he should serve the purpose of automatically registering the decrees of six or more independent Governments, even if they conflicted with the interests of the people of the United Kingdom, apart altogether from the delay and inconvenience involved in sending documents to London for formal signature.'[2]

As Sir Harrison Moore has pointed out, the existence of that 'monstrosity' at which Keith had expressed such horror was 'affirmed by the Imperial Conference of 1930 in the very matter of the appointment of the King's representative in a Dominion'.[3] For paragraph VI of the Report of the 1930 Conference certainly secures to the Dominion Ministers direct access to the King himself for the purpose of the King's acting on their advice in relation to the appointment of the Governor-General, His Majesty's Government in Great Britain being neither interested nor concerned in such appointments. And the new method of appointing the Governor-General, exclusively upon the advice of Dominion Ministers, has been adopted in appointments since 1930.

It should not be assumed, however, that even under this modern technique of appointment there will be an elimination of all possible disputes between Ministers and the

[1] *Cambridge Law Journal*, vol. iii (1927), p. 21.

[2] A. B. Keith, *Responsible Government in the Dominions* (1928), Preface, p. xiii.

[3] Melbourne *Argus*, March 25th, 1933.

Governor-General. The affirmation of the 1930 Report of 'the constitutional practice that His Majesty acts on the advice of responsible Ministers',[1] does not necessarily exclude attempts by a Governor-General to exercise some reserve or discretionary authority. If such cases arise, and if there is, e.g., a dismissal of Ministers by the Governor-General, or a refusal by the latter to dissolve Parliament upon the advice of Ministers, there being in each case an acute difference of opinion between Governor-General and Ministers, what is to be done?

Now Jenks's logical inference from the 1926 Report, that the *appointment* of a Governor-General is exclusively a matter of Dominion concern, seems to justify the further inference —equally logical—that the *termination* of the appointment of a Governor-General is also a matter exclusively of local or Dominion concern. So far as the position of strict law is concerned, it is well established that, in the absence of a controlling Statute, a person holding such a position as that of Governor or Governor-General holds it at the pleasure of the Crown. It would seem, therefore, that Dominion Ministers must possess sufficient 'constitutional' authority to approach His Majesty directly, i.e. without any intervention by Ministers in Britain, for the purpose of advising the King that the appointment of the Governor-General should be terminated. This course was apparently the procedure adopted when the De Valera Government of the Irish Free State secured the termination of Mr. McNeill's appointment as Governor-General in the year 1932.

But the possibility of the dismissal of a Governor-General illustrates the serious position which may arise when a Governor-General who has been nominated by Ministers representing one political party is holding office during the administration of other political advisers. Serious disputes may easily arise under such circumstances, and the new Ministers may, in order to prevent any dispute arising which could lead to the exercise by the Governor-General of reserve powers, procure the latter's dismissal at the commencement of their term of office. If such a practice is adopted by one political party, it will undoubtedly be followed by the other

[1] *Parliamentary Papers*, vol. xiv (1930–1), para. (*g*), p. 595. Cmd. 3717.

or others. The result will probably be that, unless the precise extent of the Governor-General's reserve power is defined by law so as to be capable of immediate enforcement, or covered by authoritative declaration, or unless the whole of such reserve powers are entirely swept away, the office of Governor-General will become a mere reflection of the existing Dominion administration, and consequently, during the life of each successive administration, no exercise of any reserve power will take place. This may be thought satisfactory, because the inevitable result of the process will be that all reserve or prerogative power will fall into desuetude, and the problem will, by an indirect method, be solved.

Yet situations may arise in which the exercise of reserve power will be the only possible method of giving to the electorate an opportunity of preventing some permanent and far-reaching constitutional change. A convenient illustration of this is afforded by proposals of Dominion Governments to extend the life of the Legislature, and indirectly their own lives. If given command over the parliamentary position, there is no saying to what lengths certain persons may not be prepared to go in the exercise of legislative power. During the War of 1914–18 the life of Parliament was extended in the State of New South Wales, although the entire responsibility for the conduct of defence was committed by law to the Commonwealth Parliament. More recently, there has been an extension by the South Australian Parliament of its own life from three years, the normal period, to five years. It was argued that 'a mandate' had been obtained for the adoption of such a course by the Ministry from the people. On the other side such 'mandate' was alleged to be non-existent, the question being so confused and commingled with other legislative proposals that there was at least a grave doubt whether the popular vote of a General Election was intended to endorse the proposed extension of the life of Parliament. One further aspect of the matter was that the Legislature did not pass a general law extending the life of all South Australian Legislatures from three years to five, but limited the alteration to the existing Parliament. This qualification of the 'mandate' was demanded by the Legislative Council which, for the time being, happened to be of similar political complexion to the dominant party in the Assembly. What would happen if the present Assembly were replaced by an Assembly of opposing political opinion and proposed a Bill to extend its own life. Would the Council agree to the proposal? And if the 'mandate' is insufficient, what course should a Governor take?

It is sufficient to make the point that, in the interests of the people, and because of the absence of controlling constitutional provisions requiring great changes to be endorsed by vote at a referendum, some reserve authority may have to be exercised to prevent the abuse of legislative power, and to require great changes to be submitted for popular approval. Keith says that 'to extend the life of a legislature without a mandate is clearly a strong step, justified, if at all, only by war'.[1] He pointed out that there were bitter complaints by the Labour party in New Zealand at the recent decision of the Government to extend the life of Parliament 'for which it was declared it had received no possible mandate'.[2]

So far as has been ascertained, it appears that the only occasions upon which Dominion Legislatures have extended their own lives have been occasions when the Radical or Labour party was in Opposition. In no case, however, has the representative of the Crown intervened to prevent the carrying out of such extraordinary legislation, except in New South Wales in 1916–17, when Sir Gerald Strickland, threatening to dismiss Ministers or refuse assent to the Bill, was recalled by the Imperial Government.[3] Accordingly an interesting constitutional expedient has been adopted by the Labour party under Mr. Forgan Smith's leadership in Queensland, where the Constitution has been effectively altered so as to prevent the extension of Parliament's life without the express approval of the electors at a referendum held for the purpose. This device was made possible by the Privy Council's affirmation of the decisions of the Australian Courts upholding the validity of an analogous provision which prevented the alteration of the Constitution of New South Wales by abolishing the Upper House without the approval of the electors.[4] Curiously enough, Mr. Forgan Smith also induced

[1] A. B. Keith, *The Constitutional Law of the British Dominions* (1933), p. 170. [2] Ibid. [3] See *ante*, Chap. XVII. [4] See *ante*, pp. 10, 157–8.

the Queensland Legislature (which is uni-cameral) to pass a constitutional amendment preventing any reconstitution of the Legislative Council in the future without an approving referendum of the electorate.

This question of the extension of Parliament's life is quite sufficient to illustrate the somewhat dangerous position which now exists, for a Governor-General certainly runs the risk of immediate dismissal if, in any circumstances, he runs counter to the will of the Ministers holding office. For no impartial holder of the position of the Sovereign's personal representative can face with equanimity (say) a proposal analogous to that which Sir Gerald Strickland desired to veto in 1916. Such proposals may, under certain circumstances, be nothing less than attempts to cheat the electors of their right to control the Legislature. Certainly a high-minded Governor may occasionally take such a view. At present, however, he is placed in the dilemma of being summarily removed from office if he seeks to protect the people, or of yielding to what may be an impudent attempt to thwart their will by a *coup d'état* under the forms of law. The best way out of the situation is to ascertain, define, declare, and enforce rules which can be applied to govern the exercise of the reserve powers of the Crown's representative. If the precise position of the Sovereign himself as to his exercise of ultimate prerogatives were known and accepted, there might be no occasion for any special declaration of the constitutional rights of the Governor-Generals or the Governors. But no such agreement exists in relation to the Sovereign and his Ministers and the same questions may arise in Britain as in the Dominions themselves. And the Imperial Conference Declarations of 1926 and 1930 have not solved the problems which may arise in relation to the exercise of a real discretionary authority by the Monarch or his Governors in the Dominions.

XXII

THE CONSTITUTIONAL STATUS OF THE AUSTRALIAN STATES AND CANADIAN PROVINCES

IT is necessary to give close consideration to the question of the general constitutional status of the Australian States and the Canadian Provinces. As we have noted, references to his earlier writings show that Keith at first made no attempt to distinguish between the relative constitutional status of the States or Provinces and that of the central Governments in the two Federated Dominions. About 1926, however, his opinion seems to have altered. In 1933 he went to pains to point out that the declaration of equality of status contained in the 1926 declaration of the Imperial Conference 'has no application to the Governors of the States or Lieutenant-Governors of the Provinces'.[1] At the same time he asserts that the Governor in the Australian States 'still acts as an agent of the Imperial Government in addition to his normal function as constitutional head of the State'.[2] And he elaborates this view later, saying:

> 'In the States of Australia and the Provinces of Canada, the Governors and Lieutenant-Governors are still able to act as agents of the British and the Dominion Governments. Moreover, in the case of New Zealand and Newfoundland the same principle is observed, as neither Government has shown any desire to act on the resolution of the Imperial Conference of 1926. In none of these cases, however, is there much important work to be done, save that the Governments of New Zealand and Newfoundland are thus kept in effective touch with the views of foreign affairs of the British Government.'[3]

In striking contrast with this assertion is the whole tenor of Keith's former treatment of the problem of Dominion status. In addition to references given elsewhere, it may be noted that in a work of 1918 Keith discussed the status of the Dominions and regarded the position of 'the Governor'

[1] A. B. Keith, *Constitutional Law of the British Dominions* (1933), p. 150.

[2] Ibid., p. 136.

[3] Ibid., p. 160.

not only as indistinguishable from, but as including that of Governor-General. Thus he said that

> 'even in matters wholly of internal interest the Governor may refuse Ministerial advice if he thinks fit, provided that he can find other Ministers to accept office and to assume responsibility for his action *ex post facto*.'[1]

And he proceeded to illustrate important aspects of the problems of constitutional practice by referring indifferently to the dispute which arose in 1914 between the Governor of Tasmania and his Ministers (involving the position of a State),[2] and to that in relation to the double dissolution granted by Sir Ronald Munro Ferguson in 1914 (involving the position of the Commonwealth).[3]

The fact that the position of the Australian States and the Canadian Provinces was not specially dealt with by the Imperial Conference should not be regarded as diminishing their constitutional status, if it is reasonably clear otherwise that no valid legal or constitutional distinction between their status and that of the respective Federal authorities can be successfully drawn. The States were not represented at the Imperial Conference because, since 1911, such Conferences have been mainly concerned with external and foreign affairs, in respect of which either predominant or exclusive legal authority has been committed by the two Constitutions to the central, not the local, Governments of Canada and Australia. These central Governments, like the Governments of South Africa, the Irish Free State, and New Zealand, have gradually obtained recognition of their international status in relation to other members of the League of Nations and to foreign powers generally. In this important development neither the States nor the Provinces participated, because the relevant topics were outside their legal authority under the Canadian and Australian Constitutions.[4] But when the doctrine of complete Dominion autonomy was being put

[1] A. B. Keith, *Selected Speeches and Documents on British Colonial Policy*, vol. i (Preface), p. x. [2] See *ante*, Chap. IV. [3] See *ante*, Chap. V.

[4] See the writer's discussion of the constitutional basis of the exercise by the self-governing Dominions of authority in relation to Mandates issued by the League of Nations: 'The British Dominions as Mandatories', *Proceedings Australian and New Zealand Society for International Law*, vol. i.

into formal shape in a legal enactment, both the States of Australia and the Provinces of Canada suddenly realized that they also might be affected by the altered situations. And Keith seems at this stage to have deprecated, as he duly noted, 'the general inclination in the United Kingdom to overlook the position of the States in Australia'.[1]

Before dealing with the manner in which the States and Provinces intervened in relation to the Statute of Westminster, a short reference to the legal relation of the States and Provinces to the respective central authorities in the two Federations should be made. Fortunately the legal position is not in doubt, either in Canada or in Australia. In each case the Judicial Committee of the Privy Council has declared the law in judgments which leave no room for argument or misunderstanding. Thus Lord Watson in *Liquidators of the Maritime Bank of Canada* v. *Receiver-General of New Brunswick* said, in reference to the Canadian Provinces:

> 'A Lieutenant-Governor, when appointed, is as much the representative of Her Majesty for all purposes of provincial government as the Governor-General himself is for all purposes of Dominion government.'[2]

Lord Haldane said in 1916 that

> 'the effect of these sections of the British North America Act is that, subject to certain express provisions in that Act and to the supreme authority of the Sovereign, who delegates to the Governor-General and through his instrumentality to the Lieutenant-Governors the exercise of the prerogative on terms defined in their commissions, the distribution under the new grant of executive authority in substance follows the distribution under the new grant of legislative powers. In relation, for example, to the incorporation of Companies in Ontario with provincial objects the powers of incorporation which the Governor-General or Lieutenant-Governor possessed before the Union must be taken to have passed to the Lieutenant-Governor of Ontario so far as concerns companies with this class of objects.'[3]

Later in the same judgment, Lord Haldane added:

> 'Whatever obscurity may at one time have prevailed as to the position of a Lieutenant-Governor appointed on behalf of the

[1] *Journal of Comparative Legislation*, vol. xiv (1932), p. 104.

[2] [1892] A.C. 437, at p. 443.

[3] *Bonanza Creek Goldmining Company Limited* v. *Rex* [1916] 1 A.C. 566, at p. 580.

Crown by the Governor-General has been dispelled by the decision of this Board in *Liquidators of the Maritime Bank of Canada* v. *Receiver-General of New Brunswick*.'[1]

In 1924 Mr. Justice Duff, speaking for the Privy Council, said:

'And indeed, to hold otherwise would be incompatible with an essential principle of the Confederation scheme, the object of which, as Lord Watson said in *Maritime Bank of Canada* v. *Receiver-General of New Brunswick*, was "not to weld the Provinces into one or to subordinate the Provincial Governments to a central authority". "Within the spheres allotted to them by the Act, the Dominion and the Provinces are, as Lord Haldane said in *Great West Saddlery Coy.* v. *The King*,[2] "rendered in general principle co-ordinate Governments".'[3]

Much the same general principle of co-ordinate authority results from the division of powers and functions under the Australian Constitution, although the method of demarcation adopted is different. Thus in *Attorney-General for the Commonwealth of Australia* v. *Colonial Sugar Refining Coy.*, Lord Haldane said:

'Their Lordships will now examine the Commonwealth Constitution Act in the light of these observations with a view to answering the question whether the Royal Commissions Acts of the Australian Parliament were within the powers which by this instrument were transferred by the federating Colonies to the new central Parliament. It is plain that, excepting in so far as such powers were so transferred they remained exclusively vested in the States. This results not merely from the broad principle laid down in section 51 to which reference will presently be made, but from section 107, which enacts that "every power of the Parliament of a Colony which has become or becomes a State, shall, unless it is by this Constitution exclusively vested in the Parliament of the Commonwealth or withdrawn from the Parliament of the State, continue as at the establishment of the Commonwealth, or of the admission or establishment of the State, as the case may be".'[4]

These decisions of the supreme Judicial tribunal make it abundantly clear that, within their constitutional sphere,

[1] *Bonanza Creek Goldmining Company Limited* v. *Rex* [1916] 1 A.C. 566, at pp. 580–1.

[2] [1921] 2 A.C. 91.

[3] *Attorney-General for Ontario* v. *Reciprocal Insurers* [1924] A.C. 328, at pp. 342–3.

[4] [1914] A.C. 237, at p. 254.

which in general is limited and defined by reference to subjects committed to their charge, both the States of Australia and the Provinces of Canada possess legal and constitutional authority which is of precisely the same nature and quality as that of the central or Federal authority within its lawful sphere.

There is, of course, one important distinction between the two Federations. In Canada exclusive jurisdiction over specified subjects has been given both to the Dominion and to the Provinces. The two lists of subjects are set out in section 91 and section 92 of the British North America Act. But it is also provided that, if a subject does not come within either section 91 or section 92, the legislative jurisdiction may be exercised by the Dominion Parliament. In Australia a different method of allocation has been adopted, and sections 51 and 52 of the Constitution specify the subject-matters as to which the Commonwealth may legislate. Unless there is to be found an express grant of power to legislate upon a subject-matter, the Commonwealth Parliament cannot lawfully deal with the subject-matter at all.[1] Without specifying the heads of power, i.e. the subject-matter, in detail, it may be said generally that social questions, the regulation of industry, employment and unemployment, education, agriculture, land settlement and ordinary criminal and civil law are *not* subjects committed to the Commonwealth, and thus, by section 107 of the Constitution, remain within the exclusive competence of the States.[2]

Somewhat unfortunately the misunderstanding of certain observations made in a judgment of certain Justices of the High Court of Australia to the effect that the States of the Commonwealth are not 'Sovereign States'[3] has had the result of leading many lay persons, and perhaps a few lawyers,

[1] Viscount Haldane, L.C., said '. . . the burden rests on those who affirm that the capacity to pass these Acts was put within the powers of the Commonwealth Parliament, to show that this was done' (*Attorney-General for Commonwealth* v. *Colonial Sugar Refining Co.* [1914] A.C., at p. 255).

[2] None of the enumerated specific subjects within Commonwealth jurisdiction relate to the 'general control over the liberty of the subject' (ibid., at p. 255).

[3] *Commonwealth of Australia* v. *State of New South Wales* (1923), 32 C.L.R. 200, at pp. 210, 218.

to suppose that the Commonwealth itself possessed 'Sovereignty' *to the exclusion of the States.* But Vinogradoff was correct when he stated that, in relation to the Commonwealth of Australia, sovereignty was divided.[1] To the same effect is Dr. Baty's statement that 'some portion, though not the whole of the internal sovereignty, resides in the component Provinces'.[2] In *New South Wales* v. *Commonwealth of Australia*,[3] it was said of the doctrine of sovereignty:

> 'The phrase is most ambiguous. In some aspects, both the States and the Commonwealth are bodies which may lawfully exercise sovereign powers. The Governors of the States are as much the representatives of His Majesty for State purposes as the Governor-General of the Commonwealth is for Commonwealth purposes. The subjection of the States to the jurisdiction of the High Court is accompanied by a perfectly "equal and undiscriminating" subjection of the Commonwealth to the same jurisdiction. For all purposes of self-government in Australia, sovereignty is distributed between the Commonwealth and the States. The States have exclusive legislative authority over all matters affecting peace, order, and good government so far as such matters have not been made the subject of specific grant to the Commonwealth. And the authority of the State covers most things which touch the ordinary life and well being of their citizens—the maintenance of order, the administration of justice, the police system, the education of the people, employment, the relief of unemployment and distress, the general control of liberty. Speaking generally, all these subjects are no lawful concern of the Commonwealth.'[4]

That the Legislatures of the Provinces of Canada may be said to possess 'sovereignty' in certain respects appears clearly from the recent judgment of the Judicial Committee delivered by Lord Atkin (*Lymburn* v. *Maryland*).[5]

In this elaborate division of power and authority between central and local governments it is necessary, of course, to have a tribunal vested with authority to determine whether any disputed enactment is within or without constitutional power. Further, both in Canada and in Australia, the full area or content of internal self-government is divided between

[1] Vinogradoff, *Historical Jurisprudence*, vol. i, p. 122.

[2] *Journal of Comparative Legislation* (1930), vol. xii, p. 167.

[3] 46 C.L.R. 155.

[4] 46 C.L.R., p. 220 (*per* Evatt J.).

[5] [1932] A.C. 318, at p. 326.

the central and local Parliaments, so that in general the power to legislate must reside in one quarter or the other. Therefore it is impossible, either in Canada or in Australia, to make any general statement as to the authority which lawfully controls 'domestic affairs' without further elaboration and differentiation of the powers committed to the Provinces and to the States on the one hand, and to the central authorities on the other. Further, executive authority is divided, speaking broadly, in accordance with the principle upon which legislative authority is divided.

The argument of the Dominion Prime Ministers at Paris in 1919 upon the occasion of the Peace Delegation was expressed with great precision in Sir R. Borden's memorandum of March 12th, 1919. This memorandum of the Dominion Prime Ministers as to the principles of constitutional government obtaining throughout the Empire declared that

> 'the Crown is the supreme executive in the United Kingdom and in all the Dominions, but it acts on the advice of different Ministries within different constitutional units.'[1]

Now this statement was directed to external affairs mainly, and may be regarded as treating Canada as one entire unit and Australia in the same way. But this was only because the authority over external affairs was regarded as legally vested in relation both to the whole of Canada and to the whole of Australia, in the central government of each Dominion.

But the principle laid down by the Dominion Prime Ministers is of general application. In reference to many, perhaps most, matters of internal self-government, the Crown, both in Canada and in Australia, acts upon the advice of provincial Ministers and State Ministers, and upon that advice exclusively, because the Federal authority has no concern with the question, be it one of legislation or administration. The Borden memorandum accurately describes the constitutional position both in Canada and in Australia, so long as it is remembered that, for a very large number of purposes, many of vital importance, the constitutional unit in which the Crown acts, if it acts at all, is the

[1] A. B. Keith, *Speeches and Documents on the British Dominions (1918–31)*, p. 14.

local unit within the Federal system. The question whether the State or Province is, in any given case, the proper authority to act, depends mainly upon the subject-matter dealt with, and the question is determinable in any given case of dispute by the King's Courts.

Therefore there can be no possible doubt that, in relation to internal affairs, speaking both legally and constitutionally, both the Provinces of Canada and the States of Australia were as much entitled to inclusion in the general declaration of 1926,[1] which concerned 'domestic' as well as 'external' affairs, as were the central authorities of each Federation. That is only to say, after all, that, following the words of the Judicial Committee, both the Governor of each State and the Lieutenant-Governor of each Province is just as much the representative of the King for State or Provincial purposes as is the Governor-General for Commonwealth or Dominion purposes.

Undoubtedly there was a failure on the part of the Canadian Provinces and the Australian States to appreciate that their own status might possibly be regarded as being affected adversely as a consequence of the declaration of status made in the year 1926.[2] Fortunately the Conference on the Operation of Dominion Legislation came to be convened in 1929, in pursuance of the recommendation of the 1926 Conference.[3] This was done to meet the position that existing legal forms and doctrines were out of harmony with the 1926 declaration of complete Dominion autonomy in every aspect of public affairs—external and internal.

The Report of the 1929 Conference is also of general significance. For it completely destroyed the inferences drawn by Professor Keith from the declarations and resolutions of the 1926 Conference, viz., that the definition of Dominion status was in some way qualified by the references made to function. This is evidenced by Keith's vehement

[1] The vital declaration is as follows: '*They are autonomous communities within the British Empire, equal in status, in no way subordinate one to another in any aspect of their domestic or external affairs, though united by a common allegiance to the Crown, and freely associated as members of the British Commonwealth of Nations.*' *Parliamentary Papers* (*Commons*), vol. xi (1926), Cmd. 2768, p. 547.

[2] See note on p. 216.

[3] *Parliamentary Papers* (*Commons*), vol. xi (1926), paragraph IV (c).

criticism of the work of the Conference of 1929. 'As it is,'[1] he said:

> 'the Conference contented itself with destroying the legal unity of the Empire without evolving anything to encourage co-operation. It marks clearly the driving force of the Prime Minister of the Union and the Government of the Irish Free State, and their determination to secure autonomy without at the same time committing their Dominions to co-operation in maintaining Imperial interests.'[2]

Keith attacked the recommendation of the Conference of 1929 that the proposed Statute should both declare and enact extra-territorial powers of the Dominion,[3] describing it as 'vague' and asserting that the Conference in this respect exceeded its terms of reference.[4] He conjured up fearsome possibilities as a result of the exercise of extra-territorial authority, asking:

> 'Does it mean that Canadians and other British subjects may be bound in respect of acts done in the United Kingdom by Canadian laws, so that a British subject, born and resident in the United Kingdom, may be subjected to criminal proceedings if he ever visits Canada in respect of some act done in the United Kingdom which may be deemed inimical to Canadian interests, e.g., depressing the price of Canadian wheat, or supplying incorrect invoices for production to the Canadian Customs Service?'[5]

Keith was also disturbed about the possibility of the Commonwealth Parliament's legislating in respect of Merchant Shipping. He prophesied that the Commonwealth Parliament 'will be compelled, even if the Government should be reluctant to act, to deal with shipping questions from the point of view of Australian Trade Unionism'.[6]

Altogether, Professor Keith, who had sought in his comments to submerge the 1926 declaration as to the extent of Dominion status beneath the incidental references in the

[1] *Journal of Comparative Legislation*, vol. xii (1930), p. 278.

[2] Ibid.

[3] *Parliamentary Papers*, vol. xiv (1930–1), Cmd. 3717, pp. 586–7.

[4] Keith's view is not supported by Sir John Latham. See *Australia and the British Commonwealth* (J. G. Latham), at pp. 79, 82. See also *The British Dominions as Mandatories*, by the author, at pp. 26–31.

[5] *Journal of Comparative Legislation*, vol. xii (1930), p. 279.

[6] Ibid., p. 282.

Report to 'functions' actually exercised by the Dominion,[1] found himself, temporarily at least, overwhelmed by the decisions of the 1929 Conference, the proceedings of which he characterized as 'perhaps a rather disappointing outcome for the labours of a body whose work extended from October 8 to December 4, 1929'.[2]

But the work of the 1929 Conference obtained authoritative recognition on December 11th, 1931, when the Statute of Westminster, 1931, became law. It was passed, as appears upon its face, to give effect to the declarations and resolutions of the Imperial Conferences of 1926 and 1930. And the Conference of 1930 had accepted the work of the experts concerned in 1929.

In the Report of the 1929 Conference it was pointed out that:

> 'The report of 1926 dealt only with the constitutional position of the Governments and Parliaments of the Dominions. . . . The federal character of the Constitutions of Canada and Australia, however, gives rise to questions which we have not found it possible to leave out of account, inasmuch *as they concern self-government in those Dominions*.'[3]

For reasons I have given above, the passage I have italicized fairly sums up the constitutional position in the two Federations. This part of the Report of 1929 was mainly the joint work of the Canadian and Australian members of the

[1] My views as to this are expressed elsewhere: 'It has always seemed clear to me that the distinction made in the Report is between the existence of Dominion power and its actual exercise. As to the former, no question can be raised, "Every self-governing member of the Empire is now the master of its destiny. In fact, if not always in form, it is subject to no compulsion whatever", and further "every Dominion is now, and must always remain, the sole judge of the nature and extent of its co-operation". (Cmd. 2768, section V (*c*).) This language conveys that the Dominions possess the constitutional right *as against Great Britain* (1) to exercise full legislative executive and judicial authority in respect of their domestic affairs and also (2) to deal fully with external affairs and for that purpose to enter to the extent they think fit into all or any relations with foreign powers.' (*The British Dominions as Mandatories*, p. 13.)

[2] *Journal of Comparative Legislation*, vol. xii (1930), p. 278.

[3] *Commonwealth Parliamentary Papers* (1929–31), vol. ii, para. 68, p. 1352; *Parliamentary Papers (Commons)*, vol. xvi (1929–30), Cmd. 3479, para. 68, p. 193.

Conference, who were well acquainted with the position.[1] The Conference, in dealing with the question of extra-territorial legislative power of the Dominions of Australia, said: 'the most urgently required field of extra-territorial power is criminal law which, in general, is within the State power in Australia'.[2] It might have been added that criminal law, also speaking generally, is in Australia (in this respect unlike Canada) *not* within the power of the central Government. The Report said that the question whether the extra-territorial power should be granted to the State Parliaments 'is a matter primarily for consideration by the proper authorities in Australia'.[3] Inasmuch as the British North America Act commits jurisdiction over criminal law in general to the central Parliament, the question of extra-territorial legislative jurisdiction was not a matter of direct concern to the Canadian Provinces.

The 1929 Report discussed the Colonial Laws Validity Act, 1865, by virtue of which Provincial or State legislation, if repugnant to Acts of Parliament of the United Kingdom, is rendered void and inoperative. Here, as was stated, 'the question . . . presents the same problems in Canada and in Australia',[4] and here also it was

> 'a matter for the proper authorities in Canada and in Australia to consider whether and to what extent it is desired that the principles to be embodied in the New Act of the Parliament of the United Kingdom should be applied to Provincial and State legislation in the future.'[5]

It is clear that the legal experts who attended the 1929 Conference realized that, if it was desired to carry out the 1926 principles in a way most consistent with the existing legal position in the two Federations, some attempt should

[1] *Commonwealth Parliamentary Papers* (1929–31), vol. ii, p. 1369 (Covering Report of Sir William Harrison Moore).

[2] *Commonwealth Parliamentary Papers* (1929–31), vol. ii, para. 69, p. 1352; *Parliamentary Papers* (*Commons*), vol. xvi (1929–30), Cmd. 3479, para. 69, p. 193.

[3] Ibid. (*Commonwealth Parliamentary Papers*), p. 1353; ibid. (*Parliamentary Papers* (*Commons*)), p. 194.

[4] Ibid. (*Commonwealth Parliamentary Papers*), para. 71, p. 1353; ibid. (*Parliamentary Papers* (*Commons*)), para. 71, p. 194.

[5] Ibid.

be made to include the States and the Provinces in the ambit of the then proposed Statute of Westminster.

In the Commonwealth of Australia action was not taken to include the States within the scope of the Statute of Westminster. This was due in part to the sudden dissolution of the Federal Parliament towards the end of the year 1931, in part to the absence of unanimity amongst the States, and in part to the undoubted fact that several of the State Governments were not sufficiently seized of the importance of protecting their relative status in the polity of the Commonwealth. Further, the failure of the Federal Parliament of 1931–4 formally to adopt the Statute of Westminster has lessened the significance that might otherwise be attached to the absence from the Statute of any mention of the powers or status of the Australian States. Sir Robert Garran has emphasized that one objection made by several of the States to the application within the Commonwealth of the Statute of Westminster was that the provisions dealing with the Colonial Laws Validity Act and with the declaration of the removal of extra-territorial restrictions, were not applied to them as well as to the Commonwealth.[1] He concedes that internal self-government should be shared by the States, as also does Keith himself when he states that

> 'nothing has been done to assure to the States an extension of their powers. The Colonial Laws Validity Act, 1865, still binds them, and they have no concession of extra-territorial authority.'[2]

So soon as it is remembered that, while the Australian Constitution retains its present form, the States are partners with the Commonwealth in the rights and duties of responsible self-government in Australia, no action of general constitutional significance can fairly be taken without participation on the part of the States. Of course the Statute of Westminster was directed to the removal of certain legal rules which contradicted the 1926 declaration of full Dominion status. The Statute was not concerned with the task of expressing the relative constitutional position either of the State Governor and State Ministers, or of the Commonwealth Governor-General and Commonwealth Ministers. But in-

[1] *British Year Book of International Law* (1932), p. 116.

[2] *Journal of Comparative Legislation*, Feb. 1932, p. 104.

asmuch as, in respect of legislative and executive authority, the Australian States and Canadian Provinces are partners with their Federal Parliaments, the same broad position will have to be recognized when the time arrives to deal with the relation between the Crown or its representative, and Ministers or Parliament possessing authority within the relevant constitutional unit.

In Canada the relation of the Provinces to the draft Statute of Westminster was most carefully considered. As the Report of the 1930 Imperial Conference stated,[1] certain of the Provinces of Canada had protested against action being taken to implement the 1929 Report (with its draft of the Statute of Westminster), until the matter was further considered in Canada. In February 1931 the Prime Minister of Canada invited the Provinces to attend a Conference in Ottawa for the purpose of considering what action should be taken. It was unanimously decided to protect the Provinces against the possibility of an amendment of the British North America Act by the Dominion Parliament's taking advantage of the Statute of Westminster. This protection was probably unnecessary, but it was agreed to be taken by way of further precaution. But it was also unanimously agreed that the Provinces, as well as the Dominion, should take the benefit of section 2 of the Statute of Westminster, so that the Colonial Laws Validity Act ceased to apply after December 11th, 1931, to provincial laws. Therefore section 2 of the Statute of Westminster, which withdraws from Dominion legislation any application of the Colonial Laws Validity Act, 1865, and which also prevents the nullifying of such legislation upon the ground of repugnancy to existing or future legislation of the Parliament at Westminster, is expressly extended to the Provinces of Canada.[2] The important point to notice about this express recognition of the status of the Canadian Provinces is that the self-governing powers of the Provinces were extended, so as to preserve their proper relation to those of the Dominion

[1] *Parliamentary Papers*, vol. xiv (1930–1), Cmd. 3717, p. 585.

[2] 22 Geo. V, c. 4, sec. 7 (2). By this sub-section, sec. 2 of the Statute is extended not only to laws made by any of the Provinces of Canada, but also to the powers of the legislatures of such Provinces.

Parliament. Yet the legal powers of the Australian States are relatively more extensive under the Australian scheme of Government than are those of the Provinces under that of Canada, where the Governor-General in Council possesses the power of appointing the Provincial Lieutenant-Governor.

One unexpected difficulty may be raised by the removal of the application of the Colonial Laws Validity Act to Canadian Provincial Constitutions. In reference to the States of Australia it has been authoritatively decided that the power of the Legislature for the time being includes the power of placing restrictions upon its successor, providing the restrictions themselves are also placed outside the power of abolition at the hands of a later Legislature (*Attorney-General for New South Wales* v. *Trethowan*).[1] The effect of this decision may not have been fully realized at the time, and Mr. Forgan Smith, the Labour Premier of Queensland, has seized upon it in order to entrench constitutional practice against interference at the hands of any subsequent Legislature.[2] Mr. Wheare's point, that the consequences of this decision are 'clearly likely to prove somewhat strange' and may go 'far beyond the intentions of the framers of the Act itself',[3] is directed to the fact that section 5 of the Colonial Laws Validity Act requires that Dominion legislation respecting the Constitution and powers of the Legislature itself shall have been passed in such 'manner and form' as is required for the time being by the existing law of the Dominion. If, however, by virtue of sections 2 and 7 (2) of the Statute of Westminster, the Colonial Laws Validity Act has no further application to the laws of a Canadian Province, or an Australian State (if and when the Statute of Westminster is applied to the latter), upon what basis will the future constitutional settlement of the Provinces and the States rest? In other words, will it be competent to the Legislature for the time being to amend its Constitution without any observance of

[1] [1932] A.C. 526.

[2] The practice entrenched is (*a*) that the life of Parliament should not be extended without popular approval, and (*b*) that a new House of Parliament should not be added to a uni-cameral Legislature without popular approval. See *ante*, pp. 199–200.

[3] K. C. Wheare, *Statute of Westminster* (1933), p. 38.

prior laws passed by itself? Will the Legislature be rendered unable to bind its successors? The question is of importance in Canada and in Australia because the removal of the operation of the Colonial Laws Validity Act may possibly be invoked to restore to the Legislature for the time being its power of ignoring existing restrictions upon its constitutional power. The difficulty, such as it is, should be capable of solution because, once a Dominion Legislature is given complete power to determine the form of the Dominion Constitution, without prejudicing, of course, the legal division of power between itself and the other members of the Federal system, there should be implied a power to adopt a form of Constitution which is binding. In other words, if it is a 'Constitution' at all, it should, by definition, bind the Legislature for the time being, as well as every other person and corporation within the constitutional unit concerned.[1]

In the Canadian House of Commons it was explained by Mr. Lapointe, in explanation of the non-inclusion of the Provinces within the recommendation of the 1929 Conference as to the Colonial Laws Validity Act, that 'the special Conference of 1929 could not make any such recommendation because we had no mandate from the provinces to ask for such a change'.[2] This statement recognized the principle that, so soon as any of the States of Australia sufficiently indicates a desire for application of the constitutional situation defined in 1926, 1929, 1930, and 1931, that desire should be carried into effect. Even Keith says that:

> 'The Conference [i.e. the Imperial Conference] has been at pains in no wise to suggest that the privileges which it accords to the Dominions should be denied so far as is appropriate to the States.'[3]

Unfortunately, as we have seen, Keith in his 1933 work suggested, upon reasoning which it is not easy, if it is possible, to accept, that the States and the Provinces may be regarded

[1] But it will, of course, be argued that the power of the Legislature for the time being includes a power to alter the Constitution. The truth is that the Statute of Westminster proceeded rather upon the assumption that the rights of the peoples of the Dominions could be identified with the powers of their Parliaments, an assumption that is not always true in fact.

[2] A. B. Keith, *Speeches and Documents on the British Dominions (1918–31)*, p. 260.

[3] Ibid. (Intro.), p. xliii.

as not affected by, or entitled to, the status to which their partners and co-sharers of constitutional power in the respective Federations have been freely admitted. The reasoning is not sound from a point of view of strict constitutional law, and makes too much of the mere non-representation, quite explicable in the circumstances, of the States and Provinces at the various Imperial Conferences. There is really no valid argument for denying to the Australian States and the Dominion Provinces a constitutional status in respect of internal affairs completely co-equal with the status of the central Governmental authorities. For the Courts not only recognize such equality of status in reference to internal affairs, they enforce it. It follows, of course, that no valid distinction can, or should, be drawn between the position of the Governor-General in relation to Ministers whose sole lawful authority is marked out by the Canadian and Australian Constitutional Statutes respectively, and the position of the Governors and Lieutenant-Governors of the States and Provinces in relation to Ministers whose sole lawful authority is marked out by the same two Statutes.

Additional note to p. 208.

In 1907 the States feared that their constitutional status would be impaired if they were not represented at the Imperial Conference of that year. Their exclusion created 'many possibilities of inconvenience and misunderstanding' (Harrison Moore, *Commonwealth of Australia* (2nd ed.), p. 353).

XXIII

TODD'S THESIS AS TO A GOVERNOR'S POWER TO REFUSE A DISSOLUTION

THE difficulty of appreciating the existing constitutional practice in relation to the Australian States and the Canadian Provinces is accentuated by the fact that it is mainly upon very old precedents that the leading work upon the subject (that of Todd) was based. It has also to be remembered that Todd's work was in many respects controversial in character. He was concerned in rebutting the theory that the political functions of the Crown have been 'wholly obliterated wherever a "parliamentary government" has been established'.[1] He regarded the office of Colonial Governor as that of a superintendent, and 'endeavoured to point out the beneficial effects resulting to the whole community from the exercise of this superintending office'.[2] He conceded that his work would express opinions upon the constitutional precedents different from those entertained by Canadian statesmen taking part in their consideration and settlement,[3] and, as he anticipated, his work 'evoked much personal abuse'.[4] Moreover, Todd's view, like that of his son, was suspicious of 'the *levelling* spirit so characteristic of the age'.[5]

Bagehot's view was not fundamentally different from that of Todd, but he adopted a more realistic and less devotional attitude. In his work on the English Constitution Bagehot was particularly intrigued with the position of the Colonial Governor. In analysing the position of the Sovereign in England he pointed out that the intervention upon occasion of 'an extrinsic, impartial, and capable authority'[6] would prove a check upon mere factiousness in a popular Assembly. He considered whether such a Head of a State had been discovered in the Colonial Governor. Certainly such a person was intelligent, and nearly always sure to be impartial, coming,

[1] Todd, *Parliamentary Government in the British Colonies* (2nd ed.), Preface, p. xiii.

[2] Ibid. [3] Ibid., p. xii. [4] Ibid., p. vi. [5] Ibid., p. v.

[6] Bagehot, *English Constitution* (5th ed.), p. 234.

as he did, from the other side of the earth. Yet there were grave disadvantages attached even to his position:

> 'A Colonial Governor is a ruler who has no permanent interest in the Colony he governs; who perhaps had to look for it in the map when he was sent thither; who takes years before he really understands its parties and its controversies; who, though without prejudice himself, is apt to be a slave to the prejudices of local people near him; who inevitably, and almost laudably, governs not in the interest of the Colony, which he may mistake, but in his own interest, which he sees and is sure of. . . . He is sure to leave upon the Colony the feeling that they have a ruler who only half knows them and does not so much as half care for them.'[1]

But it is still of value to analyse Todd's treatment of some of the earlier precedents. We shall deal first with those relating to the Governor's discretionary power to refuse a dissolution of a Colonial Assembly:

1. In 1872 the Duffy administration was defeated in the Assembly of Victoria upon a resolution of no confidence. The Cabinet thereupon presented to the Governor, Lord Canterbury, a memorandum, which asserted that:

> 'In England it may be said to have become a maxim of constitutional law that the alternative of resignation or dissolution is left absolutely to the discretion and responsibility of ministers.'[2]

Todd said that the memorandum

> 'inferred, from this erroneous assumption (as to English practice) that a similar rule should be recognized, equally without qualification, as applicable to the colonies.'[3]

But the Duffy memorandum mentioned four conditions in which a dissolution of Parliament was said to be justifiable. They were as follows:

> '(1) When a vote of "no confidence" is carried against a government which has not already appealed to the country; (2) when there are reasonable grounds to believe that an adverse vote against the Government does not represent the opinions and wishes of the country, and would be reversed by a new parliament; (3) when the existing Parliament was elected under the auspices of the opponents of the Government; (4) when the majority against a Government

[1] Bagehot, *English Constitution* (5th ed.), p. 235.

[2] Todd, *Parliamentary Government in the British Colonies* (2nd ed.), p. 772.

[3] Ibid.

is so small as to make it improbable that a strong Government can be formed from the opposition.'[1]

The Governor's reply to the request was that the fact that the Sovereign in England had not refused a dissolution 'of late years' did not warrant the inference as to the British practice made by the memorandum. Lord Canterbury said that Colonial Governors 'are personally responsible to the Crown' and that no Governor could divest himself of such responsibility, especially in relation to dissolution. He referred to the four instances mentioned by the Duffy Cabinet, and refused to admit that any or all of the circumstances mentioned therein 'would, under all conceivable circumstances, and without any reference whatever to any other fact or facts, however important, justify a dissolution'.[2] The Governor deemed it his duty in the circumstances to decline the advice to dissolve, whereupon the Duffy Government resigned, Mr. Francis was sent for, and a new administration was formed which was found to possess the confidence of Parliament.

Todd's view of the case was that the refusal was 'a great hardship to the Duffy Ministry', because it would probably have succeeded at the polls, but that Lord Canterbury was right when he

> 'vindicated for himself a "constitutional discretion" to decide as to the expediency or otherwise, upon grounds of public policy, whether or not to grant an appeal to the country to this defeated administration.'[3]

Todd was very careful to guard against the acceptance of the view that a Ministry in England is entitled to claim from the Crown a dissolution upon being defeated in Parliament, even if Parliament has been elected under the auspices of the Ministry's political opponents. His view was that

> 'it is not a legitimate use of the prerogative of dissolution to resort to it when there is no important political question upon which contending parties are directly at issue, and merely in order to maintain in power the particular ministers who are in office at the time.'[4]

Perhaps the most important feature of the precedent is one

[1] Ibid., pp. 771–2. [2] Ibid., p. 772. [3] Ibid., p. 773.
[4] Ibid., p. 774.

to which Todd gave no special attention. Lord Canterbury's decision may have been right or wrong, but his statement was, and still is, of value in testing the theory that there exists an absolute and automatic rule which can be applied by the Governor in dealing with all questions of dissolution.

Many years later Sir Charles Gavan Duffy in discussing the case said that he 'had reason . . . to know the Cabinet in London regarded (his memorandum) as entitling me to a dissolution',[1] that the business of Lord Canterbury in the Colonies 'was to increase his balance at the Banker's',[2] that the adverse vote of the Assembly was affected by assurances from quarters close to the Governor that members 'need have no fear of a dissolution as the Governor would not grant one',[3] and that the Governor's power or prerogative 'was employed to betray the interests of the community to the opulent minority'.[4] But it cannot be disputed that Canterbury's statement of constitutional practice was most valuable.

2. In 1871 the Governor of South Australia, Sir James Fergusson, agreed to grant a dissolution to Ministers who had been defeated on a vote of no confidence, carried against them only by the casting vote of the Speaker. Both Houses of Parliament then addressed the Governor, praying him to dismiss his Ministers at once, and not to grant them a dissolution. The Governor refused this request, holding that

> 'under the existing circumstances he did not feel justified in refusing to his advisers the appeal which they desired to make to the constituencies from the vote of the House.'[5]

This precedent illustrates that under certain circumstances a popular Assembly which votes no confidence may be unable to induce the Governor to refrain from granting Ministers a dissolution. It also shows the absence of any definite constitutional rule upon the subject of dissolution, and tends to bewilder the student endeavouring to find a thread of general principle running through the precedents.

[1] Sir Charles Gavan Duffy, *My Life in Two Hemispheres*, vol. ii, p. 341.

[2] Ibid. [3] Ibid.

[4] Ibid. These imputations are occasionally inevitable. The extent of the reserve powers being undefined, a Governor is subjected to blame as well as praise.

[5] Todd, *Parliamentary Government in the British Colonies* (2nd ed.), p. 771.

3. In 1872 the Stafford administration was defeated upon a motion of no confidence carried by the New Zealand House of Representatives. The Ministry was only a few weeks old, their predecessors having resigned also upon a resolution of no confidence. Mr. Stafford argued from these facts 'that no party in the present House was strong enough to command a reliable working majority'.[1] But the decision of Governor Bowen was against a dissolution. He pointed out that the Parliament, though elected for five years, was only eighteen months old, and he was not satisfied that a dissolution would have any material effect upon the state of the parties. Thereupon a new administration assumed office, and, obtaining a working majority in the Legislature, 'proved unmistakably that the general sentiment of parliament and of the country was in favour of the course pursued by Governor Bowen on this occasion'.[2]

4. In 1877 Sir George Grey, the then Premier of New Zealand, asked for a dissolution. His predecessors had been defeated in October 1877. A vote against the Grey Ministry was defeated by the House of Representatives in November upon the casting vote of the Speaker. A second motion of no confidence was then proposed, and it was during the debate that Grey asked for a dissolution of Parliament. The request was refused by Lord Normanby upon a number of grounds. He pointed out that Parliament was only in its second session, and that no important political issue was at stake. Sir George Grey sought to bring in aid the English practice, declaring that he should be regarded as entitled to a dissolution. The Governor replied that the legal power of dissolution was, by the terms of the Constitution, vested in him, that the Royal Instructions enabled him to prorogue or dissolve the Assembly, notwithstanding the opposition of Ministers, and that he 'could not admit that ministers have an unqualified right to a dissolution when the Governor may consider it undesirable or unnecessary'.[3]

Shortly afterwards Parliament was prorogued, but the Premier soon renewed his application for a dissolution, and was again refused. The Governor submitted the question at

[1] Ibid., p. 774.
[2] Ibid., p. 775.
[3] Ibid., p. 777.

issue to the Secretary of State for the Colonies, Sir M. Hicks-Beach. The ruling was that:

'The responsibility, which is a grave one, of deciding whether, in any particular case, it is right and expedient, having regard to the claims of the respective parties in parliament, and to the general interests of the Colony, that a dissolution should be granted, must, under the constitution, rest with the Governor. In discharging his responsibility, he will, of course, pay the greatest attention to any representations that may be made to him by those who, at the time, are his constitutional advisers; but, if he should feel himself bound to take the responsibility of not following his ministers' recommendation, there can, I apprehend, be no doubt that both law and practice empower him to do so.'[1]

It will be observed that this decision of the Imperial authorities asserted in unequivocal terms that the Governor possessed a discretionary power to ignore the request of Ministers for a dissolution of Parliament. Further, the dispatch did not make it sufficiently clear that it was an essential part of constitutional practice that political responsibility for the Governor's decision should be shouldered by Ministers whether they asked for a dissolution and retained office after its refusal, or whether they succeeded to office after the former Ministers who advised dissolution had resigned. The Instructions to the Governor (which on this point are not distinguishable from those operating in respect of the States of Australia even to-day)[2] seemed rather to suggest that if the Governor, as he might, acted against Ministerial advice, and reported his action to the Colonial Office, he could assume personal responsibility for his action. The error of such 'personal responsibility' was not sufficiently emphasized before the Harcourt dispatches of 1914 (one affecting Tasmania, the other South Africa).[3]

5. In 1879 a vote of no confidence was carried against the Crowther Ministry in Tasmania, though the majority was only one. Thereupon Governor Weld was approached with a view to the grant of a dissolution. Ministers pointed out that parties were fairly equally divided and they were advocating a distinct policy calling for the decision of the country.

[1] Todd, *Parliamentary Government in the British Colonies* (2nd ed.), p. 778.
[2] See *ante*, Chap. XIV. [3] See *ante*, Chaps. IV and XX (A).

The Governor refused the advice. He pointed out that he was not satisfied that there was any sharp division between parties upon any important political issue, that the House was only two years old, that it was elected under the auspices of the party then in office, and that there was no probability that a general election would alter the strength of parties.[1] Accordingly a dissolution was refused, Ministers resigned, and the Opposition leader succeeded in forming an administration.

Previously, in 1877, a dissolution was granted by Governor Weld to the Fysh Ministry. In a dispatch to the Colonial Secretary the Governor stated that

> 'in all cases the representative of the Crown should be more careful in granting a dissolution than the Crown might be in England, as he must sometimes be advised by ministers not sufficiently determined to waive small party advantages, somewhat accustomed occasionally to the sledge-hammer style of political warfare, and not uniformly imbued with that constitutional knowledge and spirit which often seems hereditary and is generally inherent in British Statesmen.'[2]

The Governor had prepared a memorandum with reference to the question of supplies that

> 'he had no right to suppose that parliament would depart from the most usual and most constitutional course of voting necessary supplies for the period that must elapse before the meeting of the new parliament.'[3]

The Governor was of opinion 'that nothing but the most extreme and clear public necessity would justify the Crown in dissolving after supplies had been refused'.[4] In the event, supplies were granted, Parliament was dissolved, and the Colonial Secretary expressed approval of the Governor's action.

The two Weld precedents cannot be regarded as laying down any definite constitutional rule. The discretion of the Governor was asserted in each case, and certainly upon considerations which would not be open to a constitutional Monarch or Governor at the present day. How, for instance,

[1] Todd, *Parliamentary Government in the British Colonies* (2nd ed.), pp. 785–7.

[2] Ibid., p. 784. [3] Ibid., p. 785. [4] Ibid.

can it be predicted that a general election would or would not be likely to 'materially alter the strength of parties'? In truth, the Governor, at any rate up to the nineties, assumed the role of supreme political superintendent and also that of political prophet. As time went on the more preposterous reasons for the exercise of discretionary powers came to be abandoned.

6. The last precedent discussed by Todd in relation to refusals of dissolutions is that of the Joly administration in Quebec in 1879. Ministers were defeated by six votes upon a question regarded by them as a vote of no confidence. The Premier stated to Lieutenant-Governor Robitaille that he believed that his Government would succeed upon an immediate appeal to the people. The latter stated that:

> 'It must not be forgotten that the privilege of dissolving parliament is one of the most valued prerogatives of the sovereign, and that it is the right and duty of the representative of the Crown to control its exercise.'[1]

The Lieutenant-Governor pointed out that the administration had already obtained one dissolution, and added:

> 'Is it in the public interest that the province should be subjected so frequently to general elections? Is it in accord with the spirit of the constitution that parliament should be dissolved so often? Is the renewal at such brief intervals of the popular representation of a nature to ensure the stability and the good working of our political institutions? To all these questions the lieutenant-governor deems it his duty to answer—No. The wise authority awarded to us by the constitution which we enjoy has decided that general elections for this province should take place every four years, and this period is not so long that it should be still further shortened without reasons of extraordinary gravity.'[2]

The Lieutenant-Governor concluded that in all the circumstances Parliament being only eighteen months old, and the Ministry having itself procured the last dissolution, it was his duty to decline to dissolve. Thereupon the Leader of the Opposition formed an administration and the Joly Ministry resigned.[3]

It should be noted that Todd describes the statement of

[1] Todd, *Parliamentary Government in the British Colonies* (2nd ed.), p. 797.
[2] Ibid., pp. 797–8.
[3] Ibid., p. 799.

the Lieutenant-Governor as containing an 'excellent' exposition of the constitutional position.[1] It is certainly in accordance with Todd's view as to the principle applicable to requests by Ministers for a dissolution, for Todd's conclusion from the precedents is that

> 'the power of dissolution rests absolutely and exclusively with the governor or lieutenant-governor for the time being. He is personally responsible to the Crown for the lawful exercise of this prerogative, but he is likewise bound to take into account the welfare of the people, being unable to divest himself of a grave moral responsibility towards the Colony he is commissioned to govern.'[2]

Over and over again Todd takes up this position. He declares that a Governor is justified in withholding a dissolution if he thinks it is being asked for the purpose of strengthening a particular party. He is always 'free to make trial' of an existing Assembly instead of granting Ministers, who have been defeated, a dissolution.[3] On the other hand, the Governor may grant a dissolution, even though both branches of the Legislature or one branch may remonstrate against the proposed appeal.[4]

Further, he asserts that a Governor is entitled to stipulate for such conditions as he thinks fit in the public interest before he exercises the power of dissolution. In such a case, Todd asserts, he may defer his final decision until he ascertains whether the conditions which he desires to impose have been complied with.

The declarations represent fairly accurately the general attitude of the Colonial Office at the time when Todd produced his *magnum opus* on Colonial Government. But Todd is careful to emphasize the principle of ministerial responsibility which many of the official dispatches omit from mention, notwithstanding its great importance. He says that,

> 'If an existing administration be not prepared to accept the governor's decision in regard to a proposed dissolution and to assume responsibility for the same, they are bound to resign office and give place to other ministers who are willing to facilitate—and to become responsible to parliament and to the country for—the intended exercise of the royal prerogative.'[5]

[1] Ibid. [2] Ibid., p. 800. [3] Ibid., p. 801.
[4] Ibid., pp. 801–2. [5] Ibid., p. 803.

This passage of Todd, whilst referring in general terms to the Governor's decision 'in regard to' dissolution, and so appearing to include cases of a refusal of a dissolution, as well as of grants, is intended to apply to the case of the Governor's dissolving Parliament against the advice of an existing administration.

At an earlier stage of his work Todd says that

> 'whilst this prerogative, as all others in our constitutional system, can only be administered upon the advice of counsellors prepared to assume full responsibility for the governor's decision, the governor must be himself the judge of the necessity for a dissolution.'[1]

This statement is not free from ambiguity, and it also seems to suggest that Todd did not expressly direct his consideration to the case where the Governor refused the Ministers' advice to dissolve. In such an event Ministers might resign, so that the incoming Ministers could be visited with responsibility for the Governor's refusal. But what was to be the position if, notwithstanding the Governor's refusal of their request to dissolve, Ministers remained in office? The modern view in such a case was expressed in the Harcourt dispatch of 1914[2]—that Ministers must themselves 'accept responsibility' for the Governor's refusal.

Todd was concerned to emphasize that the real responsibility for the crucial decision on dissolution lay with the Governor, and not at all with Ministers. But if his decision was that Parliament ought to be dissolved, constitutional practice required that a Minister should sign the Governor's proclamation and so assume responsibility for what was in truth the act of the Governor alone. But if the Governor refused a request to dissolve, no official record or even pronouncement was required. Todd seemed to make it clear that Ministers whose advice to dissolve had been rejected were not in the position of having to accept full responsibility for the Governor's decision, although they remained in office.

In August 1892 the New Zealand Ministers appealed to the Colonial Secretary in reference to a dispute between them and the Governor as to proposed appointments to the Legis-

[1] Todd, *Parliamentary Government in the British Colonies* (2nd ed.), pp. 800–1.

[2] See *ante*, Chap. IV.

lative Council, and proceeded to justify their decision not to resign, although their advice had been declined, by reference to a statement from Todd to the effect that Ministers

> 'would be responsible for the advice they gave, but could not strictly be held accountable for their advice not having prevailed; for if it be the right and duty of the governor to act in any case contrary to the advice of his ministers, they cannot be held responsible for his action, and should not feel themselves justified in retiring from the administration'.[1]

According to Todd's view the reality of the matter was that responsibility rested upon the Governor whether he decided to dissolve against advice, or to refuse to dissolve although advised to do so. In the event of his deciding to dissolve *against* the advice of Ministers, the opponents of the latter would seldom be sufficiently disinterested to repudiate, upon purely constitutional questions, the Governor's action and to refuse to conduct the government pending the election.

It has been observed that Todd overstated the real discretionary authority and reserve power of the Governor. Bryce said that

> 'there is always a tendency in Colonists (perceptible even now in the works of such a writer as the Canadian publicist, Mr. Todd) to overestimate the importance of the Crown, whose conspicuous position as the authority common to the whole empire makes it an object of special interest and respect to persons living at a distance. It touches their imagination, whereas assemblies excite their criticism'.[2]

No doubt the real reserve authority and power of the Sovereign and of his representative in the Colonies was somewhat over-emphasized by Todd. But the opposing tendency, mainly of Whig origin, was equally calculated to produce a false impression by under-estimating the reserve powers of the Crown. A sharp check to Todd's over-emphasis was given by the answering dispatch sent by the Colonial Secretary, the Marquis of Ripon, in September 1892, to the Governor of New Zealand. As noted above, this decision of the Colonial Secretary related to the question of Legislative

[1] Todd, *Parliamentary Government in the British Colonies* (2nd ed.), p. 822.
[2] Bryce, *American Commonwealth* (2nd ed.), vol. i, p. 26 (note 1).

Council appointments, but it soon assumed general importance. It stated:

> 'When questions of a constitutional character are involved it is especially, I conceive, the right of the governor fully to discuss with his ministers the desirability of any particular course that may be pressed upon him for his adoption. He should frankly state the objections, if any, which may occur to him; but if, after full discussion, ministers determine to press upon him the advice which they have already tendered, the governor should, as a general rule, and when Imperial interests are not affected, accept that advice, bearing in mind that the responsibility rests with the ministers, who are answerable to the legislature and, in the last resort, to the country.'[1]

Now the Ripon dispatch proceeds upon a different principle from those which Todd had enunciated. The dispatch was sent about eight years after Todd's death. Broadly speaking it places the onus for the exercise of *all* legal powers vested in the Governor (including what would be, in England, prerogative or common law powers, but which, in New Zealand and the other Colonies, were usually embodied in Statute Law), not upon the Governor, but upon the Ministers. The dispatch was concerned with appointments to the Legislative Council. But such matter was itself of very great importance because control of the Council by Ministers possessing the confidence of the Lower House necessarily involved full legislative authority upon all subjects.

Yet exceptional cases were provided for in the Ripon dispatch, for the general doctrine it asserted was to apply 'as a general rule and when Imperial interests are not affected'. This still left open an area for the exercise of discretion, though a smaller area than Todd would have agreed to. It may be noted that the dispatch was sent during a Liberal administration, Mr. Gladstone having taken office in August 1892.

[1] Todd, *Parliamentary Government in the British Colonies* (2nd ed.), p. 823.

XXIV

THE GRANT OF DISSOLUTION IN VICTORIA IN 1908–9

IN December 1908 Sir Thomas Carmichael, Governor of Victoria, granted a dissolution of the Legislative Assembly to the Premier, Sir Thomas Bent, who had been defeated by a majority of twelve on a direct vote of no confidence. The latter stated to the Governor that he

'felt confident that in the event of a dissolution being granted the country would be found to side with the Government.

'He said further that he believed that if asked to do so, either Mr. Prendergast, the Leader of the (Labour) Opposition, or Mr. Murray, the mover of the resolution on which the Government was beaten, would be willing, and probably able, to form a Ministry in the present House, but in neither of these cases could such a Ministry be permanent. He could not advise the Governor to ask either Mr. Prendergast or Mr. Murray to take office, but he did advise him to grant a dissolution, as desired by the Cabinet.'[1]

The Governor gave the following written answer to the request:

'In the matter of granting or refusing a dissolution the Governor considers that he can only refuse to act on the advice of Ministers if he feels that in doing so his action would be supported by the constituencies. At the present time, especially in view of the elections involved by the recent reconstruction of the Ministry, he sees no indications to lead him to suppose that the constituencies would prefer any other set of men as Ministers to the present Ministry; the Governor, therefore, is prepared to act on the advice of Sir Thomas Bent and grant a dissolution.'[2]

After the defeat of the Bent Ministry at the general elections, the Governor, answering an address from the Assembly dated February 10th, 1909, referred to a further memorandum which he had prepared in December 1908, setting forth the considerations which had led him to decide in favour of dissolution. This may be summarized thus:

1. The Premier 'recognised that, especially on the matter of a

[1] *Votes and Proceedings, Legislative Assembly* (*Victoria*). *First Session,* 1909, p. 213. [2] Ibid., p. 214.

proposed dissolution, the advice of a Premier who had lost the confidence of the House must be received with caution; but he was prepared to support his views by argument'.

2. 'Two courses were open to me—to follow the Premier's advice and dissolve; or to reject his advice, ask him to tender his resignation, and endeavour to find a member of one of the two Houses to form an administration. My duty was to take the course which I thought most likely to meet with the approval of the constituencies.'

3. 'The majority in favour of the vote of no confidence was made up of fifteen members of the Labour Party, who never had any confidence in Sir Thomas Bent's Ministry, and 22 former supporters who had lost confidence in it; but who, both at the last general election, and apparently still, were opposed to the Labour Party. The 25 members who, by voting against the motion, showed their confidence in the Cabinet, were the most numerous section in the House. It was obvious that no Leader could form a stable Government in the Assembly then existing unless he could command support from two of these sections. The Premier assured me that his supporters would continue to oppose the Labour Party, and were not likely to be friendly to those non-Labour members who had voted against him. I carefully considered Mr. Prendergast's position as Leader of the Opposition. The Labour Party, in their attitude to politics, claim to stand exactly as they did at the last election. Mr. Prendergast, therefore, with only fifteen followers, could not command the confidence of the House, unless there had been a change in the attitude of a considerable number of non-Labour members towards him. Of this there was no evidence. It would not have been fair to the Labour Party themselves to have asked their Leader to form a Ministry, unless I was prepared to allow him to appeal at once to the electors. And, as I saw no sign that the constituencies, which had hitherto been so opposed to Mr. Prendergast's Party as to return fifty members against it and only fifteen in its favour, would like an appeal made to the country made by him, I did not feel justified in asking Mr. Prendergast to form an Administration. I could find no evidence of Mr. Murray having ever been regarded as a Leader in the House, and nothing had been disclosed in debate on his motion to show that anything had arisen to give him that position. The majority which had supported him, though large, seemed to me entirely formed to carry that one motion; two of those who voted with him deliberately expressed doubt as to following him in anything else; some were well known to be hostile to the Labour Party, with whose representatives they then voted;

others had shown by their speeches that they were divided among themselves on the land question, with which it was generally expected that the Government would shortly deal; and nothing showed that the Labour Party meant to give him further support.

In my opinion any Ministry formed at that moment by Mr. Murray could have had no real stability; and I saw nothing to lead me to think that he, rather than the present Ministry, ought to appeal to the country at a dissolution.'

4. 'To sum up' the evidence before me led me to believe that even if the constituencies, in spite of the recent by-elections which were the only clear indications of opinion, and which were in favour of the Government, did desire a change of Ministry, there was no proof that they wished for either Mr. Murray or Mr. Prendergast as Premier—that as there was no apparent probability of either of those gentlemen being able at that moment to form a stable Government, and as I knew of nothing entitling me to invite any one else to try to do so, I had no reasonable grounds for differing from the Premier's view that dissolution was inevitable; that a dissolution at Christmas time would not increase the popularity of the Government, and that, therefore, I should not give the Premier any unfair advantage, if, in the absence of clear indications of desire in the country for any other definite leader, or for a policy other than that which his Government professed, I allowed him to appeal to the electors.'

5. 'It was my duty to act in local matters on the advice of the Ministry, as expressed by the Premier, unless I was prepared to find other advisers better able than they to conduct His Majesty's Government, or unless I felt that their advice was contrary to the feelings of the country. I do not believe that I could at that moment find such advisers, and I felt that if I refused to accept the advice of the Premier I should be doing so without reasonable certainty of my action being supported by the constituencies.'[1]

This memorandum has been referred to in detail because it is of significance as illustrating the technique of a Governor's method of exercising his discretion when a dissolution is requested by a defeated Ministry, at a time when the popular House does not consist of two parties only, but of three or more groups, the likelihood of whose co-operation in Government is a material question. The stated grounds for the Governor's action call for some comment.

[1] *Votes and Proceedings, Legislative Assembly* (*Victoria*), *First Session*, 1909, pp. 214-15.

1. The first statement of Sir Thomas Carmichael rejected the theory that an existing Ministry possessed an absolute right to a dissolution. A contrary view was accepted by both Premier and Governor, viz. that the advice of Ministers after their defeat 'must be received with caution'.

2. The second proposition that 'approval of the constituencies' was to be the guiding consideration for the Governor is very difficult of application because, if a dissolution is to be refused, no consultation of the constituencies can take place at all. Further, the electorate, if consulted, will not necessarily, or at all, be expressing any opinion of the Governor's action in having accepted advice to dissolve. Modern experience suggests that, whatever the circumstances which lead to a dissolution, the electoral verdict will be determined at least as much by ordinary considerations of rival policy as by the supposed merits or demerits of the Governor's constitutional opinions or action.

3. The third statement of the Governor is given at length in order to illustrate how carefully he considered the possibilities of an alternative Government, which might be able to stabilize the parliamentary situation. It may be observed that the Governor did not consult with the leaders of the parliamentary groups as to the chances of their successfully forming an administration. This illustrates the danger of assuming that, in cases where the Monarch or his Dominion representative has granted a dissolution and there has been no consultation of other party leaders, there has been no full consideration of the parliamentary situation. In particular, why should it be assumed that, when the King granted a dissolution to Mr. MacDonald in 1924, he did not consider all the possibilities of an alternative Ministry, just as Sir Thomas Carmichael did in 1908?[1]

4. The fourth statement of the Governor sums up in a convenient form many of the considerations which led to his decision.

5. The fifth statement of Sir Thomas Carmichael is somewhat confusing, as suggesting that the advice of Ministers to dissolve might properly be refused so long as there was 'reasonable certainty' of the Governor's action being 'sup-

[1] See *ante*, pp. 63 and 66.

ported by the constituencies'. The Assembly had been elected in March 1907, so that about half the duration of its normal life remained. If the Governor refused a dissolution, the constituencies would not, or might not, be appealed to until after a considerable lapse of time. It is easy enough to understand, if not to accept, the theory that, when a dissolution is requested, a relevant consideration is that the Ministers who advise such act will probably be returned to power. But the theory of popular endorsement can hardly apply to a case where the decision that no dissolution should be granted prevents the possibility either of popular approval or disapproval.

XXV

TWO RECENT EXERCISES OF THE POWER OF DISSOLUTION IN THE COMMONWEALTH

SINCE the Imperial Conference of 1926 there have been two dissolutions of the House of Representatives which should be considered.

In September 1929 the Prime Minister, Mr. Bruce, obtained a dissolution from Lord Stonehaven. The latter was informed by the Prime Minister that, in Committee of the House, the Maritime Industries Bill, which altered the existing system of Commonwealth industrial arbitration in certain respects, had been amended by a vote declaring that the Bill should not be brought into operation until submitted to a referendum or an election. Mr. Bruce pointed out to the Governor-General that:

> 'The Constitution makes no provision for a referendum of this description, and the Commonwealth Parliament has no power to pass effective legislation for the holding of such a referendum. The Government is, however, prepared to accept the other alternative, namely, a general election.'[1]

The Prime Minister's request for a dissolution then proceeded:

> 'I therefore formally advise Your Excellency to grant a dissolution of the House of Representatives, and I now inform you that I propose to ask Parliament for the necessary financial provision to carry on the public services until after the election has been held.'[2]

The Prime Minister's memorandum dated September 11th, 1929, was replied to by Lord Stonehaven on the following day. He said that he 'had carefully considered the question which it (the letter) raises',[3] noted the proposal to ask for supply, and concluded: 'In view of this assurance I accept the advice tendered by you.'[4]

The existing parliamentary situation was as follows. Parliament was but ten months old. Mr. Scullin, the leader of

[1] *Commonwealth Parliamentary Debates*, Sept. 12th, 1929, p. 873.
[2] Ibid. [3] Ibid., pp. 873–4. [4] Ibid.

the Labour Opposition, said that the Prime Minister 'has accepted a grave responsibility in advising the Governor-General to dissolve it, and His Excellency a grave responsibility in accepting the advice'.[1] The Government had been defeated because a number of its supporters took the view that the Government possessed no electoral mandate for the proposed legislation. Under the circumstances it was highly improbable that Mr. Scullin, the Labour leader, could have formed a Ministry which would have been able to carry on in the House of Representatives. Neither the Prime Minister nor the Governor-General, so far as their correspondence discloses, paid any attention to the 'parliamentary situation' in the older sense of the doctrine that the House should be exhausted before a dissolution is granted. But it should be pointed out that the form of the amendment carried by the House of Representatives itself suggested a submission of the Bill to the people, either at a referendum or at a general election. In the circumstances the House could properly be regarded as having not only authorized, but invited, its own dissolution, especially as the Bill had previously been declared by the House to be an urgent measure. The precedent is very special in character, and no general inference can safely be drawn from it.

The next precedent to which attention should be called is the dissolution of the House in November 1931. Mr. Scullin was then Prime Minister, being supported by the majority of the Labour party. A separate group of Labour members from New South Wales, led by Mr. Beasley, was, at the time, acting independently of the Government, and giving general support to the financial proposals of Mr. Lang, the New South Wales Labour Premier.[2] Mr. Beasley moved the adjournment of the House of Representatives in order to discuss the method adopted by the Government in selecting men for employment under the terms of a Federal grant for unemployment relief. The motion was directed towards the holding of an inquiry, by Select Committee or otherwise, as to the allegation that discrimination was being exercised by the Government against those unemployed persons who were supporters, not of the Federal, but of the New South Wales,

[1] Ibid., p. 874.

[2] Cf. *ante*, p. 157.

Labour organization. The then Federal Treasurer, Mr. Theodore, dismissed the allegation as 'puerile'. But the Prime Minister, in his speech, said that 'if Honourable members wished to take the business of the House out of the hands of the Government they can have an election'.[1] The motion for adjournment was carried by a majority of five votes. The Prime Minister, on November 26th, informed the Governor-General that the adjournment motion was carried 'by a combination of the Nationalist party, the Country party, and the group led by Mr. Beasley'.[2] He then asked the Governor-General (Sir Isaac Isaacs) to grant a dissolution of the House of Representatives.

The Governor-General granted the request in a communication made on November 26th. He stated that 'in view of the present constitutional position of the Governor-General of a Dominion, as determined by the Imperial Conference of 1926, confirmed by that of 1930',[3] it was his duty to accept the advice tendered.[4] He then proceeded to state two separate grounds for his decision.

First of all, the Governor-General said,

> 'For the principles upon which I act, I make reference to various works by Professor Berriedale Keith, in which passages occur relating to the duty of a Governor-General in such a case as the present.'[5]

One of the passages from Keith referred to by the Governor-General, which contained the reference[6] to Mr. Asquith's 'obvious . . . decline in mental power' has been mentioned earlier in this work. So far as Keith asserted in unqualified terms that neither the Sovereign nor his representative was endowed with any discretion to refuse a dissolution—his assertion has already been analysed and criticized.

But, in considering whether the grant of a dissolution by Sir Isaac Isaacs was justified, the most significant passage in the Governor-General's memorandum on the question is the last sentence, which suggests that, apart from the general principles adopted since the Canadian crisis of 1926,

> 'there are considerations in the known circumstances which tend to

[1] *Commonwealth Parliamentary Debates*, vol. 132, Nov. 25th, 1931, p. 1899. [2] Ibid., p. 1926. [3] Ibid. [4] Ibid. [5] Ibid. [6] *Ante*, pp. 4, 66.

support the acceptance of the advice tendered to me. They are such as the strength and relation of various parties in the House of Representatives and the probability in any case of an early election being necessary.'[1]

The factors in the parliamentary situation not already referred to were that the House of Representatives had run two years of its normal period of three years, that, in any event, it was necessary that an election for eighteen of the thirty-six senators should be held early in the year 1932, and that it was agreed on all sides that, in order to prevent waste of public money, the House of Representatives should be elected at the same time as the Senators. In all the circumstances the Governor-General felt able to infer that no alternative Ministry was reasonably possible.

Whilst, therefore, it is quite impossible to say that the Governor-General's action was not warranted, he would certainly have been justified in getting in touch with the other party leaders, including Mr. Beasley, particularly as the latter disclaimed any intention of doing more than forcing an inquiry into a subordinate aspect of Government administration. The Governor-General's failure to take these steps cannot be imputed to him as error, particularly in view of the grave lack of certainty as to the constitutional position. An unfortunate aspect of the precedent is the Governor-General's expressed reliance upon an opinion which so unfairly attacks a great Prime Minister and constitutional authority.[2]

[1] Ibid., Nov. 26th, 1931, p. 1927.
[2] Lord Oxford and Asquith. See *ante*, pp. 4, 66, 236.

XXVI

TWO OLDER PRECEDENTS AFFECTING THE GOVERNOR'S POWER OF DISMISSAL

1. IN 1878 the Governor of Cape Colony, Sir Bartle Frere, dismissed the Molteno administration, after a prolonged dispute had arisen in relation to the military authority exercisable by the Governor. At the time the Colony was threatened with a Kaffir outbreak. The Premier advised the withdrawal of the Imperial troops from the Colony, and was of opinion that the Colonial forces should be under the control of Ministers. Further, a member of the Ministry was actually appointed to take charge of the forces. The Governor asserted that, as Commander-in-Chief, he could not be stripped of his individual responsibility for the military situation; and he expressed the opinion that it would be utter madness for him to accept Ministers' advice to send away the Imperial troops, and to depend entirely upon the Colonial forces to suppress rebellion. Ministers ignored the protest, and proceeded to direct certain military operations, and make certain military appointments without the Governor's approval. Finally, on February 2nd, 1878, the Ministers were dismissed. In March 1878 a dispatch from the Colonial Secretary pointed out that the Governor also occupied the position of Queen's High Commissioner in respect to territories adjacent to Cape Colony, and that these territories were also threatened with invasion by hostile tribes. In these circumstances the Colonial Secretary stated that:

> 'In civil matters lying entirely within the Cape colony, I desire of course that the responsibility of your ministers, for the time being, should be as full and complete as in other Colonies under the same form of government, but in affairs such as those in which you have recently engaged, your functions are clearly defined by the terms of your commission.'[1]

The new Premier, Mr. Sprigg, readily accepted responsibility for the Governor's action in dismissing his predecessors,

[1] Todd, *Parliamentary Government in the British Colonies* (2nd ed.), p. 383.

and, upon the meeting of the Assembly, the action of the Governor was endorsed. Mr. Merriman moved a resolution directed against the Governor, but the latter relied upon

> 'the constitutional power of the governor to inform ministers that they have lost his confidence, and to summon other ministers to office, subject to the necessity of their securing the support of parliament'.[1]

This is an interesting precedent. The Conservative party held office in England. The Secretary of State, in dealing with the Governor's first Report, said that it was

> 'of the first importance that the earliest possible opportunity should be taken of affording such full explanations to your parliament as may enable a clear and impartial judgment to be formed upon the course adopted'.[2]

Precisely the same condition—that of parliamentary support—was emphasized by Governor Frere himself in his own dispatch of May 1878. In the final Report the Governor referred to his having taken 'the extreme step',[3] but considered that he had not trespassed beyond

> 'what, in the estimation of the colony and its representatives, was necessary to uphold the authority of the Crown . . . when circumstances did not admit of an immediate appeal to the parliament of the colony'.[4]

The period which elapsed between Mr. Molteno's dismissal and the meeting of the Assembly was three months.

The case should be carefully distinguished from those cases in which the Ministers who are dismissed not only possess, but are reasonably certain of retaining, the confidence of the existing Assembly. Governor Frere's action is occasionally relied upon as establishing a very general principle, but all it seems to show is that, under such special circumstances as existed in 1878, especially when Parliament is in recess, a Governor may even dismiss Ministers and assume primary responsibility for a grave military decision, providing that his action is approved by the Assembly after it meets. The action of dismissing Ministers in such special circumstances, though admittedly quite outside the ordinary domain

[1] Ibid., p. 387.
[2] Ibid., p. 383.
[3] Ibid., p. 387.
[4] Ibid.

of constitutional practice, does not involve so violent an exercise of the prerogative as where the legal power of dismissal is exercised against a Ministry although it is quite certain that the Governor's action would be immediately repudiated by Parliament. In the latter case, one grave act of personal prerogative must necessarily be followed by an even graver—dissolution must follow upon dismissal.

2. A very important case of the exercise of the power of dismissal was the Canadian constitutional crisis in 1878, when Lieutenant-Governor Letellier (of the Province of Quebec) dismissed the De Boucherville Ministry. According to Todd the Lieutenant-Governor was aggrieved because his recommendations on public affairs had not received proper consideration from Ministers, and the latter, both in regard to administration and legislation, acted not only against the Lieutenant-Governor's will but often without his knowledge.[1] The Lieutenant-Governor also believed that Ministers had yielded to pressure exerted by members of the Legislature in order to procure the expenditure of public money upon the construction of certain railways. The leader of the Opposition, M. Joly, was commissioned to form an administration. He was unable to do so; supply was refused by the Assembly by a majority of 32 to 13, and M. Joly at once applied for a dissolution, which was granted. The new Assembly met in June 1878, parties were evenly balanced, but the Joly administration gradually increased in strength and continued to carry on the Government.

The Conservative party of Canada immediately identified itself with the cause of M. De Boucherville, and, ultimately, when the Executive Government of the Dominion became Conservative in character (the Prime Minister being Sir John Macdonald), it dismissed the Lieutenant-Governor of Quebec from office, after the proposed action had been referred by the Governor-General of Canada (the Marquis of Lorne) to the Colonial Office.

The course of events is important to trace.

(*a*) No resolution hostile to M. Letellier was carried by the Quebec Assembly.

(*b*) The Lieutenant-Governor of a Canadian Province is,

[1] Todd, *Parliamentary Government in the British Colonies* (2nd ed.), p. 601.

under section 58 of the British North America Act, an officer appointed by the Governor-General in Council. By section 59 he holds office during the pleasure of the Governor-General, but is not removable within five years of his appointment except for 'cause assigned' to be communicated in writing to the Canadian Senate and House of Commons. It is well established that, whilst holding office, the Lieutenant-Governor of a Canadian Province is as much the representative of the Crown for Provincial purposes as the Governor-General is for Dominion purposes.[1]

(*c*) A petition was addressed to the Governor-General in Council by members of the dismissed De Boucherville Ministry, praying for the dismissal of the Lieutenant-Governor. The Governor-General forwarded the petition, together with statements of their respective cases by the petitioners and M. Letellier, to the Senate and House of Commons of Canada. At this time the Conservative party was in a majority in the Senate, but in a minority in the House of Commons, Sir John Macdonald being leader of the Opposition.

(*d*) In April 1878 Macdonald moved a resolution that the action of Letellier in dismissing his Ministers was subversive of the principles of responsible Government. The motion was negatived.

(*e*) Simultaneously the Conservative leader in the Senate moved a similar motion which was carried.

(*f*) A dissolution of the Dominion Parliament led to the formation of a Conservative Government under Macdonald. The Parliament assembled in February 1879. An ordinary member of the House moved a motion identical in terms with Macdonald's motion which had been defeated in the last Parliament. On this occasion the motion was carried by a large majority.

(*g*) Macdonald then informed the Governor-General (the Marquis of Lorne) that 'the usefulness of M. Letellier, as lieutenant-governor of Quebec, was gone'.[2] Ministers recommended his removal from office, the Governor-General objected, and it was agreed to refer the matter to the British Government for an instruction.

[1] See *ante*, pp. 203–4.

[2] Todd, *Parliamentary Government in the British Colonies* (2nd ed.), p. 604.

(*h*) Memoranda were forwarded to the Imperial authorities from Dominion Ministers, and also from M. Letellier. M. Joly, the Quebec Premier, proceeded specially to England to watch the interests of the Province, and a Dominion Minister also visited London. M. Joly suggested a reference of the question to the Judicial Committee of the Privy Council, but the Secretary of State for the Colonies would not agree.

(*i*) In a dispatch dated July 3rd, 1879, the decision of the British Government (then Conservative in character) was announced to the effect that

> 'Her Majesty's Government did not find anything in the circumstances which would justify him [i.e. the Governor-General] in departing in this instance from the general rule, and declining to follow the decided and sustained opinion of his ministers, who are responsible for the peace and good government of the dominion to the parliament, to which [according to the 59th section of the statute] the cause assigned for the removal of a lieutenant-governor must be communicated.'[1]

The dispatch also pointed out that the application to the Colonial Office for instructions was approved because the case was exceptional in character, but it stated that the rule generally applicable was that 'whatever affects the internal affairs of the Dominion should be dealt with by the government and parliament of Canada'.[2] The dispatch stated further that,

> 'there can be no doubt that the lieutenant-governor of a province has an unquestionable constitutional right to dismiss his ministers, if, from any cause, he feels it incumbent upon him to do so. In the exercise of this right, as of any other of his functions, he should, of course, maintain the impartiality towards rival political parties which is essential to the proper performance of the duties of his office; and, for any action he may take, he is [under the 59th section of the British North America Act] directly responsible to the governor-general.'[3]

The dispatch also suggested that the Governor-General should ask his Ministers to review their proposed action, having regard to the long interval which had elapsed since the dismissal. In July 1879 the Governor-General made this request to his Ministers, and emphasized that the Lieutenant-

[1] Todd, *Parliamentary Government in the British Colonies* (2nd ed.), pp. 606–7. [2] Ibid., p. 606. [3] Ibid., p. 606.

Governor's action had the support of the Legislature of Quebec and of M. Joly, 'the Minister who is by constitutional practice responsible for the action of the lieutenant-governor'.[1] But the Macdonald Ministry repeated their former advice to the Governor-General, and on July 25th, 1879, M. Letellier was removed from his office. The 'cause assigned' under section 59 of the British North America Act was that 'after the vote of the house of commons . . . and that of the senate . . . M. Letellier's usefulness as a lieutenant-governor was gone'.[2]

This precedent was rightly regarded by Todd as of very great importance. He emphasized that it required careful examination 'lest it should seem to justify dominion interference in provincial affairs under unwarrantable circumstances'.[3]

Further, Sir John Macdonald, during the course of his criticism of Governor Letellier, asserted that

> 'In England the power of dismissal of a government having the confidence of parliament is gone for ever, and that, if it is gone there, it ought never to have been attempted to be introduced in a colony under the British Crown.'[4]

This assertion of Sir John Macdonald aroused Todd's indignation. He thought it was an 'ill-considered declaration' and had 'no warrant either in theory or practice'. Todd insisted that 'one of the reserve powers of the Crown' was

> 'the right of appealing, at all times, from a ministry, strong (it may be) in the possession of the confidence of the existing parliament, to the electorate, whose decision must ultimately prevail.'[5]

Todd argued that such was the position in England, and it was 'equally true of the powers of a Governor in the colonies of Great Britain'.[6] Now this part of Todd's comment was in direct line with the dispatch of the Colonial Secretary which asserted the 'unquestionable constitutional right' of a Governor to dismiss his Ministers. Todd went further, however, to declare that

> 'it is the *bounden duty* of a governor to dismiss his ministers, if he believes their policy to be injurious to the public interests, or their

[1] Ibid., p. 607. [2] Ibid., pp. 607–8. [3] Ibid., p. 608.
[4] Ibid., p. 614 (Sir John Macdonald's Speech, April 11th, 1878).
[5] Ibid., p. 615. [6] Ibid.

conduct to be such, in their official capacity, that he can no longer act with them harmoniously for the public good.'[1]

I italicize the words 'bounden duty' which were (as is noted elsewhere) frequently used in the official communications of Governor Game to the Premier of New South Wales in May 1932.[2] Todd went on to contend that the one condition of such action on the part of a Colonial Governor was that the latter should be assured that he can replace the dismissed Ministers by others

'who will be acceptable to the country and to the assembly, as well as to himself, and who will be prepared to assume full responsibility for his act in effecting the change of government.'[3]

Now the general propositions of Todd went far beyond the 'constitutional right to dismiss' referred to in the dispatch of the Colonial Secretary. To make the Governor's personal belief that the policy of Ministers is against 'the public interests' or 'the public good' sufficient justification for dismissing Ministers possessing the confidence of the popular Assembly is to sacrifice all pretence of responsible or parliamentary Government to the opinion and (very possibly) the prejudice of a single individual.

Todd strongly criticized the action of the Conservatives who procured the removal of the Lieutenant-Governor, but he agreed that the arguments of their opponents—that a Lieutenant-Governor was 'irresponsible for acts performed within the legitimate sphere of the duties prescribed to him by the British North America Act'[4]—an argument advanced by M. Letellier himself[5]—was quite erroneous, and that such an officer could not divest himself of responsibility to the authority which had the right to appoint him. Todd also agreed that the removal of a Provincial Lieutenant-Governor was not a matter for the Governor-General personally, but for the Governor-General in Council, and that the advice of Dominion Ministers would be decisive.

Todd strongly attacked the action of the Macdonald Ministry in relying upon the resolutions of the Dominion

[1] Todd, *Parliamentary Government in the British Colonies* (2nd ed.), p. 616.
[2] See *ante*, Chap. XIX.
[3] Todd, *Parliameutary Government in theBritish Colonies* (2nd ed.), p. 616.
[4] Ibid., p. 608.
[5] Ibid.

Houses of Parliament, and contended that the passing of such resolutions was outside the proper functions of either House. He concluded that the action taken for the removal of the Lieutenant-Governor was

> 'at variance with constitutional law and precedent, as well as contrary to the spirit and intent of the British North America Act; inasmuch as it was initiated by parliament and not by the executive government, and did not set forth the particular acts of misconduct for which his removal was deemed to be necessary.'[1]

Todd's advice was 'to deprecate any reliance upon it (the case) as a precedent for future guidance',[2] because of the strictly party attitude taken throughout the dispute both by the Conservatives and by their opponents.

Todd did not fail to note that, in the circumstances,

> 'if any just cause of offence or complaint had arisen out of the conduct of Lieutenant-Governor Letellier towards his late ministers, the legislative assembly of the province were competent to afford redress . . . but, by the dissolution of the legislature which ensued, the electoral body of the province ratified the action of M. Letellier, and upheld him in the exercise of his lawful prerogative.'[3]

Keith, in dealing with this precedent[4] rather side-tracks it into a discussion of the doctrine that an incoming Ministry should accept responsibility for a Governor's action either in refusing to act on the advice of the Ministry's predecessors, or in dismissing such predecessors from office. He suggested that it would be more in accordance with the reality of the constitutional situation in the Dominions if 'a Ministry in fact should be held responsible for what it actually does, not for what it does not do'.[5]

But the case of M. Letellier has implications of a far more important character. The outcome of the long dispute was that a Provincial Lieutenant-Governor, never convicted of having broken any constitutional rule or undertaking, was dismissed from office by the authority lawfully entitled to exercise such power. This meant little short of disgrace. Further, the ruling of the Colonial Office, though general in its terms,

[1] Ibid., p. 614. [2] Ibid., p. 616. [3] Ibid., p. 620.

[4] A. B. Keith, *Responsible Government in the British Dominions* (1928), vol. i, pp. 126–30. [5] Ibid., p. 130.

asserted the right of a Lieutenant-Governor to dismiss his Ministers. By whatever motives he was inspired, all that Letellier did was to dismiss his Ministers, taking care to comply with the practice that other Ministers should be found ready to accept responsibility for the act of dismissal. Further, the dissolution of Parliament which he granted brought an Assembly into being which could be regarded as having ratified what was done.

Todd is more than justified in emphasizing the party atmosphere in which the whole of the constitutional conflict was waged. It seems probable that, although the Canadian Dominion Ministry had the right to advise the removal of Letellier, it was the coincidence of a Conservative Government's holding power in England and in the Dominion at the same time which proved fatal to Letellier. The Governor-General himself held a very strong opinion that Letellier was being unjustly treated, yet the Colonial Secretary almost rebuked him for not having acted upon Ministerial advice and for even referring the dispute to London. It may be conceded that Sir John Macdonald was satisfied that Letellier had abused the office of Lieutenant-Governor for the purpose of assisting the Quebec Liberals, and that an arbitrary exercise of authority was dangerous to accepted doctrines of responsible government. A close study of the case shows that the real ground of Letellier's removal from office was his original dismissal of the De Boucherville Ministry, but this ground was not that assigned by the Dominion Ministers in the Order in Council required by the British North America Act. The real reason for dismissal was deemed invalid by the Secretary of State, so far as an opinion can be gathered from his dispatch: and, if the matter can be considered *ex post facto*, the electors of Quebec could be regarded as having not censured, but endorsed, the Lieutenant-Governor's action in dismissing his Ministers.

The precedent shows that, where acute party differences exist, it is impossible for a Governor to take the responsibility of dismissing a Ministry possessing the confidence of the popular House without being regarded as a partisan by the party to which the Ministers belong. It is almost certain that such party will attack and upbraid the person who has brought into effective operation a prerogative usually regarded as having fallen into desuetude.[1]

The Letellier case also shows that the immediate electoral verdict, supervening upon the act of dismissal and dissolution, will not necessarily be accepted by defeated Ministries as an endorsement of the Governor's action; and that there may be attempts to recall or dismiss a Governor who has been regarded, by partisans, as having played the role of a partisan.

The case is thus anticipatory, in one sense, of the action taken by Mr. de Valera in 1932 when, fearing action of a hostile character from the then Governor-General of the Irish Free State, he assumed the initiative himself, and procured the appointment of a nominee of his own as Governor-General.

It also illustrates the weakness—in actual practice—of Todd's theory under which it becomes the 'bounden duty' of a Governor under certain circumstances to dismiss Ministers holding office with a definite majority in a popular Assembly. Although the documents in the Letellier case do not show that Letellier was constitutionally wrong in his original action of dismissal and dissolution, and strongly suggest the contrary, it was undoubtedly because of his original action that he was removed from office.

In considering the full implications of the Letellier case, it has to be remembered that the removing and appointing authority in relation to the office of Lieutenant-Governor of a Province was the Dominion Government of Canada itself. The case is different in the Australian constitutional system, where the Federal Government has no concern whatever with the office of Governor of the Federated States.

It is now definitely established that, so far as the Governors-General are concerned, those responsible for the appointment are the Ministers of the self-same constitutional unit in which the Governor-General acts. The McNeill–De Valera precedent shows that the same rule will also apply to the dismissal of a Governor-General. The general practice in reference to Governors-General has not yet been formally recognized in the States of Australia. If and when it is recognized in such constitutional units, a Governor who dismisses Ministers and

[1] Cf. *ante*, Chap. XIX, also p. 152.

dissolves the Parliament in which their party is in control will have to face the danger of his own removal from office provided the party which he has deprived of office secures the reins of Government. The Letellier case illustrates the intensity of feeling between Conservatives and Liberals so long ago as 1879. There is every indication that to-day party feeling is even more intensified. The only real alternative to such actions of reprisal will be the declaration and enforcement of what are still, in many respects, disputable and disputed rules of constitutional practice.

XXVII

TODD'S GENERALIZATIONS AS TO THE RESERVE POWERS OF DISMISSAL AND DISSOLUTION

THE historical importance of Todd's conclusions as to the constitutional position of a Colonial Governor is great. His work has played an important role in the development of colonial self-government. From the particular instances which he cites, it is not easy to make any very definite generalizations. But Todd boldly generalized as to the constitutional practice, and his propositions require some attention. They may be stated as follows:

1. Although Ministers possess the confidence of the popular Chamber, the Governor may decline to act upon their advice

> 'if at any time he should see fit to doubt the wisdom or the legality of advice tendered to him, or should question the motives which have actuated his advisers on any particular occasion—so as to lead him to the conviction that their advice has been prompted by corrupt, partisan, or other unworthy motives, and not by a regard to the honour of the Crown or the welfare and advancement of the community at large.'[1]

It will be observed that this rule, if acted upon, would almost completely destroy the reality of self-government in a Dominion or Colony. For it would enable the Governor to decline to act upon advice merely because, *inter alia*, he attributes unworthy motives to those Ministers who hold office. It is clear that no self-respecting Ministers could accept office if such a condition of affairs were to obtain.

2. If Ministers do not modify or abandon the policy or proceeding disapproved by the Governor, the Governor may dismiss them from office. This

> 'reserved right of dismissing a ministry must be determined by himself, with due regard to the gravity of the proceeding, and to the responsibility it would entail upon him to the Crown.'[2]

[1] Todd, *Parliamentary Government in the British Colonies* (2nd ed.), pp. 816–17.

[2] Ibid., p. 817.

This proposition is clearly unsound to-day because its validity is bound up with Todd's first proposition.

3. The reasons for the Governor's action should be capable of being explained and justified by an incoming administration to the local Assembly,[1] such administration being

> 'willing to accept entire responsibility to the local parliament for any acts of the governor which have been instrumental in occasioning the resignation or effecting the dismissal of the outgoing Ministry.'[2]

4. The Governor may insist upon the dissolution of an existing Parliament contrary to the advice of Ministers, if he can procure other Ministers to accept responsibility, and if 'he has reasonable grounds for believing' that the appeal to the electorate will result in 'an approval by the new Assembly of the policy which, in his [i.e. the Governor's] judgment, rendered it necessary that a dissolution of Parliament should take place'.[3]

There is a good deal in the precedents collected by Todd to warrant this statement; but the constitutional position which results is unsatisfactory unless more adequate safeguards attend the Governor's action.

5. A Governor has a 'constitutional discretion' to decide as to the expediency or otherwise, upon grounds of public policy, of granting a dissolution to a Ministry, but it is not a legitimate use of the power to resort to it when there is no important political question directly in issue, and merely in order to maintain existing Ministers in office.[4]

Here, again, too much is left to the Governor's decision upon what are really questions of fact and opinion. What is 'expedient'? What grounds of 'public policy' are to be recognized? Who is to determine the sufficiency of the 'political question'? Who is to decide the motives of Ministers?

6. Todd also included in the discretionary powers of the Governor a right to refuse assent to Bills passed by the Legislature. He was of opinion that, even in Britain, 'it is a fundamental error to suppose that the power of the Crown

[1] Todd, *Parliamentary Government in the British Colonies* (2nd ed.), p. 817.
[2] Ibid. [3] Ibid., p. 818. [4] Ibid., pp. 773–4.

to reject laws has . . . ceased to exist',[1] merely because the practice of veto has fallen into disuse. And he asserted that the power of a constitutional Governor in a Colony 'is greater practically than that of the Sovereign' in England, and that

> 'every statesman conversant with colonial politics is aware that in a colony very many occasions will arise where the prerogative of the Crown would need to be exercised under circumstances which would not necessitate, and perhaps would not justify, a similar procedure in England.'[2]

It has, of course, to be emphasized that Todd's opinions were expressed about a half-century ago, and were fairly well warranted by the terms of many of the dispatches forwarded from time to time to the then Colonies, and ultimately made available to the public.

Elsewhere we have quoted official Colonial Office rulings as to the existence of gubernatorial discretion. And the real basis of the supposed necessity for the reserved powers of the Crown's representative is to prevent the danger pointed out by Russell in 1839 in his dispatch to Sydenham, that

> 'every political constitution in which different bodies share the supreme power is only enabled to exist by the forbearance of those among whom this power is distributed. In this respect the example of England may well be imitated. The sovereign using the prerogative of the Crown to the utmost extent, and the House of Commons exerting its power of the purse, to carry all its resolutions into immediate effect, would produce confusion in the country in less than a twelvemonth. So in a Colony.'[3]

When Lord Carnarvon was Colonial Secretary, a dispatch of November 20th, 1866, to Sir G. F. Bowen, Governor of Queensland, contained the following statement:

> 'In practice, no doubt, the sovereign, if he disapproved of a measure introduced by his ministers, would have the constitutional right to dismiss them; but whether he would choose to exercise this right would depend upon other constitutional considerations bearing on the expediency of a change of ministers.'[4]

[1] Ibid., p. 155.

[2] Ibid., pp. 679–80.

[3] Kennedy, *Documents of the Canadian Constitution* (*1759–1915*), (1918), pp. 523–4.

[4] Todd, *Parliamentary Government in the British Colonies* (2nd ed.), p. 631.

Similarly, in March 1862, the Duke of Newcastle, when Colonial Secretary, sent a dispatch to the Governor of Queensland, laying down the rule that

> 'in matters of purely local politics he [the Governor] is bound, except in extreme cases, to follow the advice of a ministry which appears to possess the confidence of the legislature. But extreme cases are those which cannot be reduced to any recognised principles, arising in circumstances which it is impossible or unwise to anticipate, and of which the full force can, in general, be estimated only by persons in immediate contact with them.'[1]

Both these dispatches of the sixties were certainly capable of an interpretation which suggested a far greater discretionary power than was contemplated by their authors, having in view the particular matters under consideration at the time. But subsequently there has been a recognition first of the expansion of Colonial self-government, and finally of a special Dominion status which cannot be reconciled at all with the earlier precedents, even if they are interpreted as being limited to the facts of the particular dispute.

Lowell, writing in 1908, was of opinion that the Governor's position 'is still a delicate one that may require much sound judgment and tact', but, on the whole, he summed up the situation by stating that 'the Governor, although as yet at some distance, is taking more and more the position of the English King'.[2] Like most definitions of the subject, this is incomplete. 'More and more' is a vague phrase, and the exact position as to the reserve powers 'of the English King' is by no means fully ascertained.

[1] Todd, *Parliamentary Government in the British Colonies* (2nd ed.), p. 630.

[2] Lowell, *Government of England* (1914), vol. ii, p. 404.

XXVIII

LEADING TEXT WRITERS ON THE RESERVE POWER OF THE CROWN

I. TODD

TODD himself is an authority who may always be cited by those who at any time desire to assert the 'constitutionality' of the Sovereign's retaining and exercising wide reserve powers. Todd's work on Parliamentary Government in England was referred to with approval by Anson in his *Law and Customs of the Constitution*, when published in 1892.

Todd's attitude to the precedent of 1784 is, on the whole, one of approval of the dismissal of the Coalition, but he stresses the fact that Pitt's 'acceptance of responsibility' for the removal of his predecessors regularized the King's own 'irregular acts' in intriguing to deal with the India Bill in the House of Lords to secure its rejection. Todd quoted Lord Campbell's approval of the King's conduct in the emergency.[1]

Spencer Walpole also contributed a valuable note upon the point, asserting that:

> 'In the present day, no monarch would even venture on parting with a ministry which retained the confidence of the House of Commons. The dismissal of the Melbourne Ministry in 1834 was the last, and will probably remain the last, example of such an exercise of the prerogative. . . . The fact that [in 1784] the country ultimately adopted the views of the sovereign should not blind the student to the true constitutional objections to the sovereign's conduct.'[2]

This point of Spencer Walpole—that the electoral verdict should not be regarded as necessarily determining the question of the correctness of the Sovereign's act—is valuable, but continually lost sight of. Of course, if Dicey's statement of general principle were accepted, the vote of the electorate would of itself furnish a final and complete justification for the exercise of the prerogative.

[1] Todd, *Parliamentary Government in England*, vol. i (ed. Walpole), pp. 62–3 (note 1).

[2] Ibid.

William IV's dismissal of Melbourne is regarded by Todd as

> 'an instructive illustration of the effects of the Reform Act, in diminishing the ascendant influence of the crown. In George III's time the dismissal of a ministry by the king, and the transfer of his confidence to their opponents—followed by an appeal to the country —would certainly have secured a majority for the new ministers.'[1]

This last comment of Todd approaches the reality of the matter. For in the situation which faces the electors after an exercise by the Sovereign of the extreme prerogative, the latter is supposed to be committed to one of the parties. As the defeat of the Ministers upon whom the Sovereign has seemed to bestow his personal preference and favour may, and probably will, be regarded as a rebuff, every doubtful elector will tend to have his doubts resolved for him by his sentiment of loyalty and affection to the Monarch.[2]

Todd asserts that the Sovereign's power to dissolve 'may properly take place in four circumstances', viz. (1) After the dismissal of Ministers by the Sovereign, as in 1784, 1807, and 1834. (2) On account of disputes between the two Houses. (3) In order to ascertain popular opinion in relation to any important act of the Executive Government if 'some question of public policy' creates a dispute between Ministers and the Commons. (4) 'Whenever there is reason to believe that the House of Commons does not correctly represent the opinions and wishes of the nation.'[3]

The last instance of Todd does not seem to be distinguishable from the first, because Todd limits its application to cases analogous to the dissolution granted to Pitt in 1784, when the Coalition still had the support of a majority of the Commons. Both the first and fourth cases of Todd assume that the Sovereign has dismissed Ministers at a time when they possess the confidence of the Commons. The case where Ministers and the Commons differ is covered by the third example, and, as to this, Todd is really guarding against the notion that the Ministers for the time being are at all times

[1] Todd, *Parliamentary Government in England,* vol. i (ed. Walpole), p. 74.

[2] See *ante,* p. 106.

[3] Todd, *Parliamentary Government in England* (ed. Walpole), vol. ii, p. 126.

entitled to a dissolution, because not only does he limit the occasions, but he also insists that 'the prerogative of dissolution should be exercised with much discretion and forbearance'[1] and that 'it must be clearly approved by the Sovereign after all the circumstances shall have been explained to him, and he shall have duly considered them'.[2]

Todd adds that when the Sovereign is asked to dissolve, he

> '*ought by no means to be a passive instrument in the hands of his Ministers*; it is not merely his right, but his duty, to exercise his judgment in the advice they may tender to him. And though by refusing to act upon that advice he incurs a serious responsibility if they should in the end prove to be supported by public opinion, there is perhaps no case in which this responsibility may be more safely and more usefully incurred than when the ministers ask to be allowed to appeal to the people from a decision pronounced against them by the House of Commons.'[3]

Keith, who at one stage took a very different view, now agrees that 'even the Crown in the United Kingdom is not merely an instrument in ministerial hands'.[4]

As has been shown,[5] Keith's hand was forced by the very important discussion in the Canadian House of Commons after the Mackenzie King crisis of 1926. He now states, in reference to the King as well as to the Governor-General, that:

> 'It is obvious that only one dissolution can be asked for by the same ministry within a limited period; if it fails to secure a majority at a dissolution, it cannot imitate continental practice and endeavour to secure a complacent legislature by a series of dissolutions . . . but it may be hoped that neither in the Dominions nor the United Kingdom will any Government venture to disregard the result of an election.'[6]

With these opinions that the discretionary power of the Sovereign has not vanished may be contrasted the opinion of Gladstone, who asserted that, under the British Constitution,

[1] Ibid. p. 127. [2] Ibid., p. 128.

[3] Ibid., pp. 127–8 (quoting Wellington in Peel's *Memoirs*, vol. ii, p. 300). The italics are mine.

[4] A. B. Keith, *The Constitutional Law of the British Dominions* (1933), p. 139. [5] See *ante*, Chap. VII.

[6] A. B. Keith, *The Constitutional Law of the British Dominions* (1933), pp. 150–1.

the proper sphere of the Sovereign's action was reduced to that of influence, so that all modern constitutional arrangements 'completely shielded the Sovereign from personal responsibility' whilst the advisers of the Crown bore 'undivided responsibility'.[1] It is clear that, in spite of the verbiage in which his opinions were so often concealed, Gladstone leaned towards the Whig view that the Monarch could not constitutionally exercise any real discretionary power or authority.

The great practical importance of the Sovereign's position in political affairs was stressed by Lord Elgin at a time when the limits to be ascribed to the demand for responsible Government in the Colonies were being discussed. For Elgin wrote to Earl Grey in 1850:

> 'You talk somewhat lightly of the check of the Crown, although you acknowledge its utility. But is it indeed so light a matter, even as our constitution now works? Is it a light matter that the Crown should have the power of dissolving Parliament; in other words, of deposing the tyrant at will? Is it a light matter that for several months in each year the House of Commons should be in abeyance, during which period the nation looks on Ministers not as slaves of Parliament, but servants of the Crown?'[2]

II. MAY

May considered that the crisis of 1784 showed 'the paramount influence of the Crown'.[3] He regarded George III's method of organizing the defeat of Fox's India Bill as 'bold and unscrupulous', because the King had authorized Temple to say that every Peer who voted for it 'would be considered by him as an enemy'.[4] But May also emphasized that the House of Commons greatly injured their cause by openly evidencing their dread of a dissolution, especially as 'constitutionally the King had a right to dismiss his Ministers, and to appeal to the people to support his new administration'.[5] May deprecated Fox's attempt to coerce the King by threatening to refuse supplies.

May, in summing up the precedent of 1834, said that it

[1] Gladstone, *Gleanings*, vol. i, p. 41.

[2] Kennedy, *Documents of the Canadian Constitution (1759–1915)*, (1918), p. 588.

[3] May, *Constitutional History of England* (7th edn.), vol. i, p. 44.

[4] Ibid., pp. 46–7.

[5] Ibid., p. 58.

was not directly alleged that Ministers had lost the confidence of the King, and certainly they had not lost the confidence of the Parliament. He concluded: 'its impolicy was so signal as to throw into the shade its unconstitutional character.'[1]

Lord Campbell, who was Attorney-General in Melbourne's administration, referred to William IV's forcing the Prime Minister out as being 'preposterous'.[2] Campbell considered that Peel would have had a better chance of ultimate success if he had imitated Pitt and faced Parliament, and kept a dissolution in reserve instead of dissolving immediately. After the election the strength of parties was tried upon the election of the new Speaker, and Peel was defeated. Campbell says that when William IV 'heard the fatal news, he exclaimed, "But why did you deceive me?" In truth the good old gentleman had only to blame his own rashness.'[3]

May's comment upon the King's action included the assertion that:

> 'The right of the King to dismiss his Ministers was unquestionable; but constitutional usage had prescribed certain conditions under which this right should be exercised. It should be exercised solely in the interests of the State, and on grounds which can be justified to Parliament—to whom, as well as to the King, the Ministers are responsible.'[4]

It is difficult to gather any precise rule from May's language. When May uses the phrase 'the right', he may even be referring to the legal, as distinct from the constitutional, position. But if this is not so, May does not define the conditions which hedge round the constitutional exercise by the Sovereign of his undoubted legal right. The phrase 'in the interests of the State' is too vague. All parties profess to be acting at all times in the interests of the State, and a difference of opinion as to whether in fact a party is so acting is usually a difference merely of political opinion. May seems to contemplate that some precise ground should be capable of being assigned for the dismissal of Ministers, presumably by their successors, in order that the dismissal should be justified

[1] Ibid. (7th ed.), vol. i, p. 100.

[2] Hon. Mrs. Hardcastle, *Life of Lord Campbell*, vol. ii, p. 58.

[3] Ibid., p. 62.

[4] May, *Constitutional History of England* (7th ed.), vol. i, pp. 99–100.

'constitutionally'. This seems to imply a reference of the ground of dismissal to the existing Parliament. Then what is to happen if such Parliament expresses the opinion that the grounds of dismissal are unjustified or not substantiated? If, on the other hand, there is to be a reference to the new Parliament, the electoral verdict itself would undoubtedly determine Parliament's attitude both to the grounds of dismissal and to those who advised it.

May considered that the Commons' weapon of stopping the supplies 'lies rusty in the armoury of constitutional warfare',[1] not having been used even once since the reign of William III. As he says, it failed the Commons in 1784 'at their utmost need, and the experiment has not been repeated'.[2] The reason is, May points out, that 'the establishments and public credit of the country are dependent on their votes; and are not to be lightly thrown into disorder'.[3]

III. HALLAM

Hallam's treatment of the Crown's reserve power is as vague as that of May. He says that

> 'it is to the high prerogative of the English Crown, its exclusive disposal of offices of trust, which are the ordinary subjects of contention, its power of putting a stop to parliamentary disputes by a dissolution, and, above all, to the necessity which both the peers and the commons have often felt, of a mutual good understanding for the maintenance of their privileges',[4]

that general harmony prevails between the two Houses.[5] This generalization is of little assistance in the practical task of measuring and applying reserve powers. How unreal Hallam's views are to-day is shown by his statement that 'the happy graduation of ranks, which renders the elder and younger sons of our nobility two links in the unsevered chain of society',[6] constitutes one of the principal reasons for the working of the English constitutional system.

Hallam, attaching great significance to the fact that the Commons might be 'annihilated by a proclamation'[7] was

[1] May, *Constitutional History of England* (7th ed.), vol. i, p. 377.
[2] Ibid. [3] Ibid.
[4] Hallam, *Constitutional History of England* (7th ed.), vol. iii, p. 16.
[5] Ibid. [6] Ibid. [7] Ibid., p. 297.

very puzzled as to what might occur upon the accession of 'a King at once able, active, popular and ambitious, should such ever unfortunately appear in this country'.[1] Certainly, in his view, such a Sovereign would endanger 'the present balance of the Constitution'.[2]

IV. MARRIOTT

A modern view, that of Marriott, is that

> 'the King has . . . the right of appeal from Parliament to the masters of Parliament, from his own advisers to the political Sovereign before the expression of whose deliberate will the legal Sovereign must bow.'[3]

Marriott adds that in the event of the dismissal of Ministers possessing the confidence of the Commons,

> 'an adverse verdict [that is, adverse to the King] would create a situation almost intolerable. The position of the King would be that of a master who has given notice to servants and has been compelled by circumstances to retain them on their own terms.'[4]

Marriott illustrates his view that the King may dismiss Ministers, although they possess the confidence of the Commons, by reference to the attempt, in the autumn of 1913, to induce the King to exercise his prerogative against the Asquith Ministry.[5] He said:

> 'It would . . . have been within the undoubted right of the Sovereign to have sought the advice of an alternative Ministry, and in the event, certain under the circumstances, of their immediate defeat in the House of Commons, to have dissolved Parliament.'[6]

Yet Marriott admitted that, if the electorate returned the Asquith Ministry to power after such a dismissal and such a dissolution, there would have arisen 'a position of some embarrassment'.[7]

Marriott accepts the position that the King has a constitutional right to refuse a dissolution to Ministers. Reference has already been made to his approval of Mr. Asquith's statement of the position in 1923.[8] Marriott identifies the King's

[1] Ibid., p. 294. [2] Ibid.
[3] Marriott, *The Mechanism of the Modern State* (1927), vol. ii, p. 32.
[4] Ibid., p. 32. [5] See *ante*, Chap. X.
[6] Marriott, *The Mechanism of the Modern State* (1927), vol. ii, p. 33.
[7] Ibid., p. 34. [8] See *ante*, pp. 5, 65.

power to refuse a dissolution to Ministers with the King's right to appeal to his Parliament against his Ministers. He says:

'Another constitutional right . . . belongs unquestionably to the King. He is entitled to appeal from his Ministers to Parliament. This is in effect to refuse to an existing Ministry a dissolution.'[1]

It is, of course, apparent that the Sovereign could not persist in the refusal of a dissolution to Ministers who were already assured of Parliament's support; such a condition of affairs would at once exclude the possibility of any alternative Ministry, so that, sooner or later, the King would be compelled to grant the dissolution if both Ministers and the Commons persisted in their desire to dissolve.

V. BAGEHOT

Bagehot points out that if the King is to dismiss Ministers, great judgment is required. Upon such occasions

'to do so with efficiency [the Monarch] must be able to perceive that the Parliament is wrong, and that the nation knows it is wrong. Now to know that Parliament is wrong, a man must be, if not a great statesman, yet a considerable statesman—a statesman of some sort.'[2]

Bagehot's conclusion is that

'the power of dismissing a Government with which Parliament is satisfied, and of dissolving that Parliament upon an appeal to the people, is not a power which a common hereditary Monarch will in the long run be able beneficially to exercise. Accordingly this power has almost, if not quite, dropped out of the reality of our Constitution.'[3]

VI. LOW

General statements as to the constitutional practice not only leave many particular difficulties unsolved, but they are apt to be coloured by very special circumstances. As Sidney Low pointed out, many of the assertions made as to the English Monarchy have been based upon the special position occupied by Queen Victoria. He says:

'It has never been contended by English critics, as it is by some

[1] Marriott, *The Mechanism of the Modern State* (1927), vol. ii, p. 34.

[2] Bagehot, *The English Constitution* (5th ed.), p. 237. [3] Ibid., p. 240.

foreign observers, impatient of the mysterious half-lights and vague shadows, in which our system moves, that the transfer [that is, of power from the Sovereign to Ministers] has been complete. . . . Though the King does not govern the country, he does still have a share in the control of Government, which may be greater or less, according to circumstances, but is in any case substantial.'[1]

Low declares that

> 'within certain limits, the King may also require the acting chief of the executive to seek a fresh mandate from the electorate. Power, of a genuine kind, must rest with the Sovereign, so long as it is at his discretion to "send for" the leader of the Opposition, and so long as he can—under favourable circumstances—demand, or refuse, a dissolution.'[2]

VII. LASKI

Recently, so acute an observer as Professor Laski has said of the Monarch: 'It is true that the King can no longer dismiss a Ministry or refuse his assent to an Act of Parliament.'[3] But this statement has to be qualified in some way. For much authority to the contrary can be cited, and might, if any sufficiently urgent occasion arose, be relied upon. Thus, with reference to the reserve power of the King, Keith says, writing in December 1931, shortly after the formation of the Ramsay MacDonald–Baldwin–Samuel Alliance, that

> 'In the United Kingdom, by his hereditary tradition of authority, and by long experience, the King has a measure of power which is wholly different from that enjoyed by any Governor-General in the Dominions, and he is able, as has recently been seen, to exercise a deep influence on the course of government in cases where no political party in Parliament has a clear control and where crises of a national character emerge.'[4]

Laski himself fully recognizes this element of uncertainty in his discussions of the constitutional position which might be created in the event of a demand by a Labour Government for the creation of sufficient Peers to carry out important measures of policy.[5]

[1] Sidney Low, *The Governance of England*, p. 262. [2] Ibid., p. 263.

[3] Laski, *The Crisis and the Constitution*, p. 31.

[4] A. B. Keith, *Speeches and Documents on the British Dominions (1918–31)*, Intro., pp. xxviii–xxix.

[5] Laski, *The Crisis and the Constitution*, pp. 51–2; see *ante*, pp. 10–11.

VIII. LOWELL

Lowell regarded William IV's ridding himself of the Melbourne Ministry as not being a dismissal strictly speaking.[1] Whilst he says that the right of dismissal seems to be now regarded as 'practically obsolete', he is careful to add:

> 'As in the case of some other powers, however, it is hardly safe to predict that it will never be used again, for circumstances might arise in which it was evident that the Ministry and the House of Commons no longer represented the opinion of the country.'[2]

He mentioned the House of Lords' action in rejecting the Home Rule Bill of 1893, and in destroying the Education Bill in 1906, and added:

> 'It is conceivable that under similar conditions the Crown might, by dismissing a Ministry, force a dissolution, and appeal to the electorate. Such an event, though highly improbable, cannot be said to be impossible.'[3]

Lowell's view was that the Sovereign might, by refusing to assent to Ministerial advice, bring about a change of Ministry. An illustration of such action was the refusal of Ministers' request for a dissolution. But he then states:

> 'Nor is it probable that it [the dissolution] will be refused, because the rules of political fair play are so thoroughly understood among English statesmen that the power is not likely to be misused for party purposes.'[4]

This emphasis by so acute an observer as Lowell does not lack the element of irony. It illustrates the present difficulty, not only of measuring the actual extent of the royal reserve authority, but of forecasting with any certainty that general agreement as to the propriety of its exercise can be reached. For it was after Lowell's work (of 1908) that the great constitutional struggles developed during the years from 1909 to 1914. Within that comparatively short period of time the good faith of party leaders was very seriously brought into question. Appeals to a spirit of 'fair play' were seldom made, and, when made, ignored to such an extent that the

[1] This matter is referred to earlier at p. 32, n. 1. Both Grey and Melbourne regarded the affair as a dismissal.

[2] Lowell, *Government of England* (1908 ed.), vol. i, p. 32.

[3] Ibid.

[4] Ibid., p. 33.

ultimate responsibility for several most crucial decisions had to be accepted by the Sovereign himself.

IX. ANSON

1. The opinions pronounced by Anson during the controversy of 1913 are referred to elsewhere.[1] Previously he had pointed out that Queen Victoria considered the instrument of dissolution to be

> 'a most valuable and powerful instrument in the hands of the Crown, but which ought not to be used except in extreme cases, and with a certainty of success. To use this instrument and be defeated is a thing most lowering to the Crown and hurtful to the country.'[2]

The Queen's view as to the dissolution power was derived, to some extent, at least, from Lord Melbourne. But Anson adopts a more modern view, stating:

> 'the prerogative of dissolution is one which the King exercises on the advice and at the request of his Ministers and . . . a request is not refused. It remains to consider when this request may properly be made. Shortly it may be said that a dissolution is rightly demanded whenever there is a reason to suppose that the House of Commons has ceased to represent the opinion of the country.'[3]

2. But this statement is not consistent with the first dissolution of 1910, when the Asquith Ministry dissolved in order to secure the predominance of the Commons in matters of finance. Anson is forced to treat such dissolution as 'altogether exceptional', owing to the implied claim of the House of Lords itself, when it rejected the Finance Bill of 1909 'to compel a dissolution'.[4] Anson's suggested limitations upon the Ministers' right to *ask* for a dissolution is not recognized to-day. It is quite inconsistent with Mr. Ramsay MacDonald's being granted a dissolution in 1924.[5]

3. Although Anson at first asserts that 'the direct action of the Crown in causing or refusing a dissolution may be

[1] See *ante*, Chap. X.

[2] Benson and Esher, *Letters of Queen Victoria*, vol. ii, p. 108 (Letter to Lord John Russell).

[3] Anson, *Law and Custom of the Constitution*, vol. i (Parliament) (5th ed.), p. 327.

[4] Ibid., p. 328 (note 1).

[5] *Ante*, Chap. VIII.

said to have ceased',[1] he immediately qualifies his statement by adding:

> 'but the prerogative exists. Where the King has thought that his ministers and his Parliament were alike out of harmony with the country he has dismissed his Ministers.'[2]

He illustrates this position by saying, with the emphasis of understatement, that William IV 'promoted if not suggested a change of Government'. Accordingly Anson concludes that the prerogative 'might conceivably be a resource' when both Ministers and the Commons are 'alike out of harmony with the country and were unwilling to admit the fact'.[3] He also states:

> 'The prerogative of the Crown might still be brought into play to dismiss a Ministry, or to dissolve a House of Commons whose docility in support of the Government of the day arose from a knowledge that the House and the ministers alike had ceased to represent the wishes of the people, and that a dissolution would involve the retirement of many of its members into private life.'[4]

4. With reference to the King's legal power to decline to assent to Bills passed through both Houses, Anson states that, in modern times, if the King disapproved of legislation to such an extent as would warrant the exercise of his subsequent veto, he would commence his opposition long before the Bill was submitted for Royal Assent. He says that it is open for the King

> 'if the Ministers insist upon their measure . . . [to] dismiss them and employ others, in the hope that those others may be supported by Parliament. . . . If Parliament, in its desire for this particular measure, refuses its confidence to the new Ministers and puts them in a minority on divisions upon important questions, the King has one more resource. He can dissolve Parliament and appeal to the country. If the constituencies return a new Parliament pledged to the measure of which the Crown disapproves, this last resource has failed. It remains for the Crown, in the words of Lord Macaulay, "to yield, to abdicate, or to fight".'[5]

5. This last startling comment by Anson upon such an issue shows the folly, not to say the recklessness, of allowing

[1] Anson, *Law and Custom of the Constitution*, vol. i (Parliament) (5th ed.), p. 329. [2] Ibid. [3] Ibid., p. 330.
[4] Ibid., vol. ii, part i, p. xxix (Preface). [5] Ibid., vol. i, p. 336.

the King and his people to be embroiled in matters which are quite capable of reasonable solution, without bringing the King into the political arena as an interested party, or throwing the electorate into repeated turmoil.

6. As he boldly asserts the vitality of the reserve powers of the Monarch, it is somewhat surprising to find Anson also stating that

> 'it would seem, therefore, that a dissolution is now invariably granted on the request of the minister, and involves no rebuff to the Sovereign if the minister is defeated at the polls.'[1]

In making this statement in 1907 Anson again referred to Queen Victoria's letters, where the opposite view was recorded, namely, that there was 'no doubt' as to the power and prerogative of the Crown to refuse a dissolution, providing that, if Ministers resigned, their successors would bear the responsibility of the Sovereign's action, and be prepared to defend it in Parliament.[2]

Expressing such strong views as to the reality of the reserve powers in Britain itself, it may be noted that Anson found little difficulty in holding that the Colonial Governor possessed a wide discretionary power to act against ministerial advice or to decline to act on ministerial advice when 'Imperial interests are in issue'[3] or when the Governor was 'prepared to appeal from them [i.e. Ministers] to the colonial Parliament and, ultimately, to the colonial electorate'.[4]

X. BRYCE

Bryce has pointed out that, once Parliament succeeded in prevailing over the Crown and its Ministers, and the Executive Government thus became 'fairly bitted and bridled',[5] the result—that the Ministry held office at the pleasure of the House of Commons—tended to deprive Parliament of any motive

> 'for seeking to restrict the discretion of the ministers of the Crown by minutely particular legislation, for Ministers had become so accustomed to subjection that their discretion might be trusted.'[6]

[1] Ibid., vol. ii, part 1, p. xxxi (Preface).
[2] Ibid.
[3] Ibid., part 2, p. 79.
[4] Ibid.
[5] Bryce, *The American Commonwealth* (2nd ed.), vol. i, p. 215.
[6] Ibid.

But this discretion itself tended to balance Parliament's control of the Executive; accordingly Bryce adds that an English Ministry finds its strength not only in the frank acknowledgment of its dependence upon the Commons, but also because

> 'it may dissolve Parliament, and ask the people to judge between its views and those of the majority of the House of Commons. Sometimes such an appeal succeeds. The power of making it is at all times a resource.'[1]

According to Bryce, Ministers had, by the year 1888, become 'a mere Committee of Parliament dependent upon Parliament'.[2] He adds that:

> 'It is not easy to say when the principle of the absolute dependence of Ministers on a Parliamentary majority without regard to the wishes of the Crown passed into a settled doctrine.'[3]

Bryce also emphasizes the important fact that, until 1827, there had been a very long period during which the wishes and interests of the Crown had coincided with those of the parliamentary majority under Pitt and his Tory successors. This should have warned Bryce that fifty of the sixty years elapsing since 1827 were accounted for by the reign of one Sovereign, and that a Queen. But, on the whole, Bryce accepted the Whig tradition that the English 'system' of Government was inconsistent with any real authority remaining reserved or vested in the Crown.

This stripping of the Crown's prerogative is not an unmixed blessing, for Bryce sees a 'real danger' when a Ministry supported by a parliamentary majority is acting contrary to the wishes of a large majority of the electorate. He illustrates this by reference to the position of the Beaconsfield Government from 1876 to 1880. He says that:

> 'It followed, during the years 1877 and 1878, a foreign policy which the bulk of the electors apparently disapproved . . . but which Parliament sanctioned by large majorities.'[4]

Whilst, theoretically, it was open to Queen Victoria to follow the precedents created by George III and William IV and

[1] Bryce, *The American Commonwealth* (2nd ed.), vol. i, p. 217.
[2] Ibid., p. 273.
[3] Ibid. (note 4).
[4] Ibid., p. 280 (note 1).

insist upon a submission of the Government's foreign policy to the decision of the electorate at a new general election, the published correspondence of the Queen and Beaconsfield shows that the Prime Minister retained the Queen's unswerving support; any possibility of dismissal and dissolution was quite out of the question, and the Government retained office until it was defeated at the general election of 1880.

Bryce regards the English system of Parliamentary Government as one of 'delicate equipoise', even 'exquisite equipoise',[1] which depends, to a large extent if not wholly, upon the existence of two great political parties, each being 'strong enough to restrain the violence of the other'.[2]

XI. HEARN

1. Hearn stresses the vitality of the royal reserve power. He follows Burke in saying that the power of dissolution is 'the most critical and delicate' of all trusts vested in the Sovereign. He opposes the theory that a defeated Ministry has a right to 'appeal to the country',[3] by means of a dissolution. His view is that:

> 'The King is by no means bound to follow that advice. The refusal . . . would indeed be a sufficient ground for the resignation of ministers; but, on the other hand, compliance with the request can only be meant to assist them against the hostility of Parliament. Such assistance the King cannot and ought not indiscriminately to give.'[4]

2. Hearn's general view is that it is a necessary consequence of the Monarchical system of Government that 'a large discretion must rest with the Crown'.[5] Accordingly, the King may 'dismiss the Parliament whose advice he no longer finds suitable to his requirements'.[6] But, as penal dissolutions cause exasperation of the public mind, the verdict of the constituent body in favour of the dissolved House of Commons should be accepted. He says that

> 'experience has fully shown that penal dissolutions, when the public mind is bent upon any object, only serve to exasperate the quarrel. It is therefore understood that if the constituent body support the

[1] Ibid., pp. 280–1. [2] Ibid., p. 281.
[3] Hearn, *The Government of England* (2nd ed.), p. 162.
[4] Ibid., p. 163. [5] Ibid., p. 124. [6] Ibid., p. 157.

representative body, if the new House of Commons remain of the same opinion as its predecessor, that opinion shall prevail. Ministers must yield to Parliament, and Parliament is not to be new-modelled until it is fitted to the purposes of Ministers.'[1]

3. Hearn says that it is now

'definitely settled that . . . no Ministry can satisfactorily serve the Crown unless it also possess the confidence of Parliament, that if the King continue his confidence in his servants, although no such confidence be felt by the House of Commons, the proper mode of terminating the difference is by an immediate dissolution of that House; and that the Ministry must abide by the results of the general election.'[2]

It is abundantly clear from the opinions of text-writers that there will seldom be lacking 'authoritative' support for those who suggest that the Crown should, upon some given occasion or crisis, exercise a reserve power in relation to dissolution or dismissal. No doubt the employment of the weapon may be accompanied by grave dangers, particularly as other text-writers may, very likely, take a view which is hostile to the exercise of the reserve power in question. But the existence of those dangers will not, in themselves, prevent those interested in promoting or obtaining a desired exercise of the prerogative from advocating such an exercise. Amongst the text-writers on the subject of constitutional conventions those interested will usually be able to find support for (or against) almost any proposition.

[1] Hearn, *The Government of England* (2nd ed.), pp. 157–8.
[2] Ibid., p. 162.

XXIX

THE ARGUMENT IN FAVOUR OF THE 'ELASTICITY' OF THE RESERVE POWERS

THE vagueness and uncertainty of the rules governing the exercise of the reserve powers of dismissal, dissolution, and veto by the Crown in England, or its representative in the Dominions, has now been sufficiently demonstrated. Even when May wrote that

> 'the unwritten law of the British Constitution assumes the mutual forbearance of the bodies among whom power is distributed, and had gradually shaped itself at Westminster in usages and constitutional conventions, which indicated clearly when and how this forbearance should be exercised',[1]

the 'clearness' of the usages was greatly overstated. But to-day the position is befogged by conflicting authority, and by inconsistent or ambiguous precedent.

Yet it is the 'elasticity' of both British and Dominion constitutional usages which is said by many distinguished publicists to constitute their greatest merit. Thus Mr. Hughes, representing Australia at the Imperial Conference in 1921, said:

> 'The difference between the status of the Dominions now and twenty-five years ago is very great. We were Colonies, we became Dominions. We have been accorded the status of nations.'[2]

But he did not favour the proposal to hold a constitutional conference for the purpose of defining constitutional relations, saying:

> 'Let us leave well alone. That is my advice . . . I know of no power that the Prime Minister of Britain has, that General Smuts has not.'[3]

Substantially the same point of view was expressed by Mr. Lloyd George when he said in relation to the Irish Free State Constitution:

> 'What does "Dominion status" mean? It is difficult and danger-

[1] May, *Constitutional History of England* (7th ed.), vol. iii, p. 303.

[2] Keith, *Speeches and Documents on the British Dominions (1918–31)*, p. 56.

[3] Ibid.

ous to give a definition. When I made a statement at the request of the Imperial Conference to this House as to what had passed at our gathering, I pointed out the anxiety of all the Dominion delegates not to have any rigid definitions. That is not the way of the British Constitution. We realise the danger of rigidity and the danger of limiting our constitution by too many finalities.'[1]

In the same speech Mr. Lloyd George referred to the limits upon the power of the Crown:

'It is something that has never been defined by an Act of Parliament, even in this country, and yet it works perfectly.'[2]

Mr. Lloyd George then asserted that, as Ireland was about to acquire the same status as Canada, Australia, New Zealand, and South Africa:

'Wherever there is an attempt at encroaching upon the rights of Ireland, every Dominion will begin to feel that its own position is put in jeopardy. That is a guarantee which is of infinite value to Ireland. In practice it means complete control over their own internal affairs without any interference from any other part of the Empire. They are the rulers of their own hearth, finance, administration, legislation, so far as their domestic affairs are concerned—and the representatives of the Sovereign will act on the advice of the Dominion Ministers.'[3]

In certain quarters the same distrust of definitions was expressed in reference to the Statute of Westminster passed in December 1931. Mr. Winston Churchill,[4] for instance, took much the same view as Lord Buckmaster, who thought that it was 'a grave mistake' to express the relationship between the self-governing Dominions and the Parliament at Westminster in the 'unyielding form of an Act of Parliament'.[5] In Australia this view was stated by Mr. Latham, K.C.,[6] who said:

'I regard the relations of the self-governing parts of the Empire *inter se* as corresponding closely in the political world to the relations of the members of a family in the personal world. . . . I do not desire such things to be made rigid by legal rules and enactments. On many political and constitutional matters the British Constitution,

[1] A. B. Keith, *Speeches and Documents on the British Dominions (1918–31)*, p. 84. (Speech in the House of Commons, Dec. 14th, 1921.) [2] Ibid. [3] Ibid. [4] Ibid., pp. 276–7. [5] *Parliamentary Debates (Lords)*, vol. 83, p. 195. [6] Now Sir John Latham, C.J.

as applied not only to Great Britain but throughout the Empire, has been a success largely because it has been loose and elastic, and has left things to be determined by the commonsense of statesmen as emergencies arise, instead of being decided with the precision of lawyers in the interpretation of written documents. . . . I should therefore prefer very much to leave things as they are.'[1]

It is interesting to note a somewhat modified view, which resembles those already mentioned above by its distrust of *legal* rule as such, but does admit the desirability of written definition of constitutional usage.

In his work *The British Commonwealth of Nations*, Duncan Hall, in 1920, propounded the theory that there was a dilemma between absolute equality of status of the Dominions and the formal unity of the Empire, which depended upon 'the legal authority possessed by the Imperial Crown and by the Imperial Parliament in every portion of the Empire'.[2] Referring to prior declarations as to their 'constitutional right' made by several of the Dominions in reference to one or more aspects of their powers, he concluded that

> 'by developing to its logical conclusion the ancient and well-known distinction of the British Constitution between legal power and constitutional right, it will be possible, without destroying the legal unity of the Empire, to secure to the Dominions the absolute equality of nationhood which they desire.'[3]

He considered that the great virtue of the British Constitution was 'its elasticity and its power of adaptation to new conditions'. He proposed that there should be a '*formal general and authoritative declaration of constitutional right*' in relation to Dominion powers. This method was more in accord with the spirit and tradition of the British Constitution, and should be adopted, at a special Imperial Conference,[4] in respect of legislative, executive, and judicial authority.

It is interesting to observe what followed. In 1926 a general declaration of equality of status was made in the Report of the Balfour Committee. But, immediately this was done, it was found that varying interpretations could be

[1] Keith, *Speeches and Documents on the British Dominions (1918–31)*, pp. 264–5.

[2] Duncan Hall, *The British Commonwealth of Nations*, p. 229.

[3] Ibid., p. 230.

[4] Ibid., pp. 236–7.

given to the declaration. For instance, the governing declaration as to status was printed in italics in order to stress its importance. It seems almost incredible, but Professor Keith actually criticized the

> 'unfortunate employment of italics[1] to emphasise the declaration of autonomy of the parts of the Empire and the omission of this mechanical and unscientific aid in stating the equally fundamental principle of differentiation of function.'[2]

Keith added:

> 'the view taken in this work (completed in November 1926) of the significance of the Report of the Conference of 1926 as sentimental rather than substantial was expressed in the contribution which appeared in the *Glasgow Herald* simultaneously with the text of the Report on 22 November, 1926, and in my articles in the *Outlook* of 8 January and 5 February. The passage of time has only served to confirm me in this opinion.'[3]

Duncan Hall therefore overlooked the fact that there would always exist parties and persons ready to minimize the importance of any declaration of equality of status, especially if they deprecated its existence. So the application of the declaration of 1926 to particular problems came to be affected by the preconceived opinions or the immediate thesis of the commentator. Keith himself often provides an instance of this tendency. Further, the modern precedents have not solved much more than their own particular controversy. And we find that political parties have supported constitutional doctrines so long as, in particular circumstances, it suited them; and have done so without the slightest regard to the principle which was being applied.

Circumstances such as these rendered it inevitable that the Statute of Westminster should be passed. First in one Dominion, then in another, either the Courts would not fully or sufficiently recognize the changed status of the Dominion,[4]

[1] The words italicized in the Report were those containing the central and fundamental declaration as to the status of the Dominions. Keith also pounced upon the reference in the Report to functions performed by the Dominions, treating it as a qualification of the central declaration. See *ante*, pp. 208–10.

[2] Keith, *Responsible Government in the Dominions* (1928), vol. i, p. xiv (Preface).

[3] Ibid., p. xviii (Preface).

[4] See for instance the case of *Tagaloa* v. *Inspector of Police* [1927] New Zealand Law Reports 883; and contrast *R.* v. *Christian* [1924] South

or some particular issue arose in which political parties could not, or did not, agree as to how the general declaration of 1926 was to be applied. The passing of the Statute has a double significance. It not only evidences the recognition by the Parliament at Westminster of the increased political power and legal authority of the Dominions; more important for present purposes, it also evidences that constitutional conventions cannot, of themselves, be depended upon in times of crisis or emergency; so that the tendency is for them to be replaced by Statutes, which have to be recognized by all, including the Courts of the land, and even learned commentators and text-writers.

No doubt practical difficulties may arise in any attempt of the Parliament of the United Kingdom to elevate rules of practice into rules of law, and to safeguard the latter against the action of subsequent Parliaments. For instance, will the recording in the form of the Statute of Westminster of the self-denying ordinance of the Imperial Parliament that no Act passed by it shall extend or be deemed to extend to a Dominion as part of the law of the Dominion, unless the Act specially declares that the Dominion has requested and consented to such extension, be regarded by the Courts as valid and effective? If so, a newer and more modern view will have to be adopted as to the binding effect upon its successors of an Act of the Parliament of the United Kingdom. For it is usually asserted or assumed that the second Act of the Parliament of the United Kingdom may set aside any restrictions imposed by the first Act, entirely defeating the attempt to impose any fetter upon the action of the subsequent Parliament. But, as Anson stated or implied in connexion with the first Home Rule Bill,[1] the question should not be answered without closely considering the form and character of the Statute which the subsequent Parliament is endeavouring to alter. It should not be assumed that the legislative jurisdiction, formerly regarded as belonging exclusively to the Imperial Parliament, is incapable of being permanently and effectively surrendered to another authority having jurisdiction

African Law Reports, 101. The question is elsewhere discussed by the present writer (*British Dominions as Mandatories*, pp. 16–21).

[1] *Law Quarterly Review*, vol. 2 (1886), p. 427; *post*, pp. 308–9.

over some prescribed portion of the British Dominions. During the argument before the Privy Council in the case of *Attorney-General for New South Wales* v. *Trethowan*,[1] where the power of the Legislature of New South Wales to bind its successors in relation to a particular matter (the abolition of the Legislative Council) was affirmed, it was suggested that the Parliament at Westminster would be capable of acting in an analogous manner. But, if it is so capable, in relation to the internal affairs of the United Kingdom itself, that must be so under a far broader doctrine than the precise ground upon which the New South Wales legislation was deemed valid (i.e. the mere meaning and application of a section of the Colonial Laws Validity Act, 1865). The broader doctrine must be that the Parliament is itself capable of establishing a 'Constitution', and a 'Constitution' by reason of its very nature must necessarily bind each and every portion of the constituent elements of Parliament, and Parliament itself.[2]

Dicey's exposition of the subject is very familiar. But his opinion is usually misunderstood. For Dicey at least conceded that the Sovereign power could divest itself of authority by the method of a permanent transfer of part of its authority to another person or body of persons.[3] He added that:

> 'If indeed the Act of Union had left alive the Parliaments of England and of Scotland, though for one purpose only, namely, to modify when necessary the Act of Union, and had conferred upon the Parliament of Great Britain authority to pass any law whatever which did not infringe upon or repeal the Act of Union, then the Act of Union would have been a fundamental law unchangeable legally by the British Parliament.'[4]

The mere form of section 4 of the Statute of Westminster may suggest that an Act of the Parliament of the United Kingdom can legally extend to a Dominion so long as it contains a declaration that the Dominion has requested and consented to the legislation. But the substance of the section is that such a request and consent must be obtained before any Act of the United Kingdom Parliament can be deemed to extend to a Dominion. And this is in accordance with

[1] [1932] A.C. 526. [2] See note on p. 281.
[3] Dicey, *The Law of the Constitution* (8th ed.), pp. 65–6 (note 3).
[4] Ibid., p. 67.

'the established constitutional position' referred to in the preamble to the Statute, viz. that no law of the Parliament of the United Kingdom shall extend to any of the Dominions as part of its law 'otherwise than at the request and with the consent of that Dominion'.

For the Commonwealth of Australia, the further question as to how the Dominion's 'request and consent' is to be expressed is determined by reference to the 'request and consent of the Parliament and Government of the Commonwealth'.[1] In the other Dominions the matter is not so expressed, although, in practice, the Legislature would be consulted. It is one of the paradoxes of the constitutional position evidenced by the Statute of Westminster that, without the slightest reference of the issue to the people of the Dominion, the status of any of the Dominions may be formally surrendered by its Parliament (for the time being) requesting the necessary constitutional legislation from the Parliament of the United Kingdom. That this is not a mere hypothesis is shown by the diminution of constitutional status accepted by the Parliament of Newfoundland without any express consultation of the people of that Dominion.

The notion of 'sovereignty' is extremely difficult to apply to modern States, and particularly in the case of such a body as the British Commonwealth of Nations. Few are likely to find satisfaction in Bacon's pontifical utterance to the effect that 'a supreme and absolute power cannot conclude itself, neither can that which is in nature revocable be made fixed'.[2] The truth is that 'Sovereignty' is, as Sir Frederick Pollock has pointed out,

> 'a generalisation from the "omnipotence" of the British Parliament, an attribute which has been the offspring of our peculiar history, and may quite possibly suffer some considerable change within times not far distant.'[3]

It may be worthy of note that the statement of Keith in relation to the Statute of Westminster, that sovereign power cannot be surrendered because 'Legally, as Bacon long ago perceived, the Imperial Parliament cannot limit the power of

[1] 22 Geo. V, c. 4, sec. 9 (3).

[2] Dicey, *The Law of the Constitution* (8th ed.), p. 62 (note 2).

[3] *Harvard Law Review*, vol. viii, p. 251.

any successor',[1] is a somewhat inadequate treatment of a complicated problem.

Therefore it should not be assumed that the Parliament of the United Kingdom is incapable of creating a binding Constitution which will clearly define 'the established constitutional position' governing the relation between the Sovereign, the Parliament, each House of the Parliament, and the electors themselves, and which will enable the Courts to declare and enforce any disputed matter which arises. Nor should it be assumed that Statutes of the special character of the Statute of Westminster, 1931, can be set at nought by another Parliament at Westminster.

Keith's view is that the Imperial Parliament

> 'still possesses a pre-eminence over all the other parliaments in the Empire, a fact which the Statute of Westminster solemnly acknowledges, in two ways. In the first place, it recognises its right to legislate for the Dominions with the assent of their governments or parliaments, whose concurrence the Commonwealth formally requires. Secondly, it maintains intact the constitutional restrictions on the alteration of the Canadian, Australian and New Zealand constitutions, thus perpetuating the restrictions imposed by earlier Imperial Acts.'[2]

These two references do not bear out Keith's thesis. With regard to the first, the significance of section 4 of the Statute of Westminster is that the Parliament of the United Kingdom surrenders its right to govern a Dominion unless at the request, and with the consent, of the Dominion. This does not warrant the inference of pre-eminence but rather suggests a restriction upon power. If a Dominion Parliament desires legislation by the Parliament at Westminster it may express its desire, and the legislation—the form of which will clearly be in the control of the Dominion—will be passed. Unless such desire exists no such legislation will (or perhaps can) be passed.

Keith's observation that the Statute of Westminster is careful not to prejudice the existing restrictions upon the alteration of the Constitutions of some of the Dominions

[1] Keith, *Speeches and Documents on the British Dominions (1918–31)* (Preface), p. xxx.

[2] Ibid. (Preface), p. xxix.

(section 7 as to Canada and section 8 as to Australia and New Zealand) is hardly borne out by those sections which afford little evidence of pre-eminence. The form of the Statute of Westminster is negative in this respect, i.e. 'Nothing in this Act shall be deemed to apply to' (section 7 (1)) and 'Nothing in this Act shall be deemed to confer any power to' (section 8). In other words, the rights and immunities elsewhere conferred by the Statute do not affect the constitutional restrictions existing in the Dominions concerned. These provisions are merely inserted by way of precaution in order to preserve and maintain the internal limitations governing the alterations of the Constitutions of the Dominion concerned.

It follows that the supposed merits of 'elasticity' in constitutional understandings should not be regarded as including the legal difficulty or impossibility of defining such understandings and enforcing them. Uncertainty, and even tyranny, may be the direct result of continuing in legal force an undefined discretionary authority. As Paley said in relation to criminal law:

> 'Either the law must define beforehand and with precision the offences which it punishes or it must be left to the *discretion* of the Magistrate to determine, upon each particular accusation, whether it constitutes that offence which the law designed to punish or not; which is, in effect, leaving to the Magistrate to punish or not to punish, at his pleasure, the individual who is brought before him; which is just so much tyranny.'[1]

This principle should be applicable to the civil as well as to the criminal law, and particularly applicable to the more important and far-reaching matters which depend upon that relationship between the supreme powers in a State which some are content to leave entirely dependent upon mere constitutional conventions and maxims. The result of not defining, and so confining, such conventions and maxims may easily be to transfer political contests into something like civil war; so anarchy may breed anarchy.

For the raising of fundamental issues is not unrelated to the changes in the character and objects of modern political

[1] Paley, *Works*, vol. i, p. 3. Italics are mine.

parties, and particularly to the development of the Labour movement. In 1842 Lord Abinger C.B. said in reference to the demands of the Chartists:

'The establishment of any popular Assembly entirely devoted to democratic principles, elected by persons the vast majority of whom possess no property, but live by means of manual labour, would be inconsistent with the existence of the monarchy and the aristocracy. Its first aim would be the destruction of property and the overthrow of the Throne.'[1]

Although modified, the same violent class outlook is observable in the work of such a constitutional authority as Bagehot. He said:

'I do not consider the exclusion of the working classes from effectual representation a defect in *this* aspect of our parliamentary representation. The working classes contribute almost nothing to our corporate public opinion, and therefore the fact of their want of influence in Parliament does not impair the coincidence of Parliament with public opinion. They are left out in the representation and also in the thing represented.'[2]

It was Bagehot who suggested, after the extension of the franchise in 1867, that 'the higher classes' should so act as to prevent the 'working classes' from combining. He said:

'But in all cases it must be remembered that a political combination of the lower classes, as such and for their own objects, is an evil of the first magnitude; that a permanent combination of them would make them (now that so many of them have the suffrage) supreme in the country; and that their supremacy, in the state they now are, means the supremacy of ignorance over instruction, and of numbers over knowledge.'[3]

A similar point of view, though directed to a different goal, is seen in the observations of Lord Balfour. He supposed that the political parties were reduced to two, but that 'the chasm dividing them' was so profound

'that a change of Administration would in fact be a revolution disguised under a constitutional procedure. . . . Is there any ground for expecting that our Cabinet system, admirably fitted to adjust political action to the ordinary oscillations of public opinion, could

[1] Lord Abinger C.B. to the Grand Jury at Liverpool, Oct. 9th, 1842. 4 State Trials (N.S.), p. 1421.

[2] Bagehot, *The English Constitution* (5th ed.), pp. 166–7.

[3] Ibid. (2nd ed.) (Intro.), pp. xxiii–xxiv.

deal with these violent situations? Could it long survive the shock of revolutionary and counter-revolutionary violence? I know not. The experiment has never been tried. Our alternating Cabinets, though belonging to different parties, have never differed about the foundations of society. And it is evident that our whole political machinery presupposes a people so fundamentally at one that they can afford to bicker.'[1]

The same curiosity as to the future development of the English system of parliamentary government was shown by Lowell in 1908. He pointed out that, in the absence of a rigid constitution,

> 'party activity must be limited to a conventional field, which is regarded by public opinion of the day as fairly within the range of practical politics. Clearly the issues must not involve vital matters such as life or confiscation. When, during the progress of the French revolution, an orator argued in favour of the responsibility of Ministers, and added "by responsibility we mean death", he advocated a principle inconsistent with the peaceful alternation of parties in power.'[2]

Lowell's opinion was—in 1908:

> 'the upper classes in England rule to-day not by means of political privileges which they retain, but by the sufferance of the great mass of the people, and as trustees for its benefit. . . . Most . . . have fought together in the sports of schools and colleges, and are constantly meeting in the society of London. This in itself tends to make them play the game fairly and observe the conventional rules of honour of the day.'[3]

The situation has altered since Lowell wrote. A Labour party, aiming at Socialism, and recruited very largely from the ranks of the working class, has risen to office, if not to power, and is one of the two leading parties in England. It is no longer possible to say as Lowell did that 'the connexion of fashionable society with politics is still very close',[4] if he intended to include, as he clearly did, the two leading political parties. Lowell's view was that the system of parliamentary government worked in England because 'the immediate

[1] Laski, *Crisis and the Constitution*, pp. 49–50.
[2] Lowell, *Government of England*, vol. i, p. 438.
[3] Ibid., vol. ii, p. 508.
[4] Ibid., p. 509.

direction of affairs is still mainly in the hands of a smaller governing class'.[1]

Sidney Low emphasized a somewhat analogous point of view, and he pointed out some of the dangers of the situation. He prophesied that:

'Our modern wealth, kindlier, more self-restrained, less arrogant than in the past, yet lives under the curious gaze of a giant, always armed, and sometimes hungry. Democracy in England has not used its powers; it has indeed scarcely been conscious of them. But that is due to circumstances and conditions which are not sempiternal and may not much longer endure.'[2]

Low's later observation upon the subject of the Constitution made in 1914 was that:

'A revolution, as comprehensive as that which ultimately abolished predial and domestic servitude, seems to be entering upon its initial stages. The passion for material equality, which has succeeded that for political equality, will hardly be satisfied without many strenuous attempts to transfer property and all the amenities and opportunities which go with property, from the Few to the Many. The value of our Constitution will be tested by its action in the presence of these aspirations and impulses, and by its capacity to shape them to a favourable issue, without the disasters and disorganisation by which revolutionary changes in the social structure, and in its ethical and economic basis, have so often been attended.'[3]

Accordingly it is not surprising to find that some responsible Labour leaders express their anxiety and concern at the vague and indefinite constitutional position which will obtain, should they be returned to power with effective control over the House of Commons.[4] Professor Laski, using Lord Balfour's statement, makes the point that the action of the Crown would, or might, be called for if the legislation of such party was rejected by the House of Lords. Referring to the exercise of the prerogative of creation of Peers, he says that:

'Were it refused, or were a general election demanded on the precedent of 1910, the neutrality of the Crown would be so gravely

[1] Lowell, *Government of England* (1908), vol. ii, p. 538.

[2] Low, *Governance of England*, p. 312.

[3] Ibid. (2nd ed.) (Intro.), pp. xxxvii–xxxviii.

[4] See e.g. *Problems of a Socialist Government*: Attlee, p. 186; Cripps, pp. 41–50; Trevelyan, pp. 27–9.

impaired that a new metaphysics of limited monarchy would become necessary. And it is doubtful if such a metaphysics is now available.'[1]

Laski's inference is, as was that, I think, of other constitutional students, that:

> 'In any country where either a party, or an influential section of the citizen body, will not accept the right of Parliament to legislate in terms of the power confided to the Government of the day, the peaceful compromise of political issue is impossible.'[2]

But there should not be any insuperable difficulty in reaching agreement as to the rules governing the exercise of royal powers and prerogatives, either in England or in any of the Dominions. As yet, no party denies the right of a majority of the electors to enforce their will upon all political subjects, providing it appears that such majority is sufficiently informed, and its will sufficiently ascertained. Even if special safeguards are wanted, they might be agreed upon. If agreement upon constitutional practice is rendered impossible, the near future must see the end of political democracy.

[1] Laski, *Crisis and the Constitution*, p. 52. [2] Ibid., p. 45.

Additional note to p. 274.

In 1803 Chief Justice Marshall said in the famous case of *Marbury* v. *Madison* (5 U.S. 137 at 176): 'Certainly, all those who have framed written constitutions contemplate them as forming the fundamental and paramount law of the nation, and consequently, the theory of every such government must be, that an act of the legislature, repugnant to the constitution, is void.' Every such 'Constitution' must have a commencing point, and there is no reason why it should have to commence in a revolution. The recent cases of *Moore* (1935 A.C. 484) and the *British Coal Corporation* (1935 A.C. 500) do not preclude the future consideration of such a question. (See *post*, p. 309, n. 3.)

XXX

THE IRISH FREE STATE'S CONTROL OF THE RESERVE POWERS

THE Constitution adopted by the Irish Free State forms an interesting precedent so far as it sets up a definite scheme of controlling the exercise of the discretionary authority of the representative of the Crown. By Article 28 of the Constitution Dáil Eireann (the popular Assembly or Chamber of Deputies) 'may not at any time be dissolved except on the advice of the Executive Council'. The Executive Council consists of Ministers appointed by the Governor-General on the nomination of the President[1] and includes the President of the Council, the Vice-President, and other Ministers, all of whom (except one Senator) are required to be members of the Dáil.[2] The President of the Council must be appointed 'on the nomination of Dáil Eireann' and the President nominates a Vice-President.[3] The President and the Ministers nominated by him 'shall retire from office should he [i.e. the President] cease to retain the support of a majority in Dáil Eireann'.[4] It is further expressly provided that 'the Oireachtas [i.e. the Legislature] shall not be dissolved on the advice of an Executive Council which has ceased to retain the support of a majority in Dáil Eireann'.[5]

From these closely related provisions it is clear:

1. That the Governor-General cannot dissolve Parliament after dismissing a President (and Ministers) who retains the confidence of the Dáil.

2. A Ministry which has lost the support of the Dáil cannot secure a dissolution, whatever may be the supposed justification for an appeal to the electors.

3. A Ministry which retains the support of the Dáil has the legal right to ask for a dissolution.[6] There is no express provision that the Governor-General shall grant a dissolution to such a Ministry, whatever may be the existing circumstances;

[1] Constitution of the Irish Free State, Article 51. [2] Ibid., Article 52.
[3] Ibid., Article 53. [4] Ibid. [5] Ibid.
[6] Ibid., Articles 28 and 53.

but, as has been illustrated elsewhere, such a result must follow where both Ministers and the popular Assembly are agreed, and there is no statutory bar.

4. The request for a dissolution proceeds on 'the advice of the Executive Council'.[1] The doctrine of 'collective responsibility' (which is expressly mentioned in Article 54) would seem to suggest, as Kohn states, that 'the power to advise a dissolution rests with the Executive Council as a whole'.[2] In practice, the result of a dispute between the President and other Ministers as to a proposed dissolution would depend upon the extent of their respective following in the Dáil. It may be added that Kohn says that the Irish Constitution is distinct in this respect from the practice which enabled Mr. Ramsay MacDonald to retain the strategic initiative for himself in the Coalition Government formed in August 1931.[3]

The other matters which call for comment are:

1. From the position of the Governor-General there is a 'radical exclusion of all discretionary authority'.[4] Since 1933 the intervention of the Governor-General in relation to money votes has been terminated. They are now recommended by a message from the 'Executive Council signed by the President of the Executive Council'.[5] Previously the Governor-General, though 'acting on the advice of the Executive Council', had to send the message, and, in theory at least, might in an emergency prevent an appropriation of which he disapproved.

2. Kohn asserts with reference to dissolution that the Executive Council still 'retains the initiative and the monopoly of surprise'.[6] He adds at once that 'it loses that position of vantage only when a decisive part of its majority has deserted it'.[7] It should, however, be added, that under the conditions of the modern party system, a Ministry would hardly dare to dissolve without consultation in advance either with its

[1] Ibid.

[2] Kohn, *Constitution of the Irish Free State*, p. 291 (note 1). [3] Ibid.

[4] Ibid., p. 270.

[5] Constitution of the Irish Free State, Article 37 (as amended by No. 20 of 1933).

[6] Kohn, *The Constitution of the Irish Free State*, p. 291. [7] Ibid.

parliamentary supporters or, what amounts to the same thing, with those who control its general policy.

3. Under the British Constitution, by contrast with that of the Irish Free State, what Kohn describes as an 'historical process', 'reached its consummation when the right to advise a dissolution was effectively asserted even by a minority Ministry.'[1] In discussing this 'consummation', Kohn is on firm ground in his emphasis upon the absurd and contradictory character of the modern British theory (as he supposes it to be) of the 'anarchical prerogative of dissolution'.[2] He points out that there was no alternative to the possession of a right of dissolution by a minority Ministry (or even by a minority Prime Minister in a minority Ministry) if 'the personal power of the Monarch was not to be revived'[3]—that the result was that, 'in this instance the Prerogative of the Crown was not converted into a Privilege of the People', that it was 'fundamentally inequitable' that such a power should be exercised by a 'Prime Minister who inevitably views every question affecting the issue of power from the angle of the party he leads', instead of by 'a supreme organ which, while enjoying impartial authority, would yet be qualified to adjudge on an essentially political issue'.[4]

Kohn's acceptance of the theory of the automatic and unqualified right of the Prime Minister (or the Ministers) to extract a dissolution from the Monarch may be questioned; but his criticism of the position shows the absurd lengths to which the theory has to be driven. In truth, until there is an authoritative definition of the conditions (if any) under which it is just and expedient that a Parliament should, and should not, be dissolved—the only available impartial adjudicator of such issues is the Monarch himself or his representative in the Dominion. Kohn himself approaches this position when, in a footnote to his valuable discussion of the situation of a minority Ministry, he suggests that perhaps a solution of the problem of finding a *via media* between such a system as that of France—where the restriction upon the President's right of dissolving the Chamber (that of obtaining the assent of the Senate) has resulted in the supremacy of Parliament over the

[1] Kohn, *The Constitution of the Irish Free State*, p. 292.
[2] Ibid. [3] Ibid., p. 292. [4] Ibid., pp. 292–3.

Executive—and that of England—where the Prime Minister or Ministers retain the right of dissolution—may under the Irish Free State Constitution,

> 'be found in investing the Governor-General with a limited and well-defined measure of discretion. He might be authorised to grant a dissolution either in the case of parliamentary *impasse* or when issues of such novel and fundamental character had arisen as clearly to require a new expression of the will of the electorate, the cause of the dissolution to be specifically stated in the proclamation.'[1]

The difficulty of regarding this as a satisfactory solution of the exercise of the reserve power is that questions of law and fact and a just discretion may all be involved in the decision reached by the Governor-General. Stating the specific cause of the dissolution in a proclamation will avail but little. It was stated in the proclamation of Sir Ronald Munro Ferguson of July 1914, when he granted a double dissolution of the two Houses of the Australian Commonwealth Parliament. It is probable that not one elector in a hundred paid much regard to the particular dispute which was so specified, and that almost all of them decided the election upon the grounds of more general policy.

In truth the task imposed upon the Monarch or his representative in deciding such issues is too great to be borne. So soon as there is a sufficient definition of the extent of the discretionary authority and the nature of the occasions when its exercise is justified or required, there is no reason why recourse should not be had to the organs exercising the judicial power, or to a specially constituted tribunal.

[1] Ibid., p. 297 (note 1).

XXXI

SOME PRACTICAL ASPECTS OF THE PROBLEM OF DEFINING THE RESERVE POWER

THE difficulties existing in England and the Dominions include the following:

1. It is not certain to what extent, and under what conditions, the Sovereign or his representative possesses the right to refuse a dissolution of Parliament to Ministers.
2. The power of dismissal of Ministers possessing the confidence of the majority of the popular Assembly is not precisely ascertained.
3. The power of the Crown or its representative to insist upon a dissolution against the will of Parliament and Ministers alike, a power connected with 2, is also undefined.
4. The conditions of the exercise of the prerogative of appointments of Peers in the United Kingdom cannot be precisely stated.
5. The ultimate right of the Sovereign or his representative to 'veto', i.e. refuse assent to legislation, is still asserted to exist.
6. There is no clear understanding as to the precise constitutional relation between the Prime Minister or Premier on the one hand, and other Ministers on the other.

If the situation is allowed to continue without any alteration, the Sovereign, Governor-General, and the Governor will have to determine for themselves, on their own personal responsibility, not only what the true constitutional convention or practice is, but also whether certain facts exist, and whether they call for the application of the rule which is alleged to be derived from, and consistent with, all constitutional precedents. Even if, upon the given occasion, no extraordinary exercise of the Crown's prerogative results, the possibility of its exercise has always to be reckoned with, and this inevitably creates uncertainty and distrust.

This feature of the existing position is well illustrated by the references in the Irish Free State Assembly during the debate upon the Statute of Westminster. Mr. McGilligan said:

> 'Nobody has dared to say that at present the constitutional relationship between this country and the King is such that the King can deviate in the slightest way from the advice tendered to him on any and every point by the Government of this country—
>
> Mr. de Valera—Suppose he did?
>
> Mr. McGilligan—Suppose he did. Suppose the President of the Republic also failed to recognise the will of the country?
>
> Mr. de Valera—Keep to the King.
>
> Mr. McGilligan—The situation applies to both, the one is as likely to err as the other.
>
> Mr. de Valera—And suppose he did?
>
> Mr. McGilligan—I ask the Deputy to face up to the same question with regard to the President. Then the situation would have changed, and—
>
> Mr. de Valera—That would be easily dealt with.
>
> Mr. McGilligan—And the other would also easily be dealt with.
>
> Mr. de Valera—How?'[1]

Mr. McGilligan dealt in a striking way with the constitutional practice as to Treaties, and thus stated the position of the King in relation to the Irish Free State.

> 'The King, acting on the advice of the British Government, can no more contract for the Irish Free State than can the King of Italy or the Mikado of Japan. The conclusion of the Treaty in the Heads of States form is merely an old-established international usage. In its binding force it differs in no way whatever as a matter of international law from an inter-governmental agreement.'[2]

But Mr. de Valera was concerned with the legal results which might follow if the constitutional conventions were broken.

Moreover, it is plain that, upon certain occasions, the failure of the Sovereign or his representative to protect the people against acts of tyranny or usurpation on the part of Government and Parliament, such as the extension by

[1] Keith, *Speeches and Documents on the British Dominions (1918–31)*, pp. 247–8.

[2] Ibid., p. 240. Speech delivered by Mr. McGilligan on July 16th, 1931.

Parliament of its own life against the popular will, may be just as detrimental to the true interests of the Crown, although the prerogative is *not* exercised, as its exercise may be upon other occasions. The real trouble is that no one can lay down the true constitutional practice with binding authority: hence the uncertainty illustrated by Mr. de Valera's words 'Suppose he did?', to which one may add 'Suppose he did not?', in reference to other occasions and other problems.

It has been made abundantly clear:

1. That there is no generally recognized or binding rule to govern each situation of crisis.

2. That no independent tribunal is vested with any authority to determine either what the general rule is, or how it should be applied to the particular case.

3. That even where a general rule is recognized, no sanction is attached to secure its performance or to prevent its breach.

4. That as the Crown and its representatives cannot avoid being embroiled from time to time in the controversies created by a political crisis, the tendency to weaken the Crown as an institution is almost inevitable.

5. That, in the case of the self-governing Dominions, it is the very uncertainty as to the possible exercise by the Governor for the time being of prerogative or statutory powers which is likely to lead to the recall of the Governor by the King, the latter being advised to act by the Dominion Ministers, who tender it solely because they are not prepared to accept the risk involved if a constitutional crisis suddenly arises.

6. It follows that the tendency will be for the position of Governor (if it remains at all) to be filled at all times by the nominees of the Ministry in power, such nominee retiring from office when the Ministry is displaced.

7. That, in the event of a Governor's dismissing Ministers who retain the confidence of Parliament and dissolving Parliament upon the advice of new Ministers, it is possible that the failure of the latter at the ensuing elections will be visited by some sanction. It cannot be supposed that, so long as parliamentary Government remains, members of Parliament may openly and with impunity flout the majority of an

existing Parliament, who not only appear to represent the majority of the electors, but who are proved to do so.

The best methods by which the constitutional practice, determining the relationship between the Crown, the first and other Ministers, the Parliament and each House thereof, and the electorate, may be defined and controlled is by the passing of legislation by the Parliament possessing jurisdiction within the appropriate constitutional unit. For instance, the Legislature of an Australian State may pass an enactment itself declaring (say) the rules which are to govern the appointment and dismissal of Ministers of the Crown, the dissolution of Parliament, and the special position, if any, of the Premier in the Ministry. There is no difficulty whatever in attaching binding force to legislation of this character. It has been ruled by the Australian Courts that the remedy of mandamus is inapplicable in proceedings directed against the Governor of one of the States,[1] but the writ there in question was a prerogative writ. The case does not lend support to Keith's very broad generalization that 'it is not for the courts to seek to control the highest form of executive authority'.[2] All that is necessary to make legislation of the kind already indicated valid and effective, is to specify the remedies obtainable against the Governor and Ministers if the constitutional rules laid down are broken. In *Attorney-General for New South Wales* v. *Trethowan and Others*,[3] which is discussed elsewhere, an Act of the New South Wales Legislature had provided that Bills of a certain character should not be presented to the Governor for the Royal Assent until a condition precedent had been fulfilled.[4] As the condition had not been fulfilled in reference to the particular Bill and as it was alleged that its presentation was threatened and intended, the Supreme Court of New South Wales seemed to find no difficulty in issuing an injunction restraining Ministers from presenting the Bill to the Governor for the Royal Assent. The case was carried on appeal, ultimately, to the Privy Council, but, after the proceedings before the Supreme Court, the question of remedy was canvassed no further, the High Court restricting

[1] *Rex* v. *Governor of South Australia* (1907), 4 C.L.R. 1497.

[2] A. B. Keith, *Constitutional Law of the British Dominions* (1933), p. 145.

[3] [1932] A.C. 526. See *ante*, pp. 199, 200, 274. [4] Ibid.

the appeal to the real controversy, which was whether the prior legislation, in terms preventing such a presentation until approval by the electors at a referendum, was itself valid. The original issue of the injunction has been criticized in some quarters. It is certainly unsafe to rely upon the precedent as establishing a general right to an injunction, merely because a breach of statutory constitutional law is threatened; and if the very just and convenient remedies of injunction and mandamus are to be made available in enforcing statutory rules as to constitutional relationship, express references to the remedies should be made in the constitutional statute.

An illustration of legislation by a constitutional unit controlling the exercise of its own Executive power is provided by an Ontario Act,[1] which provided that, in matters within the jurisdiction of the provincial Legislature, all powers and functions exercisable at the time of the passing of the British North America Act, 1867, by the Governors or Lieutenant-Governors of the several Provinces, should be vested in and exercisable by the Lieutenant-Governor of the Province of Ontario, in the name of the Crown or otherwise, as the case might require. A special section provided that the power of commuting sentences for offences against the laws of the Province should be included. It was contended by the Dominion that the power of commuting sentences was a prerogative right of the Crown, exercisable exclusively by the Governor-General. But, as Mr. Blake argued for the Province, the prerogative of pardon 'is divisible and passes by right direct from the Crown to the governor-general, or to lieutenant-governor as the case may be, but not through the former'.[2] Blake also stated that the British North America Act operated to divide Executive, as well as Legislative, powers between the Dominion and the Provinces, and that the declaration in the British North America Act that 'The Executive Government and authority of and over Canada is hereby declared to continue and be vested in the Queen'[3]—implied that the word 'Canada' included the Executive of the Provincial, as well as that of the Federal, Government.

[1] 51 Vic., c. 5 (Ontario Act).

[2] Todd, *Parliamentary Government in the British Colonies* (2nd ed.), p. 368.

[3] Ibid., p. 369.

This argument was upheld,[1] and it seems to be in strict line with the later decision of the Privy Council in the Bonanza case (1916).[2]

The competence of a Dominion Legislature to confine the discretion or duty of the Governor within prescribed limits was also recognized in a dispatch of Earl Granville, bearing date January 7th, 1870, and dealing with the expenditure of public money under the warrant of the Governor without sanction of law. The dispatch was to the following effect:

> 'But if both branches of the legislature should agree to dispense with this injunction of the law, and desire that the governor should hereafter be guided by the advice of his ministers in the performance of this duty, her Majesty's Government would not object to this conclusion and would then free the Governor from personal responsibility in the matter.'[3]

It must also be emphasized that there is no greater difficulty in investing a proper tribunal with jurisdiction to determine questions of internal constitutional law, in the sense of usage, than there is in the determination of such questions of international law as are covered by the words of Article 13 of the Covenant of the League of Nations, viz.

> 'Disputes as to . . . any question of international law, as to the existence of any fact which, if established, would constitute a breach of any international obligation, or as to the extent and nature of the reparation to be made for any such breach.'

All such disputes are recognized as generally suitable for arbitration or judicial settlement. This general recognition has been supplemented by subsequent recognition of the jurisdiction of the Permanent Court of International Justice. This recognition, made by declarations under Article 36 of the Statute of the Permanent Court, known as 'signing the Optional Clause', has been made by all the members of the British Commonwealth of Nations who 'signed the Optional Clause' in respect of a period of ten years. It is true that the jurisdiction of the Court was not accepted as to (*inter alia*) disputes between the Dominions and the United Kingdom *inter se*, though this exception was not made by the Irish Free State. But the point to remember is the general acceptance

[1] Ibid. [2] [1916] 1 A.C. 566.

[3] Todd, *Parliamentary Government in the British Colonies* (2nd ed.), p. 635.

of the situation that questions of international law and questions of fact relating to such disputes are not only susceptible of judicial settlement and determination but are determinable by a permanent International Tribunal. Questions of International Law are in many respects analogous to those which arise in relation to British Constitutional usage and practice.

XXXII

CONSIDERATION OF SOME RELATED PROBLEMS

MATTERS which may arise for consideration in defining constitutional practice include the following, some of which have already been discussed in a different aspect.

1. The conditions under which the normal duration of Parliament should be lessened. This is the problem of dissolution. It invites a number of possible solutions, (*a*) that the right of dissolution should be committed to the Monarch or his representative; (*b*) that the right of dissolution should be subjected to the consent of Parliament itself; (*c*) that the right should be vested in the electorate itself by adopting some appropriate method of recalling all sitting members.

2. The conditions under which the life of Parliament may be extended. In the case of a controlled Constitution, where the overriding Charter fixes the duration of Parliament (e.g. Commonwealth of Australia Constitution Act, section 28 as to the House of Representatives), the problem is solved. In the case of an uncontrolled Constitution there is a temptation for a Legislature to postpone dissolution and, taking advantage of some actual or alleged crisis, extend its own existence in order to avoid popular disapproval. There are very dangerous possibilities in such an abuse of legal power, and the right and duty of the Crown in relation thereto are of the utmost importance.

3. The problem of the individual member of the popular Assembly. To what extent should law compel the individual to give faithful support to the party upon the platform of which he has been elected? Should the remedy for alleged breach of such duty depend upon electoral recall at the instigation of electors, or should the mere fact of voting upon an important division contrary to his party's wishes itself create a vacancy?

4. The relation of the Upper House to the popular Assembly. Should the power of the former be allowed to extend beyond the suspensive veto, should the Upper House be itself dissoluble, and how should it be composed?

5. The relation of the Ministers *inter se*, particularly the special position and status of the Prime Minister or Premier.

Morley said that the Head of the Cabinet occupied a position of 'exceptional and peculiar authority',[1] that he 'chooses his own colleagues and assigns to them their respective offices',[2] and that, in an emergency, he may 'take upon himself a power not inferior to that of a Dictator, provided always that the House of Commons will stand by him'.[3] An illustration of this special predominance of the Prime Minister took place in 1931, when Mr. Ramsay MacDonald formed a Government with four only out of twenty-one Labour Ministers, and the support of only a handful of his party. Professor Laski criticized the action taken, saying

> 'A Cabinet treated as Mr. MacDonald treated his late colleagues cannot avoid the feeling that they have been tricked by the employment of a weapon devised for quite different purposes. For the whole essence of the right to resign or to dissolve is not to permit a Prime Minister to appeal from his colleagues to his opponents; it is to permit a Cabinet defeated in the House of Commons, or desiring a refreshment of its authority, to seek a new mandate from the electorate. No Cabinet in the past would have accepted the operation of that power by the Prime Minister alone on any other terms. And from this the inference should surely be drawn that its operation cannot now safely remain the sole prerogative of the Prime Minister. He must share its exercise at least with the Cabinet.'[4]

In Australia the Labour parties have chosen Leaders and Ministers by ballot of all Labour members of Parliament. Other parties have been more controlled by the discretion of their Leader, though often enough nowadays a parliamentary leader is chosen by ballot. In England Asquith asserted that 'Such a question as the dissolution of Parliament is always submitted to the Cabinet for ultimate decision'.[5]

These divergent views both as to the actual and the desirable constitutional position make it essential that some more definite rule or understanding should determine the relationship between Prime Minister or Premier and his colleagues.

6. Important questions arise as to the enforcement of the electoral 'mandate'. There are two main possibilities. The

[1] Lord Morley, *Walpole* (1921 ed.), p. 144. [2] Ibid.

[3] Ibid., p. 145. [4] Laski, *Crisis and the Constitution*, pp. 17–18.

[5] Earl of Oxford and Asquith, *Fifty Years of Parliament*, vol. ii, p. 194.

'mandate' may be exceeded by an attempt to pass legislation never approved of by the people. On the other hand, the popular will may equally be defeated if the promised electoral programme is not carried into effect. Of course there is a school which still asserts that the will of Parliament, not of the people, should prevail. But, on the whole, parties now seem to be agreed that consultation of the electorate is an essential condition to great and important changes in the law. In other words, the main principle of the 'mandate' is almost universally accepted.

It follows that the conditions under which the popular will is expressed should be such as will secure a real freedom of choice to each elector, and this involves providing a reasonably equal opportunity to parties to place their views before the electors. In Australia, when important proposals were submitted to the electors at a referendum, it was for some time the practice for each political party concerned to compile a written case. A pamphlet was sent by the electoral office to each elector containing the opposing cases. It is obvious that, under modern conditions, newspaper and broadcasting propaganda may create great confusion and even panic and may become as great a menace to a free vote as bribery or intimidation of individual electors under older conditions.

7. The question whether, and to what extent, Parliament should have constituent power is directly related to the legal question whether it should be regarded as capable of binding its successors. It is too late in the day to deny that the British peoples should be accorded full rights of self-government. But those rights may be delayed or defeated if constituent power is exercised by Parliament without restriction. The recent case of Newfoundland seems to illustrate this point. Whatever political justification there was for the action taken, in fact the Legislature of Newfoundland surrendered powers which, according to ordinary notions of modern constitutional practice in political democracies, belonged to the citizens of that State. This illustrates again the special, and perhaps a dangerous, feature of the Statute of Westminster which I refer to elsewhere. In the main the Statute commits powers to 'the parliament of a Dominion'.[1] It thus identifies

[1] See secs. 2 (2), 3 (5), 9 (3), and 10 (1) and (2).

the Dominions with their Parliaments for the time being, so that the destinies of the peoples of the Dominions, being committed to, may also be prejudiced by, a Legislature which, in relation to some great question, has no mandate and knows that it cannot obtain one.

8. The powers of a Legislature may be used in such a way as to destroy in advance the effectiveness of subsequent electoral verdicts. Parliament may bind its successors, and by creating unfair or even grotesque restrictions upon change, make the alteration of certain laws virtually impossible. One way of doing this is by passing a law which will be certain to escape future repeal or amendment because of the known political composition of, and the relative permanence of, an Upper House of Parliament. Further, Parliament may manipulate electorates, employing the device of the 'gerrymander', so that the will of a minority shall usually prevail. The question of giving each vote its fair representative value throughout the electorate involves consideration of such proposals as that of proportional representation. As Lowell said:

> 'The English practice of rearranging the constituencies, and apportioning the representatives among them, only at long intervals, of treating a Bill for the purpose as an exceptional measure of great public importance, instead of the natural result of each new census, has the advantage of preventing frequent temptations to gerrymander. But, on the other hand, it raises the matter of electoral districts to the height of a constitutional, and almost a revolutionary, question, preceded sometimes by long and serious agitation, and always fought over on party grounds. This is a perpetual difficulty, for the shifting of population, which must always be changing the ratio of representation, will from time to time make a redistribution of seats inevitable.'[1]

By contrast, an excellent system obtains in the Commonwealth of Australia. Electorates are redistributed after each census, and the adjustment of new boundaries is committed to skilled and impartial officers. The same assertion cannot be made in respect of some of the States where the Parliaments have directed, or at least invited, a very unfair distribution of the electorates quite inconsistent with the principle of 'one vote, one value'.

[1] Lowell, *The Government of England*, vol. i, p. 202.

APPENDIX

THE NEW STATUS OF SOUTH AFRICA

SOUTH AFRICA was one of the self-governing Dominions which provided the motive power which resulted in the Imperial Conference decisions and declarations of 1926 and 1930, and in the passing by the Parliament at Westminster of the Statute of Westminster, 1931. Further, General Hertzog, the Prime Minister of the Union, has been equally prominent in the tendency to translate mere declarations of constitutional status and constitutional practice into statutory and indisputable form. But as will appear, although 'South Africa', regarded as an abstract entity, has now been elevated by Statute into the highest legal status, there has been no binding definition of the respective powers *inter se* of the Crown, the Ministry, the Parliament, and the electorate within the constitutional framework of the Union itself.

Legal Effect of Future Acts of the United Kingdom

The Status of the Union Act, 1934, provides by sec. 2 that 'The Parliament of the Union' shall be 'the sovereign legislative power in and over the Union'. It also provides that:

> 'No Act of the Parliament of the United Kingdom and Northern Ireland passed after the eleventh day of December 1931[1] shall extend, or be deemed to extend, to the Union as part of the law of the Union, unless extended thereto by an Act of the Parliament of the Union.'

Sec. 4 of the Statute of Westminster, 1931, had provided that:

> 'No Act of Parliament of the United Kingdom passed after the commencement of this Act shall extend, or be deemed to extend, to a Dominion as part of the law of that Dominion, unless it is expressly declared in that Act that that Dominion has requested, and consented to, the enactment thereof.'

The verbiage employed in sec. 4 of the Statute of Westminster suggests that a mere declaration in an Act of the Parliament at Westminster to the effect that the request and consent of the Dominion concerned had been obtained would be sufficient to secure the extension to such Dominion of the particular Statute. Of course, the substance of sec. 4 is that the request and consent of the Dominion must actually be obtained before, and as a condition of, the applicability to the Dominion of the legislation of the Parliament at Westminster. The question of the binding force of sec. 4 upon the Parliament at West-

[1] The day upon which the Statute of Westminster, 1931, was assented to by the King.

minster is quite distinct and all that need be said at present[1] is that it may be erroneous to assume that even the Courts of the United Kingdom would treat the restriction upon power as of no effect. Sec. 2 of the Status of the Union Act secures that, in the Courts of South Africa at least, the absence of an express Act of the Union Parliament will successfully prevent any Act of the Parliament at Westminster, passed since the Statute of Westminster, 1931, from operating in South Africa.

The Legislature Supreme, not the Electorate

This illustrates the development of South Africa's constitutional status in relation to the United Kingdom. But what is 'South Africa'? What is a 'Dominion'? An essential but always overlooked feature of the Statute of Westminster is that great powers are either committed to, or recognized as existing in, either the Parliaments or Legislatures of the Dominions (see secs. 2 (2), 3, 5, 7 (2) and (3), 9 (3), 10 (1) and (2)), or, as in sec. 4 itself, 'the Dominion' itself. The Statute of Westminster does not define the elements of a 'Dominion' except that, in sec. 9 (3), it is identified, in the case of the Commonwealth of Australia, with 'The Parliament and Government of the Commonwealth'. No doubt the reference, in the case of the Commonwealth, to its Parliament and the requirement in sec. 2 of the Status of the Union Act, of a special Act of the Union Parliament, are considerable improvements upon the position which might exist if the mere consent of the Executive Government for the time being was regarded as sufficient to bind the people of a Dominion. But, even in such cases, the Parliament is the Parliament for the time being only, and it does not necessarily reflect the will of the electorate for all purposes and at all times. It will therefore have to be considered by the Dominion peoples whether special safeguards are not required to prevent a complacent Parliament from surrendering constitutional powers by the method permitted by sec. 4 of the Statute of Westminster and without the specific consent or authority of the Dominion people concerned. By way of illustration it will be remembered that the Newfoundland Act, 1933 (24–25 Geo. V, c. 2), took away from the people of Newfoundland important rights of self-government, at the request, not of the electors, but of the Parliament for the time being.

Three Leading Principles of the 'Status of the Union Act'

Sec. 4 (1) and (2) of the Status of the Union Act provide as follows:

'(1) The Executive Government of the Union in regard to any aspect of its domestic or external affairs is vested in the King, acting on the advice

[1] The matter is referred to *ante*, pp. 274–6.

of his Ministers of State for the Union, and may be administered by His Majesty in person or by a Governor-General as his representative.

'(2) Save where otherwise expressly stated or necessarily implied any reference in the South Africa Act and in this Act to the King shall be deemed to be a reference to the King acting on the advice of his Ministers of State for the Union.'

These two important subsections may be said to perform three distinct functions. In the first place, they elevate the doctrine of ministerial responsibility for the acts of the Crown into a statutory requirement which, as a general but not universal rule, excludes personal action on the part of the King or the Governor-General. In the second place, they ensure that, in the application of the doctrine of ministerial responsibility, the Ministers who are to be responsible for the acts of the Crown in relation to South Africa are the Ministers of the Union itself. In the third place, they permit of the exercise by the Governor-General of the whole content of the royal prerogative of the Crown in relation to the constitutional unit of South Africa. This third aspect will be considered separately.[1]

The Reserve Powers Unaffected

The first and second aspects of these subsections might be thought at first glance to safeguard both Ministers and Parliament against the possible exercise by the Crown of its reserve powers of dismissal and dissolution. This, however, is not so. The provisions are quite consistent with the exercise by the Governor-General of such reserve powers, so long as he can discover other Ministers ready and willing to vouch for the necessary executive acts, to 'carry on', and so accept 'responsibility' for the Governor-General's actions. This important aspect of the matter is placed beyond doubt by sec. 4 (3) of the Status of the Union Act, which says:

'The provisions of sub-sections (1) and (2) shall not be taken to affect the provisions of sections *twelve*, *fourteen*, *twenty*, and *forty-five* of the South Africa Act and the constitutional conventions relating to the exercise of his functions by the Governor-General under the said sections.'

The provisions of the South Africa Act mentioned in this subsection should be referred to. Sec. 12 gives the Governor-General power to choose and summon the Executive Council which is to advise him in the government of the Union, and such councillors 'shall hold office during his pleasure'. Sec. 14 deals with the appointment of Ministers of Departments and provides that they 'shall hold office during the pleasure of the Governor-General'. Sec. 20 gives the Governor-General power to summon Parliament, to prorogue it, and

[1] See *post*, pp. 310–11.

to dissolve either the House of Assembly alone, or with certain limitations the Senate and Assembly simultaneously. Sec. 45 also recognizes the power of the Governor-General to dissolve the Assembly.

The result is that the reserve powers of the Crown in relation to dismissal and dissolution may still be exercised by the Governor-General for the time being. It is expressly provided, however, that he should be bound by the 'constitutional conventions relating to the exercise of his functions . . . under the said sections'. This unusual direction is referred to later.[1] It may also be noted that the reserve power of the Governor-General to 'veto' or, strictly speaking, withhold assent from a Bill, after its passage through the two Houses of Parliament, is specially retained by sec. 8 of the Status of the Union Act, 1934. That section, however, prevents the Governor-General from reserving Bills for the signification of the King's pleasure—a procedure which would be entirely out of place in a constitutional system where Ministers in the Dominion, and they alone, are invested with the function of advising the Crown as to all its South African affairs, external as well as internal.

Royal Executive Functions and Seals Acts, 1934

The Royal Executive Functions and Seals Act, 1934, became law in South Africa on the same day as the Status of the Union Act, i.e. June 22nd, 1934. The former provided for a Royal Great Seal and a Royal Signet of the Union. The Prime Minister of the Union, or, in his absence, his deputy was made the Keeper of the Great Seal and the Signet (sec. 3). The King's will, as head of the Executive Government of the Union, is required to be expressed in writing under his sign manual and every such instrument is to be countersigned by a Minister for the Union (sec. 4 (1)). The King's sign manual is required to be confirmed by the Great Seal on all Royal proclamations, and the King may by proclamation prescribe what other public instruments require authentication under the Great Seal or the Signet (sec. 4 (2)). Where the instrument has to pass the Great Seal or the Signet, the keeper of the Seals is required to affix the Great Seal or the Signet, as the case may be, to the instrument bearing the King's sign manual, and the counter-signature of one of the King's Ministers of State for the Union (sec. 4 (3)).

Reserve Powers unimpaired

If these provisions of sec. 4 of the Royal Executive Functions and Seals Act stood alone, the Crown, in the person either of the King himself, or of the Governor-General, would be rendered incapable of

[1] See *post*, pp. 303–6.

exercising the reserve powers of dismissal or dissolution without the consent of the Prime Minister for the time being. But this would be inconsistent with sec. 4 (3) of the Status of the Union Act. Accordingly, it was provided in sec. 4 (4) that the sections do not affect the exercise by the King or the Governor-General of the powers under secs. 12, 14, 20, and 45 of the South Africa Act.

The King's Personal Authentication Unnecessary

Under sec. 6 of the Royal Executive Functions and Seals Act, it is provided that whenever, for any reason, the King's signature to any instrument requiring the King's sign manual cannot be obtained, or whenever the delay in obtaining it would, in the opinion of the Governor-General in Council, either frustrate the object thereof or unduly retard the despatch of public business, 'the Governor-General shall, subject to such instructions as may from time to time in that behalf be given by the King on the advice of his Ministers of State for the Union, execute and sign such instrument on behalf of His Majesty'. This very important provision furnishes machinery to carry out the Status of the Union Act so far as the latter commits to the King's Ministers in South Africa exclusive authority to advise and control the exercise of all royal prerogatives, powers, and functions appertaining to the external or internal affairs of South Africa. Moreover, it solves the possible conflict which might arise if, in relation to such affairs, the King had received advice from his Ministers in the United Kingdom inconsistent with that tendered by his Ministers in South Africa. In such case the King would be spared the necessity of a personal decision and the Governor-General is enabled to act on his behalf.

Administration of Imperial Acts still extending to South Africa

Secs. 7 and 8 of the Royal Executive Functions and Seals Act deal with the administration of Acts of the Parliament of the United Kingdom passed prior to the Statute of Westminster, 1931, and extending to the Union as part of the law of the Union. The administration of all such Acts is taken away from the hands of the King's Ministers in the United Kingdom, and transferred to his Ministers in South Africa. In the case of Acts which require the King's Orders in Council, the Governor-General in Council is empowered to act unless the Governor-General in Council determines that the exigencies of the case require an order of the King in Council. In the latter case the King in Council is to act in respect of the Union only at the request of the Prime Minister of the Union, and it is to be expressly declared in the instrument containing the King's pleasure 'that the Union has requested and consented to the King-in-Council so acting in respect of the Union' (sec. 7).

No Difficulty of Interpretation

It is now possible to venture some general observations upon these two very important Statutes. It is said that the object of General Hertzog was to secure 'the doctrines of (1) the divisibility of the Crown as regards the Union;[1] (2) the right of Union neutrality in the case of a war declared by the Crown on the advice of British Ministers; and (3) the right of the Union to separate from the Commonwealth'.[2] Professor Keith has, however, also emphasized that the legislation was passed with the approval of General Smuts and that the latter has 'in the past . . . been inclined to deny that the Union can legally be neutral in a British War or can legally separate from the Commonwealth by unilateral action'.[3] In these circumstances Professor Keith thinks that legislation 'accepted by men holding such different views must tend to be vague', and the result has been to 'render interpretation of the legislation especially difficult'.[4] The matters dealt with in the two Statutes do not, however, raise difficulties of interpretation, because in no case is the meaning of the provisions left ambiguous. The attitude which may be adopted by the Court to the legislation will depend rather upon questions of power than of construction.

The Statute of Westminster, 1931, not a Direct Source of Power

The Statute of Westminster, 1931, has not been used by the Parliament of the Union as the sole, or even as the direct, source of its constitutional power to enact the two Statutes. This appears clearly from the recital to the Status of the Union Act, which refers to the declarations and resolutions of the Imperial Conferences of 1926 and 1930 and states that such resolutions and declarations 'insofar as they required legislative sanction on the part of the United Kingdom have been ratified, confirmed, and established by the Parliament of the United Kingdom in an Act entitled the Statute of Westminster, 1931'.

The recital to the Status of the Union Act concludes by declaring that it is expedient, first, 'that the status of the Union of South Africa as a sovereign independent State . . . shall be adopted and declared by

[1] In 1904 Harrison Moore pointed out that 'the doctrine of the unity and indivisibility of the Crown is not persisted in to the extent of ignoring that the several parts of the Empire are distinct entities. To ignore it, in fact, would lead to consequences not merely inconvenient and absurd, but in the case of the self-governing Colonies at any rate politically mischievious.' (See *Law Quarterly Review* vol. xx, p. 358; *The King* v. *Sutton* (1908) 5 C.L.R. 789; and the *Engineers Case* (1920) 28 C.L.R. 129 at p. 152 to the same effect, and contrast *Williams* v. *Howarth* (1905) A.C. 551.)

[2] Keith, *Journal of Comparative Legislation*, Nov. 1934, p. 289.

[3] Ibid. [4] Ibid.

the Parliament of the Union,' and second, 'that the said Statute of Westminster, insofar as its provisions are applicable to the Union of South Africa . . . shall be adopted as an Act of the Parliament of the Union of South Africa.' Accordingly, sec. 3 of the Status of the Union Act declares that the parts of the Statute of Westminster relating to South Africa as one of the Dominions 'shall be deemed to be an Act of the Parliament of the Union and shall be construed accordingly'.

Reliance upon Status apart from Statute of Westminster

It is reasonably clear, therefore, that the two Acts of Parliament proceed upon the assumption that the Imperial Conference decisions of 1926, declaring that the Dominions and the United Kingdom are 'equal in status, in no way subordinate one to another in any aspect of their domestic or external affairs', should be regarded as sufficient evidence of South Africa's constitutional right to control all its affairs external and internal alike. Upon such assumption the two Acts of 1934 proceed to declare status and provide for a method of exercising all the powers and capacities incident to such status. From the point of view of strict law the result of this method of approach may not be different in essentials from that reached if the Statute of Westminster had been regarded as itself furnishing for the first time the necessary constitutional power.

The Reserve Powers and Constitutional Conventions

Both the Acts of Parliament passed by the Union expressly save the reserve powers of the Governor-General as the King's representative in relation to the dismissal of Ministers, the dissolution of Parliament, and the assent to Bills passed by the two Houses of Parliament. But the Governor-General, in relation to the matter of dismissal and dissolution, is required to act according to 'the constitutional conventions'.[1] This unusual requirement has its only analogy in the provisions of Articles 51 and 41 of the Constitution of the Irish Free State. Art. 51 of that Constitution, whilst declaring that the executive authority is vested in the King, provides that 'it shall be exercisable in accordance with the law, practice, and constitutional usage governing the exercise of the Executive Authority in the case of the Dominion of Canada, by the Representative of the Crown'. Similarly Art. 41 provides for the Representative of the Crown in the Irish Free State dealing with Bills which have passed both Houses by acting 'in accordance with the law practice and constitutional usage governing the . . . withholding of assent or reservation in the Dominion of Canada'.

[1] Status of the Union Act, sec. 4 (3).

Uncertainty of Application of Constitutional 'Maxims'

The great difficulty about incorporating in a Statute references to constitutional conventions, usages, maxims, and practices, is that there is the greatest uncertainty not only as to what rules are to be applied but also as to how in any particular case they should be applied. The Statute of Westminster, for instance, declared in language quite unambiguous that 'it is in accord with the established constitutional position that no law hereafter made by the Parliament of the United Kingdom shall extend to any of the said Dominions as part of the law of that Dominion otherwise than at the request and with the consent of that Dominion'. It might have been thought that a convention evidenced in such an authoritative way would be amply sufficient to preclude the Parliament at Westminster from considering any change in the constitutional position of one of the six States declared by the Commonwealth of Australia Constitution Act, 1900 (another Act of the Parliament at Westminster), to be united 'in one indissoluble Federal Commonwealth'. But there appear to be constitutional authorities ready to assert that the Petition which has been presented to the Parliament at Westminster on behalf of the Parliament and Government of one of the States of the Commonwealth, viz. Western Australia, may, without a breach of constitutional usage, be acceded to so that, by an Act of the Parliament at Westminster, the State in question will be allowed to secede from the indissoluble Commonwealth. Yet as Mr. Justice Dixon has recently pointed out:

> 'that Petition contemplates in a matter affecting the internal affairs of the Commonwealth an exercise by the British Parliament of its legislative supremacy over the law throughout the Empire; the supremacy which these provisions (i.e. of the Statute of Westminster) are expressed to restrict. It is true that the Commonwealth has not adopted the Statute of Westminster. But in this respect it does no more than restate as a legal rule an existing constitutional convention.'[1]

Difficulty not avoided by Ministers' Control over Governor-General

It is obvious, therefore, that it is never safe to rely upon the application of mere constitutional usages, no matter how authoritative the documents by which they are evidenced. In the case of South Africa the difficulty raised by the reference to the 'Conventions' is much greater because it is impossible to say what the 'conventions' are and where they may be found. Is recourse to be had to Hallam or May?

[1] University of Melbourne Centenary Lecture, March 1935; *Law Quarterly Review*, vol. li, 612. The present Appendix was prepared before the decision of the Committee appointed by the Houses of Parliament at Westminster that the petition should not be investigated.

to Hearn or Bagehot? to Bryce or Anson? to Asquith or Dicey? to Todd or Keith? to Jennings or Laski? Professor Keith avoids the difficulty by stating that

> 'the fact that any Government can provide itself with a Governor-General of its own party complexion renders these formal powers meaningless. It is noteworthy that a proposal to allow the King to act independently in the matter of the selection of the Governor-General was deliberately negatived. Yet, if the Governor-General is a nominee of the local Government and holds office at its pleasure, he departs vitally from the British parallel and the constitution ceases to provide any control over the majority party in the lower House for the time being.'[1]

But is it permissible to agree that the occasion will never arise when, in the crisis of a political controversy, a Governor-General may think it proper to exercise his ultimate authority and even dismiss a Ministry which has the support of a majority of the Assembly, appoint the Opposition Leader as Prime Minister, and grant a dissolution of Parliament to the new Prime Minister? Surely it is wrong to assume that the Governor-General for the time being will always be a mere tool in the hands of the dominant party. It is true that a Governor-General could not safely exercise his reserve powers unless he had good reason to suppose that the electorate would vindicate his action. But that the possibility of similar action by a Governor-General against the advice of his Ministers for the time being is not merely academic, was shown in May 1932, when the Governor of New South Wales dismissed from office a Ministry in full possession of the confidence of the popular Assembly. After the Governor had dismissed his Ministers the Leader of the Opposition became Premier, and being unable to face the Assembly for an hour, secured, first a prorogation, and then a dissolution of Parliament.[2] Many constitutional students have attempted to justify that particular exercise of the reserve powers. Even in the case of the Governor-General of the Commonwealth it has been stated that in the exercise of his 'discretion' under sec. 58 in dealing with Bills passed by both Houses of the Parliament, he need not always act upon the advice of his Ministers. Mr. Latham,[3] for instance, says:

> 'Exceptional cases may arise in which the Governor-General would be justified in disregarding their advice. The principles applicable for determining the existence of such exceptional cases can only be those which in fact have been applied in Australia (though not without controversy) by the Governor-General and by State Governors in dealing with advice by a Ministry that Parliament should be dissolved. Such advice has on several occasions been rejected, but only where the Governor-General, or Gover-

[1] *Journal of Comparative Legislation*, Nov. 1934, p. 292.

[2] See *ante*, chap. xix.

[3] Now Sir John Latham C.J.

nor, as the case may be, has been able to secure another set of Ministers who do not repeat the advice given by their predecessors.'[1]

No Effective Remedy against Non-Observance of Conventions

Perhaps the greatest advantage to be derived from defining the extent of the discretion as to the exercise of reserve powers is that the absence of definition may prevent an over-careful Governor-General from acting when he should, just as it may enable an imprudent or over-zealous Governor-General to act where no reasonable ground for intervention exists. In each case an error may be fatal to the best interests of the people which are committed in the last resort to the care of the Governor-General or Governor.

In such cases, moreover, it may not be possible to retrace the wrong steps which have been taken. An interesting illustration of this is contained in the recent decision of the Permanent Court of International Justice, which interpreted the Statute of the Memel territory under the Convention of May 8th, 1924. The majority of the Court held that the dismissal of the President of the Directorate in February 1932 was in order in the circumstances in which it took place, and that the Governor of the territory was also correct in appointing the Opposition Leader in his place. But it also held that the dissolution of the Chamber of Representatives of the territory in March 1932, at a time when the Directorate presided over by the new appointee had not received the confidence of the Diet, was not in order. But although the Court thus reached the opinion that the constitutional Statute had been infringed by the Governor, it took occasion to add:

'It has arrived at the conclusion that on the proper construction of the Statute the Governor ought not to have taken certain action which he did take. It does not thereby intend to say that the action of the Governor in dissolving the Chamber, even though it was contrary to the treaty, was of no effect in the sphere of municipal law. This is tantamount to saying that the dissolution is not to be regarded as void in the sense that the old Chamber is still in existence, and that the new Chamber since elected has no legal existence.'[2]

In the case of South Africa, action by the Governor-General, although 'unconstitutional' as offending against the 'conventions' of the Constitution, would be incapable of being remedied so long as the Opposition leaders accepting office were ready to accept 'responsibility' for the action taken. Similarly, if the Governor-General failed to take action to protect the electorate against a Legislature which proposed to extend its own life in order to avoid certain defeat upon the expiration of its normal period of life, the result would be irrevocable and might be disastrous.

[1] J. G. Latham, *Australia and the British Commonwealth*, pp. 65–6.

[2] Permanent Court of International Justice, Series A/B, No. 49, p. 46, 11.8.1932.

Possibility of Constitutional Restrictions in South Africa

The complete removal of the Colonial Laws Validity Act, 1865, from the constitutional system of South Africa raises the question whether it is possible for the Parliament of the Union to be bound effectively by constitutional restrictions. For instance, sec. 152 of the South Africa Act gives Parliament power to repeal or alter any of the provisions of the Act, but this provision is subject to certain exceptions. One exception is that secs. 35 and 137, which deal with the franchise and disqualification therefrom and with the equality of the English and Dutch languages in the Union, cannot be repealed or altered unless the Bill is passed by both Houses of Parliament sitting together and is agreed to at the third reading by not less than two-thirds of the total number of members of both Houses. May sec. 152 itself be repealed or altered so as to do away with the 'entrenching' of secs. 35 and 137?

Colonial Laws Validity Act

In the case of those States and Colonies to which the Colonial Laws Validity Act extends, the general answer to the question of restrictions upon the legislature's power is to be found in the decision of the Privy Council in *Attorney-General for New South Wales* v. *Trethowan*, [1932] A.C. 526. There it was held that a law passed by the Parliament of New South Wales, which required the approval of the electorate at a referendum (1) to any Bill abolishing the Legislative Council, and (2) to any Bill repealing the law containing the requirement of a referendum, was valid and effective by reason of sec. 5 of the Colonial Laws Validity Act. That section, whilst committing to the Legislature for the time being full power to alter its own constitution, adds a proviso that laws so passed 'shall have been passed in such manner and form as may from time to time be required by any Act of Parliament, letters patent, order in Council, or Colonial Law for the time being in force in the said Colony'. The conclusion was reached by holding that the laws in question constituted a 'manner and form' of passing laws, and that this requirement, being that of a 'Colonial law ... in force', had to be observed. The decision of the Privy Council has been availed of by the now uni-cameral Legislature of Queensland which has passed constitutional amendments requiring popular approval at a referendum *before* an Upper House can again be reconstituted. Further, such popular approval is now also required in Queensland before the Legislature can lawfully extend its own life. In all these cases the supremacy of the Imperial Law contained in the Colonial Laws Validity Act made it unnecessary to determine whether upon general principles of constitutional law one legislature could bind its successor.

Applicability of Decision in Trethowan's Case

It has been stated that the decision in Trethowan's Case has no application to those Dominion Legislatures which, since the Statute of Westminster, 1931, are released from the binding effect of the Colonial Laws Validity Act.

'It would seem, although there is a constitutional convention that this shall not be done, that the Union Parliament could, since the passing of the Statute of Westminster, 1931, repeal by an ordinary Act of Parliament sec. 152 of the South Africa Act, 1909, which provides for the employment of a special machinery for the amendment of certain sections of the constitution.'[1]

Is Sec. 4 of the Statute of Westminster Binding?

Professor Keith deals with the question of constitutional restrictions in relation to the operation of sec. 4 of the Statute of Westminster, 1931, upon the Parliament at Westminster. He quotes the well-known dogma of Bacon that 'a supreme and absolute power cannot conclude itself, neither can that which is in nature revocable be made fixed'.[2] Keith's conclusion is 'unquestionably in strict law, if a subsequent Act of Parliament applied nominatim to any Dominion, the omission (i.e. in the Statute of the Parliament of Westminster) of the requisite statement of concurrence would be unavailing to prevent it applying to the Dominion'.[3]

A close perusal of the arguments before and the observations of the members of the Judicial Committee in the case of *Attorney-General for New South Wales* v. *Trethowan* suggests doubt as to the validity of this sweeping assertion. Mr. Justice Dixon, in a recent analysis of the Statute of Westminster, has said of sec. 4 that it 'is a restriction upon British Parliamentary supremacy over the law'.[4]

The Views of Anson

In 1886 Sir William Anson, dealing with the Government of Ireland Bill, disputed the unqualified proposition that the Parliament at Westminster was unable to bind its successors. One exception to the general rule occurred, he considered, 'where Parliament surrenders its sovereign powers over a certain area to another person or body.'[5] Anson illustrated this exception as follows:

'Suppose that legislative independence were to be conceded to the colony of Victoria. Suppose that Parliament were to repeal the Colonial Laws

[1] *Law Quarterly Review*, vol. xlviii (1932), p. 456.

[2] Keith, *Constitutional Law of the British Dominions* (1933), pp. 38–9.

[3] Ibid. [4] Melbourne University Centenary Lecture, March 1935; *Law Quarterly Review*, vol. li, p. 611.

[5] *Law Quarterly Review*, vol. 2 (1886), p. 440.

Validity Act as regarded that colony, and the provisions of any other Act which affected the subordination of the Victorian Parliament, and that all necessary steps were taken to place Victoria in the position in which Fox desired to place Ireland. Would it be maintained that our Parliament could still legislate for Victoria, or that the Victorian Courts need regard such laws as anything but specimens of legislation, instructive perhaps, but certainly inoperative? I should be disposed to contend that Parliament could only regain its power in one of two ways. Acts passed by the Parliament of Victoria and the Parliament at Westminster might provide for a legislative re-union of the two countries on any terms to which both could agree. Or war and the suspension for a while of all legal relations might leave Victoria in the position of a conquered territory with which the Imperial Parliament could deal as it pleased.'[1]

It will be observed that there is a very close parallel to be drawn between the status of the self-governing dominions to which the Statute of Westminster applies, and the case supposed by Anson. If Anson's views were accepted, the Courts of the United Kingdom as well as those of the Dominions concerned should regard the absence from any Statute of the Parliament at Westminster of the declaration of request and consent by the Dominion to whom it is sought to be applied as effectively preventing such application.[2]

Broader Question arises in South Africa

But this does not dispose of the question of a possible repeal of sec. 152 of the South Africa Act. In that instance there is no question of any surrender of sovereign power by one authority to another.[3] Anson himself is forced to add a second exception to meet the case where two portions of a people represented in one Parliament agree for the future to have separate Parliaments. But the broader question is whether the main doctrine will itself be regarded as valid when legal thought seems no longer to debar Parliament itself from setting up a *Constitution* which, by reason of its very nature as such, is

[1] Ibid.

[2] In Moore's case (1935 A.C., p. 484) the question of the power of the Irish Free State to make its own constitution permanently binding did not fairly arise. The appeal to the Privy Council was treated as a fetter upon Ireland's judicial autonomy and as having been imposed from without by virtue of the Colonial Laws Validity Act; consequently the fetter was deemed removed by the express provision of the Statute of Westminster giving power to a Dominion legislature to pass Acts repugnant to Imperial Acts. In the British Coal Corporation Case (1935 A.C. at p. 520) it was suggested by Lord Sankey that the Imperial Parliament might repeal or disregard Sec. 4 of the Statute of Westminster 'in theory' or 'as a matter of abstract law'. This statement was a mere *obiter dictum*, and there was no analysis of the theory in its application to the changed circumstances of to-day. (See ante, p. 274.)

[3] Why should not 'abdication' or 'surrender' be possible upon a functional, as well as a geographical, footing?

intended to restrict the liberty of the legislative, as well as of all other organs within the appropriate constitutional unit. In South Africa, for instance, is it possible to deny that the sovereign Legislature could set up a constitution which would adequately and effectively define and limit the powers of the Governor-General, the Legislature and each House thereof, the Executive, the Judiciary and the electorate, and would provide for its own amendment and its own enforcement? In such circumstances it would become the duty of the Judiciary to enforce the terms of the Constitution. The fact that in other countries the Judiciary has yielded to the overwhelming pressure of the Legislature for the time being does not lead to the inference that all Courts of justice will prefer the power of the existing Legislature to the supremacy of the law. Bacon's dogma will hardly be allowed to stand in the way of modern notions of constitution making and constitution breaking.

The Grant of Royal Prerogatives to the Governor-General

The two recent acts of the Union Parliament deal with the important question of the extent to which the Royal Prerogatives in relation to South Africa may be exercised by the Governor-General. The answer is that all such prerogatives may be exercised.

A similar question was discussed in connexion with the Dominion of Canada in what is known as the *Bonanza Case*, [1916] 1 A.C. 566. There it was stated by Viscount Haldane for the Privy Council that the argument was:

> 'that the Governor-General and the Lieutenant-Governors of the Provinces, excepting so far as the royal prerogatives have been reserved expressly or by necessary implication, have the right to exercise them, as though by implication handed over and distributed in such a fashion as to cover the whole of the field to which the self-government of Canada extends.'

Delegation of Prerogatives in Canada and Australia

Sec. 9 of the British North America Act provides that the Executive Government and authority of and over Canada 'is hereby declared to continue and be vested in the Queen'. Sec. 10 of the Act assumes that the Governor-General will be exercising the authority of the Queen, but there is no special provision as in sec. 61 of the Constitution of the Commonwealth of Australia. The latter section declares that the Executive power of the Commonwealth is vested in the Queen and is 'exercisable by the Governor-General as the Queen's representative'. Sec. 8 of the South Africa Act had provided that the Executive Government of the Union was vested in the King and 'shall be administered by His Majesty in person *or* by a Governor-General as his representative'. The possibility of the exercise of the Executive power over

South Africa by the King in person remains unaffected by sec. 4(1) of the Status of the Union Act. In the *Bonanza Case* Viscount Haldane refrained from expressing an opinion upon the question of the extent to which the King's prerogatives had devolved upon his Canadian representatives. He said: 'There is no provision in the British North America Act corresponding even to sec. 61 of the Australian Commonwealth Act which . . . provides that the Executive power, though declared to be in the Sovereign is yet to be exercisable by the Governor-General'.[1] He also referred to other sections of the British North America Act which appeared to 'negative the theory that the Governor-General is made a Viceroy in the full sense'.[2]

Later, in December 1922, on the occasion of the application of the State Governments of Australia for special leave to appeal from the decision of the High Court of Australia in the Engineers' Case, Viscount Haldane said in the course of argument:

> 'Under sec. 61 it is declared "The Executive power of the Commonwealth is vested in the Queen and is exercisable by the Governor-General as the Queen's representative and extends to the execution and maintenance of this constitution and of the laws of the Commonwealth". No doubt that does not take away the powers of the Governors of the States as representing the Sovereign within their limits, but does it not put the Sovereign in the position of having parted, so far as the affairs of the Commonwealth are concerned, with every shadow of active intervention in their affairs and handing them over, unlike the case of Canada, to the Governor-General?'[3]

It may be observed that Viscount Haldane's tentative indication of opinion in relation to the exercise of prerogatives by the Governor-General was not in line with that of Clement who thought that sec. 10 of the British North America Act impliedly recognized that the Governor-General was entitled to exercise all the prerogatives of the Crown in relation to Canada's sphere of self-government.[4] Curiously enough, Lefroy regarded sec. 2 of the Commonwealth Constitution, which provides that the Governor-General may exercise in the Commonwealth 'such powers and functions of the Queen as Her Majesty may be pleased to assign to him' as being inconsistent with the theory of a full grant of the royal prerogative, and as declaratory of the theory that the Governor-General was limited as to all prerogative powers by the Letters Patent of his office and by his instructions.[5] Harrison Moore doubted this opinion.[6] And Inglis Clark, writing in 1905, also

[1] [1916] 1 A.C. pp. 586–7.
[2] Ibid., p. 587.
[3] Transcript of argument, pp. 22–3.
[4] Clement, *Canadian Constitution* (2nd ed.), p. 95.
[5] *Law Quarterly Review*, vol. 15, pp. 282–3.
[6] Ibid., vol. 16, pp. 36–7.

disagreed with Lefroy and expressed the opinion that the reference in sec. 2 was to powers and functions additional to those included in the words 'Executive power of the Commonwealth' in sec. 61.[1]

Legal Position in South Africa before Recent Acts

Prior to the passage by the Parliament of South Africa of the Status of the Union Act, the position of the Governor-General in relation to the exercise by him of the prerogatives of the Crown could be stated as follows:

1. It was established that all the royal prerogatives of the King extended to, and existed in respect of, the Dominion by virtue of its being a Dominion under the Crown. In every case of course the existence of such prerogatives could be terminated by legislation of the appropriate law-making authority.

2. The royal prerogatives in relation to South Africa, so far as they were capable of separation from the prerogatives in relation to the United Kingdom or to other parts of the King's Dominions, were exercisable by the King personally or by the Governor-General.

3. It was not impossible to separate the prerogatives of the King in relation to South Africa from those in relation to the United Kingdom or to other parts of the King's Dominions. Such a separation was not impossible even in the case of the prerogatives of the King in relation to foreign or external affairs.

Authority over Mandated Territory

In the case of *R.* v. *Christian*, [1924] S. African L.R. 101, the Supreme Court of South Africa was called upon to consider the legal basis of its control as Mandatory over the mandated territory of South-West Africa. It was held that the Government of South-West Africa set up by the Union possessed sufficient '*majestas* operating internally' to found a charge of high treason against a native chief alleged to be in rebellion. De Villiers J.A. stated that in relation to the Mandate delegated to South Africa as a member of the League, 'the Union Government as Mandatory of South-West Africa is not in any respect subject to the Imperial Parliament'.[2] From the point of view of the territory under Mandate, the *majestas* of the Mandatory operated 'internally'. But from the point of view of the Union of South Africa, the authority it exercised was 'external' to the Union, the Mandated territory not being portion of the Union properly so-called.[3] The

[1] Inglis Clark, *Constitutional Law*, pp. 65–6.

[2] [1924] S. African L.R. 101 at pp. 119–20.

[3] In the case of the Mandated Territory of New Guinea very strong, if not conclusive, evidence that the mandated territory is not part of, but outside, His

relation of Australia to the Mandated territory of New Guinea is essentially based upon the same exercise of power in relation to external affairs. I have said elsewhere:

> 'It is well established, of course, that capacity to enter into agreements with foreign powers belongs to the King and such capacity may be exercised by the King in relation to any of his self-governing Dominions. The adaptability of the common law (of which the prerogatives of the Crown form an important part) to new circumstances and conditions has allowed the prerogative to be exercised so as (*a*) to enable the King to enter into binding arrangements with foreign powers, in his capacity as head of, and with respect solely to, any one or more of the self-governing Dominions, and (*b*) to authorize the King, in right of and as representing such Dominion, to accept a Mandate.'[1]

In the case of the Commonwealth of Australia the international arrangements which were concluded in relation to the Mandated territory were not made in the name of the Governor-General but of the King although, since the Treaty of Versailles, the advice to act has come from the Ministers of the Commonwealth. A significant feature of the Status of the Union Act is that, in relation to external affairs, it will now be possible to enter into binding transactions through the agency of the Governor-General.

Position since Passing of Recent Acts

Since the passing of the two recent Acts in South Africa it would appear that all the prerogatives of the Crown in relation to South Africa are capable of being distinguished and separated from those in relation either to the United Kingdom or to the rest of the Empire or to the other self-governing Dominions. Professor Keith goes so far as to say:

> 'As the Status Act grants all executive power to the Crown or the Governor-General, the result is that in strict law there seems no obstacle to the Governor-General issuing a proclamation of neutrality in the event of the Crown declaring war on the advice of British Ministers. There seems further no obstacle to the Governor-General assenting to an Act which would sever the connexion between the Union and the Crown. General Hertzog, therefore, may claim that the measure does provide a legal means for the assertion of the doctrines of the right of neutrality and secession.'[2]

Majesty's Dominions is furnished by two Imperial Orders in Council—No. 648 of 1923, and No. 1030 of 1928. The former was made under sec. 737 of the Merchant Shipping Act, 1894, the latter under sec. 30 of the Fugitive Offenders Act, 1881. Each order not only recites, but is expressly based upon, the legal assertion that the Mandated Territory of New Guinea is a place 'outside' or 'out of' His Majesty's Dominions.

[1] *The British Dominions as Mandatories*, p. 23.

[2] *Journal of Comparative Legislation*, Nov. 1934, p. 291.

The statement of Professor Smiddy, when Minister of the Irish Free State to America that 'the only bond linking together the various nations of the British Commonwealth of Nations is the British Crown, or one might say, the person of the King'[1] has now been made to correspond with considerable accuracy to the legal position created in South Africa. Mr. Latham,[2] writing in 1929, considered that General Hertzog, who made similar statements, 'failed to appreciate the reality of other constitutional bonds of a legislative and judicial nature'.[3] In 1929, of course, it was correct to emphasize, as Mr. Latham did, that 'in the legislative sphere there is also a real bond between all parts of the Empire. The British Parliament is still legally supreme.'[4] That position has been considerably altered during the past five years. Mr. Latham's reference to 'the judicial bond' constituted by the Judicial Committee of the Privy Council is a matter in respect of which some of the Dominions have thought it desirable to overlook the delay and—in the case of ordinary litigants—the great expense of such appeals, for the sake of retaining access to a famous tribunal. But the opinion of Professor Lowell in 1928—that the result of the decisions at the Imperial Conference of 1926 appeared to be that the self-governing Dominions had 'obtained legal and political independence'[5]—has turned out to be far more accurate than the opinions ventured by those who resisted and deprecated many of the implications of full Dominion Status.[6] Indeed the recent Acts passed by the Parliament of the Union of South Africa illustrate the substantial truth of Lowell's comment.

Danger of Over-Generalization

I say 'substantial' truth because there is always a danger in a generalization as to 'status' or 'Sovereignty'. As Professor Noel Baker said of the self-governing Dominions in his 1928 work which so accurately foreshadowed many of the developments of Dominion Status in relation to International Law:

> 'If we have a precise conception of the international relations which in fact they maintain, if we have a complete and accurate idea of the legal rights and duties in International Law which they have assumed, we may confidently neglect the battle about such words as statehood, sovereignty, and independence.'[7]

[1] *Great Britain and the Dominions* (1928), p. 117.

[2] Now Sir John Latham C.J.

[3] Latham, *Australian and the British Commonwealth*, p. 22.

[4] Ibid., p. 29.

[5] Lowell and Hall, *The British Commonwealth of Nations* (1927), p. 587.

[6] Noel Baker, *The British Dominions in International Law*, pp. 358–9.

[7] Notably Professor Keith in his works as well as in his contributions to the *Journal of Comparative Legislation*.

There is also danger in over-generalization as to the precise functions of the King and his Representative, as has been stressed in the reference to the reserve powers of the Governor-General. 'The feeling of personal loyalty towards the King is something much more than a "sentimental bond". It is an integral part of the political structure of this Empire, . . .'[1]

[1] *Round Table*, Dec. 1930 (vol. xxi, p. 98).

INDEX